TUDOR RYE

Rye from Playdon Hill, 1841 (PDA 467/9)

Sheila M. Cooper

TUDOR RYE

Graham Mayhew

Falmer
Centre for Continuing Education,
University of Sussex
1987

Front cover: the John Prowze map of Rye Harbour 1572, in the
        custody of the Public Record Office: document
        reference MPF 212 (ex SP12/254(751)

ISBN 0 904242 30 7

Typeset by Oxford University Computing Service
Printed by Delta Press, Hove

To my father

The assistance of the
Marc Fitch Fund is
gratefully acknowledged

Contents

Figures

Tables

Illustrations

Foreword

I was glad to be asked to write a foreword to this interesting book. As a local and as an urban historian I welcome it as an important contribution to our understanding of towns. As former Vice-Chancellor of the University of Sussex, who took particular interest in the setting-up of a centre for Continuing Education, I was delighted to learn of the way in which the author of this book prepared it while teaching a Continuing Education lecture course in Rye. There is a long tradition of group involvement in writing local and urban history. Finally, and not least, for more than ten years I had a house in Winchelsea, and while spending many happy days there got to know Rye well. The view from Winchelsea was a very different view of Rye from the view from Brighton.

When I first moved to the University of Sussex in 1961 I was presented with J.R. Armstrong's *History of Sussex* by the Southern District of the W.E.A. It was a gift which I treasured, and although Rye figured little in it and not at all as a busy Tudor town, it too was the result of co-operation between a tutor and his extramural classes.

Since then both local history and urban history have boomed. The former has been more sophisticated and more thorough: the latter has become more organised and systematic, and during recent years increasing attention has been paid to pre-industrial towns. Their history raises issues of general historical importance. I have always believed that through local history we can develop a new version of national history: local history should never simply illustrate national history or take it as given, it should point to new interpretations. I believe equally firmly that both local history and urban history have comparative dimensions and that they call for comparisons across societies and cultures as well as within them.

This book will be of interest though not only to people who already know Rye, but people who have never seen it. I am sure it will encourage them to come.

Asa Briggs

Worcester College, Oxford
January 1987

I

Preface

The present work grew out of a much shorter projected Occasional Paper, based on much of the material I had used with a Centre for Continuing Education evening class in Rye over a three-year period between 1980 and 1983. As I began to write it, additional problems continually raised themselves in my mind until, considerably over a year after the original deadline, the project had grown to its present form. To the members of that evening class and in particular to Mrs Jo Kirkham, then Mayor of Rye and Geoffrey Bagley, curator of Rye Museum and a freeman of Rye, my especial thanks, for their continuing interest and for opening a number of doors. My thanks also to the Twenty-Seven Foundation and the Sussex Archaeological Society Margary Research Fund for grants towards my research, and to my colleagues at the East Sussex Record Office, where I found myself in the summer of 1979, a young historian in the throes of completing a doctoral thesis, who almost at once was casting around for new areas of research. My enthusiastic discovery and systematic exploitation of the Rye Corporation records housed there has no doubt been to them a source of trial as well as amusement.

Since I began working on the Rye records, I have been much indebted to two other historians working in this field. In particular I have benefitted greatly from my many conversations in the early days of research with Stephen Hipkin, whose work on early seventeenth century Rye will be of considerable interest to early modern historians when it is published; and my thanks also to Annabel Gregory for lending me first her computer cards of the sixteenth century Rye parish registers, which I'm afraid I rearranged manually as a card index, and more recently for print-outs of her index. I should also like to record my indebtedness to the many helpful comments which I received from the graduate and staff history

3

seminar at Sussex University, where I gave a paper during the early stages of my research on the problems of interpreting the Rye records.

The errors and omissions are, of course, all my own, but I would like to thank those who have commented upon earlier drafts of the text. In particular my especial thanks to Professor Claire Cross, of York University, where I read history and began research. Her continued encouragement and willingness to read a succession of articles and the present chapters, often at extremely short notice, and her many helpful comments have been one of the mainstays of my research. To Fred Gray of the Centre for Continuing Education at Sussex University, who has taken over responsibility for Occasional Papers my thanks both for his comments and his patience during a year of broken deadlines and a rapidly expanding project. I should also like to thank Joe McPartlin, formerly of the University of Malta, a friend from my several years in Oxford, who compiled the index. His insistence on my justifying the need for another full-length study of a sixteenth century English town has resulted in the present introduction. I should also like to mention my ward Rowland Coombes, who despite having the intimate details of the lives of Rye inhabitants four centuries ago forced upon him, corrected several chapters of the proofs and is now at Cambridge reading history. I thank him for his often useful comments and forebearance. Finally, my especial thanks to my father, who has once again meticulously read through the typescripts, correcting errors and pointing out inconsistencies.

In conclusion, I would like to thank David Martin for his comments on the section relating to houses and furnishings and for drawing the maps (figures 1, 2, 6 and 8) and also Pat Reaks and Sylvia Larkin, who retyped much of the revised draft. Also I acknowledge the permission of Rye Town Council and the late Vicar of Rye, Canon J.E.R. Williams for allowing me to quote from and reference parts of the Rye Corporation MSS and the Rye parish records; to the Keeper of the Public Record Office for permission to reproduce the John Prowze map of Rye (1572), which forms the cover of this volume.

Graham Mayhew
Lewes
October 1986

4

Introduction

This book is an attempt to provide a picture of Rye in the sixteenth century in its totality. Tudor Rye saw itself and indeed was a semi-autonomous self-governing entity—a 'commonweal' in sixteenth century parlance. Those who dwelt within its liberties were either freemen—'the commons'—or inhabitants. Outsiders were 'foreigners' if they came from the surrounding countryside (or elsewhere in England) or 'aliens' if they came from abroad. Entry and permanent settlement in the town was tightly controlled and the most usual final sanction against undesirables was banishment. Governed by its own magistrates, known locally as Jurats and drawn chiefly, but not entirely from the wealthier local merchants and ship owners, its status as a Cinque Port gave it virtually complete exemption from the jurisdiction of the Sussex and Kent JPs, drawn from the local gentry, who ruled beyond its boundaries.

Successive town clerks presided over an administration which kept meticulous records of its daily activities. Minutes of the corporate decisions of its freemen and the administrative and judicial proceedings of the Mayor and Jurats, the Assemblies, Hundreds and Sessions Books (RYE 1) run with gaps from 1538, continuously from 1549, important earlier decisions being recorded in the Custumals and Precedence Books (RYE 57), which refer back to the twelfth and early thirteenth centuries. The Chamberlains' Accounts (RYE 60) which began in 1446, and record daily income and expenditure are virtually complete for the Tudor period. A series of eleven 'sesses' or local rates, beginning in 1491/2 span the period to 1604. These, together with the returns of those subscribing to the 1523 benevolence, list all but the poorest sort and enable a detailed reconstruction of the social and economic structure of the town. The Churchwardens' Accounts 1513–70 (RYE 147), the most detailed in

5

Sussex, itemise the religious changes in Rye resulting from the English Reformation. Finally, the General Files, which survive from 1571 (RYE 47) and preserve much of the incoming and outgoing correspondence of the corporation, together with the Plea Rolls of the Court of Record from 1536 (RYE 35) provide a wealth of material on the occupations and business activities of many of the town's inhabitants.

Among other records relating to Rye in the Tudor period, the parish registers of Rye's only parish church (unusually for a town of its size) survive with only short gaps from 1538. Second only to the parish registers themselves as a source of information on the families of Rye inhabitants have been the 300 wills and 400 administrations, usually with inventory totals, preserved among the Lewes Archdeaconry probate records at the East Sussex Record Office and the 120 wills among the Prerogative Court of Canterbury wills registers at the Public Record Office, London. Principal among the other sources of material on Tudor Rye held there are the Customs Accounts of the Port of Chichester (E122) and the Rye Port Books (E190) which provide the major source for trade and shipping movements into and out of the port of Rye.

For a town whose population cannot have much exceeded 4,000 at its height in the mid-sixteenth century, such a range of documentation is impressive and enables a study of similar scope and depth to those already published for larger, better-known communities. Rye was a very different town in a number of important respects from places such as Coventry, Worcester, Exeter or York.[1] Firstly it was in no sense a provincial centre unlike these other towns. Its catchment area as a local market was considerably smaller and it did not serve as a centre of administration for its surrounding area. Nor, unlike towns such as Coventry and Worcester, did it have any firm manufacturing base. It was simply a port, dependent for its continued existence on a combination of fishing and trade. Perhaps most crucially for its growth and eventual decline, Rye was within 70 miles of London, whose markets it supplied with fresh fish and for which, together with other south-eastern ports, it acted on occasion as an out-port. Finally, unlike the subjects of existing studies, Rye did not overcome its economic difficulties, but entered the seventeenth century with a rapidly-silting harbour, the loss of much of its trade and fishing fleet and a sharply-reduced population which only in the late twentieth century has regained its mid-sixteenth century levels.

At the beginning of the Tudor age, Rye was already a substantial and growing south coast port. With the final abandonment of

Winchelsea by the sea in the early decades of the sixteenth century, Rye grew substantially in wealth and population, reaching a peak in the middle years of the sixteenth century. From the 1580s decline set in, slow at first, but rapidly gaining pace in the 1590s, marked by a sharp fall in the number of its inhabitants, driven out by a combination of deteriorating harbour facilities, rising local taxes and reduced trading opportunities. By the beginning of the seventeenth century, Rye's years of greatest prosperity and importance were well past and the transformation into a much smaller local market town and fishing port had been largely effected. The terminal dates of this study, 1485-1603, can therefore be seen to cover a distinct period of Rye's development as a town, although these dates have not been rigidly adhered to where particular trends could best be traced by extending the time-span a little.

Many of the themes touched on in this study will be familiar to historians of other early modern towns. Rye's social structure, for example, displays a familiar pyramidal shape, with a heavy concentration of wealth and political power amongst a relatively closely-knit and often inter-related urban elite. The occupational structure, on the other hand, heavily dominated as it is by the fishing and maritime trading activities is quite distinct. In common with other urban centres of the period, Rye suffered severe recurrent epidemic mortality, reflected in substantially more burials than baptisms throughout the sixteenth century, such that its population could only be maintained by a continuous influx of migrants, mainly from the surrounding Kent and Sussex villages. Similarly, in the vitality of its political institutions, its stubborn resistance to encroachments on its liberties by government and other outsiders and in the single-minded pursuit of the town's economic interests by its parliamentary representatives, Tudor Rye closely follows the political patterns of behaviour of the larger English corporations. Lastly, Rye typifies the religious and social experience of many English towns an its wealth of pre-Reformation activities, its religious festivals, Resurrection Play, May Game and other seasonal events, so abruptly terminated in the mid-century by the English Reformation, which split the body of the freemen and magistrates into two opposing camps and laid the foundation for the sometimes bitter factional conflict which continued into the seventeenth century.

Rye's importance as a port was linked inextricably with the often shifting patterns of trade in the Channel, which were in turn largely determined by political events in Northern Europe. In this sense Rye's function and geographical location made it vulnerable to sudden changes in its economic fortunes as a result of political decisions far beyond its control to a far greater degree than the other early modern English towns so far studied. In the first half of the period, Rye's trade was dominated by the regular provisioning of Calais, England's last continental possession, to which vast quantities of firewood and other provisions (mainly foodstuffs) were sent annually, accounting for as many as 300 ships in some years, or about three-quarters of Rye's total export trade. The loss of Calais in early 1558 therefore resulted in an overnight once-and-for-all reduction in the numbers of ships entering and leaving the port by almost two-thirds. Such a sudden change affected not only the agents and suppliers directly involved in the trade, but also the town's victuallers, brewers and bakers, who had provided for the needs of visiting seamen. From the late 1560s Rye participated in the growing cloth trade with Rouen, only to find that this, too, collapsed virtually overnight, after the declaration of that town for the Catholic League, following the murder of the Duke of Guise in December 1588. Warfare in the channel might also have a more temporary but often recurrent effect on the town's trade, as during the period of hostilities with the Netherlands following their backing for Perkin Warbeck's attempted invasion in the late 1490s, or the various wars with France of Henry VIIIs reign. Often, in times of war, the demand for ship service and the need to repair Rye's town defences might see a doubling of expenditure by the corporation at precisely the same time that trade was virtually at a standstill. In all these respects, Rye's experience, while typical of other south coast ports such as Sandwich, Dover and Southampton, was quite different to that of larger inland towns.

Rye's geographical location and role as a port no doubt also influenced its early adhesion to Protestantism, which already had a firm hold on an important section of freemen and inhabitants by the mid-1530s. Its cosmopolitan atmosphere was enhanced by the existence of a small but significant alien element among its population throughout the sixteenth century, which grew to enormous propor-tions with the influx of Huguenot refugees in the 1570s. The conflict of economic interests which this engendered between native Rye inhabitants and their foreign co-religionists, to whom they gave shelter, provides an interesting footnote to Elizabethan England's championing of the protestant cause.

In a number of important respects, therefore, the experience of sixteenth century Rye differs markedly from that of many other English towns. Its wealth of documentary sources, while weaker than

8

some of these towns in certain respects, in a number of areas provides new insights into life in the early modern town. The moral and social outlook of the town dwellers of sixteenth century England, reflected in the actions and utterances of both governers and governed are revealed especially clearly in Rye's judicial records. Its religious and social life is also particularly well documented, as are its citizens' commercial and trading activities. The main features of trends in Rye's demography and its household structure can also be outlined with more confidence than other sixteenth century English towns. If this study has succeeded in giving new insights into some of these areas, while confirming and occasionally modifying the conclusions drawn from other similar studies, it will have achieved its main task. Perhaps too it may awaken a new interest in the results of research into our less recent urban past in a wider local audience.

CHAPTER 1

A Populous Town

'your highnes said towne is a place of suche sarvice as the
lyke this realme hathe not; not only for the contynuall well
sarvinge of youre Maiestie, the citie of London, and a great
parte of this realme with the provision of fishe, for the
furnysshinge likewise of a greate countrye adioyninge to yt
with all kinde of neadefull foren comodities; and for the right
worthye and acceptable sarvice yt hathe don and may do in
the annoyinge of thenemy in the tyme of hostilitie and war;
but also for the notable refuge that aswell youre graces owne
navye as all other vessells traders by the seas have had of the
famous rode called the Camber in the tyme of stormy
tempest ...'
                Petition concerning amendment of the harbour, 1561
                                                    (RYE 99/3).

'The number of our people daily being five thowsand besides
our estrangers being resident and others in trade by see and
land.'
                        Request for licence to purvey corn,
                            September 1573 (RYE 47/7/68).

Rye in its geographical and economic setting

To the modern-day visitor approaching the town from Hastings
to the west or New Romney to the east, Rye appears at a distance
as an island hilltop, dominated by its church and covered in
houses, rising out of the grey expanse of Romney Marsh. As
Pevsner notes in his admirable county guide, the overall
impression is more 'reminiscent of the north of France'.[1]
Approached from the sea Rye still looms menacingly, the outline
of its silhouette marked by the sharp lines of its onetime defences,
Baddings Tower and the Gungarden, which guard its seaward
side, in front of which advancing shipping still has to pass, much
as it did in the sixteenth century when the town was at the zenith

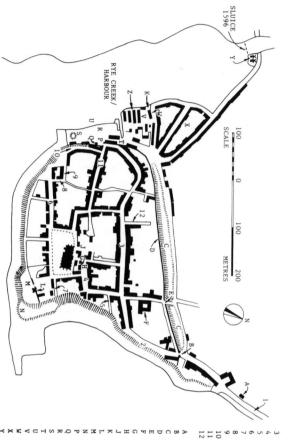

Figure 1: Sixteenth century Rye (based on Jeake's map 1666/7, copied 1728 (Rye 132/15) and John Prowze's map of Rye harbour 1572 (PRO MPF 212))

1 Causeway to Playden Hill.
2 East Cliff.
3 Lower or Longer Street.
4 Butchery.
5 Ockmans Lane.
6 Watchbell Street.
7 Baddings Lane.
8 Watchbell Lane.
9 Rucks Lane.
10 West Cliff, otherwise Baldwins Wish.
11 Middle Street.
12 Pondgarden.

A Almshouse.
B Landgate.
C Town Ditch.
D Town Wall.
E Postern Gate.
F Former Austin Friary.
G Court Hall.
H Market Place.
J Vicarage.
K Crane.
L Baddings Tower.
M Upper Gun Garden.
N Lower Gun Garden.
P Strandgate.
Q The Cage.
R Strand.
S The Mount.
T Strand Conduit.
U The Quay.
V Fish Market.
W Town Store House.
X The Wishe.
Y Strand Mills.
Z Rows of Shops.

12

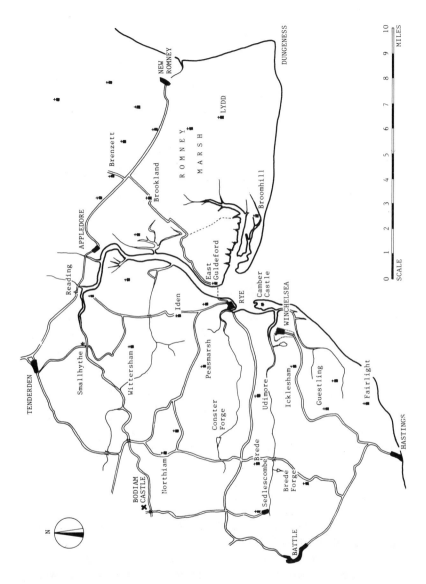

Figure 2: Rye and its environs
(based on P. Symondson's map of Rye harbour, Rother levels, Walland and
Romney Marshes 1594 (Rye 132/6) and J. Stonehouse the younger's map of
Romney Marsh 1599 (Rye 132/7))

13

of its prosperity and importance.

The town itself (see Figure 1) retains its original medieval street plan pattern within its walls, much of which remain stretching along its northern side from Landgate in the east to the site of the former Strandgate in the west. Behind its Georgian facades Rye retains many of its original timber-framed buildings, erected by the town's wealthier merchants and traders in the late fifteenth and sixteenth centuries.

In this period, before the silting up of the Camber (see Figure 2), Rye lay at the northern end of a vast tidal bay, formed out of the estuaries of the Rivers Brede, Tillingham and Rother. The town itself stood perched on a sandstone promontory at the head of a narrow isthmus, surrounded on three sides by water and to the north by saltmarsh inned at various points in the sixteenth century, which was protected by a seawall extending north-west along the banks of the Tillingham. This wall was recorded in 1528 when it was breached by the sea and again in about 1571 when the ravages of the autumn winds and tides were assisted by some of Rye's inhabitants 'of meaner sorte to the nomber of an hundred persones in evill and unlawfull manner assembled', according to a contemporary account, at the instigation of the deputy mayor, John Bayley, 'pretendinge the breche thereof to be greatlye to the amendment of the said haven'.[2] Only a narrow causeway, guarded by a series of groynes (maintained at considerable expense by the corporation) and running from the Landgate to the foot of Playden Hill, linked Rye to the mainland. Otherwise, communication was by ferry to East Guldeford to the east and the road to New Romney and Dover, or by the Town Ferry to the west, which linked Rye to Cadborough Hill and the roads to Winchelsea and Battle.[3]

Rye owed its continued prosperity to the sea. Its fishing and mercantile fleets in the early to mid-sixteenth century were among the largest on the south-east coast. Rye's rapid growth to major importance in the early Tudor period owed much to the silting up of the approach to Winchelsea some three miles to the southwest and the consequent migration of trade to its quayside. Towards the end of the sixteenth century, however, Rye fell into an equally spectacular decline, its population and corporate income falling by more than half in the last two decades of the century.

In its heyday, Rye was easily the largest and most prosperous

Table 1

Rye and leading English towns 1523-7

		£			£
1	London (and Southwark)	17,465	22	Hereford	273
2	Norwich	1,704	23	Great Yarmouth	260
3	Bristol	1,072	24	Hull	256
4	Newcastle	–a	25	Boston	c240
5	Coventry	974	26	Southampton	224
6	Exeter	855	27	Hadleigh	c224
7	Salisbury	852	28	Wisbech	c220
8	Ipswich	657	29	Shrewsbury	c220
9	Lynn	576	30	Oxford	202
10	Canterbury	552	31	Leicester	199
11	Reading	c470	32	Cambridge	181
12	Colchester	426	33	Stamford	c180
13	Bury St Edmunds	405	34	Dover	–a
14	Lavenham	402	35	Northampton	180
15	York	379	36	Windsor	178
16	Totnes	c317	37	Durham	–a
17	Worcester	312	38	Plymouth	163
18	Gloucester	c307	39	Maldon	c150
19	Lincoln	298	40	St Albans	c150
20	RYE	291	41	Chichester	138
21	Chester	–a	42	Winchester	132

Notes:

a   no return available. Position estimated from population.

Subsidy paid to nearest £. Hoskins apparently based his figures on the cumulative totals of payments made by towns in the 1523 anticipation, and the 1524 and 1525 subsidies. Chichester for example paid only £62 9s 5d in 1524 and £63 2s 11d in 1525, yet Hoskins credits it with payments of £138. The difference ought to be accounted for by the anticipation, yet Chichester paid £27 14s 0d according to the surviving account. Hoskins' figures probably need to be treated with caution. For the Sussex figures see J. Cornwall *The Lay Subsidy Rolls for the County of Sussex 1524–5,* Sussex Record Society 56 (1956). Those assessed for subsidy paid in 1524 and in 1525 flat rate of 4d on wages of £1; 6d in the £ on wages of over £2 or on goods worth between £2 and under £20; or 1s in the £ on income from land or on goods worth over £20, whichever was the highest. Rye as a Cinque Port was exempt from the actual subsidy, but those assessed at £5 and upwards paid at the rate of 2s in the £, or, for assessments over £300, at 2s 8d.

Sources:

Adapted from P. Slack 'The English urban landscape', p.86 in 'The Urban Setting', *English Urban History 1500–1780* Unit 3, The Open University (1977). Slack's figures are for London and for the placings of Newcastle, Chester, Dover and Durham. The remainder of the figures and placings are from W.G. Hoskins, *Local History in England* (1959) p.177. The Rye figures are taken from two promissory letters under Privy Seal for the amounts received from Rye inhabitants May and July 1523 (RYE 81/1-2), which total £287 12s 0d plus the subsidy assessment on aliens living within Rye, amounting to £2 18s 8d (P.R.O. E179 189/156) printed in J. Cornwall *op. cit.* pp.164-5. Aliens paid at double the rate of Englishmen.

town in Sussex, and can claim to rank among the foremost provincial towns in England. In 1523 for example, as Table 1 indicates, Rye must have ranked among the top 20 English towns after London, and may well have been considerably higher on the list than the bare totals from the 1523 benevolence payments suggest. Certainly its population throughout much of the sixteenth century can have been no lower than 530 householders and 2468 'people of all sorts' (excluding strangers) at which it was put by a government survey in 1565, and may well have been considerably higher, as the quotation at the beginning of this chapter suggests.[4]

Historians can however be excused for having failed to appreciate the size and wealth of Rye in the Tudor period. Hoskins' ranking of the leading provincial towns, upon which Table 1 is based, relied largely on the 1524 and 1525 subsidy payments from which Rye, in common with the other Cinque Ports, was customarily exempt. The chance survival of the indentures for Rye's payments under the 1523 benevolence, which, like the subsidies of the following two years were based on an earlier assessment for the 1522 musters does, however, allow a rough comparison to be made between Rye and other English towns at this date. Since the first of these returns for Rye only includes those worth £20 and above, and the second, which purports to cover those worth between £5 and £20, includes only a small fraction of those at the lower end of the assessment, whereas the subsidy returns include all those worth £1 a year in wages or goods and upwards, it is clear that the total figure for Rye is substantially lower than it would have been had the town not been exempt from subsidy. In Chichester, for example, ranked 41 in Table 1, 35.6 per cent of the subsidy payments fell on those assessed at under £10. If a similar distribution of wealth held true for Rye, the amount actually paid would be increased from £290 10s 8d to £389 4s, with a corresponding rise in Rye's place in the Table from 20 to 15, immediately ahead of York.[5] Such a conclusion clearly has major implications for the placing of other leading Cinque Ports, in particular Sandwich and Dover, in this table and may well call for a substantial revision of current views on the timing of the shift in economic importance from the east coast to the west in the late medieval period.[6] It must be emphasised that such figures are only a very rough guide and need

16

Table 2

The relative wealth of Sussex towns 1523-5

	Assessed wealth £	total paid £	number of taxpayers £
RYE	2801	291	83
Chichester	1610	153[1]	301
Lewes	1042	85*	208
Horsham	645	55	107
Midhurst	410	27	103
Arundel	270	17*	76
Steyning	257	20	63
East Grinstead	155	11*	44
Shoreham	36	3	20
Bramber	38	2	17

Notes:

Amounts to nearest £. Assessed wealth and number of taxpayers based on 1524 subsidy except for Chichester, where 1524 returns appear defective. Total paid refers to sum of payments in 1524 and 1525.
[1]   sum of payments in 1524 and 1525 plus anticipation 1523.
*   returns for 1525 defective: figure therefore obtained by doubling 1524 assessment.

Sources: RYE 81/1-2; J. Cornwall op cit.

to be treated with a degree of caution.

However, a number of other surviving assessments lead to a similar conclusion concerning Rye's considerable size and wealth in the early Tudor period. In 1491/2 for example a town sesse (rating assessment) on all those worth £2 and upwards gave a total valuation for those assessed of £6803, compared to £2801 in the 1523 benevolence, indicating a deliberate under-assessment on the latter occasion. In 1595/6 a similar sesse gave a total valuation of £15,344.[7]

A brief comparison of Rye with other Sussex towns assessed for subsidy in 1523-5 indicates at once the overwhelming pre-dominance of the town as a trading centre in the county. As Table 2 demonstrates, its tax base, even ignoring the limited numbers of those assessed for the benevolence, easily outstripped those of Chichester and Lewes, the two county towns, combined. Despite its notional immunity from subsidy assessments, Rye's payment by way of benevolence equalled the combined subsidy payments of Chichester, Lewes and Horsham, the three wealthiest Sussex towns outside the Cinque Ports confederation. Indeed, Rye's contribution to the exchequer in these years was more than three times that of Lewes, then a town of some 1,500—2,000 people.

17

Among the Sussex Cinque Ports (Table 3), Rye's predominance in size and wealth is equally striking. In the forced loan of 1543, Rye paid almost 60 per cent of the total contribution of the Sussex Ports. In 1545, despite massive expenditure by the town on its defences, Rye contributed over £338, equivalent to virtually two-thirds of the entire payments of the Sussex Ports and more than any of the Sussex rapes with the exception of Chichester Rape, which included the City. Chichester's own contribution can be gauged from the fact that when a further forced loan was called for early in 1547, Chichester paid £100 3s 4d out of a total county payment of £1756 10s 6d, a figure proportionately only slightly down on the £1364 17s 8d total for four of the six Sussex rapes in 1545.[8] At the height of its prosperity, in the 1540s, Rye would seem to have been taxed at approximately three times the rate for Chichester, including the Cathedral close, whose occupants had been exempt from the lay subsidy payments of the 1520s.[9]

Rye's wealth depended on its function as a port. Its fishing fleets provided fish for the royal household, for the London fishmarket and for many of the towns and villages and for much of the noble and gentry households in eastern Sussex and the Kentish Weald. The 1565 government survey, summarised in Table 4, listed 25 fishing vessels from Rye, 'goinge dayly to the sees' and a further 24 which were laid up until the season for 'fishing for playse, cunger and mackerelles'. Of equal importance as a source of wealth, although employing rather less people, was

Table 3

The relative wealth of the Sussex Cinque Ports 1543-5

	Amounts paid £	
	1543	1545
Rye	100 0 0	338 6 0
Hastings	6 13 4	67 7 8
Winchelsea	16 13 4	67 2 0
Pevensey	33 6 8	34 4 0
Seaford	13 6 8	10 4 2
Total Cinque Ports	170 0 0	517 3 10
Total county assessment	1225 0 0	1364 17 8*

Notes: * Arundel, Pevensey and Hastings Rapes only. No returns for Bramber and Lewes Rapes.

Sources: PRO E179 190/218 (1543 loan); E179 190/197, 199-202 (1545 benevolence).

Table 4
Ships and mariners in Rye and the eastern Sussex ports 1565

Town	Households	Population	Fishermen Mariners	Ships	Tonnage
RYE	530	2468	785	66	1252
Hastings	280	-	239	32	551
Winchelsea	109	-	12	12	81
Eastbourne	141	-	12	4	25
Pevensey	64	-	0	0	0
Seaford	38	-	7	1	2

Notes: Only Rye, Hastings and Winchelsea had mariners engaged in merchant trade or passage. Rye had 60, Hastings 16 and Winchelsea 10. In Rye 13 barkes or crayers of between 16 and 50 tons were engaged in 'trade of merchauntdise and passage', in Hastings 7, and in Winchelsea one hoye of 30 tons. The residue of Winchelsea's shipping consisted of 6 cock boats of between 1 and 3 tons and 5 lighters of between 5 and 10 tons. The total tonnage for Rye does not include 8 cock boats for which no tonnages were given. No lighters are listed for Rye itself, but 4 lighters of between 8-10 tons and 2 boats of 3 tons are listed belonging to the Hundred of Goldspur, which extended north from Rye to Appledore on the Sussex side of the River Rother.

Source: PRO SP 12 38/28.

the town's mercantile trade, which in 1565 engaged thirteen of the larger vessels, 'barkes and crayers', to the total of 439 tons, and which employed some 60 mariners. Fishing was however the dominant occupation, according to the 1565 survey, accounting for 225 of the town's 530 householders. In addition there were 50 young men 'occupying themselves and no householders', presumably single, but who, having served their apprenticeships, qualified as full crew-members for their share in the catch, plus 450 'servants to fishermen', who would have worked for an annual wage.[10] Since few of these latter can have been householders either, they presumably also lived with their masters, helping to create a distinct male bias in the composition of Rye's population[11] and contributing to a higher than average mean household size. The residue of the town's population seem largely to have been engaged in such ancillary occupations as food and drink, carpentry and the building industries, clothing and distribution, such as merchants and their servants, carriers and the like. Other sources for the employment structure of Rye, such as the statistics for freemen's occupations and an analysis of the 1576 sesse bear out the 1565 survey's findings that just over 40 per cent of householders were engaged in fishing or seafaring as their primary occupation. However, such a proportion would indicate an adult male population of more than 1800, since 785 (according to the

19

Table 5

Ships and mariners in Rye and the Cinque Ports 1587

Town	February 1587			October 1587		
	Mariners	Ships	Tonnage	Mariners	Ships	Tonnage
Sandwich	106	43	1216	102	40	-
RYE	285	45	1111	325	34	-
Dover	130	33	1091	176	26	-
Hastings	121	15	478	168	20	-
Faversham	-	-	-	57	26	-
Brightlingsea	41	20	340	63	12	-
Hythe	73	11	201	22	10[1]	-
Ramsgate	32	14	189	80	12	-
Margate[2]	-	-	-	64	12	-
Folkestone	35	4	68	44	4	-
Lydd	31	8	33	30	8	-
Deal	39	6	16	35	5	-
Walmer	19	5	11	8	4	-
Winchelsea	-	-	-	6	1	-
New Romney	-	-	-	-	-	-
Pevensey	-	-	-	-	-	-
Seaford	-	-	-	-	-	-

Notes: 1 others fishing at Yarmouth
2 with St Peters.

Sources: PRO SP12 198/29; SP12 204/25.

1565 survey) were employed in fishing or other maritime activities. The total figure of 2468, given in the survey for 'people of all sorts besides strangers' can hardly therefore refer to the whole population including women and children, as these two groups would, on estimates from other early modern towns, be expected between them to account for approximately two-thirds of the total population. Under any reasonable estimates therefore, were Rye's population in 1565 to have been 2468, approximately 1600 of them would have been women and children. If 785 of the remainder were employed primarily in the fishing industry, there would have been almost none left to carry on all the other activities essential to any Tudor town. It seems likely that Rye's actual population in 1565 was nearer to 4,000, or perhaps slightly higher, which would accord more readily with the corporation's own estimate of 5,000, excluding strangers in September 1573.

Two later surveys of shipping, dating from the time of the Armada scare in the late 1580s, provide an opportunity for a comparison between the size of Rye's mercantile and fishing fleets and those of the other Cinque Ports. By February 1587, when the first of these lists was drawn up, Rye had begun its period of rapid decline. According to this survey Rye had only 45 vessels, with a

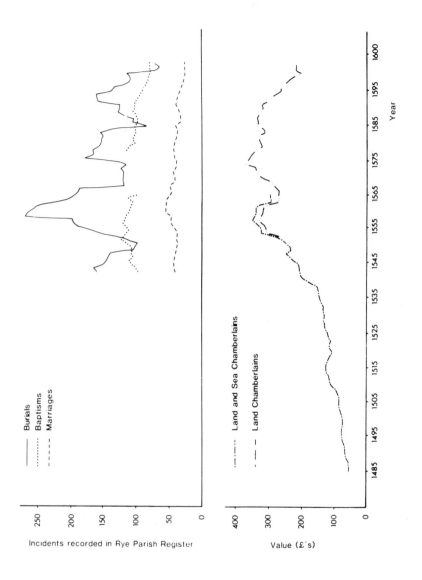

Figure 3A: Christenings, marriages and burials in Rye: nine year moving average

Figure 3B: Rye Chamberlains' receipts: nine year moving average

21

combined tonnage of 1111 tons and 285 masters and mariners, compared to the 66 ships totalling 1252 tons and 785 seamen listed in 1565. Much of the decline was clearly very recent, since another list of Rye's shipping dated November 1580, gives 458 mariners and 55 ships with a combined tonnage of 1282 tons, as Dell suggests, roughly equivalent to 'half that of Hull, Bristol and Southampton, more than Exeter, Lynn or Leigh and an eleventh of that of London itself'.[12]

Nevertheless, despite the reduction in the size and manpower of Rye's fleet in the 1580s, in 1587 the town still had the largest number of ships of any of the Cinque Ports, by far the largest number of mariners and the second largest combined tonnage (although in this respect there was little to choose between the three leading members of the Confederation at this time, Sandwich, Rye and Dover). Such figures indicate the still considerable importance of the larger members of the Cinque Ports even at the end of the Tudor era. Rye's own fortunes however continued to decline. A further survey of 1590 listed only 37 vessels and 279 mariners, while the Rye muster rolls for 1598/9 list only 149 seamen out of an apparent adult male population (notionally aged between 16 and 60) of 429, indicating that the overall population of the town may have fallen to little more than 1500 by the end of the sixteenth century.[13]

Demographic and economic developments

Overall population figures for communities in the period before the introduction of censuses are notoriously difficult to calculate with any great degree of exactitude, particularly where, as in the case of Rye, the surviving evidence is often contradictory. However the survival of Rye's parish registers from 1538 and the fact that, unusually for a town of its size, the town had only one parish church, enable a reasonable degree of confidence in calculating the underlying trends in Rye's population. Figure 3A graphically illustrates the trends in recorded christenings, marriages and burials, using a nine-year moving average to smoothe over any short-term aberrations. The annual totals on which it is based are in Appendix 1.

The most striking feature of the figures is the high degree of fluctuation and overall high levels of burials throughout the period, indicating the impact of major epidemic mortality throughout the sixteenth century, which necessitated continual immigration on a considerable scale in order to maintain the town's population.[14] Nevertheless, even the annual burial totals give clear indication of the decline both in the peaks caused by major epidemics (the early 1560s, the late 1570s and the early 1590s) and in the troughs resulting from their absence for a period (around 1550, the early 1570s, the mid-1580s and the early years of the seventeenth century). Between 1559 and 1564, for example the nine-year moving averages for burials ranged between 267 and 201, whereas the mortality crises of the early 1590s only resulted in a peak rate of 157 recorded burials. Similarly the absence of major epidemics in the late 1560s produced an eight-year trough where annual burial rates fluctuated between 114 and 118. A similar lull at the beginning of the seventeenth century resulted in average rates of between 65 and 70 burials per year, an average burial rate 40 per cent lower than thirty years previously.

A similar trend is revealed by the baptism and marriage rates. In the case of christenings, a gradual decline is observable from the high levels of the 1550s, when annual baptism rates fluctuated between 110 and 120. By the 1580s these had fallen to just below 100. The biggest decline, however, came in the 1590s, the annual rate dropping from 100 in 1590 to 77 in 1600, representing a decline of more than 20 per cent in a single decade and of more than one third compared to the 1550s. Marriage rates tell much the same story, with a gradual rise to a peak of 52-4 marriages per year in the early 1560s, followed by a steady decline to around 40 throughout the 1570s, 31-7 during the 1580s and 25 between 1599 and 1603, the latter representing a fall of more than half since 1560 and approximately 40 per cent from the 1570s.

Allowing for such special factors in Rye's population structure as the sexual imbalance in the population, resulting in a below average birth rate; and the presence of numbers of strangers and foreigners passing through the port, causing an above average death rate, it would seem reasonable to assume a crude baptism rate of perhaps 25 per thousand and a crude burial rate of at least 40 per thousand.[15] Such figures agree in producing an estimate for the town's population of just under 5,000 in the 1550s and 1560s, falling only slightly, to perhaps 4,000 by 1580 and to little more than 2,000 by the end of the century, although as Rye's decline becomes more marked in the 1590s it is clear that there is a growing tendency for burial and baptism rates to converge, with the reduction of employment opportunities for young men and a fall in the number of vessels visiting the port. Marriage rates may well have been as high as 11 per thousand throughout the period. However all three series (christenings, marriages and burials) clearly demonstrate, with only a very slight variation in degree, the rapid decline of Rye's population in the 1590s, so that by 1600 the town can have numbered little more than half its population in the two peak decades either side of 1560.

Further confirmatory evidence of these trends in Rye's fortunes is provided by the annual receipts of the two chamberlains, recorded in the chamberlains' account volumes. Again a nine-year moving average has been used to reduce the distortion of freak years. The results, set out in Figure 3B, suggest a steady growth in the town's fortunes to 1558, after which there was a short-lived minor recession, followed by recovery lasting well into the early 1570s. From 1574 however, the trend is noticeably downwards, with a distinct acceleration during the 1590s. The trends in corporate income closely mirror the pattern established from the parish registers and add further weight to the view that Rye reached its peak in size and prosperity in the 1550s and 1560s, began a period of slow decline in the later 1570s to 1580s, which accelerated in the 1590s, resulting in a fall in corporate income levels from an average £366 in 1574 to £211 by 1603, a drop of well over 40 per cent and very much in line with the fall in population.

The chamberlains' accounts provide detailed evidence of the sources of corporate income and expenditure throughout the Tudor period. Generally speaking, income rose to meet expenditure, the additional revenue being generated by temporary expedients, such as the levying of special sesses or rates, of which eleven are recorded between 1491 and 1604, mainly to meet increased wartime expenditure[16] but also for other major items of expenditure, as in 1576, for harbour works, or in 1581 and 1598 to pay the parliamentary expenses of the town's MPs. Other such expedients included the borrowing of money, as for example the £100 lent by the mayor on the occasion of Queen Elizabeth's visit in 1573; and, at the end of the period, the selling-off of town properties, a particularly short-sighted policy which sacrificed future income to short-term financial gain.

In normal years, however the chief sources of revenue were a variety of taxes on economic activity in the town and the rents from corporation properties. Throughout the Tudor period, the most important single sources of revenue were the quarterly dues of the great and lesser boxes and the dues paid by fishermen, representing a portion of their catch. The dues of the great box were paid by shopkeepers, the victualling trades—innkeepers and beer tipplers, butchers, bakers and brewers—and by local fishmongers or 'feters'. The lesser box covered maltodes (dues on goods, passengers and animals passing through the port) and consisted chiefly of quayage on wares and livestock, measurage on salt and grain, grand and petty passage (tolls on ships and passengers) and the dues of 'osts' or agents chiefly of the London fishmongers but also the royal purveyor of fish, together with dues of 'marketmen' (outsiders) on fish bought for local consumption in the neighbouring towns and villages. Together these items, including the maltodes on the fishermen, accounted for over £46 of the total income of the corporation of £53 15s 1½d in the financial year[17] 1485/6, and although their proportionate contribution to the town's finances fell somewhat in the middle part of the period, as, increasingly, other items of income were exploited, in real terms they continued to rise, contributing over £75 of the £123 12s 4d income in 1525/6 and more than £141 of the total income of £319 0s 1d in 1575/6. However, at the end of the period, even these sources of income suffered a substantial decline, with the proceeds of the great and lesser boxes together falling from £102 1s 3½d in 1593/4 to £76 9s 6d by 1600/1—a drop of over 25 per cent in seven years, and of more than 45 per cent from the 1585/6 total of £140 18s 5d. An apparent recovery to £124 5s 7d in 1602/3 was in fact achieved only by a substantial increase in the rates of the maltodes on goods coming into or going out from the town and the introduction of additional taxes such as the new payments of quarterage by craftsmen (master carpenters, shipwrights, masons, tanners and the like) for occupying their trades, which the assembly decreed in November 1602.[18] Such measures may have provided short-term relief for the corporate finances, but their longer-term effect can only have been to have driven some of these occupations elsewhere by reducing still further the economic attractiveness of a rapidly declining port.

A second source of income that assumed a growing importance in the early sixteenth century was the town rent roll, which stood at only £1 12s 4d in 1485/6. With the building of new shops by the quayside at Strand in the mid-1480s, this figure more than doubled, to £4 2s 4d by 1487/8. Further investment raised that figure still further, to £10 16s 4d by 1515/6 and to between £24 and £27 from the shops at Strand alone from the 1550s to the 1590s, £17 14s 6d of this amount coming from the two new rows of shops erected in the mid 1540s, which were generally let for 8s or 16s depending on size. Other developments which contributed to the growing importance of rents as a source of corporate income included the letting to farm of the town ferry, the income from which rose from £4 in 1527 to £26 13s 4d by 1548; the farming out of the town storehouse at the Strand, erected in 1552, which brought in between £25 and £33 from mid-1550s until the early 1590s; and the farming out of the dues from the grand and petty passage (tolls on ships and passengers using the port), which brought in a further £20 in 1555/6. As these last three items were generally let on short-term leases of from one to three years, the changing levels of income from them provide a reasonably sensitive guide to the ups and downs in Rye's economic fortunes. In the early 1590s for example, the price paid by the farmers (lessees) of the ferry to the town fluctuated from £17 15s in 1593/4 to £28 5s a year later and only £14 2s 6d in 1595/6, before recovering to £28, at which annual total it remained for the rest of the reign. During the same period the farm of the storehouse fluctuated between £5 (1595/6) and £20 (1594/5 and 1596/7), although by 1601/2 £10 10s was all that the town could get for it. Overall, rents and farms of corporation property formed a major part of corporate income in the later part of the period, the proportion rising sharply from only 3 per cent in the 1480s to between approximately 25-40 per cent in the second half of the sixteenth century, compared to between 40-60 per cent from the taxation of the economy during the same period. The residue was made up of miscellaneous items. These ranged from such constants as £4 dues paid annually by Tenterden as a limb of Rye throughout the sixteenth century and the profits of the courts, to such extraordinary sources of income as the 'hed money' (a form of poll tax) paid by French prisoners in time of war, which accounted for almost one sixth of total income in 1545/6. The

26

occasional collection of 'arrerages' from past chamberlains and churchwardens might also considerably distort a particular annual total, as in 1585/6 when they amounted to £80 10s, over 20 per cent of that year's total income.

Nevertheless, despite such annual fluctuations, the decennial totals provide clear evidence of the trends in Rye's fortunes. After half a century of expansion, corporate expenditure in Rye in the 1540s stood at an annual average of £211, compared to that of £227 by Exeter, a comparable western port. By the 1550s, Rye's expenditure had risen significantly, to £307 a year, but Exeter's had risen faster, to £356. By the 1570s, when Rye's economy had ceased to grow, the comparable figures were £536 for Exeter and £356 for Rye. By the last decade of Elizabeth's reign, they had diverged still further, to £847 for Exeter and only £245 for Rye, which was now experiencing a decline in absolute and not just relative terms, providing a clear example of the differing fortunes of the east and west coast ports in the late sixteenth century.[19]

Corporate expenditure

The annual pattern of expenditure is more difficult to characterise in detail as major outgoings in a particular year could so easily distort the figures, but major recurrent items included wages and liveries of town officers, the costs of repairs to the harbour jetties and the conduits which provided the town's water supply, and the maintenance of Rye's defences (a wartime activity that could account for half of total corporate income in crisis years such as 1557/8).[20] Lesser items of expenditure of a recurrent nature included annual attendance at brotherhoods and guestlings, maintenance of highways within the town and a measure of poor relief. Occasional expenditure of a substantial nature could occur without warning such as the summoning of Parliament and the consequent payment of MPs' wages, or visits to the town by important dignitaries—including Henry VIII, the Duke of Somerset and Elizabeth I, as well as lesser figures as the Lord Warden and the Bishop of Chichester—for all of whom suitable feasting and entertainment had to be provided at the town's cost.

In each aspect the inflationary trends of the mid-Tudor period added substantially to costs, causing the corporation to be looking continually for new sources of revenue and for means of increasing existing ones which were all too often, as in the case of rents (and to a lesser degree, maltodes) fixed by custom. Labourers, who could be hired in 1485 to work on the jetties at 4d a day, cost 12d a century later. In the same period the mayor's quarterly fee trebled from 16s 8d to 50s; while that of the town clerk and lesser officers such as the two sergeants doubled, from 10s and 5s respectively to 20s and 10s. The wages bill of the corporation, which stood at £15 12s 8d in the first year of Henry VII's reign, had more than quadrupled to £63 15s 2d, in 1585/6.[21]

A similar trend can be seen in expenditure on maintaining the harbour. In 1480 a new quayside was built at the Strand at a total cost of £35 16s 4½d. In 1486 a new jetty outside the Landgate was completed for an outlay of £12 7s 2d. By the 1570s costs had risen sharply. A proposal in 1576 for a new jetty on the west side of the creek to protect the fishermen's boats from storms necessitated a sesse of £184. In 1597, it was reported, £445 10s 2d had already been spent on the latest round of harbour repairs with little apparent hope for their immediate completion. A hurried scheme of forced labour and the wholesale disposal of town property to finance further expenditure immediately followed.

In the middle years of the sixteenth century, however, the growing prosperity of the town enabled the corporation to invest in improved harbour facilities. In 1551 a new jetty and new shops were built at the Strand. In 1555 a new town storehouse was built at a cost to the corporation of just under £100. With iron grates set in brick surrounds for its windows and heavy wooden doors, it provided a place of safe storage for the large quantities of goods passing through the port. The building itself had a gallery and was tiled, and its floors and courts were paved with stone and there was a weigh beam with 1,000 lb in lead weights for weighing goods coming into it. With lead guttering alone weighing 855 lbs it must have been a very substantial building, and the long list of weekly charges for storage indicates the range of goods it was expected to serve. Rates varied from 1d for every barrell, small pack or hundred pounds of hops to 6d for a tun of wine or a thousand billets of wood, while a quarter of grain could be stored there for 2d per week. It was clear that its erection was seen as an important investment, since it was immediately rented out for £30 6s 8d a year, and later town decrees make it clear that every

28

man was to lay his stores there or to compound for laying them elsewhere at the rate of one month's charges. The following year a crane was erected adjoining it at a further cost of more than £6, Peter Rolf the carpenter having previously been sent to Sandwich 'to peruse the crane ther to make a new by'. It must, however, have proved inadequate for the town's needs, since only six years later another lessee of the storehouse undertook to erect a second crane at his own charges, in return for a five years' lease at a reduced rent.[23]

A further major source of recurrent expenditure was the maintenance of the town's water supply. The chamberlains' accounts reveal an annual expenditure by the mid-sixteenth century running into several pounds for routine repairs to the pipes, the replacement of the pumps and the cocks, together with more major works every few years. In 1550/1, for example, such repairs cost £4 13s 10d following considerably higher expenditure the previous year. As early as 1520, one such project, involving the services of a master workman from London to make the cistern, cost over £29 16s 11½d. In 1548 the visit of the Lord Protector provided an opportunity to petition him for assistance in the finishing of the new conduit, for which another cistern was built 'at the southend of the chauntrey stables', presumably in the churchyard, and for which the town had levied a special sesse, promising a 'Mr Grey', with whom they had entered into an agreement for its construction £20 in reward if he finished it during the year. Following its completion a plumber was engaged at £4 a year to maintain the system. However substantial costs were still incurred from time to time. In October 1563, for example, the assembly agreed to a payment of £24 13s 4d to a plumber for his work on the conduit. The following September a new maintenance contract was entered into with another plumber on a similar annual basis of £4 a year plus 12d for every day worked and a further 2s 4d for every hundredweight of lead cast. In 1570 another contract was entered into with a different London plumber for a further set of pipes to bring 'new water' from Leasham to the Strand.[24] The list is endless.

From the various topographical information in the accounts and from later agreements for the maintenance of the water supply, it would seem that the Old Conduit ran from the Budgewell (which derived its name from the ships' budge barrells filled there), at the foot of Playden Hill, across the causeway and along the Town Dike to the Strand. The new conduit ran from the spring heads at Leasham Hill through the Postern Gate to a cistern nearby. Various references to pumps indicate that there was a means of pumping the water up the hill, and it is clear from other references to the buying of pitch, canvas, tallow and sailcloth that these were used for minor repairs, presumably mainly to broken joints. The pipes themselves seem to have been in many places above ground, encased in wood, packed in stone and cement. Access to the water supply was controlled by the corporation, which in 1564 limited the opening hours of the Strand Conduit to from 6 to 10 in the morning and from 2 to 8 in the afternoon. A penalty of 10s was ordained for anyone who broke open or picked the lock, and the washing of clothes in the conduit was forbidden.[25]

Among the lesser items of recurrent annual expenditure, attendance at brotherhoods (meetings of the Cinque Ports) at New Romney cost sums ranging in the 1480s from 17s 10d for the mayor and three representatives in July 1488 to £3 0s 7d for attendance at a similar gathering in April 1486. Costs in 1488 included horse hire, the charges of the ferry to East Guldeford, breakfast and dinner at New Romney, horsemeat and a supper at the mayor's on their return. The variable which accounted for the large difference in costs between brotherhoods was the contribution to the common purse which paid for such charges as the legal fees of the ports in maintaining their liberties and their common interest, which 1488 stood at 5s. In 1486 costs were higher due to the necessity of an overnight stay and a common purse contribution of 30s. A hundred years later in 1586 the costs of attendance had risen to £13 7s 10d, including a common purse contribution of £3.[26]

Another minor recurrent item of expenditure was the maintenance of roads within the town. Although householders were responsible for paving the street immediately outside of their own tenements, the town had a responsibility for maintenance of the king's highways, including the road across the causeway from Playden which entered Rye through the Landgate, and also the Market Place and the Strand. In 1512 for example, the chamberlains' accounts refer to the gathering of stones for the pavers from under the cliff and to the paving of the street which ran along by the Strand, for which 'the pavers of London' were paid 26s 10d. Later the same year there are references to paving the Market; and in 1514 to 'gravelling' the way at Strand. As with other items of expenditure, inflation pushed up charges substantially, and in 1549/50 the accounts show expenditure of £5 18s 4d for 'paving the streate against Mr Woodes shops', a total of 489 yards. Following a 1555 Act of Parliament, householders had to provide a labourer to work four (or from 1563, six) days on the highways, usually in Rogation Week or at Whitsuntide. Those defaulting paid an additional highway rate, which by the 1570s was bringing between £4 and £6 a year. Such small sums, however scarcely began to meet the costs involved, which in 1584, for example, ran to £13 9s 0d, compared to only £5 15s 10d collected from the highway rate.[27]

Of rather less importance in terms of costs as far as the chamberlains' accounts are concerned were the charitable disbursements made to poor people, usually amounting to only a few shillings, which were paid by the mayor at each opening of the boxes. In 1485/6 such payments in total only amounted to £1 0s 6d, but they indicate the connection between office-holding and charitable distribution which was a feature of the period. Most charitable provision was made through the church, in wills and through the poor box. The custumal reveals that the chief religious institution for the provision of the poor in Rye in the Middle Ages had been St. Bartholomew's Hospital, on the roadside leading from Rye to Playden, within the parish of Rye but outside the liberties of the town. The right of appointing a chaplain was vested in the mayor and jurats, who also nominated the inmates from among the respectable aged poor of the town, the phrase used, indicating the distinction already existing in the minds of the authorities between the deserving and undeserving poor: 'among hys commons man or woman which hathe competentlye borne charges ... in ther tyme for ye welfare of ye towne and they be nowe impoveryshed and ympotent, decayed of ther goodes and catalles and lytyll goodes have to lyve wyth'.

Following the Reformation, a new almshouse was erected, on a plot of land 60ft by 30ft just outside the Landgate, conveyed to the town for the purpose in 1551 by Alexander Welles, then town clerk. The following year the chamberlains' accounts reveal expenditure of £29 15s 2½d for the erection of the building itself, including the purchase of an existing timber-framed building in the town for £3, a further £3 to a carpenter for taking it down 'and setting uppe the same howse for the newe almes howse', plus the purchase of an additional 7 tons of timber, 2 loads of lathes, 130 bushels of lime for the plaster, tiles and 10,000 bricks made locally at 'Eston's Kyllne' and bought from him for 9s a thousand, together with a further 2,000 Flemish bricks 'to make the top of the chymneye' at 6s a thousand. Provision was also made for a garden, and, later, when the building itself was extended and a further chimney stack erected, an additional piece of ground at the rear was conveyed in 1581 by the corporation and 'the donge and offall of the town shalbe there laide, and then to be inclosed' to serve as a new garden.

Later developments included the acquisition in 1580 of a separate dwelling house for 'all the poor children kept of almes by the town ... under the government of an honest man and woman' where they would be 'brought up to serve God and to be kepte to work', and an attempt in 1598 to enter into combination with neighbouring parishes 'for purchasing a house of Correction and for settinge the poore a worke', a clear indication of prevailing attitudes towards the able-bodied poor and unemployed. That same year, following the new statute, overseers for the poor were first elected at the town assembly, although Rye had had collectors for the poor since at least 1558, who levied a separate rate and kept their separate accounts, which no doubt explains the absence of expenditure on the poor in the chamberlains' accounts in the Elizabethan period. Yet despite the somewhat patchy nature of the evidence, it is nevertheless clear that provision for the poor was another important aspect of the work of the corporation, as well as being a further source of exaction, which, as Rye's economy began to contract, the town became rather less able to afford.[28]

Another lesser, but recurrent cost met by the chamberlains was the town's share of the wages of the bailiffs to Yarmouth, who went with the Cinque Ports fishing fleets to preserve order and to act as its representatives in any disputes with the Great Yarmouth authorities. In 1485 Rye's charges were £3 10s, but by the mid-sixteenth century increased expenses led to higher fees. In 1556, for example, Nicholas Mercer, a Rye jurat, received £10 for his fee, and, although this was probably an exception, rates had clearly increased. Thomas Birchett, another jurat received £5 1s for his expenses as bailiff in 1546.[29]

A more serious, but intermittent charge on the corporate finances was the cost of parliament wages, set at 2s a day throughout much of the period. A long session could cost a considerable sum, especially if the town had two MPs to support. In 1496 for example, William Barnham attended for 9 weeks and 3 days and Adam Oxenbridge for a lesser period of 6 weeks and 2 days, at a total cost of £10 14s. Barnham was paid in full, but Mr Oxenbridge had only received 40s by the end of the financial year, in two instalments of 20s each at the last two openings of the boxes that year, indicating the difficulty the town was having in meeting its obligations. In 1559, both Richard Fletcher and Robert Marche attended for the full 112 days, at a cost of £22 8s. It is hardly surprising therefore that many towns came under the sway of local gentry influence in exchange for being excused the financial burdens of independent representation. In Rye this too became the case as successive Lord Wardens sought to establish a right to nominate one of the town's two MPs. Even so, the costs of the corporation's own nominee, Thomas Hamon in the 1597 Parliament necessitated a special sesse to raise over £40, it having been agreed that he should be paid at the rate of 5s a day.[30]

A further source of unexpected expenditure, was the hospitality which customarily had to be provided for important dignatories visiting the town. Rye was especially vulnerable to such expenses since its position as a port meant that there were often government officials and foreign ambassadors passing through the town. This was particularly the case in the period before the loss of Calais in 1558. In 1500, for example, there were at least six such visits by the Duke of Suffolk (2); the Lord Warden, Mr Guldeford (3); Lord Poynings and Sir John Paston. On each occasion suitable fare was provided at a total cost of at least £5 16s. Mr Poynings passed through the town in Lent. Nevertheless the bill of fare for his entertainment was considerable, including a wide range of fish such as salmon, ling, eels, whiting, cod, sole, gurnards and salt fish. There was also an unspecified quantity of mussels (a few days earlier at a similar feast for Mr Guldeford 200 oysters had been consumed). Mr Poynings brought his own cook, and there were evidently pies with almonds, nuts, raisins and figs, spiced with cloves and mace,

33

saffron, cinnamon and ginger, washed down with beer, claret and red wine. A similar visit by the Attorney General, Sir John Baker and other commissioners for the trial and execution of three counterfeiters in 1551 was marked by a feast with shrimps, pies, a variety of meat dishes including a rib of beef, a calf, lamb, several pigs and capons with apples, oranges, cakes, vinegar and a variety of spices and large quantities of wine and beer to drink. As with all other items of expenditure, costs rose as the sixteenth century wore on. A visit by the Lord Warden and his company cost the town £6 18s 8d in September 1560. A similar visit by the Lieutenant of Dover Castle in August 1596 cost £15 17s.[31]

The largest expenses incurred on entertainment were, of course, during royal visits. When Henry VII was at Rye in August 1487, preparation included the removal of dunghills and general tidying up of the town, and there were the costs of riding to the King at Reding, just north of the town, where the royal warship the Regent was under construction. The total costs of the exercise, including the dinner given for the King and other gentlemen by the mayor and the entertainment provided elsewhere in inns for the remainder of the party came to £58 4d. However, the repayment of a further £15 for which the town was indebted to one of the wealthier jurats shortly afterwards, indicates that the real costs were substantially higher. On the occasion of the Lord Protector's visit in October 1548 the surrounding countryside was scoured for some days beforehand to provide 111 chickens, 72 rabbits, 40 capons, 10 pidgeons, 2 cygnets and a curlew in his honour, and the town's ordnance at the Landgate was made ready for a royal salute.[32]

The greatest expense of all, however, was incurred during Queen Elizabeth's visit to Rye in August 1573. Unfortunately the chamberlains' accounts are missing for the exact period of the visit, but it is possible to reconstruct at least some of the features of her three-day stay in the town. The total cost appears to have been in excess of £150, which was the level at which a sesse was agreed, and £100 was lent to the town by Henry Gaymer, the mayor. Sixty coats were provided for the town's shot, who escorted the Queen into the town, and she was presented with 100 golden angels in a purse (worth £33 6s 8d). There is a later reference to 'the silke gowne that the oration was made in' and to the sending on afterwards of 100 calivers with drum, phife and 6 holberds to guard the Queen at Dover. There is also reference to the giving of 40s between them and a livery apiece to Philip Fanefield and Angel Shaw 'in consideration of their paines taken this sommer with drome and phife when the Quenis Maiestie was here'. The evidence is scanty, but it is enough to give a general indication of this royal visit by the last of the Tudors to the town.[33]

Urban geography and economic structure

Queen Elizabeth as with other visitors coming by road would have entered Rye through the Landgate, one of the two principal gates of the town, forming part of the town defences which were still being kept in a good state of repair throughout the Tudor period. A new portcullis had been put in early in 1559, and the ability to control access into the town was a useful asset, not just in time of war. In August 1593, for example, fear of infection led to the posting of two men to guard the Landgate from the departing of the watch in the morning until the watch was set in the evening 'so none can enter which may be suspected to bringe infection'. Nor were they to allow any packs to be brought into the town without the leave of the mayor and any such brought in for merchants were to be placed in the town storehouse unopened.[34] From the Landgate, the town wall, fronted by a wide ditch, ran in a south-westerly direction to the Strandgate, with only a small entrance for foot passengers in between at the Postern Gate, reached by means of a bridge over the town ditch.

Inside the town, the land rose steeply to the churchyard and the market place, which stood at its highest point. This area formed the economic and administrative centre of the town itself, with its row of butchers' shops and market cross, with stairs leading to the court hall above, rebuilt between 1514 and early 1515, providing a meeting place for the town assembly with covered market below, while Baddings Tower to the south-east seems to have housed the town gaol and courthouse, and the churchyard provided the meeting-place of the freemen for the annual election of the mayor. Here were the principal residences of many of Rye's leading citizens. Most of the jurats lived here in large houses around the churchyard and market place or in Middle Street (present day Mermaid Street) reached by a lane on the north-west corner of the churchyard. Queen Elizabeth herself is traditionally thought to have stayed here, in the house known today as the Customs House, but in sixteenth century as Grene Hall, fronting on to the west side of the churchyard. Other large houses stood in the Longer Street (the present High Street), in the area between the Market and the Landgate, known as Landgate Ward. Further towards the Strandgate, and in the Watchbell Street, lived many of the middling citizens, craftsmen, fishing boat masters and the like. The poorer folk, ordinary seamen, fishermen and labourers lived in crowded cottages long-since disappeared, in side alleys (there were at least seven such tenements in Okeman's Lane) and in Watchbell Ward, which ran down the top of the West Cliff from the Watchbell and continued north outside the Strandgate underneath the Town Wall in the damp, unhealthy area beyond the fishmarket known as the Wish.

A stranger visiting Rye would have found a variety of inns and victualling houses in which to stay. Forty were listed in 1576 including 23 in the Lower Street (High Street) including Market Street, six in Middle Street and 11 in the Baddings (Watchbell Street, the West Cliff and the Wish). This number was larger than usual, licensing generally being restricted to between 26 and 30 in the 1580s although numbers fluctuated rather more widely in the 1560s and 1570s. In April 1574, when at the request of the leading victuallers, numbers were restricted to 26, there were 94 beds for strangers. The figure for 1588 when there were 28 licensed premises was only 51 beds, but this latter figure leaves blank some of the details of the principal inns such as the Mermaid, owned by William Didsbury, or that of his fellow jurat, William Ratcliffe. Didsbury, described as 'a man of good credytt' kept the Mermaid 'for marchantes' and the wealthier sort of visitor, the names of all his guests being registered in his book. It was there that the corporation often provided hospitality to visiting dignitaries, as in an earlier period they had done at John Sutton's house, the Crown, on the corner of West Street and the High Street, as in 1520 when Lord Dacre of the South was feted there on his way to join Henry VIII at Calais.[35] Other leading inns included the Red Lion (probably on the site of the present George) and the Three Kings, in Middle Street, kept by John Fisher, another jurat in the 1590s. There, in 1576 one Cornelis Jacobson, a master of a ship of Rotterdam stayed so long 'beinge every daye very dronke' and later, on board his ship, entertaining his countrymen and drinking large quantities of his cargo of wines from Rouen, that the Queen's officers went on board and confiscated a portion of the residue to pay the customs dues.[36] Other, lesser victualling houses included the Blue Anchor, kept by John Hamond, a carpenter, in 1592; the Swan, in the Butchery, whose proprietor, in 1581 Edward Call, was a shoemaker; and the Three Mariners, kept in 1592 by Agnes Tokey, a 60 year old widow, much frequented by foreign seamen, one of whom was arrested for dealing there in pieces of canvas stolen from a nearby shop.[37]

For those wishing to pass beyond the seas, the regular passage from Rye to Dieppe in Normandy provided one of the most direct routes linking London and Paris. In 1554, the number of such vessels was limited to four, paying between them £20 a year. The measure was apparently necessitated by the numbers of other fishermen who were carrying passengers, without having to pay any dues for the maintenance of the jetties. A later decree, extending the dues to any English vessel trading passage along the French coast from Boulogne to Honfleur and entering Rye, indicated that by then, the Rye passenger vessels were paying 5s per voyage. Later decrees, as in 1574 following the influx of French and Flemish from the religious wars on the continent restricted those whom the passengers could bring across to 'marchantes, gentlemen, common postes and messengers', while others, as in 1575, sought to protect their livelihoods by ordering that no ships coming from London or elsewhere should take on goods or passengers in Rye for Dieppe 'whereby the passengers therunto assigned shall stay upon their voyage'. Finally, following the introduction of a toll of 5 sous on Rye passenger vessels leaving Dieppe, it was agreed that every master of a Dieppe passenger ship entering the harbour should likewise come before the mayor and pay 6d for his passport before departing.[38]

The route was clearly a popular one, but the passage could be eventful. Three London merchants and one from Cranbrook deposed that on the night of 5th November 1574, in bad weather, the Helen of Rye in which they were passengers, developed a leak whereby they feared they might drown. They therefore threw a number of packs and items overboard in order to save their lives. In January the same year a Dieppe master carrying passengers to Rye was forced by bad weather to Dover, where he set his passengers ashore. On his return voyage towards Rye he was

37

boarded by a dozen English pirates off Folkestone who among other things robbed a crew member of a little purse of money and two letters which he was carrying for one Nicholas Blundell. Piracy appears to have been a particular scourge along the Sussex coast, especially during the protracted period of religious conflict from the late 1560s until the mid-1590s. Another party of merchants, three from London and one from Cranbrook, together with John le Roye 'a post, having her Maiesties packet' deposed that on 18th August 1579, between twelve and two in the afternoon, the 'passage' in which they were sailing from Dieppe to Rye was boarded by some thirty or forty English pirates off Dungeness whereby they were spoiled of their apparel and goods.[39]

Until the 1630s, a favoured route for the royal posts between London and Paris was via Rye and Dieppe. An assembly decree in September 1563 protected the town porter from having any of his horses taken to ride post, presumably as a result of earlier incidents, and in September 1589, during the last phase of the religious war in France, when Elizabeth had sent a force to Dieppe to aid the Protestant Henri IV, Thomas Randolph, Controller of her Majesty's Posts wrote to Rye ordering the laying up of horses in convenient places between Rye and London 'for better expedition of such lettres as come to her Maiestie's self or her Hignes Councell out of France'. The mayor of Rye was to choose 'the most sufficent man that either keapeth an inne or comonlie serveth suche horses as ordinarilie arrive out of France' who was to provide three sufficient and able post horses at the least in return for 20d per day 'duringe that service' plus 2d per mile for each horse ridden in post and 4d for the guide.[40]

A large part of Rye's prosperity depended upon the fishing industry. From Rye it was possible to send fish landed early in the morning so that it reached London fishmarket later the same day. The fish was carried in large baskets, known as dossers, by strings of pack horses from Rye to the capital by men known as rippiers. John Stow, in his *Survey of London* (1598) records that in 1522 'the rippers of Rye and other places, sold their fresh fish in Leaden hall market upon Cornehill'.[41] Most of the fish destined for London was however bought for members of the London Company of Fishmongers by local wholesalers or representatives, known as osts, nominated by the London Company, who were

38

among the wealthiest of Rye's citizens. In order that there should be no conflict of interests in securing the best possible price, it was decreed in 1504/5 that no fisherman having a boat at sea was to be an oste or a feter (a local wholesale fishmonger; most osts were also feters). There was also a royal purveyor of fish or his deputy, resident in the town.

Inevitably there was a clash of interests, and throughout the sixteenth century there were regular disputes between the royal purveyor and the Rye fishermen over such issues as the quality of the fish served, price and delays in payment. The height of the controversy came in October 1523, when the London fishmongers attempted to secure royal support for a series of articles designed to ensure their preferential treatment in the Rye fishmarket, immediately following the purchases made by the royal purveyor. These articles, which included provision for limiting the price paid for fish in the fishmarket to 6s a seame on Wednesdays and Saturdays, and 8s a seame each Friday and on Saturdays in Lent and for the serving of the osts of the London fishmongers after the King, Princess Mary, the French Queen, Cardinal Wolsey and the Archbishop of Canterbury, were immediately rejected by the Rye corporation as 'unreasonable and consonant to the dystruccion of this Towne'. As a result a special commission, including Sir Edward Guldeford the Lord Warden, his brother Sir Henry Guldeford the Controller of the King's Household, George Guldeford Esq and the mayor of Rye, John Edolphe, met in Rye on the 14 April 1524 and a series of ordinances were drawn up to govern the operation of the Rye fishmarket for the future. One notable feature of these articles is the absence of any references to preferential treatment of the London fishmongers or of any limitation of price. They did, however, lay down very strict conditions to safeguard the interests of the royal purveyor. In particular the Rye fishermen were to bring their best fish directly to the market without embezzelling any of the same and the mayor and jurats were to assist the King's purveyor, who was to have first choice of all the fish in the market, to ensure that he obtained his full proportion. In the case of any dispute over the price, the mayor or a jurat was to make a reasonable price between the purveyor and the fishermen. In return, the royal purveyor was always to be ready in the market to do his duty so that the market was not delayed, and was only to set his mark on the fish which he intended to buy for the King's use. If however any other boats were to come in with better fish, then the purveyor was to be allowed to provide for the King from the better fish and to re-sell the fish which he had previously purchased, either in the market at Rye or elsewhere, at no higher price than he had originally paid.[42]

Later ordinances largely confirmed this agreement, although there were clearly some difficulties in enforcing it. In 1544, for example, following complaints from the royal purveyor, it was agreed that when fishing vessels returned with their catch at night, then the following morning their wives should bring the fish to market no later than eight o'clock. In October 1545, one of the jurats, Robert Barnes, was fined 16s for selling 'certen fysshe owte of the markett, contrary to the order of the Towne'. So it is clear that the orders were by no means always kept. A further series of decrees made by the Rye assembly in March 1568 largely reiterated the agreement of 1524, although with an additional clause forbidding the fishermen to put any fish into the Queen's maundes other than what the purveyor had seen to be good. Another change was that in the event of a failure of the fishermen and the purveyor to agree a price, the mayor and the purveyor were to choose two indifferent arbiters to fix it. There were still problems however. In 1581 the fishermen complained of Mr Haynes, the purveyor's ill payment and other matters. When the purveyor in his turn in 1586 complained to the Lord Warden of his 'mislikes' of what he had found in Rye, the fishermen told the mayor that although they had bought the fish to the market within an hour, he continually delayed it. They also agreed that 'when it please the mayor or the Purveyor's deputy to have the bell ronge' they would be ready, and in answer to the complaint that not all the fish was brought on land, they argued that it had been the custom time out of mind for 'harbourmen' (ie those fishing daily just offshore) to keep their fish in their boats 'for that it will kepe the longer freshe and swete, and that her Maiesties Purveyor shall and may come aborde their boats at his pleasure' to view the same.[43]

The fishmarket itself was situated at the Strand, at a little distance from the quayside. Fronting it, according to Jeake's map of 1667, was the King's Shop, from which the royal purveyor operated. The osts and fishermen also had their shops in the vicinity, the osts nearest the fishmarket and the quay and the fishermen furthest away. As a result, it was argued in 1608 by William Angell the King's Purveyor, it was a relatively simple matter for the osts to obtain some of the best fish from the fishermen before it reached the market. A further difficulty, encountered in 1597, appears to have been a growing practice whereby some of the rippiers and market men coming into the town from outside, were buying fish for London fishmongers 'to the present decaye of the ostes of this towne which do helpe to beare the charge of this Towneshippe, and in short tyme wilbe thutter decaye and undoinge of the fyshermen of Rye'. A penalty of 40s for every such offence was therefore imposed.[44]

As well as its fishmarket, Rye also had a provisions market, held by the market cross, in the Butchery, situated approximately on the site of the present Market Street, just north of the churchyard. Market day, originally Saturday, was changed to Wednesdays and Fridays in 1561 before being fixed at Wednesdays and Saturdays from August 1564 'as is most lawdablie accustomed within the Citie of London or eny other auncient townes or cities within the realme'. Market lasted from 9am until 1pm, the start and finish of trading being signalled by the ringing of a bell. It was presided over by the two clerks of the market who kept the town's weights and measures in order that the assize should be maintained. Throughout much of the period the fee for standing at the cross was out to farm, but a list of receipts for standings at 1d a time for the mayoral year 1582/3 reveals generally three or four such payments on any one market day, the most common being usually one or two truggers, a butcher and a glover, with on other occasions during the year a coverlet-maker, a shoe seller, a scavelman, a cutler, an edgetoolmaker, and sellers of sickles, seeds, laces and glasses although it is not clear on what basis the fee for standings was charged. Occasionally there were more unusual items. In 1509 and again in 1510, a seller of printed books is listed.

For much of the time however the main items for sale were victuals of various sorts from the surrounding countryside, chief among these being bread and meat, but also butter, cheese, eggs and such like. In August 1566 nine country bakers from Hawkhurst, Sandhurst, Playden and elsewhere were listed at one Saturday market, a figure probably representative of attendances at this date. Country bread generally had to be several ounces heavier in weight than loaves of Rye bakers. An ordinance in 1561 laid down that it was to be weighed before sale. A further decree in 1588 made country bakers enter into a bond to keep the assize and to enter their names in a book. A similar ordinance in 1572 required country butchers also to enter into bonds to keep the market days and to bring their tallow and hides to be sold in the market, and when the price of beef was fixed for Rye butchers at 11d the naile (8lbs) in August 1580, country butchers were ordered to offer theirs at 10d. Hastings butchers presumably because of the latter town's membership to the Cinque Ports, were given slightly preferential treatment, paying only 1d for their standings and nothing for their occupying as others had to do. Fresh fruit was a seasonal commodity to be found in the market. A proclamation during the outbreak of plague in August 1580, specified apples, plums and pears among the fresh fruit banned from being brought into the town during the sickness. Finally, the Rye market provided a venue for the sale of livestock. At a Wednesday market in 1587, a Beckley farmer bought ten steers aged between two and four years from a co-parishioner for £37 10s; in September 1589 a Peasmarsh farmer bought six steers, a bull and a barren (cow) from a Herstmonceux farmer for £15 11s. Horses were also bought and sold, sometimes by those passing overseas. John Baptist, a Frenchman, sold his white gelding with a short mane, white saddle and bridle, to the Rector of Playden in the open market in May 1581. Several similar transactions are listed between 1578 and 1589 in the assembly books.[46]

Lack of sanitation and the spread of disease

Inevitably, the offal and filth generated by a town the size of Rye was considerable and caused the authorities some difficulties with disposal. The scouring action of the tides provided a partial solution and in September 1540 a 'pulpytt' was erected at the East Cliff 'to caste over donge there' at a cost of 5s for two tons of timber, and a man was paid 6d for a day's work 'makyng clene of the pulpett ... and horlyng over the dong'. There was apparently a similar arrangement at the Strand, since a town ordinance in December 1553 decreed that 'no person shall laye any garbage of fusshe upon the newe ground at Strand but to be cast over at the platforme ther'. The cleaning and salting of fish left considerable quantities of rotting remains, which were generally simply piled up beside the shops there. Another assembly decree, in September 1564 laid down that all harbourmen and shotters should employ a man to carry their garbage away on pain of a 3s 4d fine. The ostes similarly were to make yearly provision for the carrying away of the offal from their shops in proportion to the number of seames of fish they sold. As early as the 1490s, the corporation was paying three men between 2d and 6d a quarter to keep clean the Strand and the Market. By 1585/6 George Seare and Thomas Dawson were each being paid 10s a quarter to make clean the two market places and the cliff.[47]

Further problems were caused by the dung from the stables at the Strand and from the rippier's horses. Each of the rippiers was fined 12d in the hundred court presentments in 1556 for 'stopping the common water waye and conduitte' at the Strand with their dung. The stables were a more serious problem, and in September 1567 and again in June 1578 the assembly had to arrange for the dung there to be carried away at the charge of the occupants. Thereafter, it was ordered, they were to clear away their own dung twice yearly, between 1 March to 30 April and again between 1 August and 30 September. It seems unlikely that the ordinance had much effect. A year later the hundred presentments included Robert Carpenter, one of the jurats, for 'a very noysom dounghill' against his stable door, and in 1590, once again the assembly had to order the dunghills there cleared away.[48]

There were also large quantities of rubbish and filth from people's houses. The inhabitants of the Wish habitually threw theirs in the horseway leading to the ferry. Twenty-seven of them were presented in 1583 for 'castyng of ther durtt contenewally in the hywaye that goeth to the ferryway, so that by reason thereof any horsse canne skersly passe there.' Others simply piled theirs up underneath their houses. In the same year Richard Jacob was fined for 'makyng a prevy under his stayers wheare as he dwells by the fyshe market verry noyfull and felthey'. The wealthier occupants of the larger houses in the Lower Street, whose gardens backed on to the Town Wall often had privies built against it, with a hole running through, into the town dike, as in the case of four householders there including another of the jurats, William

Ratcliff, and Matthew Flory, a French physician 'to the annoyance of the dwellers that dwell in the wishe.' John Fagge, jurat, simply threw his filth straight over the wall.[49]

Those who dwelt in the Middle Street seem to have laid their dung and filth in Rucke's Lane, by the West Cliff. Twenty-nine householders including two jurats were presented in 1583 for having their servants lay their household rubbish there, very 'noyfull to the dwellers ther, and also to those that passeth by that place'. The poorer inhabitants who lived on the West Cliff were, however, little better. They simply hurled their waste over the cliff on to the houses below. The situation was evidently sufficiently serious for the assembly, in January 1580, to grant a licence to Francis Christmas to set up a pale on the cliff there beside the lane 'to kepe the people frome throwinge of fylthe upon his house and into his backside'. The practice evidently continued, since three years later, in August 1583, a fine of 6d was introduced for the offence and the corporation agreed to erect a new fence at the town's charge.[50]

The impression given is that any vacant plot of land was likely to become a dumping ground for refuse. In September 1583, a void plot against Robert Farley's house beside the Friars, described in the assembly books as 'nowe a dunghill' was granted to him for 31 years at 18d a year on condition it be fenced, and at the same time it was agreed that the gun platform, used in time of war to protect the Strand quay, also be fenced 'for the better kepinge of the people frome throwinge of donge, soylth or fylth there.' Typical of prevailing attitudes to refuse disposal was Richard Hardowne, who lived by the Market Place, who was presented in 1583 for habitually 'whorllyng of durt out of a chamber windowe where as he dwelleth and mak a dounghill ther' or the inhabitants against whom the order for 'better and sweter kepinge of the stretes from soylth' was directed in August 1584, specifying that when householders or their servants swept the streets and gutters before their houses, it was to be 'taken upe and caried awaye and not swepe the same downe to their neighbours'.[51]

Nevertheless, there was a growing awareness of the connection between steaming piles of rodent and insect-infested refuse and the outbreak of summer epidemics. During the exceptionally hot spring of 1574, the mayor and jurats ordered the constables of

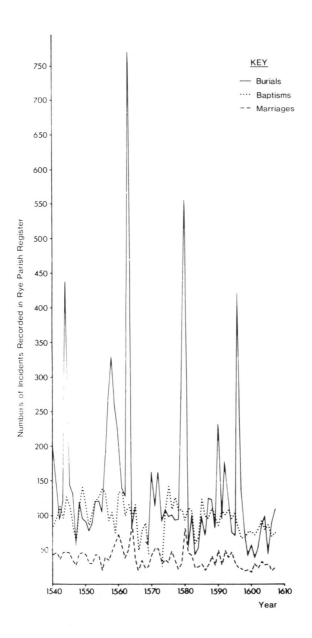

Figure 4: Annual levels of burials, christenings and marriages in Rye 1540–1608

45

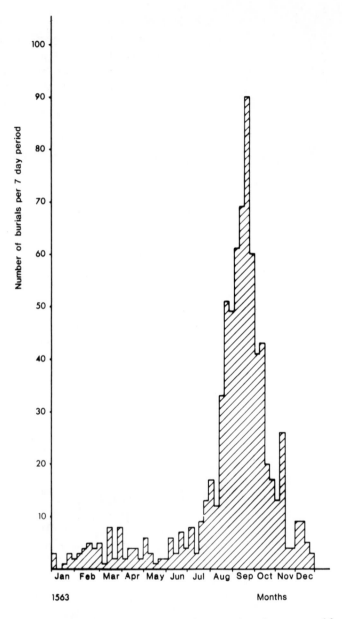

Figure 5: Profile of an outbreak of bubonic plague: weekly
burial totals from the Rye parish registers 1563

46

each ward to make a collection from each of the householders towards the making of pumps for the cleansing of the streets. Meanwhile, it was decreed that each of the four brewers, twice weekly 'shall let go a barrell of water in suche convenient places in the streates as to them shalbe assigned for the swetinge of the streates and to contynue the same during the heate of this sommer'.[52]

The insanitary conditions in towns such as Rye led to frequent outbreaks of epidemics. In 1517 the sweating sickness was recorded in Rye. In 1590 English soldiers returning home from France brought typhus to the town. Further high levels of epidemic mortality were recorded between 1557-60, caused probably by a combination of poor harvests and recurrent bouts of influenza, which reached a peak in the winter of 1558-9. But by far the most common source of recurrent outbreaks of epidemic disease was bubonic plague, which struck in the hottest months of the year, usually between July and September. Plague seems to have been present in Rye in 1532, 1540, 1544, 1556, 1563, 1577, 1579–80, 1596–7, 1598, 1604 and 1625.[53] The most serious epidemics (Figure 4) were in 1544 (436 burials), 1563 (779), July 1579—October 1580 (813) and January 1596—June 1597 (510). At their worst, such outbreaks might have accounted for as many as 25-30 per cent of inhabitants, a figure comparable to other towns. Plague outbreaks could descend upon a community with horrifying suddenness. Within a matter of days in the summer of 1563, for example, (Figure 5), the burial rate had risen from only two to five per week to weekly totals of 13, 17 and after a week's apparent respite, 33, 51 and so upwards through August and September to a peak of 90 recorded burials in the last week in September.[54]

In the face of such sudden visitations of sickness and death, there was little that the town authorities could do except to try and isolate the infected and stop any animals which might be carriers of the disease from wandering abroad in streets. In July 1563 such measures included the marking of houses visited with the plague by the sign of a cross. No member of an infected household was to go out of his house on pain of a 40s fine, and each house was to have a vessel of fresh water at its door, which was to be changed every two days and so 'kept sweet and clean'.[55] In September 1579 these regulations were extended to include the

47

appointment of two women to view the dead bodies, the killing of any dogs found wandering in the streets, the engagement of a poticiary from among the resident French exile community to prepare medicines and of three women to wash and tend the sick and to sack the dead. Special overseers were appointed for each of the six wards to see the regulations enforced and a special monthly rate was levied on the 152 wealthiest households to provide for the needy and to pay the wages of those employed,[56] Similar regulations were again in force in 1596, when the two women viewing the bodies were paid 4d per examination and hogs, as well as dogs, found roaming the streets were to be killed. On this occasion sterner measures seem to have been employed to ensure that those infected stayed indoors, the chamberlains' accounts recorded in October of that year expenditure on three locks, seven hasps and staples 'that were imployed to locke in infected persons'.[57]

Such measures availed little during major outbreaks, although they may have had a limited success in containing the spread of the disease during relatively minor visitations. The authorities clearly thought the policy of isolation had been effective when they reported in September 1596 with some satisfaction that the plague was 'as yet very little dispersed' about the town 'by reason the infected persons are for the most part shut up into their dwelling houses and are not permitted to range abroad to the spoil of others'.[58] The following month, however, the mortality rate rose from only 30 in September to 96 a month in October and December and 114 in November, before falling back again sharply as the cold weather set in. Probably a more realistic view was taken by the jurats and other wealthier inhabitants who, in the summer of 1563, retired to their houses and farms or visited relatives in the surrounding countryside during the epidemic.[59]

The daily round

During the winter months the long hours of darkness necessitated the lighting of the streets. Accordingly, various regulations were instituted during the 1570s to ensure that on nights when there was no moon, householders of ability hung a lantern out of their windows to light the way from six until eight o'clock in the evening, from All Saints (1 November) to the feast of the Purification (1 February). In 1577 the assembly decreed 'that the beadle at fyve of the Clocke every eveninge to crye for Lanthorn and Candlelight ... and that the lights be not sett in wyndowes bu hanged out of the wyndows. And this order to be proclaymed yerly by the towne sergeant in every quarter of the towne two daies before the feast of all saintes'. At eight o'clock in winter (nine o'clock in summer) the inns and tippling houses ceased serving their beer and the town settled down for the night.[60]

In winter the watch began at five o'clock, so that it was fully set by six, accompanied, during these months by the drum and phife, 'and to watche untill sixe in the morninge, and in sommer tyme the watche to begyn at viii of the clock at night, so as the same be throughly setled by nyne and so to contynue untill v in the morninge.' In 1585 it was also specified that there should always be ten persons on watch, two at the Landgate, two at the Strandgate, one at the Gungarden, two at the Mills and one in the Butchery. The other two were to walk with the search, which consisted of pairs of the more substantial commons, usually including one of the jurats or common councillors, who were chosen on an annual basis each January to walk the rounds to ensure that the watchmen did their duty. The watch itself was evidently drawn from the residue of householders, an assembly decree in January 1564 specifying 'that every land man within the said town shall fynde every night as his torne comith one able man to watche ... and ellis in default of an able man to wache hymself'.However, in May 1589 nine individuals were chosen as the town watchmen and sworn, presumably paid for by a small rate made on householders. During the Armada crisis the search was made more rigorous and the watch was ordered on pain of 'grievous punishment' not to depart in the morning until they had called at the house of the mayor.[61]

Mornings began early, with, according to a decree of October 1581, the ringing of the great bell of the church at 4 am for half an hour in the winter months. Morning prayer was at six and the evening prayer at five in the afternoon (in 1567 the respective hours of services were between seven and eight in the morning and at four in the afternoon). Every householder was expected to attend or at least to send a member of the household, the penalty for failure to do so being set at 6d in October 1567. The times of services regulated the hours of work, which were long, allowing relatively little time for other activities. Sunday was, however, a

49

day of rest and various measures were taken to ensure it remained so. In November 1583, for example, the assembly decreed a fine of 3s 4d for any beer carts, budge carts or other vehicles being used on a Sunday without special licence; and no goods, merchandise or wood was to be discharged on land at the Strand under like penalty.[62]

The chief leisure activity, for those who could afford it, was drinking in one of the many tippling houses in the town. Even on a conservative estimate there was one of these for every 15-20 households. Gaming, particularly at cards and dice, was popular—one game referred to in 1547 was 'makinge and marrynge'—and packs of playing cards could be bought from the local merchants' shops. William Bragden claimed he had lost £8 worth when his shop was broken into in January 1580. Other games which had at least a passing popularity included 'the stone' and 'coyetes' (quoits). Early in the sixteenth century the growth in popularity of tennis had spread to men's servants, who in 1504 were banned from playing that or any other unlawful game on workdays. In the Elizabethan period bowls was popular, at least among Rye's political elite. John Donnynge and Robert Jackson, both future mayors, together with William Appleton, the town clerk, John Philpot the town preacher and Thomas Fugler, wine merchant,were reported to the Sussex Assizes for having 'assembled riotously and illicitly' outside the town liberty, at Playden, to play an illegal game called 'bowles' in September 1572.[63]

Local interests and wider horizons

The cosmopolitan atmosphere of a bustling port and Rye's proximity to London helped create an awareness in its inhabitants of the important issues of the day. Rye's seamen traded throughout many of the ports of northern Europe and the Atlantic seaboard as far as Portugal, although the bulk of trade in the period before the religious wars was with the Netherlands and France, in particular Antwerp, Ostend and Dunkirk as well as Calais and Dieppe. Rye's harbour was one of the principal embarcation points for English soldiers fighting in France in 1513, 1543, 1562, 1589, 1592 and 1596. It also witnessed the arrival and departure of countless foreign ambassadors and other dignatories. Its ships served as transports on such occasions as the

Emperor Charles V's visit to England in 1522; and when Monsieur, Elizabeth's French suitor, came over in February 1582 to seek her hand in marriage five ships and more than 60 men, including the fife and drum, went forth to serve as passengers.[64] Merchants, posts, government agents and soldiers returning from the wars passed through the port, bringing news of current events, as for example in the summer of 1513 when, following Henry VIII's victory at the Battle of the Spurs, there came into the harbour three soldiers 'from Turwyn (Therouanne) with letters of tidings of the kinges good spede'.[65] Its seamen took part in military exploits, men such as John Fletcher doing valuable service observing the disposition of the French navy during the French Wars of Henry VIII's reign. One of its ships, the newly-built Hercules, at 150 tons the largest merchant vessel in Rye, crewed by Rye mariners, served in the Cadiz expedition of 1596, when the Earl of Essex destroyed much of the Spanish fleet, sacked the city and effectively ended Philip II's plans for a second invasion attempt.[66] A few chance references show that some of Rye's more adventurous seamen went on voyages of discovery into unknown parts. In 1539 William Wymond, owner of the Savyor of Rye and Nicolas Duval, owner of the Loup of Dieppe, 'as adventurers consortyd togethurs' to set forth their ships on a voyage of exploration to Brazil. In 1567, John Emery 'went into Gynney with Captaine Hawkyns' and returned after an absence of 13 years in November 1580, having long since been presumed dead, to find his wife remarried.[67] In 1581 a messenger brought news to an anxious widow that her son had come home safely to London with Captain Drake.[68]

Such a range of experiences and activities helped to create the independent outlook for which the town was noted. In Sussex, it was the first town wholeheartedly to embrace Protestantism, and the only town openly to defy the Marian government, returning Protestant sympathisers as mayors and MPs and refusing to allow the collection of a forced loan in the autumn of 1557. Its overt support for the Sea Beggars and Huguenot privateers in Elizabeth's reign despite repeated government entreaties merely continued a long tradition of stubborn resistance to government dictat. In the autumn of 1525, for example, following a dispute as to whether the demand was 'contrary the gt chatour of the portes', the chamberlains' accounts record payment of 10s to Nicholas

Sutton 'being in warde in the Castell of Dovorr ... because ther was not prepared certayne men in harnoys for the towne to do the king service in his retynewe beyonde the see'.[69]

As well as the news brought by visitors and others passing through the port, another major source of information which can be detected at work moulding attitudes was the steady succession of royal proclamations, which were such a feature of Tudor government. The regular receipt of these proclamations can be traced throughout the period in the chamberlains' accounts, which record the payment (8d each time in the 1550s) made to the 'boders' (messengers) who brought them to each of the ports from the Lord Warden's office at Dover Castle, to which they were sent direct from London. Such proclamations, from the declaration of war and the staying of merchant ships for possible military service, to orders for the enforcement of the statutes relating to vagrants, enabled the government to justify and explain its actions to the country. In many cases the Rye accounts list the actual proclamations received, making it possible to chart the receipt of the latest news in the town. Towards the end of May 1522, for example, a boder brought the proclamation 'that all Frenchmen should be put to suerte for ther goodes' at the beginning of hostilities with France. Shortly afterwards four others arrived ordering that every man should be ready at an hour's warning, that Frenchmen's goods should be distrained, 'that no men should be taken into the Kinges ships' and 'that Caleys shuld be vytailled with beere'. Later, at the end of the conflict, in 1525 there came 'a boder of Dovorr bringing a precept to make fyers lauding god of the victorye obtaigned at the obsideon of Pavea wher Frauncesse the Frenche Kinge was taken by the Duke of Burban'. Usually the passage of such information was swift. Edward VI died on 6 July 1553. Within a matter of a day or two, a boder brought letters from the Council of the death of the King, and on 21 July, the accounts record the receipt of the proclamation of 'the right heye lady Mary, Quene of England'.[70]

Many of these proclamations, from the start of Elizabeth's reign, are preserved among the corporation archives with, in a number of instances, the date they were proclaimed in the Market Place, normally on the first market day following their receipt, so that the maximum number of people would hear. Thus the proclamation of the suspension of the michaelmas law term because of the plague in the Cities of London and Westminster, dated at Windsor 21 September 1564 was proclaimed in Rye on 5 October; and the proclamation 'to admonishe all persons to forbeare traffique in the king of Spaynes countreys, with other advertisementes for aunsweryng of a generall arrest made in the lowe countreys by the Duke of Alva' dated 6 January 1568 was proclaimed in Rye on the 11th.[71] If the experience of Rye is typical, the passage of news, at least to the larger towns, was swift.

Although literacy was no precondition for being well-informed in the Tudor period, it is clear that by the middle of the sixteenth century, there was an increasing awareness of the importance of being able to read and write, particularly among the mercantile elite of the town. In April 1564, therefore, it was agreed that a schoolmaster be employed by the corporation, initially for three years, from 1st May, paid for by a voluntary levy of £25 12s 4d, on 57 of the wealthier inhabitants, including John Yonge, the former mayor, the Customer of the port and seven of the jurats. The experiment was clearly a success, since the 1576 sesse lists two schoolmasters, and the competition which they provided in the drawing up of legal documents, such as wills, leases etc, which had previously been the prerogative of the Town Clerk, led the assembly on 9 May 1575 to order:

'that none of the schoolmasters within the towne of Ry or liberties of the same shall from henceforth take uppon them to make eny wrytinges willes, or evidences betwene partie and partie, that is to saye the last willes and testamentes of any of the inhabitants within the towne aforesaid or liberties of the same, obligations, bills of debte, indentures of apprentices, leases of landes or tenementes, evidences of landes or any suche leike wrytinges whatsoever they be, uppon pain of imprisonment for every tyme so offendinge by the space of xxiiij houres and to be fyned by Mr Mayor and the Jurates as to them shall seme good.'[72]

Above all, though, Rye's inhabitants were acutely aware of their own interests and active in their defence. Nowhere is this clearer than in the activities of the town's parliamentary representatives, who were generally two of the jurats, although Rye's declining fortunes led to the gradual establishment of the Lord Warden's right to nominate one of its members and the surrender of the other to one of the local gentry by the end of the period. Thus in 1548 Rye successfully promoted an act of Parliament (2 & 3

Edward VI c.30) for the better preservation of the harbour from silting up by regulating the dumping of ballast in the haven, although they were less successful in preventing the further inning of the marshes, which they saw as the main reason for its decline. In the same parliament they also put forward a bill for the restricting of the iron mills, which were seen as a threat to the woods on which the town relied for its timber. In 1576, 1593 and 1601 they promoted bills for a tax to be levied for the construction of sluices and jetties for the rebuilding of the haven. In 1581 they promoted a further bill for the preservation of the woods in the parishes around Rye and Hastings from the iron mills, in cooperation with the representatives of other Sussex towns. In 1572 and 1581 they also promoted bills to restrict the import of foreign fish into the realm, in conjunction with the representatives of the other Cinque Ports who normally met at the start of each new session to plan their activities, joined on this occasion by members for Yarmouth and the other towns on the East Coast. Finally, in 1581 and again in 1589, when 3d a tun was levied on all shipping for the amendment of Dover harbour, they successfully obtained an exemption on the grounds of the charges in maintaining their own haven, and in 1589 attempted to gain a similar imposition for Rye's own harbour works. In all of this, Rye's MPs showed themselves fully adept in parliamentary procedures, such as the tacking on of a proviso to the government's subsidy bill, which they attempted in 1548 and, in concert with the rest of the Cinque Ports members, in 1581.[73] In all of this they did no more than many other towns. The record of York's MPs during a similar period is much the same. Clearly parliament was seen as an opportunity for pursuing local interests as much as a forum for national debate, while the regular re-election of a number of Rye's representatives over several parliaments helped make them experienced parliamentary tacticians. Significantly, when in 1588, Rye had no particular local bill which it sought to promote, the assembly accepted Mr Audley Dannet Esq, the Lord Warden's nominee, as one of its choices and instructed Robert Carpenter, jurat, his newly-elected fellow, that he should 'take his iorny no souner then nedith, nor tarry longer then is convenient after the sessions of parliament breketh uppe'.[75]

CHAPTER 2

Religion: The Making of a Protestant Town

'Rye, Hastings, Lewes and Brighthelmeston are governed
with suche officers as be faythfull favourers of goddes worde
and earnestly given to mainteyn godly orders.'
(Bishop Barlow of Chichester to the Privy Council, October
1564)[1]

Popular culture and the impact of Protestant reform

On the eve of the Reformation, Rye enjoyed a highly-developed
and complex ritual cycle of religious events which marked the
changes in the seasons and in the civic calendar by a series of
communal feast days and holy days. Many of these communal
events together with the religious ritual that accompanied them
were swept away by the Reformation so that by the beginning of
Elizabeth's reign, the town was firmly in the hands of a Protestant
magistracy determined to ensure that Rye remained a godly
commonwealth. The factors bringing about this apparently
sudden transformation can be traced back to the 1520s and the
early 1530s when the religious practices which were shortly
afterwards to be extinguished were still apparently at their height.
The growth of Protestantism in Rye owed much to the
geographical situation of Rye and its function as a port, in
particular to the impact of new Protestant ideas coming in from
outside, which found an echo in an earlier nonconformity, for
which the town's northern hinterland was well-known. The new
ideas became a rallying point for a new, younger, rising political
generation among the Rye magistracy in the 1530s and 1540s,
whose challenge for power split both the jurats and the whole
body of freemen during the formative years of the English
Reformation.

Prior to these cataclysmic events, however, the traditional features of Rye's civic and religious calendar had acquired a seemingly unshakeable vitality and sense of permanence. The annual cycle began at the end of August,when, on the Sunday after the Feast of St Bartholomew (24 August) the commons met in the churchyard after morning service to choose their mayor. A week later, the chamberlains and most of the other town officers changed, and, from 1530, at Michaelmas, the churchwardens. The coming of winter was signalled by the Feast of All Saints at the start of November and lasted through the darkest months of the year, punctuated by the religious festivals of Christmas and the Epiphany. Soon after, came Lent, a period of abstinence from meat and of preparation for the events of Palm Sunday and Easter week, in which it culminated. With the Resurrection, so the earth experienced rebirth in the coming of spring, celebrated in the secular events of May Day. This was followed by the Ascension, Whitsun and Corpus Christi, moveable feasts which took place between May and early July, concluding in the patronal festival of the parish church on 15 August, the Feast of the Assumption of the Blessed Virgin. Less than a fortnight later came the start of the new mayoral year.

And so it went on, each change in the seasons marked by secular and religious events in an unending cycle only finally broken (and then only partially) by the Reformation and the advent of Protestantism. All Saints (1 November) was marked by a special feast day, the choir being provided, as on other such occasions throughout the year, with a pottell of wine. On Christmas night, there was a special midnight service, marked, according to the entry in the churchwardens' accounts for 1516, by the sound of church bells 'ryngyng the berthe off Jesu Chryste our blessed savyor' and, in the 1550s by the decoration of brooms and a holm bush (an evergreen oak), with candles set in it for Christmas Day.

In Rye as elsewhere, Christmas was also a time for disguisings. Henry Gaymer, a future mayor, and Peter Adrian, for instance, were both fined 12d in December 1556 'for going over mummynge in maskyng'. More expenditure on wine for the singers in the choir marked the passing of Twelfth Night and Epiphany. After some weeks came the rigours of Lent, when butchers were forbidden to kill or dress meat except in cases of sickness and infirmity, and victuallers were similarly forbidden to serve it, preceded by the jollities of Shrovetide and the ritual self-abnegation of Ash Wednesday.[2]

Easter Week began with the celebration of Christ's entry into Jerusalem, with the traditional service of procession, for which the churchyard was specially made clean. Something of this event can be reconstructed from the occasional references made to the four silk streamers and the banners, which needed repair from time to time, and the expenditure in 1517 of 20d 'for amending the staves that the sacrament is borne uppon on Palme Sunday'.

On the Wednesday before Easter the evening service of Tenebrae was performed in the parish church, when the candles were extinguished and the penitential 51st Psalm was sung in the darkness, by the choir. The accounts for 1542 record the expenditure of 4s for 6lb 'of wexe candulles for tenerber Wensday and to serve the quyer at tymes.'[3]

Holy Thursday was marked by a further procession and the ringing of the church bells, while from Good Friday until Easter Saturday, a vigil was kept at the Easter Sepulchre, in imitation of the period of anxious waiting by the disciples following the crucifixion. Incense and wax regularly figure in the accounts at this time, bought for the Paschal Candle, for the celebration of Easter itself, and in 1515 the accounts reveal 12d paid 'for cooles uppon ester even for fyre to be hallowed' at the midnight vigil when the candles were lit from the holy fire, symbolising the coming back of the light into the world with Christ's resurrection.[4]

Easter, the premier feast in the church's calendar, was accorded particular significance as a popular 'holyday' in Rye by the annual performance during this time of the Rye play, in which many of the townspeople must have taken part. In 1523, the accounts reveal, 12d was paid 'for a coote made when the resurrection was playde for hym that in playing represented the part of almighty god' and a further 3s 4d for making the stage. In 1526 there is mention of 12d 'paied for plates for the play off the Resurrection', and it seems likely that it was for storing the equipment for the same that 'the pagent house at Landgate' was used, which was leased out for 13s 4d a year in 1574, when the Reformation had led to the play's suppression.[5]

The start of spring was celebrated in the secular festivities of

May morning, when, in 1556, there is reference to 'the mynstrells that pleid before the fetyng in of the maye'. In 1560 the accounts speak of payment made 'to the drume player and to mak a brekfast fór the may game'. Robin Hood was a popular figure in the early Tudor period, his association with green indicating his role as a symbol of the fertility of spring. Hall's Chronicle tells how, in 1510, Henry VIII came to his wife's bedchamber as Robin Hood, himself and his men dressed in green. In Rye the chamberlains' accounts for the third quarter (April–June) 1511 include the payment of 14d 'for a barell off byer and ij creuses for the worshipfull man Robyn Hode when he went in visitacion about the Towne uppon Churchmasse day'.[6]

Soon after came four of the principal feasts of the church calendar, Ascension Day, Whit Sunday, Trinity Sunday and Corpus Christi, each marked by ringing of the church bells and processions, the seasons of festivities coming to an end in mid-August with the patronal festival.

At many of these occasions individual minstrels or groups of visiting players added to the festivities. The 'Lord of Arundel's players' played in the church in the Christmas holidays in 1485. They came again for Christmas 1498, and various other players are mentioned at that particular season: in 1506 and 1508 the players of Dover, in 1507 two groups of players, from Malling and Chart in Kent. The King's bearward came at Shrove Sunday 1513 and at Michaelmas 1522; and the Lord of Oxford's minstrels on St Peter's Even (28 June) 1496. The bann criers of Appledore came on Holy Rood Day 1517 and the King's minstrels for St George's Day 1531.[7] Often the players performed privately before the mayor and jurats, for which they received a reward, before giving their performance publicly in the streets. Among the more notable of such events were 'the syghte off the domesday', at about Easter 1507; a group of players from Essex 'that played with swordes at the Stronde' in 1508; 'the man wiche brought the Camell' in 1510 and 1521; 'Walter the stammeryng mynstrell' who came twice in 1514; the King's juggler in 1516; and 'the morres daunsers of Mafeld daunsyng here on Church masse day' in 1534.[8]

In the decades before the Reformation, many of the towns and villages around Rye had groups of amateur players who performed religious dramas like the Rye play. Among the many such

58

groups which visited Rye were the men of Lydd 'that come to shew a contynaunce of their play in the market place' in 1486; the players of Appledore 'what tyme they cryed the banys here in the Market Place' in 1488; the players of Brookland 'proclayming ther banyes for ther stage pley' in 1520; and 'the inhabytauntes of Ivecherch beyng here warnyng to ther pley' in 1531. The last such recorded visit was by the bann criers of Romney in May 1560[9]

The numbers of different groups and individuals visiting Rye in the period before the Reformation generally varied between eight and ten in any mayoral year, although in 1516/7 it reached as high as sixteen. The religious reforms of the 1530s brought a marked reduction, with only three visits a year being recorded between 1536 and 1540. Thereafter, there was a steady decline until, by the 1570s, several years might pass without any record of visiting players. Although there was a brief revival in the 1580s with 24 such visits, mainly by the Queen's (7) and the Lord Admiral's Players (4), by the late 1590s such events were almost a thing of the past, with none at all recorded between 1597 and the end of the Tudor period. The decennial totals are set out in Table 6 below.

An early indication of the trend of events was the determined opposition, by a group of twenty or so of the younger commons of the wealthier sort (merchants, bakers, brewers and ship masters) to William Inold, the traditionalist curate, who in 1537 was still celebrating many of the abrogated 'idell holy days', including those of St Anne, the Transfiguration and the Feast of the Name of Jesus, often 'with solemn ringing, singing, procession and decking of the church ... as though they had been the highest days

Table 6

Numbers of visits of players to Rye during the Tudor period

Mayoral years	Nos	Mayoral years	Nos
1485/6-1494/5	71	1545/6-1554/5	23
1495/6-1504/5	60	1555/6-1564/5	15
1505/6-1514/5	94	1565/6-1574/5	12
1515/6-1524/5	91	1575/6-1584/5	9
1525/6-1534/5	63	1585/6-1594/5	24
1535/6-1544/5	39	1595/6-1602/3	4

Sources:

RYE 60/3-10; 61/1-10.

59

of the year.' By the end of the 1550s, this Protestant faction had secured a firm grip on the corporation, an indication of the strength of feeling being the riot in the church occasioned by the reintroduction of the mass in January 1554, in which the Edwardian vicar, two jurats and the town clerk were all involved. From this time onwards, the Protestant allegiance of the town was never in doubt, with the inevitable consequences for the traditional forms of festivities. Symptomatic of the response received by visiting players at the end of the period are the comments of a Rye innholder, Francis Daniell, who complained to a musician from Holborn who was lodging in his house in March 1610,'We have a Puritan to our mayor and therefore you may play as long as you will at his door, but he will give you nothing'.[10]

The origins and growth of Protestantism in Rye

Two prime factors which clearly influenced the receipt of Protestantism ideas in Rye from the 1530s onwards were, firstly, the town's close proximity to the traditional Lollard region of the Kentish Weald; and secondly Rye's trading links with the Netherlands, particularly Antwerp, which had been early influenced by continental Protestantism and which, from the 1520s, harboured such English Protestant propagandists as William Tyndale, the pioneer sixteenth century translator of the Bible into English.

Kentish Lollardy was centred on the clothing towns and villages just north of Rye, particularly Cranbrook, Tenterden, Benenden and Rolvenden, with all of which Rye had close trading links, facilitated by the use of barge transport along the banks of the Rother which was navigable as far as Bodiam Bridge.[11] The roots of this indigenous heretical tradition went back at least to the 1420s, and in 1511 under Archbishop Warham a network of Lollard communities was uncovered there, leading to 41 abjurations and 5 burnings. Chief among their beliefs were their opposition to pilgrimages and to the adoration of saints and relics, a denial of the carnal presence in the sacrament, and the desire to be free to read the Bible in English, all of which featured prominently among the views of the early Rye Protestants. Significantly, it was from this region that one of Tyndale's helpers in Antwerp came, Richard Harman of Cranbrook, who continued

60

to maintain close contact with sympathisers in his home town, who wrote to him concerning progress on the new translation of the Bible being undertaken.[12]

Harman was one of those involved in the smuggling of illicit Bibles and tracts into England in the late 1520s, a trade which operated chiefly through the south coast ports, principal among which in terms of size were Southampton, Sandwich and Rye, the latter, with Winchelsea, being two of the six ports watched by Wolsey's agents following the escape from custody of Thomas Garrett, Fellow of Magdalen College, Oxford, who had been apprehended there for trafficking in imported Protestant books in 1528. He later became chaplain to Bishop Latimer and was listed in a 1536 deposition as one of the preachers who had chiefly influenced 20 Rye and Winchelsea men accused of heresy for holding the new ideas.[13] That there were illegally imported Protestant books in Rye in the early 1530s is borne out by the discovery of a number of unspecified heretical works during a search by the mayor of Thomas White's house (one of those accused of heresy on the 1536 list) in June or July 1533.[14] Some years later, William Birchett, a former curate of Rye and rector of the neighbouring parish of East Guldeford (namesake of Thomas Birchett, the leader of the Protestant faction in Rye) who, at the time of his death was a married priest, left copies both of an English Bible and Tyndale's *Obedience of a Christian Man* (1528) in his will (1553), the latter being bequeathed to Thomas Birchett's wife.[15]

A further indication of the early impact of Protestant ideas in Rye was the increasing number of overtly reformist or Protestant sentiments expressed in the wills of inhabitants from the late 1530s onwards and in the parallel decline in the number of overtly traditionalist bequests (for masses, obits etc). As Table 7 shows, by the last year of Henry VIII's reign reformist and Protestant wills had already outstripped traditional formulations. By comparison with other Sussex towns, Rye, closely followed by its Cinque ports neighbours Hastings and Winchelsea, had the highest proportion of Protestant and reformist wills in the reigns of both Henry VIII and Edward VI. In Mary's reign Rye provided the lowest proportion of traditionalist preambles and of bequests for masses, indicating the relative failure of the impact of Marian Catholicism.[16]

However the clearest evidence for the growth of Protestantism in Rye is provided by the conflict within the body of freemen themselves, which resulted in a series of accusations, counter-accusations and a petition, all of which were sent to Thomas Cromwell during the years 1536 and 1538 and are now preserved among the state papers. The most serious of allegations concerned the activities of William Inold, the local curate, who openly defied the 1536 injunctions, preached publicly against the break with Rome and was in possession of a number of papalist tracts which he encouraged others to read. These activities seem to have met with the approval, or at least tacit acquiescence of the majority of the Rye magistrates at that time, since a petition dated 12 August 1537 in support of their priest from the mayor, jurats and 75 of the 'most substantial commons' was sent to the Privy Council accusing those who agitated against Inold of being mere disturbers of the peace, 'very symple and of small substance rude both in theyr communication and behaviour not only ayenst hym but also ayenst the estate of the seyd towne'. Fortunately, a detailed series of articles against Inold's opponents has also been preserved, naming 20 individuals, including one from Winchelsea and specifying the views which they reportedly held.[17]

Some of the ideas maintained by Inold's opponents were reportedly the result of the influence of itinerant Protestant preachers licensed by Cranmer, whose activities have also been noted in Kentish towns.[18] Chief among these were the denial of purgatory and consequently of prayers for the dead, the denial of pilgrimages, prayers to the saints and the Virgin and the efficacy of fasting, all of which seem to have been generally held by these early Rye Protestants. Following on from these and showing the clear influence of continental Protestantism were a belief in the priesthood of all believers, a consequent denial of the need for confession and priestly absolution, and a reduction of the number of true sacraments to only three, all of which views were held by Thomas Birchett, the leading member of the group, while the mass itself took on more the aspect of a memorial to Christ's saving passion made once and for all upon the cross, or, as Alexander Welles, a close associate, put it, 'the blood of Christ, which was shed for them, was sufficient for the salvation of their souls without any other unction'. While to Thomas Fougler, a future jurat, 'the sacrament of the aulter ys but a figure or a shadowe in comparison to the present body of God'. Some of the views expressed by these men were, however, of a more earthy nature, presumably as a result of heated debate and with the intent to shock. Thus for Robert Wymond, a future MP, 'purgatorye ys pissed owte'; while for Robert Woode, another future jurat, the images of Our Lady and the other saints in the church 'be as ydolles and have mowthes and cann not speake, here or see' and divine service sung in the church 'ys of no more effect thenn the blething of a cowe to here calff and the calff ayen to the Cowe'.[19]

Table 7

Rye wills proved at Lewes 1530-59

Year	Total	T	R	P	T/R	P/T
1530-40	4	3	1			
1541	2	2				
1542	4	2	1	1		
1543	9	6	2			1
1544	6	6				
1545	6	5			1	
1546	5	1	2	1		1
1547	4	1		2		1
1548	4		2	2		
1549	3		2	1		
1550	7		4	3		
1551	4		4			
1552	3		3			
1553	-					
1554	2		2			
1555	2			2		
1556	3		3			
1557	8	1	6		1	
1558	8	3	4	1		
1559	3		2	1		

Notes:

T	Traditional—	(A)lmighty G(od), (B)lessed (V)irgin (M)ary and (S)aint(s); and AG, Sts; and Masses.
R	Reformist—	AG alone; AG (M)aker and (R)edeemer; AG (C)reator, R and M; Jesus Christ only MR and Saviour etc, without masses.
P	Protestant –	Salvation through Merits of Christ's Passion; Election
T/R	Mixed –	AG alone etc. as above R but with Masses
P/T	Mixed –	Merits or Election plus Masses or BMV.

The wills are arranged by date of composition.

Sources: ESRO wills registers W/A 1-4, W/C4.

The development of factions within the corporation

The growing influence of Protestantism in Rye in the mid-1530s provided a major challenge to the largely traditionalist body of jurats, dominated at this time by John Fletcher, who, by the time of his death (1545) had served as mayor on seven occasions, had been one of Rye's MPs in the Reformation Parliament and was related by family and kinship ties with almost all the other traditionalist members of the jurats' bench. Within a year of the protests over Inold and the petitioning of the Privy Council in his support, Thomas Birchett, the leader of Rye Protestant faction had become mayor (presumably at Thomas Cromwell's instigation as happened elsewhere in 1538[20]) and the character of the magistracy was transformed with the addition of four of Birchett's associates as jurats to fill the vacancies left unfilled by the previous mayors and by the election of Alexander Welles as town clerk. Thereafter, as Table 8 shows, for the remainder of Henry VIII's reign, the two factions were relatively evenly matched, with the political balance being held by a small number of jurats, not particularly associated with either group. Later, in Edward VI's reign, the re-election of Thomas Birchett as mayor in 1548 at the express command of the Lord Protector, the Duke of Somerset, who favoured the town with a visit in October of that year, marked a further Protestant advance, when three more of his associates were appointed jurats at the beginning of his year in office and (following two deaths) a further two at the end.[21] By the beginning of Mary's reign the Protestants were in firm control of the Rye magistracy, while the subsequent deaths of the leading members of both factions during the mortality crises of the late 1550s transformed the jurats' bench, ushering in a new Protestant generation of magistrates at the beginning of the reign of Elizabeth.

The degree of personal animosity diplayed between the two factions, at least until the death of John Fletcher, was considerable, although apparently no more so than in other towns.[22] In October 1539, shortly after Birchett's re-election as mayor for a second term, Fletcher accused him of deliberately siding with the local fishermen to obstruct him as royal purveyor, and to raise the price. As a result, Birchett spent some weeks in gaol in Dover Castle before being released on Cromwell's instructions, follow-

Table 8
Religious divisions among the Rye magistracy 1537–1559

	1573 Petition	1536 List	1537/8	1538/9	1539/40	1540/1	1541/2	1542/3	1543/4	1544/5	1545/6	1546/7	1547/8	1548/9	1549/50	1550/1	1551/2	1552/3	1553/4	1554/5	1555/6	1556/7	1557/8	1558/9	1559/60
Traditionalists																									
John Edolf	+	+																							
John Fletcher	+	+	+	+	‡	‡	+	+	⊤⊤																
Richard Inglett	+	+	+	+		+	+																		
John Swan	+	‡	+	+		+																			
James Jetter	+	+																							
John Marche	+	+	+	+		+	⊤																		
William Oxenbridge	+	+	+	+		+	+	⊤																	
John Cornishe	+					+	+		+																
Clement Cobbe	+				+		+		+	+		+													
William Roberthes								‡																	
Thomas Fletcher									+	‡	+	+	+	+	+	+	+	+							
William Johnson	+								+	+	+	+	+	+	+	⊤									
Richard Fletcher									+	+	+	‡	‡	+	+	+									
Robert Maycott	+								+	+	+	+	+	+	+	+									
Total	7	5	5	–	6	6	–	–	–	–	–	3	5	–	5	4	4	4	4	4	4	4	1		
Protestants																									
Thomas Birchett	+		‡	‡	+	+	+			+	+	‡	+		+	+	+	+	+						
Robert Wymond	+		+	+	+	+	+			+	+	+													
William Mede	+		+	+		+	+																		
Robert Wood	+		+	+	+	+	+			+		+	+		+	+	+	+	+	+					
Robert Marden			+	+																					
Alexander Welles	+					+		+	+	+	+						+	+	+	+	‡	⊤⊤			
William Wymond										+	+														
Richard Rucke	+									+	+	‡	+	+	‡	+	+	+							
John Raynoldes	+									⊤															
John Younge	+									⊥	+		+	+	+	+	+	+	+	+	‡				
Gabriel Adams										⊥		+	+	+	+										
Nicholas Mercer												+	+	+	+	+	+	+	‡						
William Egliston																				+					
Robert Bennett	+																			+	+	+			
John White	+																			⊥	+				
Total	0	5	5	–	4	4	–	–	–	4	–	7	5	–	5	6	7	7	6	6	6	4	3		
Unidentified																									
Richard Nycoll	+	+	+	+	+	+		‡																	
Alexander Wulphyn	+	+	+		+	‡	‡		‡		+	+													
Robert Barnes	+	+	+		+	+				+	‡	+	+		+	+	+	+	+	+	+	+	+		
George Raynoldes										+		+	+		‡	‡	+	+	+	+	‡	+	+		
Robert Marche																				+	+	+			
John Sharpe																				⊥	+				
John Bredes																				⊥	+				
Richard Hillis																				⊥	+				
John Baylye																					+				
Total	3	3	3	–	3	3	–	–	–	2	–	3	3	–	2	2	2	2	2	2	3	3	7		

Notes: See Appendix 3. The 5 jurats appointed between 1557–9 were almost certainly all of a protestant persuasion. The totals refer to the beginning of the mayoral year.
‡ –mayor. + –jurat.
⊥ –jurats elected during the year.
⊤⊤ –mayor (⊤ –jurat) dying before the end of the year.

Sources: See Appendix 3.

65

ing his agent's report that Birchett was 'an honest a man as any in the town', a discreet favourer of the word of God and loyal to Cromwell and that 'Fletcher may have secured this matter against him for malice'.[23] This and similar incidents indicate the depth of feeling between members of the rival factions at this time, one result of which was an almost total breach in social relationships between the two groups. Whereas members of both the Fletcher faction and the Birchett faction can be found acting as witnesses to the wills of other members of this group, acting as godparents of and leaving small bequests to each other's children and, entering into business and marriage alliances within their own faction, there are virtually no such associations cutting across the bounds of faction.

Only a small group of uncommitted jurats show any cross-party affiliations during these years, in particular Richard Nycoll, Alexander Wulphyn, George Raynoldes and Robert Barnes and earlier James Jetter (d.1538), who first brought in Thomas Birchett as a jurat and Alexander Welles as town clerk when he was mayor in 1535. Thus Wulphyn (d.1549) when he was mayor in 1541 appointed Clement Cobbe (a conservative) as jurat and the following year brought in Alexander Welles, whom he later made an overseer of his will and left his gold signet ring. Two of the witnesses to his will were, however, conservatives, William Johnson and Robert Maycott; similarly, George Raynoldes, who survived three changes of regime to serve as mayor under Edward VI (twice, in 1551 and 1552), under Mary (once, in 1556) and under Elizabeth (twice, in 1564 and 1565). His personal bequests spanned many of the sons and daughters of leading members of both earlier factions.[24] From the mid-1530s onwards, therefore, politics in Rye was dominated by the existence of two rival groups of jurats, sharply divided by religion and also by a difference in age, with a strong element of personal animosity between them and each with its separate connections with the rival political elements at court—the reformists with Cromwell and later with the Somerset faction and the conservatives with the local Catholic gentry, in particular the Oxenbridges, the Gages, of whom Sir John Gage (d.1556) was Controller of the Household under Henry VIII and Lord Chamberlain of the Household under Mary, and the Bakers, particularly Sir John Baker (d.1559), a regular visitor to Rye, who became Attorney General in 1536 and

Chancellor of the Exchequer 1545–58.[25]

Reformation and Counter-Reformation

The summer of 1538 saw the triumph of the Rye Protestant faction, when in June, William Inold, the recalcitrant traditionalist curate was finally removed and imprisoned on Thomas Cromwell's instructions and in August, Thomas Birchett assumed the mayoralty for the first time. Birchett's election came at a time when Cromwell's campaign against continuing traditionalist dissent was at its height and mirrored similar Protestant successes at Canterbury, Sandwich and a number of other Kentish towns.[26] The Protestant hold on affairs in Rye was further strengthened in early September by the election of Richard Rucke, another of Birchett's associates as one of the two chamberlains, responsible for the town's finances and later in the month, of Robert Wymond, one of Birchett's recent appointees as a jurat, as one of the two churchwardens.[27]

Evidence of continued opposition to the more Protestant direction of national policy, however, can be found in letters issued in March 1539 by Henry VIII to the Cinque Ports and the Kentish JPs with detailed instructions for the more rigorous enforcement of the Royal Supremacy against, in particular, clerical 'mayntenors of the Bysshop of Rome's usurpyd and feynyd autorytye wyth all hys papysticall supersticions and abuses'.[28] In Rye, opposition to the Henrician Supremacy was marked by a physical attack on the priest during the celebration of the mass on the Feast of the Assumption (15 August) 1539 by one Randall Bell, capper, who was subsequently tried in Rye for treason before Thomas Birchett, mayor; Sir John Baker, the Attorney-General; and five other judges on 13 September 1539.

On that day in August 1539, Bell, with his cap upon his head, ascended the chancel on the north side of the altar, in full view of the congregation and in particular of the mayor and the jurats, whose bench was at the front of the nave, and immediately prior to the elevation of the host, proceeded to the middle of the altar 'and dyd offer to cacche and take the sacrament vyolently out of the prystes handes callyng the pryst false knave and sayd thow cannyst nott make God'. The deacon trying to restrain him, he drew his dagger and 'dyd speke many raylying wordes' whereupon Robert Wymond, jurat, left his seat and commanded him to ward. Examined later the same evening, he justified his actions by saying that he had been commanded to do so by two dissident members of the King's Council. The following day, upon further examination he amplified his protest by adding that 'the Churche dyd stande awry' and 'not as Cryst dyd leave yt but ys nowe removyd in that the pope ys refusyd to be hede of the Churche and therfore there cann be no Salvacyon nor any due mynystracyon of the Sacraments and other rytes of the Churche untyll the pope be hede of the Churche ayene ...'. It was evidently decided to make a public example of Bell, for early in September he was sent to London to be examined by the Council, subsequently being returned to Rye to stand trial.[29]

Earlier, in April 1539, the election of a new parliament saw Rye represented for the first time by two committed Protestants: the mayor, Thomas Birchett and William Mede, one of the recently appointed jurats.[30] It was, however, Thomas Cromwell's last parliament, passing the attainder against him and being dissolved on 24 July 1540, the day after his execution. Rye, as elsewhere, succumbed to the reaction which followed, and in August 1540, John Fletcher (in his absence) was once again returned as mayor.[31] The following year, Inold returned to Rye as vicar, presented by the Crown, the new patron of the living since the dissolution of Stanley Abbey in 1538.[32] The entry marking his death in the Rye burial register in March 1545 notes he was then also Dean of Battle and vicar of Boughton (Aluph), Kent—an indication of the extent both of Inold's personal rehabilitation and also of the shifting nature of royal policy.[33] However, this resurgence of conservatism could not entirely wipe out the Protestant gains of 1538–9, not least because it was customary practice for incoming mayors to renominate existing jurats, so that whilst Birchett and his associates might be temporarily excluded from the mayoralty, they retained considerable influence within the magistracy as a whole. Even before the end of the reign, Protestant fortunes revived nationally, with Henry VIII's final marriage to Catherine Parr and locally with the election in 1545 of Alexander Welles and Robert Wymond as representatives to Henry VIII's last parliament.[34] In Rye itself, another indication of the changed direction was the decision by the mayor and jurats in 1546 to sell off 'certen plate of the churches' for which they received £16 4s 10d, the sum entered in the chamberlains' accounts for 23 May of that year.[35]

The accession of Edward VI on 28 January 1547 marked the start of a throughgoing transformation of the English church. The new direction was first felt in Rye in July, when the Crown presented Edmund Scambler to the vicarage, vacant since the death of Inold's successor, Thomas Chapman. Scambler, a future Bishop of Peterborough under Elizabeth, was a staunch Protestant and was later to be married in Rye church (15 December 1552). Deprived under Mary, he went to London, where he organised clandestine services using the Edwardian Prayer Book until the accession of Elizabeth restored him to favour.[36]

Scambler's appointment provided a fresh impetus to reform, and towards the end of the financial year Michaelmas 1546–7 the churchwardens' accounts record the receipt of 4s 8d 'for iii tables that the idolles stode in at the Hiegh Aulter'.[37] Thereafter, the pace of religious change can be gauged from the detailed entries in the churchwardens' accounts, which are particularly full during the ensuing decade.

That Michaelmas, John Sharpe and John Hynxsted entered into the first year of their churchwardenship and events began to move in earnest. On 26 December, the church paid Alexander Welles 26s 8d for two Bibles which he had supplied.[38] Shortly afterwards a series of changes to the church fabric took place, necessitated by the new order of services. On 10 March 1548 the pulpit was repaired; the damage caused by the removal of the altars was made good (12 May) and the rood loft was removed (22 July). That same day a lock was bought for the poor box which had been set up following the royal injunctions of July 1547, which enjoined the giving of bequests to the poor in place of masses and obits for the dead, and on 6 June, two chains were bought for the Bible and Erasmus's *Paraphrases*, which had recently been obtained by the curate in accordance with the same injunctions.[39]

On 25 August 1548, Thomas Birchett assumed the mayoralty for the third and last time. His nomination by the Lord Protector in a letter dated 18 August urged his election as a 'veary honest, wise and discrete man ... by whom we be assured dyvers waies the same town shall have good order and rule'.[40] Once again Birchett's election heralded a major Protestant advance among the civic office-holders, with the immediate creation of three new jurats from his associates of the struggles of the previous decade, to be followed three weeks later, at an assembly on 16 September, by the removal from office of the sexton, Thomas Searles, to be replaced by one more sympathetic to reform, Peter Jamys. At the same time the assembly decreed 'that the vestments and juelles of the Churche shalbe by the said electors at their disposicion; and for the makinge of the Table of the Commynion at their discretion.[41]

A further assembly on 29 September confirmed John Sharpe and John Hynxsted in their churchwardenship for another year. Their accounts for that year (1548–9) record the sale of church plate worth £101 1s 1d, including various items of laten and silver gilt and the altar cross (alone valued at £52 15s); the money being used to meet a variety of expenses incurred as a result of the reforms, including 27s 4d on various service books, £13 10s on painting the inside of the church and a further £4 for painting where the rood loft had been, 6s 8d for the provision of the communion table and 33s 4d 'for clensying ye chaunsell from poperye'—a choice of language indicative of the prevailing outlook. However, the bulk of the proceeds went towards the costs of a new conduit and in paying the wages of Alexander Welles and George Raynoldes, Rye's two representatives at Edward VI's first parliament, who put forward three bills during the session and secured an act restricting the dumping of ballast by ships in the Camber and giving the mayor and jurats of Rye and Winchelsea the right to fine offenders.[42]

After such a spate of activity, the mayoralty of Thomas Fletcher the following year (1549–50), was relatively uneventful, with few unusual items of expenditure recorded by the churchwardens, while the records of the assemblies and hundreds, so informative for 1548–9, are virtually non-existent henceforth until 1554, though thereafter they form a continuous series. However, the election in 1550 of Richard Rucke as mayor, another of Birchett's associates from the 1530s, coincided with a further stage in the English Reformation, begun with the introduction of the first Edwardian Prayer Book by parliament in January 1549. Payments by the churchwardens in 1550–1 included 12s 4d to Alexander Welles for a Psalter, four paper books 'for songes for the churche' and 'one boke for the Communyon and of the hole services' (presumably the first Edwardian Prayer Book). Another Bible was bought from London at a cost of 12s plus 3d carriage and receipts for the year included 6s for 'pecis of Copis' bought by Thomas Fletcher during his mayoralty and the proceeds from the sale of a silk stole and quantities of lead and iron from the former site of the Friars,[43]

The churchwardens' accounts for 1551–2 record further alterations to the church fabric. The chancel was again white-limed, John Wheler the painter receiving payment for this and also for painting 'iii Tables in the church', presumably of the scriptures, since soon after he received a further sum 'for writing of ii tables in Our Ladies Chaunsell and for mending of the Ten Comaundementes and for dyvers other places in the scripture in the Church', amounting in all to £53s 4d. A *Homily Book* and another edition of Erasmus's *Paraphrases* were obtained the same year, for 16d and 6s 8d respectively, and in January 1552 another Bible 'of the largest volume' was bought for 33s 4d to be placed in the choir, followed in July by the purchase of a second *Book of Homilies*. Early that autumn, the town was visited by the Chancellor of the Exchequer, Sir John Baker, who no doubt observed the recent changes.[44]

Weekly payments for bread and wine for communion by the laity began on 6 November 1552, an innovation which lasted barely a year before a change of regime brought about the reintroduction of the Mass. On 8 December the accounts record the purchase of the second Edwardian *Prayer Book* at a cost of 4s, a second copy being purchased shortly after Christmas 'at Strand gate of a stacyoner there' for 3s 4d.[45] Its use was, however, extremely short-lived, for the reign of Edward VI was drawing to its close. The final phase of the Edwardian Reformation was marked by the payment on 27 May 1553 of 5s 6d for the expenses of the churchwardens with Thomas Birchett, riding to Hastings to appear before the King's Commissioners there, presumably with their inventory of the remaining church plate. That July, Bishop Scory visited Rye; but by then Edward VI was dead and it was only to be a matter of time before the new Queen began to impose traditional orthodoxy once again on the English Church.[46]

News of the death of the King reached Rye on 27 June. On 21 July a servant of Sir Robert Oxenbridge brought a copy of the proclamation of Mary as Queen. Events began to move with increasing rapidity as the Queen sought to impose her new policies on the nation. On 3 September the writ for the election of two burgesses to Mary's first parliament arrived from the Lord Warden, followed two days later by the proclamation 'that none shuld call other herytiquek or papist', reflecting the Queen's desire to prevent excessive public religious controversy during the restoration of the old order.[47]

In Rye, the Edwardian services remained in force until mid-December 1553, when, as a result of parliament's repeal of the Edwardian legislation (with nearly one third of the Commons voting against), the Prayer Book services lost their legal sanction and ceased.[48] On 12 December a Mass Book was obtained, a second copy being bought eight days later. Vestments were acquired and an altar set up. On 29 December the Queen's proclamation for the restoration of the Mass was bought to Rye, followed by a further proclamation on 7 January 1554 'that no man shuld speke any wordes against the quenes maiesties procedinges'.[49] At about the same time the Rye churchwardens and sidesmen travelled to the annual visitation at Hastings (an item for their expenses appears dated 10 January) at which they were presented with a list of 80 articles and injunctions (presumably to ensure that they possessed the necessary service books and other items to enable the proper conduct of the traditional services) to which they had to prepare a written bill to be delivered again to Hastings, to the Bishop's Commissary there.[50] A few days later (21 January) the churchwardens' accounts record the purchase of two Graduals, one Manual, four Processioners, three Antiphoners, three Psalters, two Hymnals, one Mass Book, one Legend and 'ii other bokes for the quyere' at a total cost of £8 16s 8d. At about the same time two candlesticks were bought for 5s and a sacring bell for 6d.[51]

The restoration of the mass in Rye did not come about without some measure of local opposition, however, for on 18 January the vicar of Rye 'and diverse other of thinhabitauntes there' were ordered to appear before the Privy Council, presumably following some kind of disturbance. Those summoned, who included not only Edmund Scambler but also Thomas Birchett, Alexander Welles, John Yonge and three others, subsequently 'being admonisshed by the Lordes to live hereafter like good and quiet subjectes, upon hope they will so do were ... dysmissed of thier further attendance' on their appearance on 20 February. Shortly afterwards, Edmund Scambler was among those clergy deprived of their benefices for being married.[52]

The familiar cycle of religious feast days was now fully restored. A series of payments to workmen in April 1554 record the re-erection of the High Altar again in preparation for Easter. For the first time since 1546, payments were made for the setting up of the Easter Sepulchre for the Easter vigil, and for a paschal candle, coals, incense and for a pair of censers (4s). Other expenses during the year, indicating the gradual restoration of traditionalism, included the provision of a holy water stoop at Whitsun and two payments for such goods formerly appertaining to the church as the Cross, censer and chrismatory 'withe other implements belonging to the Churche' for which William Parterage was paid 25s; and 'the herse clothe of velvett and gold' for which the churchwardens paid Robert Barnes 45s.[53] On 20 August, with the presentation of John Browne to the Rye vicarage, vacant by virtue of Scambler's deprivation, the incumbency was once again in the hands of a clerical conservative.[54]

Events during 1555 showed that the Protestant opposition could still muster considerable local support among the freemen. That August, Richard Fletcher was re-elected mayor for a second term. But at the hundred held on 6 October to elect Rye's two representatives to Mary's fourth parliament, the commonalty chose John Yonge, one of those summoned before the Privy Council in 1554, in what can hardly have been other than a calculated gesture of political opposition to the course events were taking nationally. Not surprisingly, Yonge's election was overturned by the Lord Warden and an outsider, Sir Reginald Moone, returned instead, together with John Holmes, the port controller.[55]

The following year marked a concerted governmental effort to reassert its authority. In June, a special court presided over by the mayor and jurats sitting exceptionally with the vicar, John Browne, ordered William Scragge, cutler, to appear before Bishop Day and other royal commissioners at Lewes to answer various unspecified charges. Among his two bondsmen was William Gibbon, blacksmith, another of those who had previously been summoned before the Privy Council for their opposition to the new regime, so there must be a strong presumption that his offence was of a similar nature. Possibly the charges against him were connected with the proceedings against Thomas Ravensdale, the only known Rye inhabitant to have been burned for heresy during the reign. Whatever the reason, shortly afterwards, Thomas Lamb, one of the Rye curates was summoned to London, appearing before the Council in late June or early July 'for the Churches matters'. Immediately following this, the church-wardens and sidesmen were summoned to Lewes 'apperyng before my lorde bysshope and the other Commyssioners the xvth of July'.[56] In August, Bishop Day again visited Rye, for the second time in two years. Possibly following upon this visit, or perhaps before, Lamb had to make another journey to Lewes 'for an answer of my lorde bysshope'.[57] Unfortunately, the records provide only the bare chronology of events, but clearly something serious must have occurred to merit this degree of concern by both the church authorities and the Privy Council.

Indicative of this continuing interest in events in Rye was the letter sent by the Privy Council on 15 August for the election as mayor for the ensuing year of George Raynoldes 'the Quenes Majesties servant, whose service shalbe to thadvancement of the common wealthe and benefite of that towne'. He was duly elected mayor a fortnight later.[58] Inside the church, 1556 saw the rebuilding of the altar in Our Lady's Chancel, followed early the following year by the re-erection of the rood screen and the obtaining of images from London.[59]

In 1557 the Privy Council again nominated George Raynoldes as mayor, he having, according to their Lordships' information 'behaved himself well in that offyce and is like to doo so agayne'. However the Rye freemen clearly thought otherwise, for at the end of August they returned Alexander Welles as mayor. The death of Thomas Birchett the previous October had left Welles, who, since 1548 had been town clerk, combining it from 1553 onwards with the office of jurat, as the effective leader of the Protestant faction. His election to the mayoralty in defiance of the Privy Council's instrucions was therefore a clear provocation to the central authorities and on 7 September, the assembly authorised 'Mr mayor, Mr Fleccher and certen of the commons' to ride up to London at the town's expense 'to answere the councelles letter brought done by Mr Raynoldes for the eleccon of the mayor', it being added in the margin, 'an evill presidente'. Between that date and the following 23 April when he was paid

74

total of £31 6s 8d expenses, Alexander Welles had to travel to London no fewer than four times to appear before the Council to 'answere certen pointes of our charter' and in mid-October 1557 he spent six days in the Fleet prison after he refused to allow the collection in Rye of the latest forced loan (to finance the war with France), being finally released on 21 October 'having a good lesson to him to beware of the like disobedience hereafter'.[60]

Welles's election to the mayoralty in 1557 saw a further strengthening of the Protestant faction among the magistracy with the appointment of three new jurats, William Egliston, a Winchelsea man who was made free and elected a jurat the same day, Robert Marche and Robert Bennett, the latter an associate from the struggle against Inold twenty years earlier, who was shortly afterwards elected one of Rye's two churchwardens, together with Robert Fowler another committed Protestant.[61] On 9 December at the election of Rye's representative to Mary's last parliament, Thomas Fletcher, who had evidently supported Welles' election as mayor, was returned as MP, the first time since March 1554 that one of Rye's two members of parliament had been a jurat. The restoration of both seats to members of the Rye magistracy had to wait until the first Elizabethan Parliament, just over one year later.[62]

In August 1558 Bishop Christopherson visited Rye, the last incidence of official interest in Rye's affairs by the outside authorities during the reign. Later the same month, Alexander Welles was re-elected mayor. In November the new Queen was proclaimed and the dismantling of the Marian structure in church and state soon followed. Welles did not live to see it, however, for he died shortly afterwards, being buried in Rye parish church on 21 November 1558, four days into the new reign. He was succeeded as mayor by John Yonge, the last surviving of Thomas Birchett's appointees.[63] The altars came down again that spring, followed in October by the levelling of the choir. On 10 December 1559 the weekly payments for bread and wine for the communion resumed and shortly afterwards the desk for the preacher was remade.

Further alterations and acquisitions followed over the next two years, including the buying of a new copy of Erasmus's *Paraphrases* in October 1560. In the same month St Crispin and Crispinian's cloth, possibly a banner or covering commemorating

75

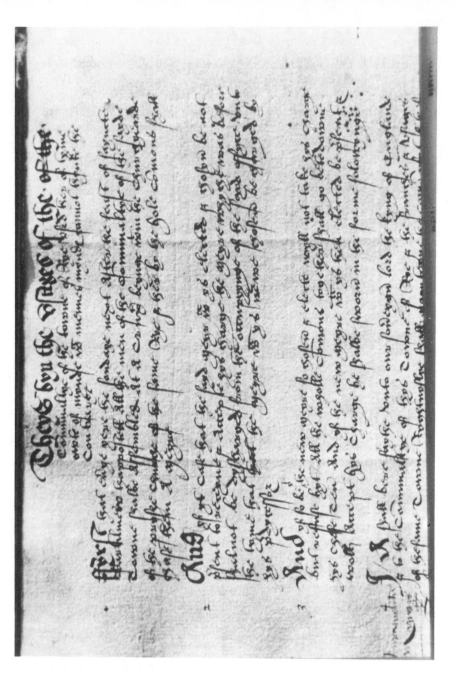

Extract from a Rye Custumal (RYE/57/1/39v)

the victory at Agincourt on that day in 1415, was removed from the church and given into the custody of one of the jurats, Robert Bennett. 'A litill homilye boke' was obtained in February 1561, followed by the taking down of the rood loft again in September and the 'writing of the scriptures in the churche' by a painter at a cost of 31s 8d in October. Three other tables of the scriptures were set up in November, for which Mr Davison received 20d 'for taking it out of the Bible and for his payne to rede it to the painter'. The poor box was set up again and the pulpit repaired the same month. This year also marked the final disposal of the remaining pre-Reformation plate and vestments, the rood coat being delivered to George Raynoldes and sold in January. At the same time 'all the churche copes and chrispinians clothe' were sold to John Yonge for £9 4s and 'certen old stoles' to Henry Kite for 12d, leaving only the four silk streamers used for processions remaining in the court hall and a single gilt chalice of 22 ozs in the hands of one of the chamberlains. Finally, in October 1562 a new 'Booke of Sermons' was acquired, presumably Cranmer's Homilies, once again ordained to be read in church on Sundays by those not licensed to preach.[64] This time, however, there was to be no going back, and as the Elizabethan age progressed external events served only to strengthen the Protestant sentiments of Rye's inhabitants.

The Elizabethan church in Rye

One indication of these Protestant sentiments was the importance attached by the corporation to sound preaching of God's word in the town. From at least 1571 Rye had a town preacher, or lecturer, appointed by the corporation. Variously described as 'Preacher' or 'Minister of the word of God', he was paid initially £10 a year in the 1570s (half by the chamberlains, half by the churchwardens), rising to £20 in 1589 and £26 13s 4d in 1591 when it was agreed by the assembly that this yearly fee be granted to the then preacher, Mr Richard Grenewood, 'to prech and catechyse here as of late he hath donne. And what tyme Mr Grenewood shall lyke of any man to rede the service here the towne will consyder thereof'. Among those who held this office can be indentified John Philpott (1571–4), Richard Fletcher (1575–81), Richard Grenewood (1581–93) and Edward Danner (1594).[65]

77

For much of this period, there was an absentee vicar, although it would appear that Richard Fletcher (a future Bishop of London and a chaplain to the Queen) did obtain the vicarage (the right of presentation to which, after the Reformation, belonged to the Sackville family) after some lobbying by the corporation. On the whole, however, relations between the vicars of Rye and the townspeople were either non-existent or unfriendly in the extreme. Following his departure in 1581, Richard Fletcher seems to have appointed John Ruck (presented to the vicarage of Icklesham 1583) to serve under him in his absence. The arrangement soon proved unsatisfactory, however, and Richard Grenewood was brought in. Between 1586 and 1590, when the town itself acquired the lease of the vicarage from a Mr Wigmore, the assembly books record the repeated difficulties to which Richard Grenewood and the corporation were put to secure him a reasonable stipend. In April 1586 the assembly voted £4 towards his charges in obtaining an order from the Archbishop compelling Thomas Heblethwaite then farmer of the vicarage, to pay him his wages. In January 1589, it was reported that he had received nothing from this source since midsummer 1587. However, when the corporation itself secured the lease of the vicarage, the half-yearly accounts for the second half of 1591 showed a profit of only £3 8s, with £8 9s 1d as yet uncollected, so it may be that the income from the living was simply inadequate.[66]

By September 1592, however, John Prescott, the new vicar, was resident in the town. His stay was not a happy one. In September 1592 he found the mayor and jurats ranged against him when he tried to overturn the commonalty's choice of Ezay Kingwood for the post of sexton. Clearly his sermons found no greater favour, for in January 1593, Richard Grenewood was again employed by the assembly at an annual fee of 20 marks 'to reade one lecture every Satturdaye in the fore none' beginning at nine o'clock. The following year, when Edward Danner, preacher, who was associated with the puritan faction among the corporation was publicly denounced by John Prescott from the pulpit as 'a mutinous person, a sower of sedition, an enemy of the state', the corporation sided with Mr Danner. The assembly, on this occasion, described Mr Prescott as 'over mutynous amonge us to the universall disquyett of this towneshippe' and voted to seek his dismissal 'for unlawfullye atteyninge this his benefice by symony'.

78

Nothing further was heard of the matter, however, and Prescott seems to have remained in the town until his death during the plague epidemic of the autumn of 1596.[67] His successor, Roger Smith, inducted in March 1597, fared little better. At Michaelmas 1599, he too incurred the wrath of the commonalty by seeking to overturn their choice of parish clerk. The following August, Mr Smith found himself in the town gaol, accused by the mayor and jurats, in a letter to the Lord Warden, of having secret catholic sympathies, evidenced by a crucifix found in a letter to his father-in-law in London. A subsequent letter from the Archbishop of Canterbury suggests that these charges were probably groundless.[68]

The continuing friction between successive vicars of Rye and the corporation, and the appointment of a succession of town preachers or lecturers, indicates the importance with which right doctrine and sound preaching were viewed by the general body of freemen. Nevertheless, there was a limit to the extent to which the more extreme forms of puritanism were tolerated. When a small group of such men sought in 1591 to secure the expulsion of Richard Grenewood as preacher for absenteeism from his rural benefice, some five miles outside Rye, the corporation was swift to act in his defence, branding them 'a smale secte ... more holy in shewe then in dede' and 'mutynous fellowes'.[69] The prevailing religious outlook in Elizabethan Rye can therefore best be characterised as advanced Protestantism, yet firmly within the anglican church and not given over much to the development of sects.

A safe haven for Protestant exiles

The Protestant sympathies of many of the town's officers and townspeople made Rye an obvious haven for their co-religionists during the religious conflict in France and the Netherlands in the latter half of the sixteenth century. The Cinque Ports were well known to the government from the late 1560s as harbourers of the Sea Beggars, privateers operating under letters of marque of the Prince of Orange, whose expulsion, under Spanish pressure, by Elizabeth in March 1572 led to the capture of Brill and the start of the Dutch Revolt. Dover and Sandwich in particular, despite royal proclamations from October 1571 onwards forbidding any provisioning of the freebooters or receiving any of their goods had in fact continued to provide 'dailie' assistance, receiving them into their ports where they were 'releaved with all necessaries, ye and lodged openlie in the houses of some officers that ought to have bene rather the punishers of them'. When Elizabeth wrote directly to the Lieutenant of Dover Castle on 21 February 1572 ordering measures for the final exclusion of the Dutch privateers from all of the Cinque Ports on pain of loss of their special privileges, and the punishment of those who had disobeyed her previous orders, her patience had clearly run out. Yet even then, the Rye authorities hesitated to act. Seizing upon the Queen's own reference to 'shippes pretendinge to serve the Prince of Orrenge', on 9 March they wrote to the Council:

'Whereas this present daye the date hereof we have received from the Livetenaunte of Dover Castle the Quenis Majesties letters for the avoydinge from the Portes of flete of shipes of thos which pretend to serve the Prince of Orrenge on the Narrow Seies, it may please your honours to be advertised that we have callid suche persons before us, which wee thought to be of that fleete remaynige in our Towne, very late thether dryven by impietosatie of wether, their ships lyinge in the Camber, and have used towardes them for their departure according to the foresaid letters, who very humbly have desired us fyrst to signifie unto your honours their licences which they have (as they saie) absolutely frome the Prince of Orenge, before their departure. And foras-muche as the Quenis Majesties said letters do concerne suche as pretend the service of the Prince of Orenge ... and theis persones, alledginge their lawfull aucthoritie as they terme it, we thought good with as muche convenient speede as might be, fyrst to signifie unto your honours their licences by this messenger and so to staie as conceringe thos persons till your farther pleasures be therin knowen ...'[70]

Among those later charged with victualling the Sea Beggars was Robert Jackson, a baker and brewer and former town clerk. Yet notwithstanding the obvious signs of royal displeasure, when a fishing vessel from Zealand came into the harbour a month later, manned by privateers under licence of the Prince of Orange the town officers allowed the majority of the crew of thirty to depart, before signifying to the council that they had stayed the ship, together with the captain and six or seven of his company 'being sicke and weke ... for at their arrivall they had nether bredd nor drink nor had eny in seven or eight daies before' and that 'it is the first time that they have ben in England as they saie and knewe nothinge of the orders late taken towchinge such persones.'[71]

Rye also provided a more permanent haven for many religious exiles, especially from France, following the outbreak of religious war there in 1562. There had probably always been a small alien community in the town. The assessment on aliens living in Rye for the 1525 subsidy, listed sixty-six, mainly French and Flemings, but including a Spaniard and a handful of Scots. When, in 1538, a dispute broke out between the Rye fishermen and the resident alien population, who were accused of damaging their livelihood by competing in the mending of nets, there were over a hundred resident.[72]

When, however, following the massacre of French Protestants during Sunday worship at Vassy by supporters of the Duke of Guise in April 1562, the first religious war broke out, Rye became a haven for fleeing Protestants. On 26 May, there was 'a grete conflycte betweene ye Protestantes and ye Papysts' in Dieppe, during which 150 of the former were slain. Many others including whole families fled to Rye, so that by 2 November, when the mayor of Rye, John Yonge wrote to Sir William Cecil to report news of the fall of Rouen to the Guises on 26 October, there were over 500 refugees in the town. The Edict of Amboise, in March 1563, granted a limited freedom of worship to the Protestant communities. Presumably many shortly afterwards returned home, although there is some evidence of the continued abode of at least a small exile community. The Rye baptismal register, for example, includes a marginal note recording the baptism of 'John de Falloyse, son of Mighell de Falloyse of Valencia', 'enhabitaunt for religious sake with his familie' by Mr Frauncis St Poul, 'Minister of the reformed Churche in Fraunce, then being there resident'.[73]

In July 1568, renewed religious conflict broke out in France, and by October large numbers of refugees were again arriving in the port, including several gentlemen, but mainly merchants and handicraftsmen 'wyche do mean to mack ther abode thire'. By 28 March 1569, when a return was made of all aliens within the town, there were 83 such households, including 10 Walloons and Flemings, indicating an alien population of around 300. Five of those households were ministers, six were from Rouen, but by far the largest contingent came from Dieppe (63), including one minister, M. St Pawle and a number of others recognisable from later sesses and other Rye records as resident in the town during much of the ensuing decades until the final triumph of Henri IV in 1594. Many of these were evidently merchants, including Allen Harry otherwise Allain Henry, who had evidently been in Rye since 1565, paid 10s in the 1576 sesse and witnessed his brother's will there in September 1580; and William Butcher, otherwise Guillaume Bucheret, assessed at 20s in 1576, who became a denizen and in 1579 was described as being among the 'cheiffe of the Frenche Churche' in Rye. By November 1571, when the next official survey was conducted, the number of alien households seems to have fallen to twenty, thirteen of which were described as being of the French Church, including Nicholas le Tellier, a minister and his wife, who also appeared on the 1569 list. Altogether there appear to have been 44 adults and 23 children then resident in Rye, chiefly wealthy bourgeois and skilled artisans, including four French and four Walloon merchants and their families, a clockmaker, a bookbinder and a locksmith.[74]

The largest influx of French Protestants, however, came in the weeks and months following the Massacre of St Bartholomew in Paris on 24 August 1572, and the mass killings which it sparked off elsewhere in France. Although few of the names of the 641 refugees who on 4 November were reported as having arrived since 27 August, figure among the later records of members of the French Church within the town, a steady flow of immigrants seems to have continued, many of them of the poorest class, so that by the beginning of 1574 the passengers had brought over 'great numbers of the Frenche beinge very poore people, both men, wemen and children, to the great crye and grieff of the inhabitants of Ry and other places about the same.' On 15 February 1574, therefore, the town assembly decreed that from henceforth 'no common passenger of the towne or fisherman which shall fortune to come frome Deipe or any parties beyond the seas ... shall bringe nor suffer to be put on land any of the Frenche or Flemishe nation ... excepte marchauntes, gentes, common postes and messengers' on pain of a 40s fine. By the autumn of that year, special provision was having to be made for their sustenance, and at a time of general crisis of provision, when special licences were being sought by the corporation for the purveying of quantities of grain into the town, was one for 100 quarters of wheat, bought in Arundel by Hance Hanson, merchant, of the French Church, 'onelie for provision of the poor French people' of whom there were 'a greate number' in the town.[75] Many of these people remained in Rye until the ending of the religious troubles in France in the early 1590s. Writing less than a century after the events he describes, Samuel Jeake, who as a town clerk and registrar must have had access to records of the corporation and the church which no longer survive, states that in 1582 there were 1534 French refugees in the town. A further influx is apparent in the autumn of 1585, when between 23 September and 17 November, the lesser box accounts record the payment of keyage on at least 66 loads of 'howshold' (goods) belonging to various Frenchmen, which was taken either to the houses of existing French residents or to various inns and victualling houses. Some, at least, of this latest wave of immigrants must have left soon after, for on 1 March 1586 the corporation wrote to Walsingham and Lord Cobham:

> 'sithens our last advertisment to their honors of the nomber there are departed so many as nowe their remaynith but xvc (1500) and odd, whereof the Frenche Churche are willinge (as they saye) towardes the springe to remove cc (200) of them to such places as their honors shall thinke goode, but yet we thinke the reste are somewhat to greate a nomber to remayne with us, divers houses beinge tomuch pesterid with them. Notwithstandinge we wold willingly shewe them all the courtecy we might without dangeringe our selves, and do thinke that one thowsand of them are as many as we may well sustaine, every thinge groweth so extreme dere ...'[76]

Throughout the 1570s and the 1580s, therefore, Rye sustained a sizeable immigrant population. Not all of these were poor, by any means, and there was always a number of more substantial merchants and craftsmen, who carried on their occupations in their new home. In 1573, the lesser box returns of maltodes paid on goods going in and out of the port reveal the names of some 13 French and Walloon merchants, including several whose trading activities can be traced into the 1580s and early 1590s; for example Anthony Coq, and Francis Maquery, who became denizens and settled in Rye for the rest of their lives. A few moved on from Rye to Protestant havens back on the continent or returned home (Nicholas Dugrange, a French merchant and sea captain listed in the lesser box returns for 1576, by 1579 had gone

83

to Guernsey; Bawdwyn Martin, merchant, of Rotterdam, listed in 1573, returned there in January 1575; and Vincent Gloria, a spinner of fine yarn from Dieppe, who came over to England in 1574, returned there in 1579). However, they were replaced by others. In 1578, the lesser box returns list at least ten, and in 1581, eleven. Among the goods in which they dealt were wine, oil, brasell, vinegar, madder and woad (both dyes) all of which figured among the items traded by Allen Harry between 1573 and 1583. He also exported glass on behalf of his brother Andrew, a glasier, who operated his business in Rye until his death in 1580. Anthony Coq, on the other hand, seems to have specialised in importing hops and exporting barrells of salt fish, mainly herrings and sprats, while Nicholas Dugrange is recorded in February 1576 as having shipped a complete cargo of herrings from Norway to Dieppe via Rye.[77]

The contribution of these immigrants to the economy of the town was clearly considerable. Not only did they increase the actual volume of trade, they also introduced new skills. In the midsummer quarter of 1575, of 91 shops listed as paying quarterage in the great box returns, at least twelve were in the hands of aliens, and (since it is impossible to identify all of these) the total may in reality have been nearer twenty. In the summer of 1579 there were at least eleven, the majority of them in the same hands as five years earlier. Among those listed on the former occasion, was a book binder, a French tinker, a French joiner, a French turner and a French shoemaker. There was also a French baker, a French poticiary or surgeon, a French cutler and a Flemish joiner, listed at various times during the ensuing decades, although by the early 1590s the number of those identifiable as aliens had fallen to only three or four.[78]

The wide extent of the immigrants' trading concerns caused occasional resentment among the English inhabitants who feared that the increased competition could threaten their own livelihoods. This resulted in a series of town decrees restricting the activities of the newcomers. In March 1578, the French baker was ordered not to bake for sale to any of either the English or French nation after the feast of the Annunciation (25 March) on pain of a £5 fine. The penalty was evidently not sufficient as a deterrent, and two years later, the assembly repeated the inhibition 'on paine of imprisonment, and suche other ponishment as the lawes will permit'. The situation evidently resolved itself, because no French baker is listed among the receipts of the great box between 1581 and 1585, although listed among the bakers whose bread was weighed in 1587 was 'the Frenche baker at the Thre Kinges', and in April 1593 'French Peter's'. By now the situation was once again getting out of hand, with two French women setting up business by July, one in Francis Maquery's house and the other 'besides John Dowce'. That there was a danger of others also establishing themselves at this time is evident from a further assembly decree in October that 'none of the French bakers' should bake or sell any bread within the liberties of the town after the feast of All Saints.[79]

A further example of the trading activities of the French is provided by the case of Guillaume Vatmere, fined 10s in July 1586 for retailing linen cloth, having previously 'uppon complainte of the commons' been charged not to do so. Again the fine proved inadequate as a deterrent, and the following year he appeared again, was fined 10 French crowns and was commanded 'aswell unto the saide Gilliam Vatmer as unto all other of the French nacion inhabytinge' in Rye, not to retail any mercery or grocery ware to any of the English nation on like penalty for each subsequent offence. The mercers had, however, secured licence from the corporation for a company, which regulated their trade and limited the numbers of those occupying it. Not so the shipwrights, eighteen of whom joined together in September 1589 to complain to the assembly that:

'the French Shipwrightes aswell papystes as Protestantes come over from Diepe and tooke awaye their occupacion. And that the Frenchmen which come hether for succor do sende for those French shipwrights and sett them on worke upon their shyppinge, refusinge to sett the Englishe men on worke, although they are contented yt the French shall sett some master workmen of their contrye shipwrightes beinge of the religion on worke. Of which ... abuse they crave remedy, unto whome the Mayor and Jurates have graunted remedye'.[80]

In such situations feelings could run high. Thomas Snodden, joiner, was probably voicing similar economic grievances when he was arrested for 'abuse in the Churche against the French congregacion' in June 1589.[81]

A large proportion of the refugees in the early 1570s were

85

mariners, mainly from Dieppe, who fled with their ships across the Channel to Rye soon after the religious troubles broke out. Dieppe itself was a huge town by English standards, almost five times the size of Rye, with a population of over 20,000 and a merchant fleet of more than 150 larger vessels in the latter part of the sixteenth century. Its sea captains, operating in partnership with Rouen merchants, traded the coasts of Africa and the Levant, explored much of the eastern seabord of North America and as far south as Peru and Brazil. From the beginnings of religious conflict in the 1560s, Dieppe seems to have been divided between Protestants and Catholics, and there had been bloody clashes in 1562. In early May 1589, when once again many of its inhabitants had fled across the seas, the English agent, Ottywell Smith, reported to Walsingham that the town was in imminent danger of falling to the Catholic League, with half the town supporting it. 'Unless her Majesty send over all those of the Religion from Rye and London, the town will fall.' Apparently the Governor of Dieppe had already written in this vein to the French, but 'I think they will not come without your commandment'.[82]

Although it is impossible to ascertain the numbers of foreign mariners in Rye in 1589, among the files of correspondance of the town in the early 1570s are various safe conducts to alien masters of trading vessels giving license to embark on voyages of merchandise as far afield as Holland, Danzig, Koenigsberg, Norway, the Azores and Guinea, and to return to Rye with their cargoes. Between 1573 and 1575, at least ten such ships, with at least 269 crew, were operating out of Rye, mainly engaged in trading operations for French and Walloon merchants resident in the town. They also acted as passengers, carrying numbers of French Huguenots from Rye to such safe havens as St Malo, La Rochelle and La Hogue.[83] Inevitably, such voyages often resulted in privateering activities against their Catholic compatriots and the latter's Spanish allies. The corporation files abound with letters relating to their activities, from which it is clear that the mayor and jurats went to considerable lengths to protect them from official wrath. Among the men, mainly sea captains ordered by the English government to be arrested on charges of piracy in November 1578, were 19 listed by the mayor as not dwelling in Rye or as having lands or properties there. At least ten, however,

86

can be shown to have operated during much of the preceding decade out of the Camber. Among those who appeared on the list were Nicholas Dugrange, described early in 1579 as 'late of Rye now of Guernsey' when his ship was arrested in Poole on charges of robbing a Portuguese ship; and Thomas Beniarde, Michel Russell and Nicholas du Cheyne, arrested in Bristol in April 1575 on piracy charges. In the latter case, the mayor and jurats, having consulted the elders of the French community, merely reported that they were honest traders, fled with their families for religion; in the former they assured the Poole authorities that the vessel concerned was known to the French community to have been in Rye when the alleged incident occurred.[84]

The situation was evidently similar throughout the Cinque Ports, for at the end of November 1578 the Privy Council ordered fines to be levied on seventeen individuals, including four in Rye and others at Hastings, Winchelsea, Lydd, Romney, Hythe and Folkestone. By the time the order came through, however, none of the accused was in the town, the corporation writing in their mitigation, 'Mihill Russell hath but his wife here with her friends and his substance is his ship, Captain Braband has departed to the seas notwithstanding his wife hath promised to pay the money, Francis Maquery is in France and Nicholas Purvage we think will not be long absent.' It is not clear whether any of them ever actually paid their fines, although Francis Maquery had been previously fined £6 13s 4d in June 1574 for going aboard the Dutch freebooters without licence. One of the two fined in Winchelsea was Francis Bolton, the town clerk, who became town clerk of Rye in 1590.[85] It is evident, therefore, that the officers of many of the ports like Rye, must have been sympathetic to the privateering exploits of their co-religionists.

As elsewhere, the French Church in Rye acted as a virtually independent, self-governing community, with its own ministers and elders, the latter mostly merchants from among the wealthier members of the community, such as James Miffant resident in Rye from August 1572 until 1578 and again in 1589, when he represented the Rye congregation at the colloquy in London in April of that year. Whenever problems arose between the English and French communities or when the corporation needed to discuss important issues with the French congregation it was always to these men that they turned as representatives of their

87

community. In the summer of 1575, for example, the elders drew up a book of all those who were then resident in the town for the mayor to send to the Council, with a request that they be allowed to stay. In civil cases these same men acted on behalf of their community, as in September 1572 when Francis Mercier, Ambrose de Moye, Robert de la Place and William Butcher acted as arbitrators in a dispute between Francis Maquery and his wife and her father, Francis Canchie; or in 1576 when Cornelis Sohier, Francis Maquery, Francis Mercier the elder and his son, Francis Mercier the younger, appeared on behalf of Bawdyn Martin of Rotterdam in a lawsuit resulting from the confiscation of part of his cargo of wines from the hoye of Cornelis Jacobson, the drunken sea captain referred to above.[86] Similarly, in March 1579, Francis Mercier, William Bucher and Cornelis Sohier 'merchants and of great credit' came before the mayor and jurats to certify on behalf of Nicholas Dugrange, while in February of that year the same three men appeared with others to certify before the mayor and jurats that James Miffant and his wife, who had recently returned home to Dieppe, during their abode in Rye had 'there lived for the cause of religion during all that time, not in any way intruding themselves into the causes of war ... but very quietly behaving themselves like honest and good people'.[87]

Although all adult members of the congregation had to subscribe to the articles of religion sent down by the court of High Commission in November 1575, they appear to have followed their own order of worship conducted by their own ministers in Rye parish church. They must also have administered their own poor relief as bequests for this purpose appear in the wills of Andrew Harry (1580) and Martine Canchie[88], Francis Maquery's widow (1588). They also seem to have kept their own registers of baptisms and marriages, since only the baptisms of ministers and a few similar leading members of the French Church appear in the parish registers, and then only as subsequent additions in a different hand in the margins of the page, usually listing the French minister who carried out the ceremony. From this and other sources it is possible to establish the names of many of the ministers of the French Church in Rye. In the early 1570s, there were evidently three, Nicholas le Tellier (1569–74), Francis St Poul (1572) and Guillaume Lasne (1573–5). Between 1583 and at least 1590 Lewis Morell appears most regularly, performing baptisms, witnessing wills and attending colloquys on behalf of the Rye congregation, although there were at least two other French ministers 'preachers of their Church in Rye', Anthony Wateble and Mathewe Cartoall who both performed baptisms in February 1588. Fifteen eighty-seven, when the national colloquy was held in Rye, marked one of the high points in the history of the French Church in the town. By 1590, Morell had to tell the colloquy in Canterbury that he would have to leave within the year as the Rye congregation had dwindled and there was no longer sufficient to support himself, his wife and family. He must have left shortly after as, in 1593, the church in Dieppe sent a M. Denis as pastor to the French congregation remaining in Rye.[89]

By the early 1590s the foreign Protestant community in Rye was dwindling rapidly, as the majority of French Protestants returned home. Most of the Dutch had left previously, following the success of the Protestant cause in the northern half of the Netherlands. Baudwin Martin, of Rotterdam, merchant, 'whose contynuance emongest us we could very well have leiked of' had returned home after only two and a half years, with his wife and servants in January 1575. Many of the French had left for the Huguenot strongholds of Brittany coast in the later 1570s, and a few, such as Daniell Mynge, merchant of Dieppe, who had conducted a lucrative trade in cider out of Rye in 1572, had returned home by 1581. Of the other leading members of the French Church throughout much of the 1570s, Cornelis Sohier seems to have left by early 1579, William Butcher died in 1580, Francis Maquery met a sudden, accidental death from the stray shot of a naval vessel in Rye harbour in 1586, and Anthony Coq died some time after 1583.[90] Although there was a further influx in the period 1585–9, many of these returned home shortly afterwards, leaving only a handful of those whose long stay had rendered them more English than French. Francis Maquery's son, William, who grew up in Rye had returned to Dieppe by 1602 when, described as a mariner of that town he received £5 10s due to him from the Rye corporation for one year's rent of £60 stock of his late father's. Moyses Coq, son of Anthony, who like Maquery had become a denizen, elected to remain, following his father's occupation of a merchant and being captured and ransomed by Catholic Leaguers while on business in Ault in 1593. He was assessed as being worth £20 in Watchbell Ward in 1596.

Perhaps representative of the many ordinary mariners who came to Rye was Anthony Bryant, a Frenchman by birth who had been in the town more than forty years, had served his apprenticeship there and been married twice, having children by both marriages, and 'divers times' had been pressed and served in her Majesty's ships, and must have been one of the last to leave, obtaining his certificate of good conduct in September 1602.[91] By the close of the sixteenth century there can have been few exiles left in Rye; nor was there any reason why they should have remained. In France, the Edict of Nantes (1598) guaranteed Protestants toleration and freedom of worship; and in the same year, the Eleven Years' Truce marked Spanish recognition of the de facto existence of the United Provinces. Yet the relative shortness of the timespan when set against the centuries which have ensued, should not blind us to the fact that for more than a generation, the town and port of Rye provided a safe haven for one of the largest foreign Protestant communities in Elizabethan England.

CHAPTER 3

Town Government and the Political Elite

Who Moste desyres the charge, this offyce to supplye
Ys most unmetst the same to have I meane, of Mairaltye.
John Donnynge, 1574 (RYE 1/4/1r)
God send us Good magystrayghtes. And well to Crye Amen.
c.August 1485 (RYE 60/3/36v)

The administrative structure

The ultimate authority for town government in Rye rested upon
the rights and privileges laid down in the General Charter of the
Cinque Ports, reissued (with occasional additions), by the Crown
at the beginning of every reign. This charter, referring back to
previous royal grants, confirmed the Cinque Ports in their
complete liberties of trade and of justice as they had existed in the
time of Henry II. Amongst these liberties, as specified in the
General Charter of Edward VI (1547), were freedom from county
jurisdiction and lawcourts in Kent and Sussex; freedom from all
internal customs dues and the like within the realm; the right to
hold leets and lawdays and have the profits from them; the right
to hear and determine all pleas of the Crown except treason and to
punish offenders by use of the stocks, pillory or the gallows and to
have the goods of convicted felons; the right to hear civil pleas;
freedom from all aids, subsidies and the like; freedom from arrests
and attachments for service; the right to have fines of regrators
and forestallers of the market and other such offenders; the right
to waifs and strays, wrecks and wardship; and, finally, the power
for mayors (or bailiffs) and jurats, with consent of the commons to
amend the customs and practices of the individual ports. In
addition, where any injustice done within a port was alleged, the
Lord Warden had power to hear and determine the case, through

the Chancery court at Dover.[1]

The precise details of the operation of these various powers is not specified in the General Charter and was left to the individual ports, who conducted their affairs in accordance with the usages 'used ther of tyme owte of mynde which mennes myndes cannot thynke the contrarye' as laid down in each town's custumal. The earliest surviving copy of the Rye custumal dates from the mid-fifteenth century, but various later copies are known, as for example that drawn up in 1550 as a result of an assembly decree ordering that the customs and ordinances of the town be gathered together in one book.[2]

According to the Custumal, the mayor, the chief officer of the town, was elected by the whole of the freemen on the Sunday immediately following the feast of St Bartholomew (24 August). This meeting, referred to in the assembly books as an open hundred, took place immediately after divine service, at a crux (or cross) in the churchyard, in fact a brick and timber framed building, as appears from decrees relating to its repair in 1567 and its demolition in July 1603, by which date it had become 'so ruinous that the same is reddy to fall downe, and withall the place by reason of such fylth and ordure, that is increased therein is become so odious, lothsome and noysome, that no person is able to indure or come near the place'.[3] No restriction was placed on the number of occasions on which an individual could hold office, although an assembly decree of 1504 prohibited mayors from again holding office within three years. This did not, however, prevent the re-election for a consecutive term of John Baker alias Chesman in 1510, nor of his successor, Robert Wymond for a second term in 1502.[4]

Immediately upon his election the mayor swore allegiance to the Crown and to the commonalty of the town and its franchises and usages and to minister justice without favour, choosing to assist him in these respects up to 12 jurats 'of the prudentes of the communaltye' who swore an oath in all respects similar to the mayor's. In practice the number of jurats fluctuated between eight and twelve, although in 1510 and 1519 they fell as low as six; and in 1508, 1511–13 and 1524 to seven. Theoretically, the mayor appears to have been free to make his own choice of jurats, but in reality, except in cases of acute political crisis, jurats could only be displaced for grave offences; usually they continued to serve until retirement or death. Exceptions were 1507, when Thomas Basden was expelled by Robert Bawdwyn; 1510, when Richard Barkeley and Robert Mede were expelled on the feast of St Nicolas by the then mayor, Nicholas Sutton, and John Dyrykson and Gabriel Wayte elected instead; 1519 when, again under Nicholas Sutton, four jurats were expelled, all of whom were subsequently readmitted (presumably after some suitable submission) within the ensuing months; in 1549 when the incoming mayor, Thomas Fletcher, refused to reappoint two nominees one of whom was made a jurat by his Protestant predecessor only a week before the outgoing mayor had left office; and in 1574 when Robert Fowler 'for divers considerations and iust causes' was dismissed from his juratship.[5]

There is no evidence of any mayor incurring the penalty laid down in the custumal for refusing office during this period, namely that 'all the wholle Commons together shall go bete downe hys chefe tenement'[6] but there are a number of instances where jurats declined office or had their oaths temporarily respited for personal reasons, sometimes for a fee. For example, William Byspyn was discharged from his juratship in January 1519 at his own request, in return for which he had paid 40s. to the corporation. He returned as a jurat in October 1524 and became mayor two years later. Similarly William Dabernell, re-elected a jurat in September 1578 'who was about his affayres all the yere past' only finally took his oath at the very end of the mayoral year on 10 August 1579.[7] Amongst those who declined office were Thomas Belveridge in 1586 and in 1593 on the grounds that as principal searcher of the port of Chichester, he could not conveniently serve also as a jurat; and Peter Keling, nominated in 1587 'who beinge sent for to take the othe, and perswadid by the Maior and jurates by all courteous wayes and meanes, and in thend chargid uppon his allegeance to take the othe, he utterly refused the same, not havinge any lawfull or iust matter to alleage to the contrary, but only that he thought him self farr unmeete for the place'.[8]

One jurat who had a particularly chequered career was Thomas Edolphe. Appointed a magistrate in February 1576, the following August he declined 'with good and frendly behavior towardes Mr Maior and the rest of the jurates' and was permitted to depart at his pleasure. He was reappointed a jurat in December 1577 by the

93

full consent of the then mayor, John Fagge, and the nine jurats present, only to be dropped from the jurats' bench in 1580 by Robert Jackson. The assembly books are silent as to the reasons for this second dismissal, although it must have been connected with the factional disputes dividing the corporation members at the time. That there had clearly been some trouble is evidenced by the entry recording his reappointment once again in December 1581. On his appearance before the mayor and jurates on this occasion 'his behavior towardes them was so modest, and so commendable that all those that were present graunted unto him the rome and place he fyrst had, and so he tooke the jurates othe'.[9] He went on to become mayor in 1586, 1587 and 1594.

Few cases were as complex as that of Thomas Edolphe. More usually, jurats served an uninterrupted term until their retirement or death. Clement Cobbe the elder, for example, retired to his farm at Brensett, Kent, where he died in 1557; Robert Jackson had his oath respited for a fee in 1586 and died four months later; and Robert Carpenter disappeared from the jurats' lists after 1601, dying virtually penniless in 1607.[10] In most cases jurats died in office, at least 75 such occurrences being recorded in probate records and in the assembly books and parish registers.

The right of all the freemen to elect the mayor was a jealously guarded prerogative which twice came under threat during the sixteenth century. In 1526 the Lord Warden, Sir Edward Guldeford, in an attempt to quell factionalism throughout the Ports, secured the enactment of a decree by the guestling, restricting the election of mayor to 37 'of the most wysist and discretist' freemen, chosen for that purpose by the outgoing mayor in the larger towns and a smaller number in the lesser ports, who were to chose the mayor from one of the existing magistrates.[11] Thirty-seven names are listed in the record of the 1527 and 1528 mayoral elections at Rye, indicating that the decree must have been in force for at least two years, but thereafter the practice appears to have ceased. On occasion, however, the government intervened directly and recommended a particular choice to the commons, as in 1548 when Thomas Birchett was chosen mayor in conformity with a request by letter from the Lord Protector, the Duke of Somerset; and in 1557 when the Privy Council's letter recommending the re-election of George Raynoldes was ignored and his Protestant opponent Alexander

94

Welles was elected instead.[12]

However, the most serious attempt at restricting the franchise came during the Elizabethan period, when, in February 1580, the Lord Warden, Lord Cobham, following several years of disputed elections and growing civil unrest in Rye, issued a series of articles for the conduct of future mayoral elections. In future the outgoing mayor and jurats were to meet together on the morning of the mayoral election, prior to the election proper and, by a majority vote if they could not agree, set down the names of three of their number from which the commons might make their choice of mayor for the ensuing year. Further clauses restricted the choice of future jurats to be made from existing members of the common council; common councillors to be chosen by the mayor and jurats and, more seriously, burgesses to parliament and all other town officers (except those appointed directly by the mayor) to be in future chosen by the mayor, jurats and common council, thus excluding the freemen from any participation in the government of the town beyond that of electing the mayor.[13] The new regulations were debated at an assembly of the mayor, jurats and common council on 8th February 1580 when, on the unanimous advice of the common council they were shelved as being 'directly against their customes and auncient usages which they be sworne to mayntaine.'[14] The following August 'accordinge to thauncient custome tyme out of mynde usid' Robert Jackson was elected mayor 'by the generall voyce of the commons of the said towne'.[15]

Among the responsibilities of the mayor was presiding over the various courts of hundred, sessions and record and over assemblies, acting as coroner and setting the price of victuals (bread, beer and beef), unless he was himself a victualler, in which case he would be assisted by two jurats who were not; as happened during the mayoralties of John Fagge, a butcher, and Robert Jackson, a brewer.[16] In each of these activities the mayor could expect the support of the jurats, often referred to in this context as his 'brethren' whose oath enjoined them to 'assist in iustice the Maior for ye time being'.[17] Office holders' duties could be fairly onerous. In the mayoral year 1563/4 for instance, by no means untypical of the middle years of the century, there were 32 assemblies, 16 courts of record (dealing with over 320 cases of debt and the like), 7 courts of strangers, 6 sessions of the peace, 2

95

hundreds, 2 meetings of the lenten jury and at least 17 other occasions on which individuals appeared before the mayor and jurats for the issuing of bonds and recognizances, apprenticeship indentures and the like.[18] In the absence of the mayor, the most senior jurat acted as his deputy.

Below the mayor and jurats were approximately a dozen town officials, paid and unpaid, at the head of which was the town clerk. As the one other member of the corporation who shared the discussions of the mayor and jurats, the town clerk was in a different category to other town officers, as was evidenced by the appellation 'Mr' which was applied to him as well as to the mayor, jurats, vicar and bailiff. Two town clerks went directly from that position to being mayor, another indication that the office ranked almost on a par with a juratship. George Mercer, town clerk from 1502, went straight on to becoming mayor in 1513 with power to put in his own nominee as town clerk. Similarly William Roberthe, town clerk in 1537 and from 1539 onwards, became mayor in 1547 without ever becoming a jurat. Two other town clerks, Alexander Welles who held office in 1538 and 1549–56 and Robert Jackson who was town clerk from 1557 to 1570, also both became jurats and served as mayor, Alexander Welles uniquely combining the offices of jurat and town clerk for three years from 1553 until his election as mayor in 1556. Such men were no mere town officials.

George Mercer owned Hawkhurst Place, which he left to his son Nicholas, who himself became a jurat and served as mayor in 1559; while Welles had important mercantile interests and had married into the local gentry and Jackson had one of the largest brewing and baking businesses in the town.[19] Their later Elizabethan successors were of lesser wealth and influence. William Appleton, town clerk from 1571 until his death in 1590 lamented in 1581 'though I be one of the courte, I am nowe a daies last of councell ... My office is waxen weker in that it was, and so farr as I se devises to make it weker ...'.[20] By the time of his successor, Francis Bolton's death in 1600, the collapse of the town's economy had still further weakened the position of the office. In a letter to the Lord Warden on 9 December informing him of the appointment of Robert Convers as town clerk, the mayor wrote 'our Towne is fallen into such decaye, as the place doth afforde but a very small lyvinge unto him that shall enioye the same, unlesse he have some other matter to stick unto ...'.[21]

The town clerk was the most highly paid of the town's officials and while the town's economy flourished, the position must have been very lucrative. In addition to a basic salary (10s a quarter in 1485, rising to 13s 4d by 1515 and 20s by 1525 where it remained for the rest of the century) the town clerk received substantial legal fees in connection with the work of the Rye courts. These varied from a mere 2d for such minor matters as an entry of plaint in general actions and every continuance, to 3s 4d for drawing up every inquisition on oath of a jury, or for any special matter when the court was held from day to day or for the levying of a fine, plus 2s for engrossing each copy. In between lay a range of charges. He was allowed 8d for taking witnesses' depositions and for making indictments and 4d for every copy of a deposition or plea answer after the rate of 12 to 14 lines. For every return of servants' wages he was allowed 6d for every 20 lines in paper engrossed. For bonds and recognizances to keep the peace or to be of good abearing he received 12d and for every letter of process with seal 2s. assize cases brought higher rates than civil pleas, reflecting the more serious nature of the charge. In such cases he was paid 2s 6d for entering plaints, precepts of summons or writs and writs of execution, and 2s for entering every plea, for the verdict and the judgment.[22] Whilst it would be difficult to provide a very precise assessment of the town clerk's income from all these sources in any one year, nevertheless the volume of business generated by the court of record alone was quite considerable, as were matters of process, resulting in often bulky annual files of process at least until the town's economy began to decline. During Rye's heyday, therefore, town clerks might expect a considerable income, placing them on an equal footing in terms of wealth as well as social status with the other members of the town magistracy.

The office of town clerk was elective annually by the mayor, jurats and commons. Not surprisingly these elections could be hotly contested. Such was clearly the case during the political and religious upheavals of the 1530s[23] and there is also evidence of contests in 1574 when Robert Jackson unsuccessfully sought to regain the position from which he had been displaced by William Appleton in 1571; and in September 1590 when an attempt was made by the then mayor, Robert Carpenter, to secure the office which had been temporarily held by Francis Bolton following William Appleton's death, for his brother John. In 1571 the mayor, William Davy, having abstained from the voting, gave his goodwill to Appleton who had received the more part of the votes of the jurats and commons, and he was sworn. In 1590, Francis Bolton received the votes of eight jurats and most of the commons and John Carpenter the votes of the mayor, two jurats and a lesser part of the commons. Since the Custumal was not entirely clear on what should happen if the mayor and jurats disagreed, legal advice was sought, and it was not until December that Bolton was finally sworn, and then only on the basis that a definitive decision would be sought from the court of King's Bench, depending upon which he would either continue in office or immediately relinquish it to John Carpenter.[24] No more was heard of the matter and Bolton remained town clerk until his death.

In addition to the town clerk there were a number of minor paid officers of the corporation. The mayor's sergeant, appointed by the mayor, was chiefly responsible for making arrests and executing writs, usually for distraint of goods in debt cases. He was paid 5s a quarter in 1485, rising to 10s by 1515. Then there was the town sergeant, chosen by the whole commonalty, whose wages seem to have risen from 3s 4d in 1515 to 6s 8d by 1525 and 10s by the end of the century. His chief responsibility was the collection of the dues of the 'little box', which consisted of the maltodes or local customs on goods inward or outward bound through the port. Indeed in the early years of the century he was known as the collector of the maltode at Strand. An inventory of his equipment made during a changeover of personnel in 1560 shows that he had 2 corn bushell measures, 4 salt bushells, one coal bushell and a gallon measure together with the little box itself.[25] A third minor officer was the scorer with the butchers, an obscure office, which is first mentioned in 1570. His main function seems to have been the sealing of leather, since an inventory of his goods in 1582 specified 'seales accordinge to thorder of theschequire' and 'a bagge of lether', and in 1571 a town ordinance was made whereby any unsold tanned hides brought into the town were to be laid up in his house in the Market Place. However, there were also three searchers and sealers of leather chosen annually from the freemen, so his role may have been to assist them. From 1572 he was also responsible

98

for making arrests in the absence of the other town officers and it appears that another of his duties was to aid the mayor's sergeant and the town porter in collecting the dues of the great box, paid quarterly by shopkeepers and certain licensed trades to the town.[26] The town porter carried incoming and outgoing goods between the Strand, the storehouse and the Landgate. He was also responsible for the carriage of the town's dung and the removal of dunghills on specified occasions. His rates for carriage were to be displayed at the Strand, outside the town storehouse and elsewhere. In 1563, charges ranged from 1d for a barrell and 2d for a horsepack to 12d for a tun of beer and 16d for a tun of wine.[27] He probably took over the work of transporting the town's dung from the scavenger, whose office was abolished in 1563.[28]

Other minor officers included the keeper of the town ordnance, who was paid £4 a year from 1570; the beadle, whose main duty seems to have been the crying of 'lanthorne and candlelight' during the winter months, for which he received 6s 8d in 1574; and the town waits, or minstrels as they were known earlier, which by 1573 consisted of a fife and a drum whose chief activity apart from ceremonial occasions seems to have been 'going abroad the winter nights with their drum and phife for the watches', for which they were paid 20s a quarter each plus provision of a livery.[29] One office which appears intermittently is that of aleconner, of which there were two appointed until 1566 at the time of election of the other town officers. After that date they appear only once, in 1573, when in January of that year, Robert Wymond and John Smith senior were appointed 'searchers and tasters of bere' with the task of ensuring the quality of the 2s beer brewed for the poor by tasting it at least three times a week although the two 'kerners' which appear amongst the annual lists of town officers may be aleconners.[30] In order that the paid officers of the corporation should be instantly recognisable it was agreed, in January 1566, that every town officer should have 10s for augmenting their liveries, all to be made into gowns by Candlemass next 'all of one sort and fashion and cloth Citezyn like'.[31]

In addition to the permanent staff of the corporation who, although subject to annual election, were generally reappointed and depended, at least in part, upon their salaries for their livelihoods, there were a number of other elective offices which were filled by freemen, usually for one or two years only. The most important of these offices was that of chamberlain, of which there were two. Although at first there was no separation between the responsibilities of the two chamberlains and the accounts were in their joint names, as early as 1517 the accounts show the appointment of one fisherman and one landsman, a process which led in 1546 to a division of the accounts between the dues on fishing vessels and their catches and the residue, comprising some 90 per cent of the town's income. From 1577 they are specifically referred to as the accounts of the sea chamberlain and the land chamberlain respectively. At the beginning of the period each chamberlain was paid 13s 4d yearly, but the splitting of the accounts created such an obvious imbalance in the responsibility and workload of the two officers that the land chamberlain came to be paid 13s 4d quarterly whilst the sea chamberlain's wages remained at 13s 4d for the whole year.[32]

Since chamberlains were held accountable for each item of the town's annual revenues and expenditure during their term of office, and were liable to be surcharged for any uncollected rents or other dues, the office of chamberlain was effectively restricted to the wealthier freemen. It seems also to have been regarded as a testing ground and preparation for those being considered for future office as jurats. Of 201 different individuals who served as chamberlains between 1485 and 1603, no less than 68, or rather more than one third, later became members of the magistracy. Indeed, of the 110 jurats elected after 1485, if we exclude those who were either sons of jurats (8), or became jurats by way of being town clerk (4), or who were royal officials or relative newcomers of gentry or similar backgrounds (10), all but 20 of the remainder are known to have served as chamberlains. As almost half of these latter come from the beginning of the period, this figure would no doubt be further reduced were it not for the fact that no accounts are extant between 1464 and 1479. Thus it would appear to have been almost a prerequisite for any aspiring candidate for high office amongst the resident freemen to be elected as chamberlain first.

Of rather lesser importance was the office of clerk to the market, of which there were two, normally elected by the commons at the time of choosing the mayor. According to their oath they were to 'foresee the just and true assize of breade, ale, beare and wine ...

all goods brought to the markett to be sould, be sould by iust weight and measure and ... all fish ... be sold by iust tale and measure' and to collect all market dues.[33] They therefore had custody of the town's official weights and measures.[34] Although the record of elections to the office are patchy, particularly in the earlier period, when they were called 'collectors of the Great Maltode', it would appear that in the period up to the 1520s, one of the two positions was usually held by the mayor's sergeant and the other by a freeman. From 1523, when the name clerk to the market first appears, until 1529 when the record again gives out, the office was held by one jurat and one commoner; and from the 1530s onwards by two commoners, including at least three who later became jurats. However, by the late 1570s the status of the office again seems to have declined and for ten of the fifteen years between 1578 and 1593 one of the two clerkships was held jointly with the position of scorer with the butchers.[35]

The opening years of Queen Elizabeth's reign saw a proliferation of town offices, chiefly as the result of parliamentary legislation. In December 1558 for the first time collectors for the poor are listed. The only surviving accounts of their income and expenditure, for the period Christmas 1580 to Midsummer 1581 indicate an income of £25 17s 4d and an expenditure of £24 16s 5d during that half-yearly period. The money was presumably raised by a rate, supplemented by a proportion of fines on malefactors.[36] In March 1559 collectors for the highways are also listed. In 1582 their expenditure amounted to just £5 11s 4d, the amount being raised by a rate.[37] From 1568 Ward Constables were elected from among the more substantial commons to aid effective policing. Each year, too, a 'Grand Inquest' or presenting jury was appointed which reported in December to detect nuisances and other petty offences, ranging from leaky gutters and broken paving to drinking or gaming during service time or unlicensed trading or victualling. This function, deriving from the ancient hundred jurisdiction, was open to non-freemen householders, and in 1586 for example, of 16 members of the presenting jury, only one was a freeman.[38] Similarly at the beginning of Lent each year, a Lenten jury was also appointed to inquire into the killing and eating of meat during Lent, which was prohibited except to those exempted on medical grounds in case of illness or infirmity. This jury was also open to non-freemen.[39] In addition, adult male householders might also be appointed to sit on trial juries.

Although not strictly town officers, the elections of the two churchwardens, sexton and sidesmen, which took place in the parish church (by custom after evening service on the Sunday immediately following Michaelmas) seems to have been presided over by the mayor and jurats at least in the decades immediately following the Reformation. It is not entirely clear whether these meetings were confined to the freemen or whether they were open to other parishioners, as the assembly books which record these elections in some years refer only to the commons and in other years specify parishioners.[40] At least one churchwarden was not a freeman at the time of his election: James Gilmer, churchwarden for the year 1583/4, is recorded as having been made a freeman at an assembly on 28th August 1584. However, he appears to have been very much an exception and the majority of churchwardens came from the social and political elite. Of the 86 churchwardens chosen between 1513 and 1590, 37 later became jurats and one other, Robert Carpenter in 1582/3 was already a jurat at the time of his election. Like the chamberlains, their accounts were divided between a sea churchwarden and a land churchwarden.[41] The sexton, amongst whose responsibilities was the keeping of the church goods and churchyard, was a paid position. An assembly decree of 29th May 1581 records that he was to be paid £5 a year out of the customary dues of the church.[42] The sidesmen, of whom there were six, were appointed according to statute to present those who failed to come to church. Two surviving lists from 1568 and 1580, show them to have been drawn chiefly from the more senior freemen.[43]

One office which strictly lay outside of the corporation as such, but which had some jurisdiction within the town, was the office of bailiff or waterbailiff, the appointment of which lay with the Crown. During the sixteenth century this office was bought and sold and was even offered to the town corporation by a former mayor, John Younge, who was in the process of obtaining it in 1564. The corporation were unwilling to agree his terms, so he acquired it for himself and his son, also called John Younge, who succeeded his father upon his death in 1565. The revenues of the office derived chiefly from the collection of the petty customs of the port, although there was also a smaller sum from the rents of assize of a number of properties in the town. Some idea of the lucrative nature of the position can be gained from the fact that when John Yonge junior sold it to his namesake, a John Younge of Chichester, he was able to secure cash payments amounting to £40 plus an annual sum of £20 to himself or his assigns throughout the lifetime of his successor and of his son, Charles Younge.[44] The bailiff also appointed a sergeant, who, according to the custumal, was to do all arrests on strangers within the liberties of the town and was also to do all executions of felons sentenced to death by the Rye courts, who were to be hanged on the saltmarsh to the east of the town.

Alongside the bailiff there was also a collector of customs for the port of Rye, an office held in the 1490s by the jurat Adam Oxenbridge and later, in the early Elizabethan period by John Donnynge, another jurat, until his death in 1579. Technically, Donnynge was customer of the Port of Chichester, under whose jurisdiction, for customs purposes only, the south coast ports from Hythe to Chichester came. There was therefore also a resident undercollector, a position held in the early 1580s by Thomas Belveridge, who later obtained the more senior office for himself. The customs office was kept in a building by the quayside at Strand, with the office of the searcher in an adjoining room, a position held by Robert Welles, one of the wealthier Rye merchants in 1575.[45]

The common council, referred to earlier, was one institution which could be seen as a deliberate attempt by the urban elite further to restrict the franchise within the town. This body, which existed from January 1575 until December 1590[46] took over from the assembly, which all freemen were entitled to attend, the power of making decrees for the better government and regulation of the town. Its 24 members were appointed by the mayor and jurats 'from the moost wisest, discretest and honest commoners' and were to meet fortnightly on Mondays or as often as need should require with the mayor and jurats in the court hall, to discuss the town's affairs. The detailed regulations made at the date of its establishment allowed for majority decisions of the mayor, jurats and common council together; laid down fines for those absent without licence (2s for jurats, 12d for common councillors), and for those common councillors whose speech was 'undecent and irreverent' towards the mayor or jurats; and the disfranchising of any, whether mayor, jurat or common councillor, 'which shall disclose or oppen at large eny thinge talked of, spoken or don emongest them selves in their assemblies, which ought not to be opened or revealed'. On festival days the common councillors were to be attendant upon the mayor, 'two and two in order decently in their gownes to bring him to churche and also frome church to his house'. Vacancies among the jurats were to be filled from members of the common council and the mayor and jurats were also to nominate persons to fill any vacancies among common councillors.[47] The institution was a clear example of a self-perpetuating oligarchy.

Nevertheless, at the assembly at which the decree to establish the common council was passed, the mayor, six jurats and 38 commoners are listed as assenting to the decree, with a further four jurats and 25 commoners giving their assents later.[48] Even so, this still leaves two jurats and around 40 commons unaccounted for. There had been open political dissensions in the town for some time, culminating in nightime disturbances following the 1573 mayoral election. An assembly decree refers to the throwing of 'filthe and ordure' over certain individuals who opened their doors to unidentified callers and the fixing of 'certeine infamous libelles and skrolles conteyninge dishoneste reproche of ye persons upon whose dores they are affixed, to the great offence of God and to ye great disturbance and disquietnes of the quiet state and peace of this town'. Clearly it was disgruntled freemen who were thought to be involved since provision was made for their immediate disfranchisement, 'without hope of ye recoverie of the same', whilst others found to be involved were to be 'strayghtlie and severlie punished to the example of others'.[49] The situation at the time of the setting up of the common council was evidently thought far worse and sufficiently serious for the corporation to seek and obtain a special commission to investigate those suspected of having some hand in the disturbances, which also included the breaking of the chamber windows of Robert Daniell, evidently a leading advocate of the common council, and the jurat George Syre, one night in early January before the decree was passed and the hanging up, above the stairs of the court Hall, an old cloth with 24 knaves of cards and the letters RD CP on the knave of clubs 'beinge the formyst carde' fastened to the cloth.[50]

Whether as the result of a revival of opposition to the

institution or because the declining fortunes of the town had simply rendered it unnecessary, the common council was suddenly abolished at an assembly on 1 December 1590 attended by the mayor, six jurats and 43 commons. Thereafter, decisions concerning town ordinances and decrees reverted to the whole assembly of mayor, jurats and commons 'as of auncient tyme hath bene accostomed', and any freeman failing to attend when warned to attend was to be fined 6d.[51]

The freemen

During its relatively short life, a total of 68 different individuals served as members of the common council. They were drawn mainly from the wealthier commons and altogether 20 of these went on to serve as jurats, eleven during the life of the common council and a further nine in the period following its demise. The freemen themselves, or commons as they were more usually referred to,[52] represented approximately one in five of taxpaying adult male householders. A list of 'freemen inhabiting' dated 12 September 1562 containing 103 names (excluding the mayor and jurats) agrees almost exactly with the 104 freemen identifiable on a cesse of the same year from the lists of those admitted as freemen or recorded as paying for their freedoms in the assembly books and chamberlains' accounts.[53]

The chief benefits of enfranchisement were economic. Freemen generally paid lower rates of maltodes on goods coming into or going out of the town. In 1550 for example the rates of maltodes issued by the assembly specified that non-free inhabitants should pay at double the freemen's rate and that denizens and foreigners (i.e. non-residents) buying or selling fish should pay treble. Similarly, when new rates were laid down in 1567, a differential was maintained between freemen, non-free inhabitants and strangers. Non-free fishing boat masters likewise paid double maltode on their catch and non-free tipplers paid 4d a bone of beer sold compared to a freeman's 2d.[55] Freemen were also beneficiaries of the trading privileges (freedom of toll and the like) throughout England granted to the Cinque Ports in the General Charter and enjoyed the right of withernam in the case of detention of their goods for debt; whilst a freemen of one of the ports was likewise free of the others.[56] Finally, freemen were free of arrest within their own houses, as the following protest of

Robert Gillam, a poor freeman, makes clear:

> 'Right Worshipfull Mr Mayor ... your Sargant, upon
> Monday last past dyd come into my howse and there dyd a
> rest me, whiche not heretofore hath byn knowne at any tyme
> by any man, so that by this meanes the benefyt of my fredom
> is nothinge ... whereof I beseche your wurshipes ... that I
> may inioye the benefyt of my fredom as other fremen do and
> not to be arested in my howse, but in any place eles where
> the Sargant dothe chaunce to mete me, for I am not fygitive
> but do as God knowthe, mene to pay all men iustly as sone as
> I am able ... I dare not come into the court before you at this
> tyme. Yf I should I knowe it ware to my utter undoinge'.[57]

In return, freemen swore to uphold the liberties of the town and
to pay such lawful scots and lots as were levied on their goods and
property from time to time.

According to the custumal, any stranger having dwelt in the
town for a year and a day occupying an 'honest crafte' and being
of 'good guydyng and conversation and desyrethe ye franches'
could go before the mayor and jurats in open assembly and
demand his freedom, the mayor and jurats deciding what he
should pay by way of entry fine. He could then be sworn as a
freeman, paying in addition 2d to the mayor's sergeant and 2d to
the town clerk for entering his name in the records.[58] In the 1480s
such fines were usually 3s 4d, rising to as much as 20s for one
merchant from St Albans. In the middle years of Henry VIII's
reign 6s 8d was the norm, with occasional exceptions up to 20s
and thereabouts. In 1562 however, the entry fine was fixed by an
assembly at a minimum of 40s for strangers and 20s for those born
not free within the town, at which level (with the exception of the
period 1570–2 during which time this rate was halved) the entry
fine for freemen remained for the rest of the century. Freemen's
sons, by custom, were admitted free by their father's copy.
However the 1572 regulations make clear that this only applied to
those sons born *after* their fathers had been made free, so this
somewhat restricted the privilege. Additionally, the mayor, with
the consent of the jurats, was from 1572 empowered to make one
freeman during his term of office annually, without any payment
to be made to the town, a right exercised almost without exception
for the remainder of the sixteenth century.[59]

On rare occasions men were made free without payment for
particular services rendered to the town, as in 1549 when Robert

Cooke received his freedom 'in recompense of his paynes and charges bestowed in the delivery of a letter to the Lorde Protectores grace concerneng our condites' (the town's water supply); or in 1558 when William Ratliff received his for keeping four prisoners eighteen weeks at his own charges.[60] From 1537 freemen paid a shilling for sealing their certificates of freedom and from 1539 there are occasional references to the provision of wine, confirmation of the custom referred to in the 1582 decree whereby newly-elected freemen supplied a gallon of wine, presumably for a special 'drinking' to mark the event; while from 1570 onwards there is usually also mention of 12d 'for hooks', a reference to the custom of providing a fire hook on a pole for pulling burning thatch off buildings.[61]

Table 9

Annual totals of new freemen admitted in Rye arranged by decade, 1485-1602

Years[1]	Freemen admitted	Years[1]	Freemen admitted
1485-9	13	1550-9	62
1490-9	29	1560-9	40
1500-9	49	1570-9	68
1510-9	49	1580-9	32
1520-9	27	1590-9	20
1530-9	38	1600-2	11
1540-9	48		

Notes: [1]Dates given are for Mayoral years, starting in August. Thus 1485-9 runs from August 1485 to August 1490.

Sources: RYE 60/3-10; RYE 1/1-7; RYE 61/1-4.

The details of all these various payments made by freemen provide a reasonable basis for estimating the changing level of enfranchisements over the period. As Table 9 shows, there is a considerable variation in the average numbers of freemen admitted in each decade, although the figures largely reflect the cycle of urban growth and decline already observed from the chamberlains' accounts, with a period of stagnation in the 1520s and 30s, followed by the prosperous decades of the mid-sixteenth century and a rapid decline from the early 1580s onwards. Indeed, in the last fifteen years of Elizabeth's reign, on seven occasions only the mayor's freeman is recorded as being admitted, and on another four occasions only one other. That this is largely *not* 'the growth of an oligarchic exclusionism' in the late sixteenth century restricting admission to those able to pay 40s and above for entry[62] is demonstrated not only by the close correlation between the reduction in admissions to the franchise and other indicators of severe economic crisis in Rye in the late Elizabethan period, but also by the obvious buoyancy of the figures for enfranchisements despite the new, higher rates in the first two decades after their introduction. Besides, the increases laid down in 1562 did little more than restore the real value of entry fines to the levels they had reached in the late 1540s when inhabitants were already paying 10s and incomers up to 20s following Henry VIII's debasement of the coinage, before the even greater inflation of the 1550s. But whatever the exact causes the effect was almost to halve the numbers of freemen between 1553 and 1596, as Table 10 demonstrates.

Table 10

Numbers of Rye freemen from sesses 1553-1596

Year	Numbers of freemen listed on sesse[1]
1553	117
1562	104
1576	107
1596	61

Notes: [1] not including mayor and jurats.
Sources: RYE 1/1/1-6; RYE 60/3-10; RYE 61/1-4.

The total number of Rye freemen who can be identified for the Tudor period from available sources comes to some 627 different individuals. No doubt this is an underestimate as prior to the Elizabethan period only rarely do the chamberlains' accounts record the admission of those who were freeborn who, in the period 1558-1603 account for approximately one quarter of all freemen admissions. Of these 627 known freemen, it has been possible (Table 11) to trace the occupations of 491, or rather more than three quarters, using such sources as the lists of annual payments by the masters of fishing vessels of a proportion of their catch during the Yarmouth and Scarborough voyages which are recorded in the chamberlains' and churchwardens' accounts; the recognizances entered into from time to time by licensed traders such as victuallers and the fines levied on such traders, including butchers, bakers, brewers, vintners and tallow chandlers for breaking the assize; the quarterly fines entered in the great and lesser boxes from 1573 for such additional occupations as osts and feters; together with more occasional evidence such as lists of

Table 11
Occupations of Rye freemen 1485–1603

Occupation		1485-1603	1562	1596
Master fisherman/mariner[1]		205[1]	39 (34)	18 (15)
Ost/feter	Fishing	57[2]	9 (8)	9 (6)
Basketmaker/dossermaker	and	2		
Hookmaker	allied	1		
Cockman	distributive	1	1	1
Lighterman	trades	3	1	
Shipwright		4	1	1
Carpenter		5	1	
Cooper		1	1	
Mason	Building	2		
Painter		1		
Glasier		1		
Merchant	Mercantile	36	7	4 (3)
Tallow chandler		6	2	2
Innkeeper		8	2	
Vintner	Victualling	4	1 (0)	2
Victualler		2	2	1
Tapster		1		
Taylor		29	10	7 6
Draper	Textile/	5	1	1
Sherman	clothing	1		
Capper		1		1
Glover		1		1
Tanner		1		
Currier	Leather	1		
Cordwainer/shoemaker		10	1	2
Sadler		1		
Blacksmith		3		
Plumber		2		
Pewterer	Metalworking	1		
Goldsmith		3		2
Cutler		1		
Butcher		25	6 (3)	5
Beerbrewer	Food & drink	14	5	4 (2)
Baker		17	5 (4)	2
Fletcher		1	1	1
Husbandman		3		1
Town officer	Other	18[3]	2	4[5]
Yeoman[4]		7	4 (3)	1
Gentleman/armiger		5		
Farmer of Rectory		1	1	
Total identified		491	103	71
Not identified		136	13	1
Total		627	116 (104)	71 (61)

Notes:
[1] i.e. masters of fishing or trading vessels.
[2] includes one Queen's Purveyor of Seafish.
[3] Town clerks 5, common sergeants 5, mayor's sergeants 2, collector of customs 1, undercollector of customs 1, waterbailiff 1, deputy waterbailiff 1, searcher 1, keeper of ordnance 1.
[4] denoting status rather than occupation.
[5] town clerk 1, undercollector of customs 1, keeper of ordnance 1, waterbailiff's sergeant 1.
( ) figure excluding mayor and jurats.

Sources: RYE 1/1-7; RYE 47/1-84; RYE 33/7-17; RYE 60/3-10; RYE 61/4-4; RYE 62/1-3; RYE 65/1-83; RYE 66/1-69; RYE 99/5-6; RYE 127/1-18; RYE 130/11-30; RYE 135/2-26; RYE 137/29-42; RYE 139/1-74; RYE 140/1-47; RYE 147/1; W/A1-7; W/B1-3.

traders from petitions, as from the mercers in 1575 and the drapers and tailors in 1577 or lists of masters and crews of trading and fishing vessels drawn up in time of war as in 1587-8; and the occupations of plaintiffs, defendants and witnesses in the records of the courts of record and sessions.

Table 12

Occupations of Rye freemen by trade groups as a percentage of all freemen

Trade group	1485-1603	1562	1596
Fishing and allied distributive	43.5	43.9	40.8
Building	1.6	1.7	—
Mercantile	6.7	7.8	8.5
Victualling	2.4	4.3	4.2
Textile/Clothing	5.7	9.5	12.7
Leather	2.2	0.9	4.2
Metalworking	1.6	—	2.8
Food and Drink	8.9	13.8	15.5
Other	5.6	6.9	9.9
Unidentified	21.7	11.2	1.4

Sources: RYE 1/1-7; RYE 47/1-84; RYE 33/7-17; RYE 60/3-10; RYE 61/1-4; RYE 62/1-3; RYE 65/1-83; RYE 66/1-69; RYE 99/5-6; RYE 127/1-18; RYE 130/11-30; RYE 135/2-26; RYE 137/29-42; RYE 139/1-74; RYE 140/1-47; RYE 147/1; W/A1-7; W/B1-3.

No doubt the more complete series for ships' masters and for licensed traders has produced some bias in their favour. Few of the 136 freemen whose occupations remain unidentified probably fall into these categories. Even so, the almost overwhelming domination of the town's economy by fishing and allied trades, chiefly distribution through the osts (buyers for London fishmongers) and feters (local wholesale fishmongers), who often combined both activities, is extremely striking. As Table 12 shows, both in 1562 and throughout the period as a whole, masters of fishing and other vessels and wholesale distributors accounted for 42 per cent of all freemen, a proportion which fell only slightly, to 38 per cent in 1596 when the fishing industry was in severe decline. When such additional groups as the merchants who depended upon the larger vessels for carrying their cargoes, the brewers and bakers who manufactured the provisions for long voyages, and the keepers of inns and victualling houses, are added to the list, the almost total dependence of Rye on its harbour is obvious.[63]

In a number of instances it has been possible to identify the extent to which freemen (including the mayor and jurats) dominated Rye's economy. Among merchants and fishing boat masters, freemen heavily predominated. A decree establishing a Company of Mercers in Rye in 1575 lists eighteen petitioners, of whom the twelve men were all freemen. Of the six women listed, two were wives of freemen, one was a widow of a freeman, one other was the wife of a Protestant French merchant from Dieppe and only two of these women's husbands seem not to have been freemen. Among the masters of fishing vessels listed in a petition of 1571, the proportion was somewhat lower, 22 of 34, but several of the remaining twelve masters were probably sons of existing freemen. Among the bakers and brewers it was rare to find a major operator who was not a freeman. The dues paid into the great box of thirteen bakers and brewers for christmas quarter 1573 shows that the six freemen amongst them were responsible for five-sixths of that trade. The proportions were only slightly less among the butchers, where five freemen out of nine butchers listed for the same quarter controlled two-thirds of the trade between them. Among osts, freemen had a virtual monopoly, ten of the eleven of those paying ostage in the quarter April-June 1573 were freemen, accounting between them for all but 28 of 1326 seams of fish, or 98 per cent of the trade. In contrast, very few of those in the generally less lucrative metalworking or leather trades ever reached the status of freemen.[64]

The jurats

In terms of assessed wealth, freemen other than common councillors or the mayor and jurats were rated at approximately double the average assessed value of other householders. common councillors' assessments were on average twice that of other freemen, whilst the average assessed wealth of the magistrates (i.e. the mayor and jurats) was approximately doubled again. The result, illustrated in Table 13, was that the freemen as a whole, who in 1576 accounted for 29 per cent of those assessed, paid just under 60 per cent of the assessment, with the mayor and jurats, who represented only 3.4 per cent of taxpayers contributing 18.3 per cent. The close correlation between wealth and political office-holding is obvious.

Such figures should however only be taken as a general indication of the relationship between political office-holding and wealth. There is considerable evidence to suggest that the mid-sixteenth century sesses considerably undervalued the wealth of

Table 13

Assessed wealth and political status of Rye inhabitants in 1576

Status	Proportion of ratepayers (%)	Proportion of assessed wealth (%)	Average individual assessed wealth £[1]
Non freemen	70.9	42.8	4
Freemen	20.1	23.5	9
Common Councillors	5.6	15.4	22
Mayors and jurats	3.4	18.3	42

Notes[1]: to nearest £.

Sources: RYE 1/4/227-232. RYE 1/1-7; RYE 47/1-84; RYE 33/7-17; RYE 60/3-10; RYE 61/1-4; RYE 62/1-3; RYE 65/1-83; RYE 66/1-69; RYE 99/5-6; RYE 127/1-18; RYE 130/11-30; RYE 135/2-26; RYE 137/29-42; RYE 139/1-74; RYE 140/1-47; RYE 147/1; W/A1-7; W/B1-3.

the urban elite, probably because there was a sufficiently broad tax-base at that time for it to be unnecessary to tax them higher. The highest individual assessment in 1576, for example, was of John Fagge, who was assessed at £80. However, when he died seven years later, his money bequests alone came to over £500, quite apart from his lands, tenements and moveable goods. A similar example from an earlier period is that of Thomas Birchett who was assessed at £40 in 1554, yet when he died two years later left monetary bequests of over £260 and lands to the value of more than £300.[65] A more reliable guide to actual levels of wealth among the jurats is the assessments for the 1523 benevolence, which lists the mayor and eight out of ten jurats, with assessments ranging from £40 to £500; and the assessments for the 1491/2 and 1596 sesses, which seem broadly in line with probate inventory totals and monetary bequests.

The high levels of disposable wealth of many members of the jurat class set out in Table 14 demonstrates the extent to which the magistracy was drawn from the wealthiest inhabitants of the town. Most were worth £100 and upwards, while valuations of £400 or £500 were not uncommon among leading members of the corporation. A small number came from well-established local gentry backgrounds, such as Adam Oxenbridge, whose elder brother, Sir Godard Oxenbridge of Brede Place served as Sheriff of Sussex. On his death in 1496, Adam Oxenbridge's will reveals extensive landholdings in Rye, Winchelsea, Hastings and eight other neighbouring Sussex parishes together with the White Horse at Southwark. He was followed as a jurat by his son John

Table 14

Levels of wealth amongst Rye Jurats from tax assessments and probate record

Assessment	1491-2	1523	1596	Probate valuations[1]
Under £10	-	-	-	2
Under £50	3	1	1	5
Under £100	1	4	1	7
£100+	3	2	2	2
£200+	-	1	2	2
£300+	-	-	1	3
£400+	4	-	4	3
£500+	1	1	-	3
£600+	-	-	-	1
£700+	-	-	-	1

Notes: [1]Inventory totals or monetary bequests in wills of deceased jurats 1541-1622.
Source: RYE 77/3; RYE 81/1-2; RYE 1/6/30-43; W/A1-4; W/B1-3; PRO PROB 11/7-124.

and his nephew William. Another relative, Thomas Oxenbridge, was also a jurat. John Shurley, who served briefly as a jurat from 1499-1502, came from the gentry family that owned Isfield Place. He rose in the royal service, ending his life in 1527 as cofferer to the king's household under Henry VIII and was buried in his private chapel at Isfield, to which he left £100 for vestments, mass books and ornaments plus £6 13s 6d for 15 years for a priest to pray for his soul.[66]

Others came from less exalted local landowning families. John Fagge, four times mayor of Rye between 1577 and 1581, refers in his will (1583) to his father's lands in Hinxhill, Kent. George Raynoldes (d.1577) refers to his brother of Brodhurst, Kent, whilst Robert Maycott in his will (1559) mentions a kinsman at Lydd. Others clearly came from farther afield. Thomas Hamon, who served as mayor on six occasions between 1595 and his death in 1607 mentions a kinsman James Hamon, of London, ship-wright and William Ratcliff, who died in 1603, had a brother of Tamworth, Staffordshire and other relatives at Bristol and Lutterworth, Leicestershire.[67]

The majority of jurats seem to have been second generation Rye inhabitants, born in the town, sons of freemen who had themselves come to Rye from the surrounding towns and villages in order to establish themselves. Men such as John Fletcher, a traditionalist who represented Rye in the Reformation Parliament and was seven times mayor of the town, or Thomas Birchett, his Protestant rival who served as mayor on three occasions and was member of parliament for Rye in 1539, were both sons of Rye freemen. Fletcher's father, Thomas, was a fisherman, into which occupation his son, John, followed him, appearing among the masters of fishing vessels in the chamberlains' accounts from 1505. Assessed at £40 for the 1523 benevolence, John Fletcher's rise was henceforth meteoric. In 1524 he became mayor, without previously having served as a jurat. In 1529 he was elected as one of Rye's two members of parliament, sitting again in 1536 and 1542. During this time he seems to have come to the notice of the royal authorities since he appears regularly in the state papers in the 1530s and 1540s gathering intelligence of hostile shipping in the Channel, and by 1539 he had obtained for himself the lucrative position of resident purveyor of fish to the royal household in Rye, in which capacity he arranged for the arrest of his arch-rival (the then mayor) Thomas Birchett, on a trumped-up charge of siding with the fishermen to set an unreasonably high price.[68] He died in 1545 an extremely wealthy man, leaving three sons, two of whom, Thomas and Richard, followed him as jurats, mayors and MPs for the town.[69]

Thomas Birchett's father, also called Thomas, a baker, first appears in 1498, when he paid 6s 8d for his hepe. In 1511 he paid a further 6s 8d for the restoration of his freedom following some offence. In 1518 he died leaving Thomas, the eldest of three sons, his brewhouse together with all the necessary implements for carrying on that trade. Although Thomas Birchett does not appear in the 1523 benevolence, by 1545 his was the highest individual assessment of any Rye inhabitant in the forced loan returns of that year. He was first elected a jurat in 1535, reappearing as mayor in 1538, a year in which, under the influence of Thomas Cromwell, many corporations were returning Protestants as mayor. He served again in the following year, last appearing as mayor in 1548, when he was elected upon the nomination of the Lord Protector, the Duke of Somerset. He remained a jurat until his death in 1556, appearing before the Privy Council together with Rye's Edwardian vicar, Edmund Scambler and two fellow jurats, also Protestant sympathisers, following a riot in the parish church in January 1554 occasioned by the reintroduction of the mass.[70] At the time of his death he still had his brewing premises, together with at least five other properties in Rye and various unspecified lands in Kent and

Sussex, those in Iden being alone worth over £300.[71]

Equally striking is the career of Thomas Hamon, beerbrewer, who served as mayor on six occasions and represented Rye in parliament three times. His death in 1607 was the subject of a famous witchcraft trial.[72] His father, also Thomas Hamon, who came into Rye from outside, began the family brewing and baking business and was admitted a freeman in 1549, by which date he was already well-established in the town. Thomas Hamon, the future mayor, was baptised at Rye on 25 January 1550. At this time the family were living in the Lower Street, where Thomas Hamon senior was assessed at £6 13s 4d in 1554 and £20 in 1558, one of the highest assessments at that date. He died during the epidemic of 1559 and was buried on 3rd September of that year. Evidently his wife must have followed him some years after, since the assembly books record that on 20th March 1566 Thomas Hamon, then aged 17, one of the sons of Thomas Hamon 'late bruer deceased' chose his father-in-law, Richard Stacey, to be his guardian. In August 1578 he is recorded as being admitted a freeman, being freeborn and therefore paying only 12d for hooks. The following year he was chosen into the common council and became a jurat in 1593. His assessment of £400 in the 1596 cesse was one of only five assessments at that level, and at the time of his death he owned land in East Guldeford, Playden and Newchurch, Kent, in addition to his property in Rye.[73]

The careers of men such as Fletcher, Birchett and Hamon demonstrate the opportunities open to young men of reasonable wealth and ability to break into the ruling hierarchy. The key which unlocked the door into the magistracy appears to have been a successful business career and a resultant relatively high level of personal wealth rather than any particular family background. Family dynasties such as the Fletchers, who dominated the corporation in the middle years of Henry VIII's reign, or the Oxenbridges, whose main period of influence was during the reign of Henry VII, were very much exceptions. Altogether only two families, the Oxenbridges and the Wymonds, could count four jurats among their numbers; and only three other families could number three jurats among them. Alone amongst these five families, the Wymonds represented a family of three generations, Robert Wymond (died 1510) being succeeded as a jurat by his two sons John (d.1529) and Robert (d.1548) and a grandson William (son of John, died 1548).

More common were fathers and sons, or pairs of brothers, but even here, of fourteen instances in which the same family name appears twice, in only five cases can relationships between fathers and sons be clearly established (John and Nicholas Sutton, George and Nicholas Mercer, John and Robert Marche, Clement Cobbe and his son of the same name, and Richard Rucke and his son of the same name); although a similar connection seems highly likely in five more cases (between Stephen and Gabriel Wayte, Henry and John Swan, Robert and William Mede, and Nicholas or Thomas White, who was probably the father of John). Other brothers who served as jurats, in addition to the Wymonds, the Fletchers and the Oxenbridges previously mentioned, included Thomas and John Fisher as may have been John and Thomas Baker alias Chesman. George and John Raynoldes may have been brothers or cousins, the two Robert Woodes were probably uncle and nephew, Clement and Gabriel Adam may have been grandfather and grandson, and since there is a gap of almost 100 years between John and Robert Carpenter any close family link is unlikely. Altogether 94 different family surnames occur amongst the 120 jurats whose careers spanned the Tudor period, of whom 75 (62.5 per cent) appear only once.

At least part of the explanation for this lack of dynasties throughout the Rye magistracy is the lack of male heirs. Of 60 jurats' wills which detail bequests to heirs of both land and goods, in fifteen cases it is apparent that there are no surviving children, and in a further eleven cases only daughters. Of the 34 instances in which sons are mentioned, in ten cases there is only mention of one son, in eleven cases two, in nine cases three and in only four cases more than three. Perhaps even more significantly, in at least fifteen of the 34 recorded instances of male heirs, it is clear from the bequests that such heirs are all under age. If these proportions were to hold good amongst the jurats as a whole, little more than half (55 per cent) could have expected to have had sons upon whom to settle their estates, and only one third (32 per cent) would have had sons over the age of 21 by the time of their deaths.[74]

In a number of cases jurats made quite specific provision for the protection of their heirs' interests. The most common method in the earlier part of the period was through the appointment of a group of feoffees, usually other jurats, to whom the properties of the party making the agreement were conveyed during his own lifetime, to be held by them for the uses specified in his will. There are six such examples of enfeoffment for uses recorded among Rye jurats, ranging in date from 1497 to 1535, four of these occurring in the decade 1497 to 1506.[75] An obvious fear, occasionally expressed by testators, was that through the remarriage of the widow, property might pass out of the hands of the intended heirs. For this reason, John Younge in his will in May 1565 provided for an inventory to be made of all his household stuff by between two and four assessors appointed by the mayor immediately upon his death. In the event of his wife's remarriage all his plate was to be put into the town treasury and his wife was to enter into a bond for the delivery of all the goods specified in the inventory to his two sons, John and Richard at the age of 21. Similarly, in the event of her death before such time as his sons attained that age, the mayor was to ensure that a bond was entered into for the delivery of the same when they reached full age.[76] In a somewhat different situation, William Wymond, whose wife had predeceased him, left £20 in his will dated 1548 to his cousin John Eston, whom he made his executor, to bring up his three sons and one daughter and to attend to their schooling until they reached full age. In the event of Eston's death this responsibility passed to each of two London merchants in turn.[77]

A growing concern among jurats was the education of their children, particularly their sons. Eight wills made specific reference to this, ranging from instructions such as those of Robert Bennett to his wife in 1564 to keep his youngest son William 'to scole', to more elaborate instructions such as those of John Raynoldes to his executors in 1548 which required that his two sons, Robert and Nicholas 'shall be brought upp eyther in the universities or elswhere to their most advauncement to good lernynge'.[78] Several jurat families seem to have sent their sons to Inns of court. The admissions register of Gray's Inn records a William Oxenbridge in 1527 (possibly the future jurat), a John Reynolds in 1530, Richard Marden (possibly the son of Robert Marden jurat, who died in 1541) and Robert Fletcher, youngest son of John Fletcher (1548). Most striking, however, was the provision made by Thomas Birchett for his sons. Thomas, the eldest, born prior to 1538, matriculated a pensioner at Jesus

College, Cambridge, at Easter 1554. His younger brother, Peter, the middle of three sons, matriculated a fellow-commoner at Christ's College, Cambridge in October 1564 aged 17 and was admitted to the Inner Temple in January 1567. A Protestant fanatic, unfortunately for his family, he attempted to murder Sir John Hawkins in mistake for Sir Christopher Hatton, in October 1573 and in attempting to escape from the Tower of London, accidentally killed a keeper. He was hanged in the Strand on 12th November, his felony resulting in lengthy legal difficulties for his brothers in Rye in the preservation of their family property from confiscation.[79] The one specific reference to the education of a daughter in a jurat's will was altogether more mundane, specifying merely that she should be 'taught to read, write and to sowe in the science of shopstery with other things belonging to huswifrye' until she came to the age of 21 or was married.[80]

As a group, the Rye magistracy exhibited close ties of friendship and kinship, in many cases reinforced by marriage. Gabriel Adams (d.1557) referred to Henry Mynge, his overseer in his will as 'my well beloved friend'; John Baylye (d.1572) in his will called his overseers, George Raynoldes and William Tolken 'my good friends'; and John Raynoldes (d.1548) left the charge of his children to his four executors, three of whom were his fellow jurats, Thomas Birchett, Alexander Welles and Robert Woode.[81] Marriages such as those between Gabriel Adams's two daughters Godly (to Richard Nicoll in 1547) and Mary (to Clement Cobbe in 1560) were not uncommon among jurats' families. Robert Maycott was the son-in-law of John Swan; Alexander Welles's wife Johane was the sister of John Raynoldes; and Robert Marche was the brother-in-law of Richard Nicoll, who had married his sister, Ellen, and the son-in-law of Robert Woode, whose daughter Anys he had himself married in 1548.[82] Altogether at least 22 jurats' families were connected by marriage and a further 66 by other close ties of friendship or business.

The figures set out in Table 15 indicate that at least 88 out of the 120 Rye jurats had marriage or friendship ties with other members of the jurats' bench. When allowance is made for the relative dearth of information in the period prior to 1538 when the Rye parish register commences and 1540 when the Lewes Archdeaconry probate registers begin, it is clear that a mean of 2.9 for the combined marriage or friendship ties of an individual jurat

Table 15:
Friendship and marriage links between Rye Jurats 1485-1603

Relationship type	Number of links between individuals[1]													
	1	2	3	4	5	6	7	8	9	10	11	12	13	14
Marriage	17	3	2	-	-	-	-	-	-	-	-	-	-	-
Friendship	20	17	13	10	9	4	5	2	2	1	3	-	-	-
M/F combined	14	20	15	9	8	7	5	3	3	-	3	-	-	1

Note: [1] does not include blood relationships
Sources: W/A 1-18; W/B 1-3; PRO PROB 11/7-124; PAR 467 1/1/1-2

is a substantial underestimate. Of the 32 jurats who cannot be positively linked by friendship or marriage to other members of the bench, 20 (or rather less than two thirds) died prior to 1540, in all but one case without leaving a will, the major source of such information. The only exception was John Shurley of Isfield Place, who, as has been noted, came from a rather higher social class than the majority of the Rye magistrates. Of the twelve later jurats for whom no positive friendship or marriage links with their fellows can be located, ten failed to leave wills, all but three served for less than ten years, men such as Thomas Belveridge, Francis Smith and William Mellowe (seven months, two years and three years respectively) serving only briefly as jurats and only John Sharpe and John Donnynges served as mayor.[83]

The majority of jurats, then, were a closely-knit group, with friendship and business connections cemented by marriage alliances, drawn almost exclusively from the town's mercantile elite, plus a handful of sons of the local gentry. They witnessed and acted as executors and overseers of each others' wills, stood godparents to each others' children[84] and even married one another's widows, the parish registers detailing eight such events in the period 1540-1601. Indeed, Thomas Fletcher actually married the widows of two former jurats, Jone Marden in 1542 and Bregett Rucke in 1561. Nor were such events confined to the magistrates alone. Margery Bolton, the town clerk Francis Bolton's widow, married his successor, Robert Convers in 1601.[85] Such a tradition no doubt helped further to maintain the social cohesion of the group and to insure some of its members against the worst effects of prevailing high mortality rates and sudden bereavement.[86]

At the centre of these networks of interrelationships stood

119

figures such as Alexander Welles, Birchett's successor as leader of the Protestant faction on Rye corporation, who first became town clerk in 1535 and died in office as mayor in November 1558. By the time of his death he was related by marriage to three other jurat families, the Wymonds, the Birchetts and the Estons, and his business and other associations linked him to eleven others, past, present and future. Among those whom he helped to establish, his protege, Robert Jackson, to whom he left his books of precedents and a dagger, followed him as town Clerk, jurat and, eventually, mayor. One of his servants mentioned in his will, William Tolken, also followed him on to the jurats' bench, serving for 37 years following his election in 1566, including one year as mayor.[87]

Another focus of such interrelationships was the Fletcher family dynasty. Founded by John Fletcher, his son Richard's connections extended to nine other jurats' families and his son Thomas's to seven. Among those who owed their future careers to the Fletcher connection were Thomas Edolphe, John Fletcher's grandson, whom Richard took as apprentice, leaving him £40 at the age of 25 and making him an heir in remainder to one third of his estate in the event of the death of his daughter and Robert Carpenter. The undoubted family relationship between Robert Carpenter and the Fletchers cannot be clearly established, but it must have been close. His parents, Robert Carpenter and Elizabeth Woode, the jurat Robert Woode's daughter, were married in August 1540. Robert, their eldest child, was baptised in July 1541. Richard Fletcher (d.1558) left him his gold ring, while Thomas (d.1568) made him his sole heir to all his lands and tenements on the death of his wife. He became a jurat three years later, in 1571 and served until 1602, including four years as mayor.[88]

Such continuing family connections belie the initial impression, from the relatively large number of different family names represented among the jurats, that wealth alone was the key to entry into the ruling elite. Family connections and patronage clearly counted for something, not least because it was the incoming mayor who appointed new jurats (after 1583 with the consent of a majority of the existing bench) and it is inevitable that opportunity should have been taken to further the careers of close associates and their offspring. Besides, the mere counting of numbers of different surnames among jurats ignores the issues of length of service and whether or not an individual served as mayor, which are important indicators of the status and influence of individual members of the magistracy.

Appendix 3 details the individual careers of the 120 Rye jurats between 1485 and 1603. Lengths of service varied from one year to 42 years, with some eighteen individuals (15 per cent) accounting for 36.2 per cent of the total years served by jurats who held office throughout these years. At the opposite end of the scale, 64 jurats (52.9 per cent) served on average less than six years each, accounting for a mere 24.3 per cent of total service throughout the Tudor period. Many of these latter were the same individuals who failed to achieve the mayoralty (62 of 120, i.e. 51.2 per cent). Forty-three served only once or twice as mayor, accounting for rather less than half (47.9 per cent) of the total, while sixteen individuals (13.2 per cent) served three times or more, accounting for over half (52.1 per cent) of all mayoralties from 1485 to 1603. The mean length of service of a jurat was 12.3 years and the median length of service 10 years. Table 16 provides a summary.

Table 16

**Length of service of Rye jurats
and numbers of times elected mayor 1485-1603**

a) Length of service		b) Numbers of times elected mayor	
Years served	No of jurats	No of mayoral terms	No of jurats
1-10	64	0	62
11-20	39	1	28
21-30	10	2	15
31-40	6	3	7
over 40	2	4	6
Total	121	5	1
		6	1
		7	1
		Total	121

Note: In calculating length of service, total length of service of jurats whose careers spanned the years prior to 1485 or after 1603, have been taken into account. Three mayors died in office, John Wymond in July 1529, John Fletcher in 1545, and Alexander Welles in November 1558.
Sources: RYE 1/1-7; RYE 60/2-19; RYE 33/7-17.

Length of service as a jurat is, of course, only one indication of status. A number of promising careers were cut short by death. John Raynoldes, for example, was buried on 4 September 1548, literally only days after becoming a jurat, while at least three mayors during the Tudor period died in office, including Alexander Welles in November 1558, within two months of his re-election. Others, such as William Tolken, survived well into old age. He died aged 84 in 1604, having served 33 years as a jurat.

Table 17

Ages of Rye jurats 1485-1603

Age[1]	30-39	40-49	50-59	60-69	70-79	over 80	total
at appointment	5	9	7	1	-	-	22
at death	-	2	9	5	5	1	22
1562 (8 of 13)	-	3	4	-	1	-	8
1579 (10 of 11)	2	1	5	1	1	-	10
1586 (7 of 9)	-	2	2	2	1	-	7

Notes: [1] figures in brackets for 1562, 1579 and 1586 give number of jurats for whom ages available compared to total number of jurats (including mayor) at that date.

Sources: Depositions in cases before the Rye courts contained on the plea rolls of the Court of Record, RYE 35/1-52, and in the general files, RYE 47/1-84.

It has been possible to identify from depositions the ages of 22 of Rye's 120 jurats during the Tudor period. The results, set out in Table 17, suggest an average age at election of 44 years 8 months and at death of 61 years 3 months. The average age of jurats in 1562 was 54 years and in 1579 53 years, rising to 58 years in 1586 and 1590. However, although the general impression is of a middle-aged magistracy, five jurats (or rather more than one fifth of the sample) were still only in their thirties when they were elected, including Thomas Edolphe and the younger Robert Wymond (both aged 30), Robert Carpenter (31), George Raynoldes (34) and John Mercer (39). Significantly, each of these came from a well-established family which numbered one or more jurats among their antecedents. Others with no such family connections, such as William Coxson, aged 64 when he became a jurat, had to wait much longer for their appointments.

Most of those elected as jurats were clearly well-established in trade by the time of their election. John Fagge, a butcher by trade as well as being the owner of at least seven tenements in the town which he leased out to sitting tenants was, according to a government return of shipping, also part-owner of two of the largest merchant ships operating out of the port in 1580.[89] Thomas Birchett, originally a brewer, later came more usually to be described as a merchant, an indication of his widening sphere of activity, as did Richard Portryffe, described in a 1586 deed as mercer and beerbrewer. Such men dominated the economic life of the town through their trading activities and through the houses and tenements which they owned and leased out. Their wills attest the multiplicity of their trading interests. John Fletcher, for example, left six tenements with gardens including three newly built and his principal tenement where he dwelt, eight shops at Strand and a new storehouse, when he died in 1545. William Mede, fisherman, left five tenements, including his principal tenement and one under construction, together with four shops at Strand when he died in 1543. Robert Bennett, butcher, in 1564 left six houses with gardens and other appurtenances in the town, including a barn and slaughterhouse; while fellow butchers Robert Woode (1557) and John Fagge (1583) left seven tenements, five stables, eight shops with other unspecified lands, and seven tenements respectively. John Sutton (d.1506), besides his other properties, owned a millhouse beside the Landgate. John Mercer, variously described as beerbrewer and mercer (d.1588) referred to his newly constructed windmill with houses and barn belonging to it on the West Cliff as well as his other properties in the town.[90] Finally, in common with other wealthier Rye merchants, individual jurats loaned money, usually to private individuals in the town, generally by way of mortgage on property, as for example, the mortgage between John Ivye, blacksmith, and Clement Hopper for £13 in 1581 or that between John Sharpe, tailor, and William Mellowe, for £40 in 1588.[91] Occasionally, however, they also made loans to the corporation in cases of emergency, as in the case of the £100 lent to the town by Henry Gaymer, mayor, on the occasion of Queen Elizabeth's visit to Rye in 1573; a similar sum lent to the town for one year by John Fagge, mayor in 1578 at ten per cent interest; or the £200 promised by Thomas Hamon, mayor, in 1597 in addition to moneys already owed him towards the completion of the harbour works then underway.[92]

Although occupational descriptions, in the case of jurats, provide only a general guide to their multifarious economic activities, nevertheless, a breakdown of their primary occupations does give a reasonable indication of the chief source of their wealth. Table 18 which provides such information for all but twelve of Rye's 121 jurats during the Tudor period, demonstrates a number of contrasts with the occupational listings for the

Table 18

Primary occupations of Rye jurats 1485-1603

Occupation		Numbers	% by trade group Jurats	Freemen
Master fisherman/Mariner[1]	Fishing and allied	36		
Ost/feter[2]	Distributive trades	21	47.1	(43.5)
Carpenter		1		
Painter	Building	1	1.7	(1.6)
Merchant[3]		8		
Tallow Chandler	Mercantile	3	9.1	(6.7)
Innkeeper		3		
Vintner	Victualling	1	3.3	(2.4)
Taylor	Textile/clothing	5	4.1	(5.7)
Butcher		8		
Beerbrewer		7		
Baker	Food and drink	3	14.9	(8.9)
Husbandman		1		
Town Officer[4]		4		
Gentleman/Armiger	Other	7	9.9	(5.6)
Total identified		109	90.1	(78.3)
Not identified		12	9.9	(21.7)
Total		121	100.0	(100.0)

Notes:
[1] three fishing masters later bought ostage.
[2] includes one Queen's Purveyor of Seafish. One ost/feter also described as a brewer and another also described as a butcher included here.
[3] includes one Factor on behalf of the King of Portugal.
[4] Collector of Customs 2, former Town Clerk 2.
Sources: As for Tables 11 and 15.

freeman class as a whole. Among the maritime trades, a small overall increase (from 43.5 per cent among freemen to 47.1 per cent for jurats) disguises a substantial shift in proportions within those trades, with the more lucrative wholesale trades showing a jump from 9.1 per cent among freemen, to 17.4 per cent among jurats. Mercantile trades were also substantially higher, accounting for the primary occupations of 9.1 per cent of jurats, compared to only 6.7 per cent among freemen. Conversely, the poorer occupations, such as the leather and metalworking trades, have entirely disappeared from the list. The largest proportionate increase, however, is in the food and drink trades, which show an increase from 8.9 per cent to 14.9 per cent with the largest increases coming amongst the brewers (up from 2.2 per cent to 5.8 per cent) and the butchers (up from 4 per cent to 6.6 per cent) again reflecting the wealthier nature of these occupations.

Jurats, inevitably, were usually among the leading members of their particular occupations. Robert Jackson paid the highest quarterage for baking and brewing of those listed in the receipts of the great box in August 1578 and in August 1585. Richard Portriffe and Thomas Colbrand also paid the highest quarterage for brewing at Michaelmas 1592 and July 1597, followed closely on the former occasion by Thomas Hamon. In times of dearth, men such as these alone were licensed by the corporation as purveyors of grain for the town. In October 1575, for example, Robert Jackson was licensed as purveyor of grain for one year, with Thomas Mathewe as his deputy. In November of the same year they were joined by John Bruster and Thomas Colbrand. Similarly in February 1587, when five purveyors of corn were licensed, two were common councillors, one of whom, Thomas Hamon later became a jurat and mayor. Of the remainder, Robert Bett was already a jurat, John Mercer was an ex-jurat and Richard Portriffe also later became a jurat. It is obvious that for those who were members of, or were in favour with, the corporation considerable additional opportunities to extend their economic activities were available.[93]

Among the butchers, jurats such as Thomas Oxenbridge, Robert Marche and John Fagge were similarly at the head of their profession. The great box returns for the christmas quarter 1573 for example show the highest quarterage among butchers to have been paid by John Fagge, while Robert Bennett, a leading member of the common council and the son of a former jurat, paid the second highest.[94] Among victuallers it is clear that jurats again dominated trade. The Mermaid, Rye's principal inn, was owned at different times by Richard Pedyll (d.1536), William Didsbury (d.1593), both jurats, and in the early seventeenth century by another jurat, Thomas Higgons.[95] John Sutton was the owner of the Crowne, at the corner of the present-day West Street and the High Street, while John Fisher was the owner of the Three Kings, like the Mermaid, also in Middle Street. In addition, jurats such as Clement Adam, John and Thomas Chesman and Nicholas Sutton all kept inns which served as venues for mayoral dinners or feasts for visiting dignatories.[96] When the numbers of vintners licensed to tavern wines was reduced to only two in September 1575, significantly the licences went to Henry Gaymer jurat and William Ratliff, who became a jurat in 1578.[97]

A similar pattern can be seen among the osts, with John Fletcher, Mathew Millis and Henry Gaymer, successively Royal Purveyors of Fish, paying the highest quarterage. Ostage also seems to have formed a secure occupation in middle age. Three former fishing masters among the jurats gave up the sea to become osts in later life.[98]

Inevitably, given the importance of fishing in Rye's economy, the largest single group of jurats comprised masters of fishing vessels (36), who were almost all owners of their own ships and possibly of several others.[99] Other, land-based jurats also acquired part-shares in merchant and fishing vessels, among them in the 1570s and 1580s Mathew Millis, William Didsbury, Thomas Edolphe and Robert Jackson as well as John Fagge.[100] It seems therefore highly likely that a similar pattern prevailed at other times.

Further opportunities for individuals to extend the scope of their economic activities were open to those with sufficient capital, by acquiring the farm of town properties, in particular the town storehouse and the ferry, which were generally let to farm for a period of years. Often these were leased to existing jurats or others with suitable connections. Among the holders of the storehouse were Henry Gaymer and Francis Harris (jointly for £20 per year in 1557), John Baylye (1561 for 5 years in return for the construction of a crane and the keeping of the building in good repair), Thomas Edolphe (for three years from 1574, paying £28 6s 8d p.a.), James Appleton, son of the former town clerk (for three years from September 1597, at £14 10s p.a.) and John Fisher for one year paying £7 in September 1600 at a time when goods passing through the port had slumped. Among those who leased the town ferry were Robert Wood, paying £26 13s 4d p.a. for two years in September 1556, and Henry Gaymer, who paid £25 10s p.a. for a three year lease in September 1574.[101]

Jurats' households tended to be large, with, in most cases, two or more servants living in, usually including a maidservant and a boy or manservant. The 1597-8 muster rolls, for example, show that eleven of the thirteen jurats had one or more male servants over the age of 16. In seven cases there was one, in two instances two, in one case three and in another, five.[102] Among jurats' wills, which include female servants, nineteen list one or more servants, in all but six cases including at least one of each sex. Of the seventeen which list female servants, twelve mention one and five name two. The number of male servants ranged from one to four. Among the largest such households were those of Robert Woode (4 male servants and 2 maidservants) and Alexander Welles (3 male servants, one maidservant mentioned by name plus an unspecified number of others).

The factionalism of the mid-Elizabethan period

At first sight the Rye magistracy appears to display an almost monolithic unity, with the powerful cohesiveness of social, family and business ties. However, at times major fissures appeared among the jurats as a body. In the period from the mid-1530s to the mid-1550s, religious, personal and age differences combined to cause two decades of factional strife.[103] In the 1570s and early 1580s new disputes arose, partly of a religious nature and partly based on the factional differences of the earlier generation.

A series of events which split open the apparent unity of the jurats' bench to reveal the latent factionalism within, began in 1571 with the displacement of Robert Jackson as town clerk and his replacement by William Appleton, a relative newcomer. In 1574, Jackson sought to make a comeback, but failed to receive more than a minority of the votes of either the commons or the jurats, the mayor, William Davy who had previously promised his vote to Appleton, having remained neutral. The following year a seemingly unconnected incident involving the breaking of one or two windows by a small group of men after a late night drinking spree provides evidence of the underlying personal antipathies among the political class. The windows concerned belonged to Thomas Edolphe, who became a jurat shortly afterwards, and to Thomas Belveridge, elected a common councillor in February 1577 and also briefly a jurat, who was undercollector of customs in the town of Rye. The perpetrators of the incident included Robert Bennett who was elected a common councillor at the same time as Belveridge and who was a frequent disturber of the peace, and his brother John Bennett, who became mayor's sergeant under John Fagge in 1577, both of whom were involved in a much more serious incident in the latter year.[104]

In October 1577 following the death of George Raynoldes, the most senior jurat, the latent factionalism broke into open conflict. Raynoldes, who had been mayor five times and had served a total of 32 years as a jurat, had sought to steer a middle course through all the religious changes and political strife of the 1540s and 1550s. His death removed the one steadying influence among the jurats' bench. His will, made shortly before his death, became a focus for the political in-fighting which followed. In it he left his principal tenement and the adjoining property, which he owned, to be sold by his executor John Heblethwaite and his overseers, John Fagge and Lucy Phillips. The proceeds were to be expended on a variety of charitable and other projects ranging from bequests to the poor to highway repairs and the construction of a new conduit head at Leasham Hill for the town's water supply. In doing so he also disinherited his nearest heir, his nephew John Raynoldes of Brodhurst, Kent, who, upon his uncle's death had made out a lease of the property to one John Rolfe, mercer, a resident in Rye since 1559.

According to Heblethwaite's testimony, immediately on George Raynoldes' death he entered the property and took possession of it as executor. Rolfe, having obtained his lease, waited until Heblethwaite was absent from the town and then employed two burly individuals to break into the premises, ejecting Heblethwaite's wife in the process. When this was safely accomplished, Rolfe himself took possession and proceeded to barricade the door, forcing William Appleton the town clerk's wife and Mrs Heblethwaite's children, who had been in the house when it was first broken into to take refuge in the loft. These events took place in the early evening of 11 November. By nine o'clock a small crowd, led by the town clerk, had gathered outside the property, intent upon its repossession. According to Rolfe's testimony

'very evill disposed and riotous persons ... in very riotous and rebellious manner ... being weaponed and arrayed with bowes, billes, holbardes, partizans, swords, bucklers, daggers, spaddes, pitchforkes, spades, axes, and other weapons ... marched thence forwardes in very riotous and rebellious manner, and into the said principal messuage whereinto they before had conveyed certaine dagges ready chargid and gonpowder, and the same in very forceable manner and riotous sort assembled and the walles thereof brake downe and by the breaches entred ... and ... did assault, beat, wound and evill entreat, crying out moost desperately with lewde voyces against your said subiecte in this sorte viz "downe with him, downe with him, kyll him, kyll him", and contynued the same ... by the space of two whole houres so that your said subiect was in dispaier of his liffe duringe which space sondry riotous persons ... unknowen adioynid them selves unto the same rioters and divers other of your Maiesties subiectes herynge theroff resorted thether in great companie, so that ther were assembled together to the nomber of CC [i.e. 200] persons ... divers of the woorshipfull Jurates of the said town beinge Justices of peace ther desirous to preserve your Maiesties peace ... gevinge straight commandment ... to cease ... but all in vayne ... sent in great hast for the said Maior, (who neither was nor could be ignorant of so great a Ryot) who (after that he was with much a do founde out) they certified of all the matter ... but he comynge thether and fyndinge the said rioters ... wold not compell them by vertue of his aucthoritie to cease ... although he were thereunto oftentymes moost earnestly desired, intreated, by the said Jurates and divers other your loving subiectes, but rather anymated and encouraged them in their malicious doinges ... yet to the end that he wold seem in shewe to do somewhat in discharginge his office, he craftely called them in your Maiesties name, to doe no more then they lawfully might, or wordes to that effecte, which his deceiptfull meaning beinge to the rioters before then, known they surceased not, nether wold the saide Maior remove by force nor compell the riotors to laye downe their weapons, until this complainant overchargid with multitude, and wearied with stripes, was inforcid for safgard of his liffe to deliver upe unto him, the said house, his longe desired praye, payinge therefore but vii li [i.e. £7] by the year, which beinge don, the ryot ymmediatly ceased, and the outrage was appeasid ...'[105]

When Robert Carpenter, jurat, and his brother John arrived on the scene, having been sent for by a maidservant, they found Appleton 'revileinge and greatly mysusinge ... Mr Fletcher, preacher of Rye'. According to John Carpenter's testimony the rioters were at this stage still outside and the mayor was already present, although he later disappeared. John Carpenter went off to fetch John Mercer, another jurat and by the time he had returned, Appleton was inside the parlour 'with his rapier drawn'. At this point, although they later denied it, John Carpenter tried to persuade the mayor to proclaim the Statute of Rebellions, and it was said 'yf the sayd Maior wolde proclaime the

129

seyd Statute, that the sayd Gayemer [also a jurat] and his companye wolde fetche the sayde complaynauntes [Hebelthwaite's] famely owt of the howse by the eares' or otherwise 'they wold fyer the howse on them and have them out'.[106]

According to the interrogatories drawn up for the star chamber case which followed, Rolfe's original forcible entry which had sparked off the riot had been rumoured to have been planned at a meeting with Mr Fletcher, Gaymer and Carpenter at the house of another jurat, Mathew Millis. There was also a suggestion that Gaymer had prepared calivers and other weapons in Millis' house, which adjoined the scene of the riot, and had arranged for the gateway between the two properties to be open to allow easy transfer of these weapons into the house by Rolfe's accomplices. It also appeared that Gaymer and Carpenter, accompanied by two other jurats, William Davye and John Mercer together with Richard Fletcher, the town preacher, had intervened at the height of the riot on Rolfe's behalf with William Tolken, the mayor's deputy while the mayor was absent from the scene, and that Gaymer and Fletcher had offered Thomas Edolphe (another jurat, whose chequered career has already been referred to), £10 if he would enter the house to help Rolfe.[107]

It is clear from Rolfe's own testimony in the case that those who supported him entertained strong suspicions that the will, which had been the immediate cause of the trouble, was a forgery, at least in part, and that Heblethwaite had added his name as executor to the draft which was all that was ready when George Raynoldes died, and had prevailed upon his servant and apprentice, Robert Convers, aged 17, together with Thomas Hart (13), Jane Coxson (17) and Jone Enge (15) to add their names as witnesses to it. When John Raynoldes decided to challenge the will, Heblethwaite apparently consulted the mayor, John Fagge, William Appleton, the town clerk and Robert Jackson, who advised proving it in the Prerogative court of Canterbury. His hostile descriptions of Fagge as 'a man of great wealth and authorite and now also Maior', of Appleton as 'yett very skylfull in shiftes connynge devises and in making of infamyous liberties' and of Robert Jackson as 'a great forger and counterfaytor of wrytinges and letters, a common cheator and spoyler of poore infantes, wydowes and simple soules, tradid and trayned in all

Table 19:

The corporation in crisis:
leading members of the two factions 1577-81

	1577 riot	1579 mayoral election	1580 mayoral election
Gaymer faction			
Henry Gaymer J	/	/	/
William Davye J	/	/	
Robert Carpenter J	/	/	/
Mathew Millis J	/		
John Mercer J	/	/	
Thomas Edolphe[1] (J 1578)	/	/	/
Richard Fletcher, minister	/		
John Rolfe, mercer	/	/	
Clement Hopper (J 1585)			/
John Fisher (J 1596)	/		
Fagge faction			
John Sharpe J		/	
William Tolken J	/	/	
Francis Harris J		/	
William Dabernell J		/	
John Fagge J	/	/	
Robert Jacson J	/		/
William Ratliff (J 1578)		/	
John Bruster (J 1579)		/	
William Didsbury (J 1579)		/	
Thomas Colbrand (J 1579)		/	
Francis Smith (J 1580)			/
William Appleton Town Clerk	/	/	/
Robert Bennett (CC 1577)	/	/	
John Bennett Mayor's Sergt 1577-8	/	/	
Uncommitted			
John Donnynges J			
George Raynolds J			

Notes:
J Jurat
CC Common Councillor
/ listed as taking sides
[1] Thomas Edolphe served as Jurat January-August 1576 and again from January 1578.
Sources: RYE 1/4; RYE 47/21,23,24,25; RYE 137/36; PRO STAC 5 H32/29, H76/38.

sortes of develishe devises, and of very ill fame and report with all suche as knowe him' indicate the strength of personal animosity involved. On the other side, Heblethwaite, a former town clerk of Lydd over some thirty years, characterised Gaymer, Davye, Carpenter and Fletcher as having 'confederated together to sett ... John Rolff aworke to molest and trouble' him 'because he will not leane to the bent of there bowe and hange one there sleves'. Such descriptions indicate that the existence of factions among the jurats was common knowledge and polarised opinion.[108]

Table 19 demonstrates that the line-up of personalities in 1577 was no isolated event. In 1579 and in 1580 disputes over the mayoral elections found similar divisions among the jurats and their followers. In 1579 the issue was whether or not it was contrary to the customs and usages of the town for an individual (John Fagge) to serve three consecutive terms as mayor. In 1580, it was alleged that Robert Jackson was elected mayor during the absence of the most part of the commons due to a plague outbreak which was ravaging the town and even then only 'by his owne great labour'.[109] In each case events found Henry Gaymer, Robert Carpenter, John Mercer, Thomas Edolphe and their supporters on the one side, and John Fagge, Robert Jackson, William Tolken, William Appleton and their supporters on the other.

The origins of the two factions were rooted in the earlier divisions of the 1530s-1550s. Among the Gaymer faction, Robert Carpenter was heir to Thomas Fletcher, one of the two jurat sons of John Fletcher, the leader of the traditionalist faction in the last years of Henry VIII's reign; and Thomas Edolphe was heir to Thomas Fletcher's brother Richard. Henry Gaymer himself had been entrusted with the guardianship of the children of Clement Cobbe, the son of his namesake, who had been a leading adherent of the Fletchers, and his mother Ann Gaymer had been godmother to one of Richard Fletcher's daughters.

On the other side, Robert Jackson had been the successor and protege as town clerk of Alexander Welles, the leader of the Protestant faction in the late 1550s. He was appointed a jurat by a former servant of Welles, William Tolken, in 1576. Among their chief supporters were the brothers Robert and John Bennett, whose father Robert Bennett had been a close associate of Welles and the Protestant faction throughout the Reformation years and had been appointed a jurat by Alexander Welles in 1557.[110]

How far the revival of factions in the 1570s was due to genuine policy differences and how far merely the result of deeply-felt family and personal antagonisms is not entirely clear. The years of Fagge's and Jackson's mayoralties were marked by a concerted attempt to maintain a godly order, and it is to these years that the special measures against perpetual drunkards and the 'decree against whordome' referred to in chapter 5 belong. However, Richard Fletcher was at least in appearance in sympathy with

132

these, and his later involvement in the Lambeth Articles as Bishop of London in 1596 which lost him Elizabeth's favour, shows him to have been notably Calvinist in outlook. Possibly he resented magisterial interference in the spiritual jurisdiction in matters such as personal morality and conduct. This could have led him to throw in his lot with those of a less dogmatically Protestant mind. More likely, given his Cranbrook origins, he was related in some way to the Rye jurat family and therefore had personal ties of loyalty which overrode mere doctrinal differences. The latter might well be inferred from a letter to the Lord Warden written by Appleton for John Fagge, then mayor, in September 1578, referring to Fletcher's continuing support for Rolfe, which implores the Lord Warden to intervene 'for without your ayde we shall in suche cases stand in a ticklishe state *whan such a person as Mr Fletcher is* shalbe a partaker against the magistrate'. Certainly, by 1581, such differrences as may have existed between Fletcher and John Fagge seem to have been settled, for in June of that year, the mayor and jurats sought Fletcher's aid to 'saie your mynde' to the Lord Admiral in the continuing dispute with his servant, John Mercer, a highly prominent member of the Gaymer faction whom Fagge had dismissed from his juratship and his freedom two years earlier for bringing an action outside of the liberties.[111]

The evidence for religion as the chief cause of differences between the two factions is rather sketchy and far from conclusive. An analysis of the wills of members of the two factions is hampered by the fact that of the leading protagonists on either side, neither Robert Jackson, nor Henry Gaymer or Robert Carpenter left wills. John Fagge's is entirely neutral doctrinally, merely leaving his soul to Almighty God. The wills of several other members of the Fagge faction are, however, distinctly more Protestant than those of their opponents, in particular those of William Dabernell, William Didsbury and William Ratcliff. Didsbury, in his will, made in 1593, calling to mind that 'all flesh shall die but nothing more uncertain than when; and that sickness is the messenger of death and death the messenger of God to call men to him' showed a distinctly Calvinist outlook in his bequest of his soul 'to Almighty God my maker and Jesus Christ my Redeemer and God the Holy Ghost who had sanctified me making hereby my protestation and confession that I hope to receive remission of my sins by the death and passion of Jesus Christ and by no other means'; while William Ratcliffe in 1603 committed his soul 'into the hands of Almighty God who gave it me, trusting to be made heirs of eternal life by the merits of my saviour Christ, by whose death I believe the sting has been taken out of death' and also left 10s apiece for three sermons by the then vicar, Mr Bracegirdle, at the time of his burial and again at the times of distribution of his bequest of £20 to the poor, on the first occasion 'exhortinge them to departe this life in the feare of God'. On the other side, Thomas Edolphe's will (1599) was only mildly reformist, with the bequest of his soul 'to Almighty God my maker and redeemer', while John Fisher's (1603) referred his soul 'to Almighty God, trusting through the merits of Jesus Christ my only Lord and Saviour to receive free pardon and remission of all my sins', a statement which fell some way short of a clear acceptance of either justification by faith or election. In this case, however, the formula is not Fisher's anyway, but rather that of Robert Convers, the town clerk, who used precisely the same formula in a number of wills which he composed for jurats at this period. Only John Mercer's will (1588) among those of members of the Gaymer faction provides clear evidence of his religious outlook, with its reference to 'my Lord and Saviour Jesus Christ, by whose death and passion I do by faith assure myself of eternal life', but his reasons for supporting this faction were altogether exceptional.[112]

The evidence from wills, then, merely confirms the Protestant convictions of the Fagge faction, while revealing very little of the religious outlook of their opponents. However, three pieces of circumstantial evidence offer at least some corroboration for the theory that religious differences played some part in the factional dispute. In 1593 Thomas Edolphe and the town's lecturer, Mr Grenewood, were involved in a sufficiently serious public dispute for them both to be called before the other jurats to settle their differences. in 1600 the then mayor, Thomas Hamon, who is listed among the freemen who supported John Fagge's election in 1579, imprisoned the vicar, a certain Mr Smith, whom he suspected of papist sympathies by virtue of a crucifix and certain letters written by him to his wife's father in London. And in 1606, Thomas Fisher the younger, nephew of the John Fisher who was implicated with other members of the Gaymer faction in the 1577 riot and later became a jurat, was arrested for publicly holding forth papist opinions in conversation at an inn in Cranbrook and in Rye. According to one deponent, Fisher 'had bene of late at Dunkeirke where he had learned yt whereby he did perceyve he was now in the right faith, wherein he was not before and yt the Pope was the supreame heade of the Church'. Among those cited against him was James Appleton, son of the former town clerk, although he later denied hearing any such utterances. Nevertheless, despite his family connections, Thomas Fisher junior seems to have spent the remaining eight years of his life in gaol in Rye, where he died in 1614. It seems not impossible that a hankering after the old ways ran in the Fisher family.[113]

But whatever the underlying reasons for the factional disputes of the 1570s and 1580s, the actual existence of factions is undeniable. In the early 1570s, the advantage seems to have lain with the Gaymer faction. Henry Gaymer was mayor in 1572 and his close associate, William Davy was mayor in 1574 and 1575. In the intervening years, 1570, 1571 and 1573, the office was held by John Donnynge, an outsider who only became a freeman in 1565, and who seems to have kept himself apart from the local factions. It was during these years that Robert Jackson was deprived of office as town clerk and William Appleton installed in his place, an event which may have been the work of the Gaymer faction. If so it evidently backfired, given Appleton's later allegiance.

However, in 1576, when William Tolken became mayor, the balance within the corporation began to swing in favour of the other faction. At the time of George Raynoldes' death in 1577 the two factions were almost evenly matched among the jurats' bench, with five members of the Gaymer faction and six supporters of John Fagge. The death of one of the only two uncommitted jurats, therefore, upset the delicate balance by allowing Fagge to bring in another of his associates, William Ratcliff, so giving him and his supporters a clear majority among the magistrates. In this situation he retained the mayoralty for an unprecedented three consecutive terms, before giving way to Robert Jackson, another of his associates, whose votes, 'threeskore persons' out of approximately 80 freemen present in 1580 (there were approximately 100 freemen at this date plus the jurats), tally closely with the figure of 62 commoners and 7 jurats who comprised Fagge's supporters the year previously. By implication the arithmetic of the situation shows that the Gaymer faction could rely on the support of around 40 freemen and 4 jurats during this period. Such advantage as the Fagge faction had was therefore by no means overwhelming, and a handful of untimely deaths among the freemen or one or two changes of heart could soon reverse the situation. This appears to have happened in 1583 when Robert Carpenter began his first two-year term. Although William Ratcliff succeeded him in 1585, thereafter, for the next six years, first Thomas Edolphe (1586 and 1587), then Henry Gaymer (1588 and 1589) and finally Robert Carpenter again (1590 and 1591) held office in turn.[114]

This apparent victory of the Gaymer faction was however also by no means absolute. In September 1590, for example, when John Carpenter, the newly-elected mayor's brother, contested the town clerkship with Francis Bolton who had taken over the office earlier in the year on the death of William Appleton, he could only muster the support of the mayor and two other jurats (presumably Edolphe and Gaymer) plus the lesser part of the commonalty. The rest of the jurats and commons voted to retain Bolton. That this was no mere reaction by the corporation to the prospect of too close a family relationship between the town clerk and one of the magistrates is demonstrated by the fact that Francis Bolton was the nephew of one of the other jurats, William Didsbury.[115] As the 1590s proceeded, the influence of the Gaymer faction weakened still further. Neither Carpenter nor Gaymer held mayoral office again, and Thomas Edolphe was mayor only once more, in 1594. Although Thomas Fisher, one of Gaymer's and Carpenter's supporters, was mayor in 1601 and 1602, both John Bett (1593) and Thomas Hamon (1595, 1596, 1599 and 1600) had been among Fagge's supporters in 1579 and Thomas Colbrand (1592) was an overseer of Fagge's will. Finally, John Fowtrell, mayor in 1597 and 1598, seems also to have had most in common with the survivors of the Fagge faction. In 1595 he married William Didsbury's widow, Cicely, and another member of this group, William Ratcliff referred to him as 'my friend' in his will in 1603 and made him an overseer.[116] By now, most of the leaders of the earlier factions were dead. Following Henry Gaymer's death in 1596, only Robert Carpenter remained of the four main protagonists of the 1570s. John Fagge (d.1583) and Robert Jackson (d.1586) had predeceased him. Carpenter's own retirement from the jurats' bench followed in 1601. By the close of the Elizabethan period therefore, the old order was changing and a new generation of men such as Thomas Hamon and John Fowtrell had taken over, who would guide the town's declining fortunes into the new century and the Jacobean age.

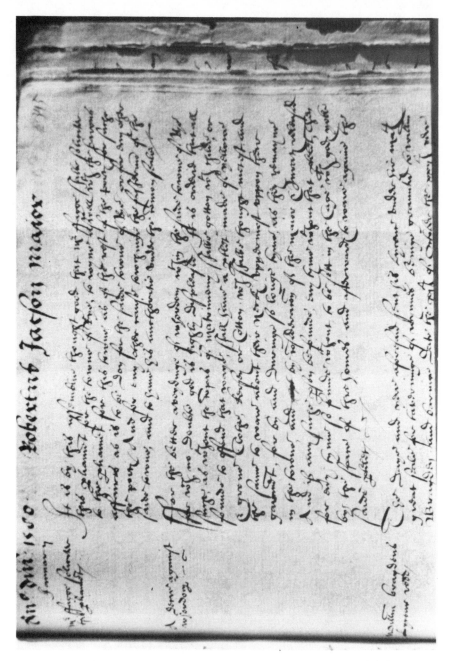

Extract from the 'Decree against Whoredom', 1581 (RYE/1/4/345)

138

CHAPTER 4

Occupations and the Division of Wealth

'the said towne and harbour of Rye is one of the auncient
townes of the Cinque Portes and hath binne of great
consequence to this State both for the convenient scituation
thereof for trade and greate provision of fishe ...'
Preamble to draft Parliamentary Bill for amending
Rye haven, March 1624 (RYE 47/98/15)

The social geography of Tudor Rye

The economy of Tudor Rye was almost entirely dependent on its
function as a port, both in terms of trade in goods and the town's
fishing industry, making it an important regional centre in south-
eastern England. In order to explore the occupational and social
structure of the town more fully, a detailed analysis of the 1576
sesse has been undertaken, in particular by linking it with
occupational lists from the assembly books, depositions, probate
records and the like, to produce a clear impression of the town at a
particular moment in time. The 1576 sesse was chosen as being
the first sesse after the formal ward structure was introduced in
February 1574, and the closest in date to the time of Rye's
greatest prosperity for which a sufficiently wide range of sources
for individuals' occupations survive (the annual clerk's files of
letters, including depositions (RYE 47) which provide one of the
major sources in this respect, have only survived continuously
from the early 1570s).

Town sesses (rating assessments) are extremely useful as a
guide to the relative wealth of those listed, but they need to be
used with great caution, as Table 20 indicates. They were an

Table 20
The division of wealth in Rye 1482-1596

Year				Assessment					
	£1	£2	£3-9	£10-19	£20-49	£50-99	£100+	£500+	Total Valuation
1492	-	53	28	27	45	7	14	1	£6303
1523	-	-	15	26	26	9	7	-	£2801
1542	-	-	-	-	-	-	12	-	£1500
1545	-	-	-	1	69	33	18	-	£6751
1576	57	78	177	67	33	8	-	-	£3278
1596	80	86	91	39	58	30	34	-	£15344

Notes:
The figures for 1492, 1576 and 1596 are taken from town sesses (rating assessments), which in 1492 and 1596, give valuations and amounts levied. The 1576 sesse gives only the latter, but an assembly decree granting the sesse stated that it was to be at the rate of 12d in the £ on goods or 2s in the £ on rents. The figures in the table are based on the assessments for goods.
The figures for 1523, 1542 and 1545 are taken from the records of the collection of benevolences and forced loans.
The valuation totals for 1576 and 1596 exclude non-residents, who seem to comprise those assessed on rents.
Sources: RYE 77/3; RYE 81/1-2; PRO E179/190/200; PRO E179/231/218; RYE 1/4/227-232, RYE 1/6/30v-43r. For the rates of assessment in 1542 and 1545 respectively, see *L.P.* vol. 17 no. 194; *L.P.* vol.20 pt.ii appendix no. 4.

extraordinary source of additional revenue, raised only intermittently, and then with a specific amount in mind, to meet a particular item of expenditure. In the middle years of the sixteenth century the overall wealth of Rye's inhabitants was such that sufficient could be raised without fully assessing each individual's wealth. In this respect, the 1576 sesse represents a considerable undervaluation of individual levels of wealth. Clearly the town was larger and more prosperous in 1576 than in either 1492 or 1596, as virtually every other indicator demonstrates. The combined wealth of Rye's top 121 inhabitants alone in the assessments for the 1545 benevolence which comes to more than double that of all 417 ratepayers in 1576, indicates the magnitude of this underassessment. Nevertheless, as an indicator of relative (as opposed to absolute) divisions of wealth at a particular date, individual sesses can be of considerable value. What Table 20 clearly demonstrates is the pyramidal structure of the division of wealth in Tudor Rye, in common with other towns of the period. Evidence from the Rye parish registers, from the burial registers in particular, also suggests that a considerable proportion of householders (33 per cent of those in the 1576 sesse, 28 per cent of those listed in 1596) were simply too poor to pay any rates at all.

Again, this figure, representing the poorest among the labouring classes, is comparable to the results of similar studies for other Tudor towns.[1]

At the apex of the social pyramid stood the wealthier merchants and traders, from whom the political elite were chiefly drawn. In 1492 a mere fifteen individuals (8.6 per cent of taxpayers) including all but two of the ten jurats, assessed at £100 in goods and upwards, owned 61.2 per cent of assessed wealth. In 1576, which saw an increase in those at the lower end of the social scale who were brought into the assessment and the inclusion of those worth only £1, the figures are only slightly less dramatic. Then, 41 individuals, including half the common councillors and all but two of the jurats, assessed at over £20, representing 9.8 per cent of taxpayers, were assessed at 43.6 per cent of taxable wealth. At the upper end of this group, eight men, including five jurats, representing a mere 1.9 per cent of taxpayers, owned 13.5 per cent of assessed wealth, among them two butchers, a brewer, a vintner, an ost and a fisherman. This group, assessed in 1576 at £50–99 was roughly equivalent to those assessed at £100 and upwards (7) in 1523; at £200 and upwards (5) in 1545 and £300 and upwards in 1596 (6).

The full extent of the under-assessment of wealth in 1576 can be gauged from the comparison made in Table 21 between the valuations placed on the goods of 55 of those assessed (13.2 per cent) who died within seven years of the 1576 sesse and for whom probate inventory valuations are available. In only three cases was the probate valuation less than that given in the 1576 sesse, while in the remaining 52 cases the probate valuation was higher, by an overall factor of 5.9. Nor was there any discernible variation in this factor between those probate valuations which took place within three years of 1576 or those which took place later. However, there is a noticeable difference in the degree of under-assessment of different social groups, those in the middle bracket (£2 10s–£9) appearing most successful at disguising the real value of their goods, while the poorer class, and above all the wealthiest were taxed on a higher percentage of their true wealth. The overall degree of under-assessment in the 1576 sesse revealed in Table 21 should serve as a warning to those who would take early modern rating assessments at face value.

The economic divisions between the different social classes

Table 21

A comparison of the 1576 sesse valuations and probate inventory totals

sesse valuation	Probate valuation expressed as multiple of sesse valuation														Total	Median	Mean
	¾	1	1½	2	3	4	5	6	7	8	9	10	11-19	20+			
£1-2	1	-	3	-	2	2	1	2	-	-	-	1	2	-	14	4	5.6
£2 10s-£9	1	1	5	6	2	1	2	2	1	1	1	3	2	1	29	3	6.6
£10-£19	-	1	-	2	-	-	1	2	-	1	-	-	-	-	7	5	4.8
£20+	1	-	-	-	2	-	-	1	1	-	-	-	-	-	5	3	4.3

Notes: The probate inventory totals cover the period 1576—end 1582 inclusive, i.e. seven years from the sesse.

Sources: RYE 1/4/227-232; W/B 1.

Table 22

The 1576 sesse: distribution of wealth by ward

Ward	Valuation (£)								Mean household assessment
	Poorer		Lower middle		Upper middle		Urban elite		
	1	2	2 10s-5	6-9	10-19	20-29	30-39	40+	
Landgate	8	19	21	4	12	7	2	1	9s 0d
Market	-	3	17	5	8	3	1	4	14s 10d
Strandgate	3	7	24	11	12	2	1	3	9s 0d
Middlestreet	6	6	21	5	16	2	4	5	11s 10d
Baddings	20	19	34	6	12	2	1	1	5s 2d
Watchbell	20	24	23	3	7	1	1	-	3s 6d
Total	57	78	140	34	67	17	10	14	
Totals by social group	135		174		84		24		

Notes: excludes assessments on rents paid by non-residents.

Source: RYE 1/4/227-232.

were broadly reflected in the ward structure. At the top of the social pyramid were Middlestreet and Market wards. These were the wards at the top of the hill on which Rye was built, in the area around the Market Place and churchyard. Here the majority of Rye's jurats lived (nine of 12 in 1558, nine of 13 in 1576) as did the majority of Rye's mercantile elite (nine of 14 assessed at £40 and above and five of ten assessed at £30–39 in 1576). At the other end of the social scale, only three of the 135 assessed at £1–2 in the same year lived in Market ward and only twelve in Middlestreet, as Table 22 demonstrates. Strandgate and Landgate wards were more mixed, almost certainly reflecting the differences between the wealthier High Street properties and the poorer lanes leading down to the town wall. Two jurats had their houses in Strandgate ward in 1576, while conversely there were only ten of the poorer sort. Landgate ward had a rather higher proportion of poorer inhabitants (36.5 per cent of the ward's ratepayers) than Strandgate (15.9 per cent) but slightly more of those in the upper-middle wealth bracket (15.7 per cent compared to only 22.2 per cent of ratepayers living in Strandgate ward), a difference masked in the average household assessments for the two wards which are virtually identical. Finally, at the bottom of the social scale were Baddings and Watchbell wards, where 61.5 per cent of the poorest ratepayers in the town lived, and only three members of the urban elite.

The boundaries of Rye's six wards are indicated in Figure 6. Landgate ward ran from the boundary of the town on Playden Hill, across the causeway and through the Landgate, taking in both sides of the present High Street (then known as the Lower or the Longer street) as far as the corner of the present-day West Street (then generally referred to as 'the street leading from the Lower Street to the Middle Street') on the south side and to the corner of, but not including, the street leading to the pound (known as Pondgarden) on the north side. Included in this ward were a collection of poorer houses 'in the Friary' (the present-day Conduit Hill).

Strandgate ward comprised the remainder of the Lower Street as far as the Strandgate, plus any properties on the north side (such as the houses in Pondgarden, between the High Street and the town wall. The ward then continued through the Strandgate in a south-easterly direction underneath the West Cliff, ending at Francis Christmas's house, which according to a corporation lease of 1577, stood next to the gun platform at the end of the quay.[3]

Market ward comprised the present East Street, Market Street and Lion Street then known respectively as 'the street leading from the Lower Street to the Butchery', 'the Butchery' and 'the street leading from the Lower Street to the church', together with a group of poorer properties in Okeman's Lane which has retained its original name, and the rather larger, wealthier properties on the east and north sides of the churchyard, as far as the junction with Watchbell Street to the south and including the vicarage to the west.

Middlestreet ward began with the large merchants' houses on

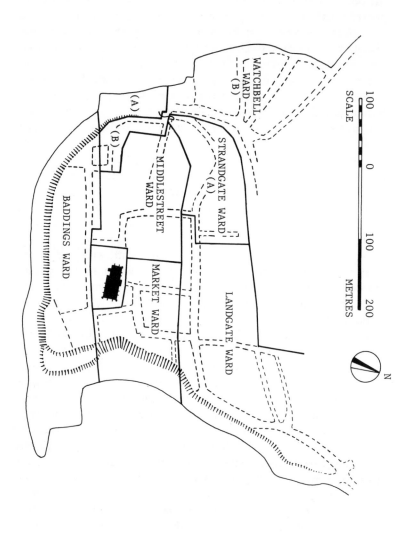

Figure 6: Rye wards 1574

the west side of the churchyard, running from the junction with Watchbell Street down into Church Lane ('the lane leading from the church to the Middle Street') and including the whole of West Street ('the street leading from the Lower Street to the Middle Street'), before finally passing down Mermaid Street ('Middle Street') to the junctions with the West Cliff and the Lower Street on the south and north sides respectively.

Baddings Ward, named after Baddings Tower, used by the corporation as a courthouse and prison, included the properties adjoining the Gungarden and all the houses in the Watchbell Street and in the lanes leading to the south cliff, in particular in Dyrrickes Lane (mentioned in the 1576 sesse and now known as Sharpe's Lane).[4]

Finally, Watchbell Ward, which took its name from the Watchbell which stood at the end of Rucke's Lane (still known as such today) included all the properties on the West Cliff (often referred to as Baldwin's Wishe after John Baldwin, who had a house there in 1513) and continued through the Strandgate in a north-easterly direction, taking in all the poorer properties around the fishmarket and underneath the town wall in the damp, low-lying area known as 'the Wishe'.[5]

An analysis of the occupations of inhabitants paying the 1576 sesse bears out the findings of the 1565 government survey, which showed that 42.5 per cent of Rye's 530 householders were mariners or fishermen. In 1576 as Table 23 shows, the comparable figure was 40.8 per cent of the 361 ratepayers whose primary occupations have been identified, almost certainly an underestimation, since the majority of those not identified were of a relatively low level of wealth, as were those fishermen and mariners who were not masters of vessels, and came from the wards in which these occupations predominated. The dominance of the seaborne trades in the urban economy is shown in a still more dramatic light when such land-based ancillary trades as osts/feters, shipwrights, hookmakers, basketmakers and rippiers are taken into account, bringing the total of those wholly dependent upon the sea for their living to 183 ratepayers, 50.7 per cent of those identified. In addition, a high proportion of the demand for the goods and services of those engaged in the clothing, woodworking, leatherworking, and food trades would have been generated by mariners and fishermen, in particular by their need for

Table 23
The 1576 sesse: the occupational structure by ward

Primary Occupation	Landgate	Market	Strand-gate	Middle street	Baddings	Watch bell	Total
Fisherman	7	5	15	14	29	24	94
Mariner	11	2	4	5	15	13	50
Mercer	10	6	6	11	3	1	37
Feter/Ost	3	2	1	3	8	4	21
Tailor/Draper	2	1	4	6	2	-	15
Shipwright	-	3	1	-	2	6	12
Baker	3	-	3	2	2	2	12
Butcher	-	4	-	1	6	-	11
Beerbrewer	4	2	3	1	-	-	10
Cordwainer[1]	3	1	3	1	1	-	9
Carpenter	3	2	1	-	2	-	8
Beer tippler[2]	2	-	1	2	-	2	7
Blacksmith	2	2	-	-	-	2	6
Innkeeper	2	1	2	-	1	-	6
Yeoman	2	-	-	-	2	-	4
Cooper	1	-	1	-	1	-	3
Labourer	-	1	-	-	1	1	3
Vintner	-	1	1	1	-	-	3
Chandler	-	-	-	2	1	-	3
Goldsmith	-	-	2	-	-	1	3
Lighterman	1	-	1	-	-	-	2
Joiner	1	-	-	-	1	-	2
Gent	-	-	1	1	-	-	2
Fletcher	1	-	-	-	-	-	1
Upholsterer	1	-	-	-	-	-	1
Basketmaker	1	-	-	-	-	-	1
Carrier	1	-	-	-	-	-	1
Locksmith	1	-	-	-	-	-	1
Surgeon	1	-	-	-	-	-	1
Glasier	1	-	-	-	-	-	1
Husbandman	1	-	-	-	-	-	1
Tapster	-	1	-	-	-	-	1
Cutler	-	1	-	-	-	-	1
Mason	-	1	-	-	-	-	1
Capper	-	1	-	-	-	-	1
Hookmaker	-	1	-	-	-	-	1
Brasier	-	-	1	-	-	-	1
Waterbailiff	-	-	-	1	-	-	1
Customer	-	-	-	1	-	-	1
Schoolmaster	-	-	-	1	-	-	1
Deputy bailiff	-	-	-	-	1	-	1
Painter	-	-	-	-	1	-	1
Cockboatman	-	-	-	-	-	1	1
Rippier	-	-	-	-	-	1	1
Other shops	1	-	3	3	1	-	8
Widows[3]	1	1	1	-	2	3	8
Unknown	6	3	9	7	13	18	56
Non-resident	1	11	2	2	5	2	23

Total residents	416
Total identified	360 (87%)
Total not identified	56 (13%)

Notes: [1] includes shoemaker, cobbler and 1 currier
[2] those tipplers without another, primary, occupation
[3] those widows for whom there is no evidence of occupation

Sources: As for Table 11

working apparel, and the repair and provisioning of their ships. Many of the merchants, too, the third largest occupational grouping, would have been chiefly dependent for their livelihood on Rye's seaborne commerce; while the keepers of Rye's inns and victualling houses would have relied for much of their income on the passing trade of visiting merchants, passengers passing to and from the continent and the crews of foreign ships and coastal trading vessels coming into the harbour.

Within the town as a whole, there was a clear zoning of occupations by ward, those nearest the Strand being chiefly inhabited by householders engaged in maritime pursuits, while conversely, at the north-eastern end of the town, in Landgate and Market wards, the land-based trades predominated. Here, for example, were to be found such specialist occupations as fletcher, upholsterer, locksmith, surgeon, glazier (Landgate ward) and cutler, mason and capper (Market ward). All but one of Rye's eleven butchers lived around the market place and Butchery, in Market ward and at the eastern end of Baddings ward, no doubt because town ordinances forbade the opening of butchers' shops elsewhere in the town.[6] Other occupations were more evenly spread. All but Market ward had at least two bakers; and all but Watchbell ward had at least one tailor and one cordwainer. Inns and victualling houses were likewise spread throughout the town and there were merchants and osts/feters resident in every ward, although in each of these cases, the wealthiest tended to live in Market and Middlestreet wards or along the Lower Street in Landgate or Strandgate wards. The brewers, too were confined to these four wards, while conversely, 56 per cent of Rye's mariners and fishermen lived in Baddings and Watchbell wards, accounting for 55 per cent and 63.8 per cent respectively of those identified (excluding widows) in the two wards.

The occupational structure

As Table 24 shows, it has been possible to identify the primary occupations of 86.5 per cent of ratepayers, who between them accounted for 95 per cent of the assessed wealth of residents in 1576. From this evidence the proportionate share of individual wealth owned by each occupational group has been calculated. By far the largest share of wealth is represented by the fishing and allied trades. However, this share of wealth (34.7 per cent) is

Table 24
A comparison of the share of wealth and numbers engaged in each trade among Rye ratepayers 1576, arranged by occupational group

Primary occupation		sesse payers No	%	assessed wealth £	s	d	%
Fisherman		94		683	13	4	
Mariner		50		190	0	0	
Ost/feter		21		244	3	4	
Basketmaker	Fishing and	21		3	6	8	
Hookmaker	allied trades	1		3	6	8	
Cockboatman		1		1	0	0	
Lighterman		2		8	6	8	
Rippier		1		3	6	8	
Total		**171**	**41.1**	**1137**	**3**	**4**	**34.7**
Shipwright		12		60	6	8	
Carpenter		8		22	10	0	
Joiner		2		4	6	8	
Cooper	Building/	3		9	16	8	
Upholsterer	woodworking	1		3	0	0	
Mason		1		10	0	0	
Painter		1		6	13	4	
Glasier		1		10	0	0	
Total		**29**	**7.0**	**126**	**13**	**4**	**3.9**
Merchant		37		529	16	8	
Tallow chandler	Mercantile	3		7	0	0	
Total		**40**	**9.6**	**536**	**16**	**8**	**16.4**
Innkeeper		6		25	10	0	
Vintner		3		105	0	0	
Tippler	Victualling	7		42	16	8	
Tapster		1		3	6	8	
Total		**17**	**4.1**	**176**	**13**	**4**	**5.4**
Tailor/draper		15		139	6	8	
Capper	Clothing	1		5	0	0	
Total		**16**	**3.8**	**144**	**6**	**8**	**4.4**
Cordwainer	Leather	9	2.2	52	0	0	1.6
Blacksmith		6		21	13	4	
Goldsmith		3		9	16	8	
Locksmith	Metalworking	1		2	0	0	
Cutler		1		13	6	8	
Brasier		1		6	13	4	
Total		**12**	**2.9**	**53**	**10**	**0**	**1.6**
Baker		12		91	13	4	
Butcher	Food and drink	11		175	10	0	
Beerbrewer		10		246	0	0	
Total		**33**	**7.9**	**513**	**3**	**4**	**15.7**
Fletcher		1		13	6	8	
Labourer		3		4	0	0	
Husbandman		1		1	0	0	
Carrier		1		3	6	8	
Surgeon		1		2	0	0	
Schoolmaster		1		2	0	0	
Town officer	Miscellaneous	3		52	0	0	
Yeoman		4		57	6	8	
Gent		2		85	16	8	
Other shops		8		85	16	8	
Total		**25**	**6.0**	**310**	**16**	**8**	**9.5**
Widows		8	1.9	61	16	8	1.9
Unidentified		56	13.5	164	13	4	5.0
Total		**416**	**100.0**	**3277**	**13**	**4**	**100.1**

Source: As for Table 11.

considerably below these trades' proportion of ratepayers (41.1 per cent), indicating that many of those pursuing these occupations were among the poorer inhabitants. Other groups which had a disproportionately low share of assessed wealth were those engaged in the building and woodworking trades, the leather and metalworking trades. Among these occupational groups, only a few individuals, representing the more specialised occupations, such as the mason and glazier from the building trades and the cutler from the metalworkers were assessed among the upper middle class (i.e. those worth £10 and upwards). The great majority of the remainder were assessed at between £2.10s–£5, mostly from the lower end of this scale.

At the other end of the scale of wealth stood the mercantile and food and drink trades. These two groups between them owned 32.1 per cent of assessed wealth, (almost as much as the wealth of the much larger number of fishermen) while representing only 17.5 per cent of ratepayers, considerably less than half the number of fishermen and allied trades. If the wholesale fishmongers (the osts and feters) were added to these groups as representing land-based entrepreneurs, then the contrast with the strictly maritime occupations would be even more stark. Clearly, then, it was these groups, the merchants and wholesale fishmongers and the beerbrewers, butchers and bakers, a relatively small proportion of the working population (94 individuals or 22.6 per cent of ratepayers), which controlled the largest share of the town's economy (39.5 per cent), rather than the numerically much larger group of mariners and fishermen[7] (147 individuals or 35.3 per cent) who between them were only worth 26.9 per cent of assessed wealth. Only the victualling and clothing trades had a share in wealth nearly proportionate to their numbers. However these groups were relatively small, representing rather less than one twelfth of residents assessed (7.9 per cent) and just under one tenth (9.8 per cent) of wealth, although in the former group, the three vintners alone accounted for almost 60 per cent of the assessed wealth of all victuallers.

Table 25 sets out the relative wealth of the fourteen most numerous trades in 1576, comparing their mean assessments with the average probate valuations of Rye inhabitants pursuing the same occupations in the period 1540–1603. The results are broadly similar for the two valuations, although again the degree

Table 25

The relative wealth of the major occupations in Elizabethan Rye

Occupation	1576 Mean assessment			no	Occupation	Probate valuations 1540–1603 Mean assessment			no
1 Beerbrewer	£24	12s	0d	(10)	1 Beerbrewer	£292	7s	0d	(3)
2 Butcher	£15	19s	1d	(11)	2 Tailor[2]	£ 94	9s	4d	(18)
3 Yeoman	£14	6s	8d	(4)	3 Mercer	£47	6s	8d	(10)
4 Mercer	£14	6s	5d	(37)	4 Butcher	£46	10s	7d	(4)
5 Feter/Ost	£11	12s	6d	(21)	5 Fisherman	£41	12s	8d	(106)
6 Innkeeper[1]	£11	2s	7d	(14)	6 Feter/Ost	£40	5s	3d	(19)
7 Tailor[2]	£9	6s	3d	(15)	7 Yeoman	£37	0s	4d	(6)
8 Baker	£7	12s	9d	(12)	8 Shipwright	£32	16s	1d	(6)
9 Fisherman	£7	5s	6d	(94)	9 Innkeeper[1]	£32	6s	10d	(9)
10 Cordwainer[3]	£5	15	8d	(9)	10 Cordwainer	£29	14s	5d	(8)
11 Shipwright	£5	9s	8d	(12)	11 Baker	£26	13s	9d	(9)
12 Mariner	£3	16s	0d	(50)	12 Mariner	£16	11s	7d	(19)
13 Blacksmith	£3	12s	9d	(6)	13 Carpenter	£14	0s	9d	(3)
14 Carpenter	£2	16s	3d	(8)	14 Blacksmith	£6	13s	2d	(3)

Notes: [1] includes tipplers and vintners.
   [2] includes drapers.
   [3] includes a currier.
   Yeoman is an indication of status rather than occupation.

Sources: see Table 11.

of underassessment in 1576 is considerable. In each case, beerbrewers, butchers and mercers account for three of the first four places in the table with the brewers being by far the wealthiest; while at the opposite end of the scale, mariners, carpenters and blacksmiths account for three of the four poorest occupations. Among the middle-ranking trades, osts/feters are in the upper half of both lists (fifth and sixth respectively) and cordwainers are near the bottom (tenth in both cases). Among the woodworking and building trades, shipwrights appear to have been worth slightly more than double the wealth of carpenters, both in the levels of their assessments and in probate valuations. The most noticeable difference between the two tables is in the rankings of tailors and fishermen. In the case of fishermen this is largely explained by the fact that most of those who left wills or whose heirs sought administrations were master fishermen who were part owners of the vessels which they captained, whereas many of those on the 1576 sesse were ordinary crew members, lists of whom survive for 1587 and 1589. Those described as mariners were also largely ordinary seamen, mainly employed in the merchant shipping operating out of the town, hence their average wealth was only about half that of the fishermen.

These mean assessments for the major occupations however can only be a very rough guide to relative wealth and often disguise widespread variations in fortune between members of a particular trade. Among the tailors for example, three men out of the 15 listed in the 1576 sesse accounted for 59.8 per cent of the collective assessment for their occupation including two assessed at over £30, members of the urban elite. At the opposite end of the social scale one poor tailor was worth only £1 in goods, while eight more were assessed at between £2 10s and £5, among the less wealthy artificers and tradesmen. The enhanced ranking of this occupation from probate valuations is due to the presence among the sample of two men worth over £400 each in goods and three others worth between £120 and £240 who between them accounted for almost exactly 80 per cent of the total probate valuations on the estates of this group.[8]

The same situation applied among several other key trades. Among the fishermen, seven men assessed at over £20 in 1576 (7.4 per cent) were between them valued at £210, accounting for 30.7 per cent of the combined assessment of the wealth of Rye's fishermen. Three of the 21 osts/feters assessed at over £20, similarly accounted for 54.6 per cent of the combined wealth of their occupation. The wealth of the merchants was slightly more evenly spread. Even so, those nine who were worth over £20 each jointly accounted for 52.8 per cent of the total assessment for the 37 merchants. Another trade in which wealth was more evenly spread was brewing, whose members needed a measure of capital for the purchase of the necessary equipment. Here only one assessment fell below £13 6s 8d, and he was a mere employee, Anthony Vines, 'chief brewere to John Mercer', assessed at £1 in Strandgate ward. Of the remainder, two were assessed at £13 6s 8d, one at £15 and the residue at £20 upwards. Even so, the four wealthiest brewers, assessed at over £30 each accounted for 63.7 per cent of the combined wealth of their occupation. Among shipwrights, a much poorer occupation, the situation was much the same, with two men assessed at over £10 each, jointly accounting for 55.2 per cent of the combined wealth of Rye's shipwrights.

The most striking degree of concentration of wealth in the hands of one or two members of a particular occupation, however, occurred among the butchers. Here two men, each worth over

£40, accounted for 74.1 per cent of the combined wealth of their trade. Rye's butchers, like the town's bakers were divided between rich and poor, with five butchers assessed at £2 10s and under. Among the bakers, five were worth £10 and over accounting for 85.5 per cent of the combined wealth of this occupation. At the other extreme, four bakers were assessed at only £2 and two at £1, making them among the poorest of Rye's inhabitants. The contrast between rich and poor in the food and drink trades could not be greater.

Thus far the emphasis has been on primary occupations. However, there is sufficent evidence to indicate a degree of secondary trading among particular occupational groups. The assembly books, for example, record the protests of the bakers against the brewers in 1566 and again in 1575 for baking without having been apprenticed to the trade. Despite fines on offenders and the issuing of prohibitions, the practice seems to have continued.[9] Both occupations were reliant on the same raw material, grain, so the blurring of the boundaries of demarcation is understandable. A similar situation endured among those engaged in trade in cloth. In April 1575, John Dowce, a capper, successfully complained to the corporation about the activities of the town's mercers, who were thenceforth forbidden to make or retail caps. A month later the mercers complained of the tailors for retailing goods pertaining to mercery who were similarly forbidden to sell such goods.[10]

There was also an inevitable element of diversification of economic activity among the urban elite. John Mercer, brewer, engaged in mercantile activities, describing himself as a merchant in 1575. William Ratliff, tailor, had also acquired a vintner's licence by 1575. A number of land-based traders acquired shares in the ownership of merchant ships, including three shipwrights; John Fagge, butcher; William Didsbury and William Bragden, merchants; Thomas Edolphe, Gent; and Francis Christmas, innholder.[11] One occupation which particularly lent itself to the nature of a secondary employment was the keeping of inns and victualling houses. Altogether 36 keepers of tippling houses were licensed in December 1575, all but one (widow Fisher) appearing on the 1576 sesse. Of these, six were merchants, four were feters, there were two cordwainers, two vintners, two widows, a lighterman, a fletcher, a tailor, a baker, a shipwright, a tapster, a chandler, a painter, a rippier and a mariner, making a total of 26. The residue either styled themselves innholders/innkeepers (4) or had no other known occupation.[12]

Many of those who worked in the town were, however, not independent traders and craftsmen, but were employed for a fixed term as journeymen or covenant servants, or as casual labourers by the day. An assembly decree in September 1561 forbade young umarried men from setting up shop as independent traders or craftsmen 'because it is a great hindrance to such as be charged with household', and in March 1583 John Ravin a tailor from Great Yarmouth, presumably young and unmarried, 'who workith for him self contrary to the statute' was ordered to complete his work within a fortnight and depart the town 'excepte he serve as a jorny man or covenant servant'.[13] In addition there were numerous apprentices (the assembly books list 448 apprenticeship indentures between 1562 and 1602, rather more than an average of ten each year, which at a usual term of 7 years suggests the presence of at least 70 indentured apprentices in the town at any one time, together with many others, no doubt, whose apprenticeships are not recorded). In September 1576, for example, 43 boys went with the fishing fleet to Yarmouth, yet few, if any, of them were indentured apprentices.[14]

Then there were those engaged in maritime commerce—a total of 168 men (not including masters) and 10 boys according to the 1580 survey of Rye shipping, only a few of whom can have been part-owners of these larger vessels in which they sailed.[15] The Rye chamberlains' accounts also reveal that many of those engaged in the woodworking and building trades were employees of master craftsmen. Between September and December 1575, for example, the accounts record payments to Roger Hever, sawyer 'and his man', to John Pye, carpenter, 'and his man' to 'John Stonham's ij men' and to Robert Berde, mason and John Clere 'his laborer' for their work repairing town property.[16] At the opposite end of the social scale, many of the wealthier inhabitants employed a maidservant and a boy, and sometimes a manservant, while occupations such as brewing had the appearance almost of a small factory. A series of depositions in a debt case reveals, for instance, that John Mercer in 1572 employed a minimum of four people in his brewing business: two servants, a chief brewer and a clerk.[17]

Table 26
Rye wage rates of urban workers 6 June 1563 (reissued 22 April 1566)

	Foreman taking charge[1]		Journeyman[2]	
	With meat and drink	Without meat and drink	With meat and drink	Without meat and drink
Artificers by the year:				
Baker, brewer	£4	£4 6 8d	53s 4d	£3
Dier, currier	£3 6s 8d	£3 13 6d	40s	46s 8d
Shoemaker, glover, sadler	53s 4d	£3	40s	46s 9d
Hosier, tailor	53s 4d	£3	40s	46s 8d
Blacksmith, cutler	53s 4d	£3	40s	46s 8d
Corn miller	53s 4d	£3	40s	46s 8d
Tanner, pewterer	50s	£3	40s	46s 8d
Butcher, bowyer, fletcher	50s	56s 8d	40s	46s 8d
Arrowheadmaker, cook	50s	56s 8d	40s	46s 8d
Wheelwright, cooper	50s	56s 8d	40s	46s 8d [3]
Hatter, capper	46s 8d	53s 4d	36s 8d	40s
Clothier, clothworker	40s	50s	33s 4d	40s
Weaver, tucker, fuller, sherman	40s	50s	33s 4d	40s
Spurrier, turner	40s	46s 8d	30s	36s 8d
Lime burner, earthen potter	40s	46s 8d	30s	36s 8d
Women servants	—	26s 8d	—	20s
Boys, 14 to 18 years (quarterly)	6d	20s[4]		

	Chief sort		Second sort	
	With meat and drink	Without meat and drink	With meat and drink	Without meat and drink
Labourers by the day:				
Carpenter and wheelwright	7d	12d	5d	9d
			4d	8d
Bricklayer, tiler and sawyer				
* Easter—Michaelmas	6d	10d	5d	9d
Winter season	5d	9d	4d	8d
Freemason summer	8d	12d	—	—
Freemason winter	6d	10d	—	—
Glasier	6d	10d	—	—
Joiner and carver summer	7d	12d	5d	10d
Joiner and carver winter	6d	11d	4d	9d
Shipwrights master hewer	13d	18d	8d	12d
Shipwrights able clincher	10d	15d	8d	12d
Shipwrights holder	6d	10d	—	—
Shipwrights master caulker	12d	18d	8d	12d
Shipwrights apprentice	4d	5d	—	—
Thatcher	—	6d	—	4d
Plasterer summer	6d	11d	—	—
Plasterer winter	5d	10d	—	—
Artificer apprentice summer	4d	7d	—	—
Artificer apprentice winter	3d	6d	—	—
Labourers Easter—Michaelmas	5d	10d	—	—
Labourers Michaelmas—Easter	3d	8d	—	—
Plumber laying and carting 1cwt	8d	13d	—	—
Sawyers for 100 of borde	—	20d	—	—
Sawyers for shitting wurke the 100	—	22d	—	
Thatchers by the 100	10d	20d	—	—
Brickmaker by the 1000 with digging the earth. making, striking and turning, having all other necessaries brought to him	—	2s	—	—

Notes: [1] corn miller: 'loder and grinder'; lime burner, earthen potter, women servants: 'best sort'.
[2] Cornmiller, wheelwright and cooper, lime burner, earthen potter, women servants: 'second sort'.
[3] 16s 8d
[4] without food?

Source: RYE 1/3/208-12.

The survival of a set of wage rates issued by the corporation under the provisions of the Statute of Labourers and Artificers in 1563, set out in Table 26 for urban occupations, enables some comparison to be made between the respective prosperity of different groups of employees. Under the terms of the Act, county justices and borough corporations were to fix annually the maximum levels of wages of artificers, labourers and other servants, having regard to the prevailing level of prices in their locality. The Rye rates are somewhat high, due, according to the preamble issued by the corporation, 'in that all thinges in the same Towne and liberties be more excedinge dere then in any Town in the Countie of Sussex Adioyninge'.[18]

In the table of rates a clear distinction is made between the more skilled 'artificers by the year' and day labourers, whose situation was more precarious. In the former category, baking and brewing appear to have provided the highest levels of financial reward, followed by the leatherworking, metalworking and clothing trades. Among the building and woodworking trades, only the realtively specialist wheelwrights and coopers, spurriers and turners, lime burners and earthen potters are listed among those paid by the year, and these are at the lower end of the scale. The remainder of these trades: carpenters, sawyers, joiners, carvers and the more specialist shipwrights were paid by the day, the shipwrights (master hewers, master caulkers and able clinchers) being consideraby better paid than other building workers. At the bottom of the wages league were the unskilled labourers, who were, however, only marginally worse off than plasterers, bricklayers, tilers or sawyers.

Unfortunately, comparable wage rates for Sussex do not survive. However, a comparison with those issued for the county of Kent in the same year confirms that Rye wages were high, with labourers up by 1d a day, as were master hewers among the shipwrights. Master caulkers were up by 2d compared to Kent. Most of the servants to artificers, paid by the year, were also up: brewers and bakers by £1 for foremen and 6s 8d for journeymen; cutlers, blacksmiths, saddlers, turners, butchers, corn millers and many others by lesser amounts. In only a few instances were wages lower in Rye than in Kent: clothiers, weavers, fullers, glovers and shearmen were all down, but few, if any, of these trades operated in Rye.[19]

Wage levels in Rye were in fact more comparable to those in Lydd, a neighbouring Kentish Cinque Port. There, the wages laid down for shipwrights, bakers, brewers etc. were broadly similar to those in Rye. The Lydd rates are also useful in that they include two groups important to Rye's economy which do not appear to have been included in the latter return: common servants to fishermen and rippiers. In Lydd a fisherman's servant, with his sea-boots, fell and other apparel might earn 30s, and without apparel 53s 4d, placing him at the bottom of the wages scale; a rippier's servant could earn 53s 4d.[20]

Actual wages paid to labourers and artificers varied, as can be seen from the various contracts of employment between covenant servants and their masters entered in the Rye assembly books, of which 39 detail the amount of wages to be paid, usually for one year's service following completion of an apprenticeship. Maid-servants, usually young women in their late teens or early twenties were among the poorest paid. Elizabeth Robinson, aged 11, a poor child, was apprenticed in September 1585 until the age of 18 to Edward Beale, fisherman, and his wife, thereafter to serve him for a further five years as a maidservant at 20s a year. Only slightly better off was Susan Morell who in January 1585 entered service for six years as a covenant maidservant to William Thorpe, linendraper, and his wife in 'seamestry worke' for 26s 8d a year.[21] Another poorly-paid occupation was that of bricklayer, in which John Welles of Fulham agreed to serve Philip Maynerd, bricklayer, for a year for 26s 8d from October 1567. A similar rate of pay was agreed between an apprentice shearman and his master in 1578 for his year's covenant service, as also between an apprentice tailor and his master in 1569, although in the case of tailors there might be other benefits to be considered. George Amere, for example, at the end of his term as apprentice to Robert Daniell, tailor and woollen draper, agreed in March 1577 to serve for a further year from the following August as a covenant servant for 20s plus 'one coate, two dobletes, one paier hoose, a paier of breches, one hatt, one shirt with bandes and roffes (and) a paier of shoes, good and decent for suche a servant'. Tailors were, nevertheless among the poorer paid; another apprentice agreed in 1593 to serve his master at the end of his eight-year term for one year for only 40s.[22]

In the case of carpenters, there is strong evidence of the

156

relationship between the level of wages offered and the skills of a covenant servant. In November 1585, for example, John Hamon, carpenter, took on three covenant servants: Richard Deane, sawyer, for one year at £5 plus a new whipsaw worth 10s; George Smith, sawyer, for one year at £3 plus a bonus of 6s 8d should he prove a diligent workman; and a younger man, John Butcher, aged 18 for three years at 40s a year with a similar bonus of 6s 8d at the end of his term. Another carpenter, Richard Dove, agreed to serve his master, John Pye, for five years at 42s a year for the first four years and 50s in the last year.[23]

Other occupations represented included a cooper (40s in 1567); a joiner (£3 in 1594); a shoemaker (50s in 1567); two mercers (20s in 1579 and 50s for two years in 1583); and among the food and drink trades, a brewer (40s in 1567), two bakers (50s in 1593, £3 in 1594) and three butchers (50s in 1569, £3 in 1570 and 5 marks in 1588). Almost half of these agreements related to fishermen or mariners. In the former case twelve fishermen agreed to wages as covenant servants ranging from 46s 8d in 1567 to £3 13s 4d in 1588, although the norm appeared to be 53s 4d in the 1560s and £3 in the 1570s and 1580s. Again there is evidence of wages rising with experience and length of service. In 1585, for example, Thomas Raynold agreed to serve John Frauncis, fisherman, as his covenant servant, for three years at £3 a year for the first two and £3 6s 8d for the third. Similarly William Androes agreed to serve John Osborne, fisherman, for three years from March 1594 at 40s, 50s and 60s respectively for each year's service.

In the 1590s, with the town's economy in decline, wages appear to have been depressed. John Baker, apprenticed to William Belveridge for six years in February 1595 was also only offered 50s for his covenant year. Even so, on these figures fishermen, somewhat surprisingly, appear among the better-off covenant servants, certainly up to the early 1590s, and in addition to their basic wages, they were also entitled to certain traditional rights, both as apprentices and covenant servants, as in the case of William Androes, whose indenture specified 'halfe his fyndells and halfe his sole money at Trammell fayre'. Only mariners engaged in merchant voyages appear to have been better paid. Three received £4 between 1578 and 1593, although by 1595 this sum seems to have fallen again to £3, and William Parker, whose terms of service to William Harman, mariner, included that he should be instructed in the occupation, agreed in 1588 to serve his master for four years for double apparel and 40s at the end of the first three years and 40s more at the end of the fourth.[24]

Most mariners were, however, probably hired for the voyage. Details of their wages during this period are, inevitably, rare. however, the accounts for the setting forth of a number of Rye ships for military service, have survived, providing evidence of the wages paid to the different members of ships' crews during the Tudor period. These are set out in Table 27. Allowing for the fact that most mariners probably spent as much as one third or one half of their working lives ashore, the rates of pay for ordinary

Table 27

Wages paid to the crews of Rye ships 1544-1596

	1544 James Pottem's boat (weekly)		1558 The Saviour 50 tons (weekly)		1588 The William (monthly)		1596 The Hercules 150 tons (monthly)	
Captain		-		-		50s		66s 8d
Master		3s 6d		5s		40s		40s
Master's mate		3s 6d		2s 6d[1]		30s		25s
Pilot		-		-		29s 6d		25s
Quartermaster		-		-		-	(4)	17s
Master gunner		-		2s 10d		17s		17s 4d
His mate		-		-		12s 6d	(2)	14s
Quarter gunner		-		-		-	(4)	12s
Boatswain		-		2s 8d		22s		17s 4d
His mate		-		-		-	(2)	13s 4d
Surgeon		-		-		11s 6d[2]		20s
Trumpeter		-		1s 8d		-		20s
Steward		-		-		17s		13s 4d
His mate		-		-		12s 10d		-
Cook		-		-		12s 10d		13s 4d
His mate		-		-		9s 6d		-
Swabber		-		-		-		13s 4d
Mariner	(10)	1s 9d	(11)[3]	1s 8d	(30)[4]	9s 6d	(27)	10s
Boy		10½d	(2)	10d	(7)	5s		-
Purser		-		1s 8d		-		-
Ship's carpenter		-		1s 8d		14s 6d		-
His mate		-		-		12s 10d		-
Total crew	(13)	-	(20)		(51)		(50)	
Victuals per man		1s 8d		1s 6d[5]		-		18s

Source: RYE 60/6/72; RYE 60/7/108v; RYE 72/1; Kent Archives Office, CP/Br 5,3.
Notes:
1 William Hasillden, Master's mate and steward.
2 Part payment only.
3 10 mariners paid 1s 8d, one paid 1s 9d.
4 19 mariners paid 9s 6d, 3 paid 10s, 2 paid 7s 6d, 2 paid 3s 6d, 1 paid 14s 4d, 1 paid 12s, 1 paid 11s, 1 paid 3s 4d.
5 estimate to nearest 1d.

158

mariners appear to have been roughly in line with the amounts paid to covenant servants. Although inflation doubled wages between 1544 and 1588, the much greater rise in the cost of victuals (mainly bread or ship's biscuit, salt beef, butter, cheese, stock fish and beer) meant that whereas in 1544 the cost of hiring an ordinary mariner and of providing his victuals were roughly comparable, by the end of the sixteenth century the cost of feeding him (just over 7d a day), was considerably greater than his hire (approximately 4d a day).[25]

Such evidence is inevitably impressionistic. Nevertheless it is clear that in the Elizabethan period, at least, the wages of most servants of artificers and craftsmen range from 26s 8d a year for maidservants, bricklayers and suchlike to perhaps £3 or £4 for fishermen and mariners, with the leather, clothing and food and drink trades in the middle range, between £2 and £3 a year, depending on such variable factors as the skill and experience of the workman and with a general tendency for wages to rise between the 1560s and the 1580s, followed by a fall in the early 1590s. Since covenant servants lived in and had their food, drink, lodging and washing provided in addition to their wages, these wage levels are not inconsiderable, especially as the cost of providing food and drink alone must often have amounted to not far short of the wages themselves, which as Table 26 indicates, were, in the mid-1560s, 4d or 5d a day. Those who were married, renting a house or tenement, who had the responsibilty of providing for their families, would have needed to have earned proportionately more, simply in order to have been able to provide the basic necessities for their wives and children. Labourers and those paid by the day, must have been extremely vulnerable to fluctuations in the level of trade.

At the lower end of the social scale, three men, possibly maimed in the town's service, were granted annuities of 40s a year for six years in September 1562. Slightly higher up the social scale, Jheram Nashe received £4 for trimming the town's ordnance in 1564 and his successor John Prowze £6 13s 4d a year for life from 1579. John Roberts the sexton received £5 a year in 1581 and a plumber hired in 1564 to maintain the town's water supply received £4 a year plus 12d a day for major repair work. Towards the top of the wages league, Philip Symondson, a surveyor, received £5 in 1594 for his map of Rye and the surrounding area, 'whereby the harbour may be amended'; and Mr. Grenewood, the town preacher, was paid 20 marks (£13 6s 8d) in 1593, his predecessor, Mr. Richard Fletcher, having received a stipend of £10 as the town's minister in the late 1570s.[26]

Out of their wages, however, journeymen and covenant servants were expected to provide and maintain their own tools and working apparel, a set of which was initially provided by their masters at the completion of their apprenticeship. Such equipment could prove extremely costly to replace. Among the more specialist working gear was that needed by those engaged in maritime pursuits. John Wood, mariner, estimated the value of the contents of his seaman's chest, lost by the negligence of Ralph Hawle, master of the Ellin of Rye in March 1568 at just under £5, made up of the value of the chest itself (13s 4d), two pairs of mariner's breeches (30s), two shirts (16s), a fryse jerkin (3s 4d), a canvas doublet (2s 4d), two pairs of short hose (5s), a pair of boots (4s), a red cap (2s 6d), three pairs of new shoes (3s), two 'cards for the sea' and two pairs of compasses (20s)[27] the total cost of replacement of all these items must have been as much as a year's wages.

Apart from such occasional detailed inventories of working gear, many of the apprenticeship indentures found in the Rye assembly books list the journeyman's tools to be provided at the completion of a young man's apprenticeship. Among mariners the provision of the necessary clothing plus 'a mappe for the sea and a paier of compasses' seems to have been the norm. Among fishermen it was usual to provide a new tramell net, an oar, a barrell, a vennett, four new lines and four old lines 'of one winter's wear', together with the necessary apparel. The most expensive item of a fisherman's equipment was clearly his nets. According to the apprenticeship indenture of John Dawson to Robert Wyllison in 1579, which gave the option of a new trammell net or the cash, such a net was worth 40s. Earlier, in 1548, John Potten had left his son Thomas 'a manfayre of flewes' (flewe nets) with 'a warrappe' worth four gold angels (26s 8d). Next, in terms of expense, came a fisherman's apparel. Thomas Townesend, apprenticed to Robert Beale in 1585 was promised at the end of his nine-year term at 'the Yermouth voyage next before thend of the said ix yeris or els at thend of thoes yeris a newe paier of bootes, a paier of newe lethern breches and a paier of newe letherne sleves'. [28]

Among the land-based crafts, and in particular the woodworking and building trades, a journeyman's tools were a much less major item of expenditure. A cooper might expect to have to provide an axe, an adze and a 'hedding' knife; a feter would need a hatchet, a sledge, a wimble, and a knife; a fletcher might need as many as six shaves, a plane, a paring knife and a 'thwytinge' knife. A shipwright's tools were rather more considerable. An apprenticeship indenture in 1564 specified an axe, an adze, a sledge, a clench hammer, a clean hammer, a handsaw, an auger and a wimble.[29] None of the apprenticeship indentures of carpenters mention tools, so it may be that these were usually provided by the master. A detailed inventory of the goods of John Jenevere detained by Henry Byler for debt in June 1580 indicates the range of specialist tools which might be owned by a master craftsman.[30]

> In primis x gonstockes
> It one caliver
> Itm ix Rampses
> Itm a vile
> Itm a morrice sawe
> Itm a France sawe
> Itm a Cloke
> a dublett
> a paire of hose
> a shirt
> a bond and Ruffes
> xvi Loges of plumtree
> xlti peces of Walnottree
> vi Carvinge tolles
> ii paire of Compasses
> a booke
> x panters
> vi plaines
> a strekinge square
> a trienge square
> ii gages
> iii wimbles
> a chissell
> a hammer
> a Robbinge stone
> a Wodden vice
> 4 knifes
> 2 tolles to Kot bone
> iii pecys of blakwod.

In occupations such as those of mercer, or draper, tools were at a minimum. Here the need was more for capital for the purchase of stock. It is therefore not surprising that these professions numbered among them many of the wealthier inhabitants in Rye. Indeed, the Statute of Labourers and Artificers forbade the taking on of apprentices into such occupations except their own sons unless the parents of the boy had freehold land worth a minimum of 40s a year. Those apprenticed to mercers in Rye included James Appleton, son of the town clerk, who in 1585, aged 17, bound himself for seven years to William Didsbury, jurat, at the end of which term he was to receive the relatively large sum of £5. Another occupation which appears to have been restricted to the wealthier sort was that of brasier, to which James Etuere, aged 17, son of a London merchant, apprenticed himself in February 1582. At the completion of his term his master, John Scrugham, was to give him 'a rasinge studdy, a burbeatinge studdy, a paier of sheres, a rasinge hammer, one other hammer, a plainshinge studdy, a fyle, a paier of compasses, a paier of pliers and a clement' all tools pertaining to that occupation, together with double apparel and £6.[31]

Another occupation which was similarly largely restricted to the wealthier sort because of the initial outlay for essential equipment was that of beerbrewer. In 1551 it cost John Colbrand £56 to purchase his brewery from Thomas Birchett. A summary of the equipment which went with the buildings easily explains the cost.[32]

> one great fornes of Copper
> thre bruing tonnes
> ii Colbackes
> x last of barrelles
> tow long settilles
> a horsemill
> a carte
> vi geldinges
> iii urking ketilles
> iii sesternes of leade
> (whereof the one standith in the malt
> howse the other in the brew howse)

A generation later, in 1585 Thomas Heblethwaite leased his brewery on the north side of the Lower Street in Strandgate ward, which had formerly belonged to Robert Jackson, for one

year to John Duron for 8s a week plus a kilderkine of $1\frac{1}{2}$d beer, a
pin of double beer and three gallons of yeast (or four if he were to
brew twice in one week) plus two half tubs full of coals from the
furnace and two swaddes of grains from every brewing—
amounting to an annual rental of more than £20 plus payments in
kind. The size of the operation is indicated by the description in
the lease itself:

> 'A Brewhouse, Malthouse, Malt mill, three malte loftes and a
> chamber belonging to one of them, also a malte byn, the
> fyrkynhouse, Cowpers house, hoppehouse and stable under
> the hoppehouse together with half the backside... to lay his
> wood and other necessary things with right of entry at the
> Budgegate to the foresaid half of the backside and to the
> stable, cowpers house and hoppehouse with men, carts, horse
> and carriages between the hours of four in the morning and
> nine o'clock at night ...[33]

Only the larger merchant ships constituted a greater capital
outlay. Peter Keling's 60 ton Blessing of God, was sold to the
corporation for £200 in September 1587 to do service against the
threat of Spanish invasion and re-sold to William French for
£108 in January 1595 having meanwhile been put to freight at the
town's own charges. During that time it netted more than £280
profit for the town, an indication of the high profits open to
shipowners. The town's pinnace, built in 1587–8 cost just over
£53 to complete; Peter Phillippson's hoye of Flushing was
apprised at £27 in May 1569, when it was sold to Robert Welles;
John Welles' barke was sold for £30 10s to Richard Portriffe in
October 1594 after Welles had hanged himself; and John House's
share in his barke, sold on his death from plague in February 1581
was £26. It would seem, then, that in the latter half of the
sixteenth century for which these figures are available, a smaller,
older, merchant vessel might be obtained for about £30, while
newer and larger vessels could cost considerably more.[34]

Unfortunately no such figures for the average-sized fishing boat
(14-20 tons) survive for Rye, although a 6-ton boat belonging to
John Engram, stolen by two Frenchmen and sold at Quilleboeuf
was valued at £24 in April 1575 and a 'small bote' bought by
Martin Havard from John Belveridge in April 1575 cost £9. At
the bottom end of the scale, a cockboat belonging to John House
was sold for £4 5s in February 1581 and a 'little cockeboat' for
35s.[35]

The distinction between fishing and merchant vessels, particularly in the 20–30 ton range is somewhat arbitrary, and there is some evidence that at least a few vessels might be used as either. Among a list of 20 masters of merchant ships from Rye in 1580, at least three, Markes Sergeant, Thomas Stride and John Sawnders took part in the Yarmouth voyage in that and previous years. The Yarmouth voyage may well have demanded larger vessels and may therefore be an exception. What is perhaps more significant is that of 65 masters whose names appear in lists of Rye merchant ships for 1565, 1572, and 1580, only 22 appear among the annual lists of fishing masters in the assembly books and the chamberlains' and churchwardens' accounts for the period 1560–80. Of these, only three, John Belveridge, John Bull and Robert Holnes took part regularly in anything other than the annual Yarmouth voyage, and of those taking part in the latter, three went to Yarmouth only once and a further two others, William Fyrrall (eight times between 1561 and 1569) and John Fawcett (twice, in 1560 and 1562) had ceased to appear among the masters of fishing vessels more than ten years before their inclusion on the 1580 list as masters of merchant ships. Apart from the occasional Yarmouth voyage, the evidence, perhaps surprisingly, suggests that there was little overlapping between the Rye fishermen and those engaged in seaborne commerce.[36]

Among the fishermen themselves there was a definite division between those masters who went on the annual Yarmouth and Scarborough voyages and those who fished the home waters. An analysis of 191 fishing masters who appeared in the Rye churchwardens' and chamberlains' accounts for the same period paying duty on their catch revealed that no less than 58 names occurred only once. Of the remaining 133, slightly more than half (78) went to Yarmouth at least twice, 95 went once and 38 never went to Yarmouth at all. These latter were almost entirely coastal tramellers and flewers (37) although there was one hookman who had also been to Scarborough. Of the 95 who had been to Yarmouth, 16 took part in no other fishing seasons and another one went only to Yarmouth and Scarborough. A further 24 went predominantly to Yarmouth and took part only rarely in coastal fishing, while 21 were regular coastal fishermen who participated only once or twice in the Yarmouth voyage. The remaining 33 participated fairly equally in both coastal and deep sea fishing.[37]

The scale of Rye's fishing activity can be seen in the tables of masters and men engaged in fishing in Appendix 5. The assertion in Rye's draft parliamentary bill for the restoration of the harbour in 1624 that the town had of late 'furnished to sea thirtie fisherboats and upwards, manned with above fower hundred men and youth' was little exaggeration. Between 1575 and 1595 an average of 25 fishing boats and 324 men and boys went on the annual Yarmouth voyage, the largest number, 407, in 1579. By the end of the sixteenth century, numbers had fallen to an average of only 19 boats and 250 men and boys. Earlier in the century the numbers had been even greater. In September 1554 41 fishing vessels made the voyage to Yarmouth and in the following June the same number went to Scarborough with perhaps as many as 500 crew. Allowing for the fact that between a third and a quarter of those fishing masters who went regularly to Yarmouth did not go in a particular year, and that, according to the 1565 and later surveys of Rye shipping at least 150 mariners were engaged in merchant trading, the total numbers of fishermen and other mariners in the town in the middle years of the sixteenth century, was probably nearer to 700 than 500. This figure agrees well with the 725 (including 225 fishermen householders) given in the 1565 survey, particularly as the numbers of fishing vessels engaged in coastal and deep sea fishing in that year show a falling off of almost a third from the peak years of the mid 1550s.[38]

Gilds and the growth of protectionism

The Rye fishermen and mariners, like a number of other occupations in the town were organised into a gild or company. The earliest reference to this body in the assembly books was 14 April 1567 when, it is recorded, the fishermen's agreements and constitutions were confirmed and sealed with the common seal of the town, the seamen having assembled for the purpose of agreeing a series of regulations for their company, including the times of fishing and for boats to issue and return and the size of nets, on 29 March. Under these regulations, the seamen were to assemble each Easter Monday for the purpose of electing four wardens to govern their affairs, and a petition to the corporation shortly after, calling for a new timber jetty on the west side of the haven for the protection of their vessels from storms, subscribed by Thomas Chesewell, Davy Hatchet, Thomas Noven, and Mr

Fowler, wardens of the seamen, and 30 others shows that the company took an active role in prosecuting the fishermen's interests.[39]

The Rye Company or Fellowship of Fishermen had evidently been under consideration for some time prior to its foundation. Richard Hillis, jurat, a fisherman, whose will was proved in March 1566, left 20s to the fellowship 'if they go through with it'. As with similar organisations elsewhere, the company had a charitable as well as a regulatory function. Among others who left sums of money to it for the benefit of the poor were a number of jurats. John Cheston (1573) and John Julyan (1574) left 20s each and George Raynoldes (1577) left 40s to the Wardens of the Company of Fishermen in Rye 'to be bestowed amongest the poore people of ther company'. The company also acquired a piece of land from the corporation in July 1573, 54ft in length, underneath the town wall at the Strand, for the fishermen to lay their masts. By the early 1580s however, with many of the signatories to the original regulations dead and many others having come into the town who were not bound by the agreements, the company appears to have fallen into disorder. An attempt was therefore made to obtain letters patent to the then wardens, Edward Beale, Thomas Chiswell, William Coxson and Robert Bett, and twenty other fishing masters henceforth to be known as the elder brethren to reform the 'Brotherhood of Seamen' and to take possession of its lands. The wardens and elder brothers were in turn to choose eight younger brothers from the rest of the fishermen to be assistant to them in the making of new statutes among the seamen to govern their trade. They were also to purchase or hire a hall as a Seamen's Hall, to have power to order recalcitrant members to ward, to maintain a light on Fairlight Point and to erect another at Camber Castle, and were to provide relief for their poorer brethren levying the necessary charges among their company. An attempt to obtain a royal charter for this new company having failed because of the opposition of the corporation, a new set of articles for the Company of Seamen was confirmed by the Rye assembly in March 1583.[40]

Other occupations which were organised into gilds or companies along similar lines were the tailors and drapers (1571), the mercers (1575) and the cordwainers or shoemakers (1576). The tailors paid 40s a year to the corporation for their grant and the mercers £4, the mercers' last recorded payment being in the chamberlains' accounts for 1579/80, and the tailors', in 1580/1.[41] These companies were primarily restrictive in nature. Thus in July 1577 the Company and Fellowship of Drapers and Tailors complained to the corporation that notwithstanding their grant 'that none shold occupye or exercies any of the said mysterye or occupacion either of wollen draper or tayllere within the said towne other then such as hade ether bene aprintice within the same with some one of the said company, or being freborne, but that the said personne shold fyerst make gree with the said company apon a certayne payne for every day occupinge as in the said grant is specifyed ... thier is at this present dyveres which have interpreted to sett uppe and exercise ye said occupacion ... withowt any agrement made ... to the utter undoinge of dyvers pour inhabitantes of this towne of the said company ...'[42]

The Company or Fellowship of Cordwainers or Shoemakers was equally protectionist in origin, resulting from competition to established householders from newcomers to the town, both English and French. They therefore secured a grant of a fellowship or company with a master and two wardens with the power to regulate the trade in the same way as the tailors and mercers. The mercers themselves sought to obtain their grant as a result of competition from the tailors who were retailing 'velvet, silkis, whit clothe, canvas for doblettinges, moccadoes, chambletes, buttons, lace, soinge silke, fringe (and threde),' all things 'perteyninge to the Mercers or Chapmens trade'. Their grant likewise specified that they should elect a master and two wardens at Michaelmas with the power to make ordinances to govern their trade and with the power to search out those occupying the same, assisted by the sergeant-at-mace, warning those found to desist until they made composition with the company, on pain of a 40s fine for each day's resistance.[43]

Such organisations were part of a wider protectionist attitude. In April 1575, John Dowce, capper, secured a decree aimed chiefly against the mercers, that no-one should make or sell caps unless brought up in the trade. In September, the town's bakers secured a similar decree against the brewers baking bread, although Robert Jackson, brewer, made his opposition clear and engaged the support of the Lord Warden to ensure at least a

167

temporary reprieve. Finally, in November of the same year, the smiths, cutlers and tinkers complained to the assembly that foreigners were taking away their livelihood by using their occupation in the town.[44]

The mid-1570s saw a crisis in living standards for many occupations in Rye with the effects of a stagnating urban economy coupled with a sudden large influx of highly skilled French Protestant artisans. In such a situation, restrictive measures were seen as essential to maintain the incomes of existing householders. Underlying each measure was a fear of the poverty which might ensue unless entry to many of these occupations was rigidly controlled. An indication of this type of thinking was the explanation given by the corporation for acceding to 'the pytifull complainte' of the bakers, since:

> 'it manifestly apperith that the bakinge of breade and bisket by the brewers of the same towne, who have not ben lawfully traynid upe to the occupacion of bakinge is and leike to be the utter overthrowe and impoverishinge of the saide bakers, their wyves and children, a thinge to be foresene, sith they are divers householdes ... and are to lyve by their trade and callinge. And sith not only the statutes of this Realme, dothe order that the subjectes in the same shuld lyve by that they have lawfully bin brought upe in, but also in all good orderid Cities and townes it is seldome senne that the brewers are also bakers, two sondry sciences and eche a sufficient lyvinge ...'[45]

Attitudes such as these were neither new nor confined to towns such as Rye. The Statute of Artificers and Labourers restricted the use of 'any Arte, Mysterye or Manuell Occupacion' from May 1563 onwards, to those who had served at least a seven years' apprenticeship on pain of a 40s fine per month, a prohibition which was only selectively enforced in Rye. Thus although a baker and fifteen tallow chandlers were dismissed from their occupations in 1566 and a further two bakers in 1567, for trading having not been apprenticed, by the 1570s such offences were clearly regarded as of minor concern, the same names appearing in consecutive years in the hundred presentments, and incurring only a small fine which amounted to little more than a licence to continue trading. In April 1583 for example, seven mercers and a tailor were fined amounts varying from 6d to 10s for occupying trades to which they had not been apprenticed. Six of the mercers compounded with the corporation, agreeing to pay amounts varying between 4s and 13s 4d yearly to continue.[46]

Some occupations had long been the subject of controls. Osts had to buy their 'hepe' of ostage, an entry fine payable to the chamberlain, usually 6s 8d throughout much of Henry VII's and Henry VIII's reigns rising to as much as 16s as a result of the inflation of the mid-sixteenth century. Tailors too, in the early years of Henry VIII's reign paid a special fine of 6s 8d for setting up shop.[47] The number of bakers and brewers was regulated by the granting of licences upon payment of quarterages related to the size of the operation. Victualling houses were likewise regulated by annual licensing and in April 1574 there was a short-lived attempt to restrict them to 26 at the request of the existing tipplers who agreed to pay the full £26 6s 8d yearly which had previously been paid by the town's alehouses.[48]

Trends in wages and prices

Baking and brewing or victualling traders were among those which were regulated by the corporation which fixed the maximum prices which could be charged for bread, beer, beef, wine and other essential commodities such as billets of wood for fuel. As a result it is possible to construct a series of price indices from the early 1550s for a number of essential commodities. In the case of bread the arrangement was slightly different to other consumables with the weight of a loaf of bread of any particular type or price varying according to the prevailing price of grain. It has also been possible to construct a wages index for labourers from the payments to labourers and other building workers by the chamberlains. The results are set out in Table 28, which confirms the general rise in wages and prices in the latter half of the sixteenth century well-known to economic historians.[49]

The figures show a rise of 33⅓ per cent in wages among the poorer paid building labourers during the period. Unfortunately it has not proved possible to provide annual series for the more skilled groups of workers (sawyers, carpenters, tilers, masons and the like) although the chamberlains' accounts do indicate a roughly parallel rise in wage rates. Carpenters, for example, seem to have generally received 12d a day throughout the late 1550s and early 1560s, rising to between 12d and 14d depending on their individual skills in the 1570s, 14d to 16d in the late 1580s

Table 28:
Labourers' daily wages and maximum prices
of household goods in Rye 1553-1602

Year	Bread 2d household loaf (weight)	Beer Double beer per 1d indoors	Beef per naile (8lbs)	Candles price per lb	billets price per 1,000	French wine price per quart	Labourer's daily wages[1]
1553			6d				9d
1554	82 oz		6d				9d
1555	66 oz	1 quart	9d				9d
1556	40 oz		13d	2¼d			9d
1557	72 oz		9d				9d
1558					3s 4d		9d
1559	76 oz	1 quart					9d
1560							9d
1561	66 oz						9d
1562	66 oz			2½d			8d-10d
1563		3 pints					10d
1564		3 pints					10d
1565	76 oz						10d
1566	44 oz		10d				10d
1567	64 oz			2½d			10d
1568	64 oz			3d			10d
1569	53 oz		9d				10d
1570	56 oz						10d
1571	48 oz						10d
1572				2½d			10d
1573	43 oz		11d				10d
1574	37oz		13d	3½d			10d
1575	59½oz		13d	3½d		4d	10d
1576	50¾oz		14d	3d			10d
1577			14d	3d		4d	10d
1578	58 oz			3½d			10d
1579	58 oz						10d
1580	56 oz		11d	3½d	4s 2d		10d
1581	49 oz		13d	3d			10d
1582	43 oz		12d	3d		4d	10d
1583	49 oz		15d	3d			10d
1584	53 oz		15d				10d
1585	48 oz		12d	3d		4d	10d
1586	30⅞oz		16d	3d	5s		12d
1587	24-29 oz		16d				12d
1588	53 oz		14d	4d			12d
1589							12d
1590	48 oz						12d
1591	42 oz						12d
1592	59 oz	1 quart					12d
1593	52 oz	1 quart		4d	5s 6d		12d
1594	35 oz	1 quart	14d				12d
1595	35½oz		4d				12d
1596	25½oz			4d			12d
1597	16¾oz						12d
1598							12d
1599	32 oz						12d
1600	28½oz						12d
1601	35½oz						12d
1602	54 oz						12d

Sources: RYE 1/1-7: RYE 60/7-10; RYE 61/1-2.   *Notes:* [1]Without meat and drink.

and a uniform 16d in the late 1590s. Masons' wages rose in the same period from 12d a day in the 1570s to 13d in 1585, 14d between 1586 and 1590 and 16d in 1596–8 before falling back to 14d in 1602. The general rise in the wages of these more skilled groups was again in the region of 33⅓ per cent during the same period.

Generally speaking, the level of price rises for basic commodities seems to have been considerably greater, although the picture is complicated by sharp fluctuations due to poor harvests and temporary shortages. This was particularly the case with the price of bread, where the size of a 2d household loaf could vary quite dramatically from one harvest to another. There was, however, a steady fall in the average size of a 2d loaf throughout the period. In the 1550s, for example, the weight of such a loaf was in the range of 40–82 oz. By the 1570s this had fallen to 37–59½oz. and in the 1590s to between 16¾–59oz, with a maximum weight of 35½oz between 1594 and 1601.

Beef prices showed a similar trend, rising from a general level of 6d–9d per naile (8 lbs) in the 1550s to between 11d–14d in the 1570s and 11d–16d in the 1580s. The movement in the price of candles was similar, with ordinary wick candles rising from 2d a lb in 1556 to 2½d a lb in the 1560s, 3d–3½d a lb in the 1570s and 4d a lb in the late 1580s and 1590s. The price of household fuel rose similarly, a thousand billets costing 4s 2d in 1580, 5s in 1586 and 5s 6d in 1593.

Overall these price rises were considerably greater than the rise in wages. In the case of bread, the weight of a 2d loaf fell by more than half, from an average 68 oz in the decade 1557–66 to only 33 oz in the decade 1593–1602, equivalent to a price increase of over 100 per cent. Average beef prices rose from just over 8½d a naile in the period 1553–7 to slightly under 14d in the decade 1579–88, an increase of 60 per cent while the price of candles rose by 78 per cent between the 1550s and the 1590s.

Such averages ignore the even greater effects on real wages of sudden temporary price fluctuations, as in the period 1554–6 for example, when bread and meat prices more than doubled without any corresponding increase in daily wage rates. A similar crisis in 1585–7 led to a 20 per cent increase in daily wage rates, but this was insufficient to offset the doubling of bread prices and an increase in meat prices of at least a third. The worst crisis, however, was undoubtedly in the late 1590s, when bread prices rose to an all time high in early 1597, as a result of a succession of bad harvests culminating in the disastrous harvest of 1596, as a result of which bread prices almost doubled between September 1596 and May of the following year, representing a price increase of nearly 350 per cent since 1592 and leading to a mortality crisis in the same winter and a growing threat of social unrest.

The crisis of the 1590s was to a great extent the product of exceptional circumstances, in particular the combination of a series of poor harvests coupled with a sudden decline in the economic fortunes of the town itself. Nevertheless it is clear that in the second half of the sixteenth century as a whole, there was a progressive reduction in real wages by as much as a third, as a result of the much greater rises in commodity prices than in wages during these years, confirming the trends in wages and prices throughout the south-east discovered by Phelps Brown and Hopkins.[50] It was, however, a crisis from which Rye never recovered.

CHAPTER 5

Housing and Living Conditions

'Riches geven by God ar geuen to thonest for thincrease of
theire godlines, to the wicked for the heaping up of theire
dampnation, to the simple for the recompence of other lackes
and to the wise for the greater setting out of godes goodnes.'

(RYE, 57/4/23v)

Houses, house prices and rents

There are, in Rye today, something approaching 100 houses,
substantially, or in part, dating from the sixteenth century or
earlier. Even where these have not survived, the property
boundaries have often remained largely unaltered. The streets
themselves have kept their original directions and width, as can be
seen from surviving mediaeval and Tudor frontages. From the
tower of St. Mary's church, the discerning visitor will observe the
many ancient red tiled roof structures, characterised by their
irregular, often concave ridges, the product of timbers settling
over the centuries, and the numerous eighteenth century facades
literally stuck on to much earlier buildings. Around the churchyard and in Mermaid Street in particular, sufficient timber-
framed buildings have been preserved or restored to their former
glory to give a good impression of the houses of the more
substantial merchants and tradesmen from the end of the fifteenth
century until the close of the sixteenth century. Such properties
vary in design and size from the two-storied hall house of the late
fifteenth century and the three-bay, three-storied town house of
the Elizabethan period, to more modest two-storey, jettied
properties with much narrower street frontages which probably
originally served as shops with living accommodation above.[1]

In addition to the surviving structures, a large number of deeds and a total of some 40 partial or complete inventories of household goods, mainly the result of testamentary and debt cases in the Rye court of record survive from the Tudor period in the County Record Office and the Public Record Office, enabling a detailed reconstruction of the furnishings and fittings of sixteenth century houses representative of all but the poorest classes.[2] The household inventories range in value from 34s 6d at which sum the goods of Alice Aubons, a poor widow, who died in 1580, were assessed, to £73 2s 11d for the total value of the household goods and shop merchandise of Mistress Castleton, widow, who died in 1592. Among the occupational groups included in them is a vicar of Rye, a member of the common council, a carpenter, a tailor and a number of fishermen, small masters and mariners.[3]

House sizes themselves varied considerably, from the hall, chamber and garrett of Thomas Roben, a poor fisherman worth 35s 4d in goods on his death in 1594 to the sumptuous town house of James Pearsall, Gent, a member of the common council, deceased in 1593, with its six chambers, hall, two parlours, kitchen, cellar, stables and seven other service rooms whose very names (Lyon Chamber, Starr Chamber, Greene Chamber, etc.) help conjure up a visual image of its internal decor. This particular house was also exceptionally well-heated, with fireplaces (indicated by the presence of andirons) in the hall and both parlours (there were brass andirons in the Great Parlour), in the kitchen and Greene Chamber together with 'a joyned garth to burne coles' in 'the old chamber'.[4]

James Pearsall's house was in Market Street. A comparable property with a substantial garden in the High Street fetched £86 in 1575. One of the houses of a former mayor, Thomas Birchett, in Mermaid Street, was sold by his son for £90 in 1585, whilst a second of Birchett's houses in the same street fetched £80 when it was sold to William Didsbury, jurat, in 1586.[5] Such house prices compared with the £18 spread evenly over nine years which Richard Mayler, mariner, agreed to pay for two tenements in the Wish occupied by himself and Robert Tomson, fisherman, in 1582.[6]

A similar range of variations can be found in house rents. At the poorest end, four widows are each listed in 1594 renting lofts in the fishmarket at 6s per year from the town.[7] John Ripley, a poor man, was pardoned the 8s per year rent he owed the town for the garrett where he dwelt in 1565.[8] At the other extreme, William Ratcliff, jurat rented a messuage complete with 'sellers, solers, backsides, outhouses and gardens' in East Street to Edward Turner, baker, for 10 years at £6 per year, and Robert Wyman of Midhurst, yeoman, leased his principal messuage in the lane leading from the west side of the churchyard to Middle Street to James Millis, merchant, together with his shops at Strand for 21 years at £6 6s 8d per year.[9]

Such rents were exceptional, however, the majority falling within the range of £1 to £4 per year, such as the house in Middle Street leased by Davy Hatchard to William Appleton, town clerk, in 1582 for 21 years for £4 a year, and the tenement, possibly an inn, at the Strand, leased to Christopher Scott, innholder by Robert Jackson, jurat, for an annual rent of £4 for 7 years in 1585.[10] More modest properties fetched lower rates, such as the messuage, stable and close on the corner of the High Street and East Street leased to Anthony Coq, merchant, for 21 years in 1582 at 33s 4d per year, or the rather smaller messuage, garden and appurtenances on the south side of Watchbell Street leased to Clement Hopper, yeoman, by the town corporation in 1585 for 55 years at 23s per year.[11]

In many cases larger properties were subdivided into separate tenements, such as the messuage on the east side of the High Street which in 1589 was the subject of an agreement to partition between the two sons and coheirs of Edmund Bell, feter, deceased. At that date it was already divided into three separate occupancies: a messuage occupied by John Bannister, a shop with a garden occupied by Martin Hayward and a third part occupied by a cooper named Gillam.[12] A similar example is given by the corner messuage in the High Street, part of which ('the Hall, parlour, kitchen, sellor with chambers over them and one moietie of the Little Buttery with free egresse ...' to go through it to the kitchen, together with the whole backside and 'herbour garden' belonging) was rented by Henry Upjohn, tailor, from Nicholas White, feter, in 1582 for 10 years at £3 per year.[13] Such properties being timber-framed, it was a relatively simple operation to remove or insert partition walls or doorways to create separate or single dwellings.

It was also quite possible physically to relocate such structures. In 1582 for example, Nicolas Wolpet, mason, was granted a

175

messuage together with an orchard and garden, situated outside the Landgate, against the Town Dike for 31 years at a rent of only 18s per year on condition he remove the building which measured 37 ft by 15 ft from its original site and set it up again on another part of the garden plot away from the Town Dike, renewing timbers as necessary, tiling it and erecting within it 'a duble chymney of bricke with three fyer romes at the least'.[14]

Prior to the sixteenth century, most houses built in Rye were hall houses, without chimneys, often with open hearths into which were sometimes inserted smokebays[15] and, in the sixteenth century, timber or brick chimneys. The earliest documentary evidence for the construction of a brick chimney in Rye is in a bond of September 1504 specifying 'a chymney with lyme, sande and breke' to be erected in a property owned by Mr. John Shirley within one month of the following Easter.[16] Brick chimneys were not cheap. In December 1552 the chamberlains' accounts record payment for 10,000 bricks at 9s per thousand for the construction of the chimney in the new almshouse together with 2,000 Flemish brick at 6s per thousand 'to make the toppe of the chymney in the Almes howse', a total expenditure of £5 2s. In 1577 the will of George Raynoldes, jurat, provided £6 13s 4d towards erecting a further chimney at the almshouse with two fireplaces along the north gable head, whilst the lease already referred to between Robert Wyman and James Millis obliged the latter, within four years, 'to newe builde, erect and sett up a good and substantial chimney of bricke with two fyer roomes in the hall' in return for an annual reduction of rent of 6s 8d or 10s until the full costs of its erection had been met.[17]

Wooden chimneys were a potential major fire hazard. In 1556 four householders were fined 3s 4d each for firing their chimneys and a fifth, Paul Wymond, was fined a shilling for 'an olde, rotten chimneye in his tenemente wherein John Priclove dwellithe, to the greate daunger of the towne'. A further five persons were fined for firing their chimneys in 1574. The next set of surviving presentments, in 1578, show wooden chimneys attracting a nominal fine of 4d each. A total of thirteen individual owners of property plus the town corporation, which had three such chimneys in different tenements were listed for 22 wooden chimneys in such diverse locations as the Strand (5), outside the Landgate (3), in a lane off Watchbell Street (3), on the south side

176

of the churchyard (2), in the Lower Street (2), in the Butchery (1), at Pondgarden (1), in the Friars (1) and in Watchbell Lane (1). Amongst these the tenement in Watchbell Lane owned by John Potten's widow and occupied by mother Whyt was singled out as being 'very dangerous and the house is thatched'. Two years later, in 1580, a total of 31 property owners including the town corporation were presented for 40 wooden chimneys together with 'a frenche man dwelling in Mr. Spelstedes tenement in the Lower Streate for making a fier against a waule joynyng to Skynner, indaungeryng the howse therby if no redress be had'. Later presentments, in 1583 listed only six persons with wooden chimneys including two whose chimneys had caught fire who were fined 6s each and in 1586 five persons for seven wooden chimneys, perhaps indicating either a reduction in the numbers of such structures, or, alternatively a reduction in concern about them on the part of the town authorities.[18]

In addition to the fire-risk caused by wooden chimneys, another major concern of the town corporation in this connection was the prevalence of thatched roofs in the town. As early as 1561 the assembly moved to prohibit the renewal of any thatch once it had been taken down from any house within the town or within 200 feet of the walls on pain of a 3s 4d fine. Three years later this decree was reinforced by an additional prohibition on any thatcher laying any thatch within the town or within 200 feet of its walls on pain of a 20d fine. However, the presentments of 1578 indicate how long a policy based on renewal and replacement might take, so every opportunity was taken in the letting of property to speed up the process by the making of appropriate conditions, as in 1587 for example when it was made a condition of Thomas Heblethwaite's lease of a number of church houses that the thatch be taken off and replaced with tiles and that suitable improvements be made to the oven in one of them so that the danger of fire might be avoided.[19]

Apart from the insertion of chimneys, the sixteenth century saw other major improvements in the structure of houses in an attempt to improve heating and comfort; in particular the fixing of wainscot panelling on the walls and the insertion of glass windows to replace the diamond mullioned unglased windows with shutters of the previous century.[20] Such fittings were regarded as moveable objects, as can be seen by various deeds and other documents specifying their retention or removal on changes of tenancy. Thus in 1577 when a new Town Sergeant was elected, the former incumbent, William Geire, was paid 46s 8d by the corporation for the 'waynescott work, portalls and a small bedsteddle' set up by him in the Court House. Similarly an award of rent arrears of a property in Middle Street in the 1570s specified that at the expiry of the lease 'all settells, shelves, benches and other things affixed' were to remain.[21]

Sometimes clauses relating to such fittings were inserted in wills, as for example in 1603 when William Ratcliff, jurat, left 'all my waynscott stuff—viz portall, studye, setels and other wainscott' in his principal messuage in the Butchery to his cousin, William Grafton of Bristol. George Raynoldes, jurat, on the other hand, specified in his will in 1577 that the fittings inside his principal messuage, which included the glass windows, the 'portals with latches, lockes, hapses, hinges, bolte, staples' and the 'long settle of wainscott fixed to the walls or the timberwork of the same' together with the shelving and a 'presse in the chamber over the hall' be not altered or removed by his executor.[22]

A standard clause in leases related to the maintenance of the glass windows for the term of the lease by the lessee after they had been first put into a state of good repair by the lessor. Four leases of properties within the range of £3 to £6 annual rent dated between 1579 and 1585 include this clause, whilst a civil action brought in the court of record in 1572 by Robert Wymond for the recovery of goods left in the house of Francis Harris, specified 'the glasse in the wyndowes which the said plaintiff bought and sett upe when he dwelled there' valued at 40s together with other items to a total value of £10 including five locks, 3s; 'a dogges kennell in the backesyde of ye howsse', 10s; and 'two Jackes howsses viz preveys on the backesyde', 20s.[23] Privies, too, it would seem, were regarded as moveable possessions!

In rarer cases, houses had their own water supply, tapped from the town's main conduit pipes. Amongst the 1556 presentments was an item relating to the premises of the late Thomas Birchett, jurat, which had 'pipes laied in the hiegh strete from the olde conditte to his house', for which it was agreed his heirs should be annually amerced 10s. In 1591 it was agreed that William Frenche should pay 4s per year for the use of the waste water running from the conduit near the Postern Gate into a house of his lately built.[24]

Finally, in 1597, for £20 the town granted Thomas Lashinden the right to lay a small pipe from the main water pipe to his tenement known as the Woode house, probably just outside Landgate, with the proviso that he shut off his water cock to avoid waste when he had drawn sufficient water.

Watercourses for drainage purposes were another consideration amongst householders. In 1580, for example, Thomas Tokey, tailor, had to obtain an easement from his neighbours for a paved watercourse through their yard to join up with the common gutterway in Middle Street, for which he paid 2d per year and a lump sum. He also had to undertake 'to make a grate of iron at the issuing out of the water from his tenement and not to cast out any soil or filth through this grate'. A more complex agreement existed, according to George Raynoldes's' will, 1577, which referred to a longstanding arrangement whereby a lead gutter and pipe ran from his principal tenement across the neighbouring tenement of Paul Wymond for which no rent was due, 'in consideration part of his parlour chimney stands on my ground'. Overhanging roofs caused a particular problem with regard to drainage. The owners of a house newly-erected adjacent to that of John Sharpe, jurat, had to be taken to court in 1581 to ensure that they altered the eaves of their tenement on the side adjoining his property in order to convey the surface water into their own grounds, 'so as not to be of annoyance to John Sharpe or to his house or grounds'.[25]

Many of the larger properties had extensive grounds, comprising gardens, herbers, orchards and closes, usually including stables and outhouses. The probate inventory of John Clarke, 1558, whose property was situated on the High Street, referred to his stable, together with a gelding vaued at 20s and a supply of hay. Francis Daniell's inventory, 1592, which listed a mare, two colts and a nag, valued at £13 13s 4d referred to a hay loft, as did James Pearsall's inventory, 1593, which also mentioned a stable and an ostry. Two other inventories, and a considerable number of wills, mentioned horses, as for example that of the former mayor, John Fletcher, who died in 1545, leaving his sons, Thomas and Richard, his two geldings, for which they were 'to caste lots insteded of choyse ... and eache of them to stande contended with him that shall heppen to him by lott'.[26] Such stables necessitated rear entrances, or, more usually, narrow passages from the street, most often running alongside the houses, as can be seen, for example, in present day Lion Street and West Street.[27]

A few larger properties, mainly inns, had vaulted stone cellars, often pre-dating the houses above them, and which were, on occasion, in separate occupation or ownership from the property above [28] There are a number of such cellars particularly in Market and Middlestreet wards and along the High Street. In the case of one property adjoining Baddings Tower, sold to the corporation in 1517, the house itself had long since disappeared, leaving the cellar under a garden plot.[29] At Grene Hall, by the churchyard, the necessity of maintaining a pre-existing entrance to the cellar led to the somewhat unusual construction of a brick doorway through the Elizabethan chimney stack which was built against the north side of the house.[30]

Cellars were primarily used for the storing of barrells. The Vine Inn, sold by the corporation for £56, in 1600, had more than one, and the Mermaid Inn, in Middlestreet has a fourteenth century wine cellar.[31] James Pearsall's cellar, in 1593, contained 'a tonne and a half of ale and beare and stallages' valued at 40s.[32]

Internally, the walls of Rye's Tudor houses were generally plastered, often with comb decoration.[33] In rarer cases there was painted decoration, as for example at the present day Flushing Inn with its painted partition wall containing a complex of animals amidst a scrollwork of branches, leaves and flowers, surmounted by pairs of cherubs holding cartouches containing the Magnificat in English, which almost certainly dates from the reign of Edward VI, and the mid-sixteenth century view of Rye and Winchelsea painted in plaster on a wall in a house in West Street.[34]

Household goods and furnishings

House furnishings varied considerably with wealth. Among the poorer sort, Thomas Swayne, fisherman, whose goods escheated to the town for felony in 1584, had in his dwelling house only 'two chests, a little table with two trestles, a bad fetherbed and a bolster, an old covering and two straw beds, three bad bolsters, four painted cloths, two pieces of fishermen's lines, a meale syve, an old settle of wood and an old (clothes) presse'. Another fisherman, found hanged in his garrett in the Longer Street in the same year had only 'one old bedsted with an old bedd, an old table and a lyttle cubberd, two old basons' and two manfare of nets unmade.[35] Widows were often particularly poor. One Prophette's wife, who died in 1567, left goods in the house of Fyndall's widow, where she had presumably been lodging, valued at 55s 4d which consisted of little more than her own personal flock bedding together with a blanket, coverlet, pillowcote and four pairs of sheets, a carpet, her spare clothing, three candlesticks, nine items of crockery, a brass pot, a little pan, a little kettle, a cauldron and a chest.[36]

Debts might often account for any remaining household goods, as in the case of Richard Goodwins, fisherman, who died in 1583 owing £3 16s. His goods were 'copped' (auctioned off) in the Market Place on two separate occasions, by order of the court and fetched £4 9s 6d which was entirely accounted for by the outstanding debt and court charges. Apart from two bedstedles, one of which was described as 'ould', one with a featherbed and bedding, the other with a flock bed, which between them fetched 38s 8d, his other furniture consisted of two cupboards, 'an ould table and a fourme', three chairs and five chests. He was, however, better off than many, with 21 assorted pewter dishes and a dozen (probably wooden) trenchers, and a 'lyttell tanckard', together with a pair of bellows, a gridiron, spit, two kettles and an iron pot for cooking purposes, a small amount of clothing and 'half an ould tramel nett' with an old net rope. The only decoration in his house consisted of four or five 'ould payntid clothes', which were a common substitute for tapestry hangings at this time, and occur in ten Rye inventories. These fetched between 2d and 5d each.[37]

Somewhat higher up the social scale was John Hamond, carpenter, assessed at 2s 6d in Baddings ward in 1576. His house consisted of a hall, parlour, three chambers (including one over his shop), kitchen and buttery. Furnishings in the hall comprised a long table with a frame, a long form, a cupboard, two chairs and two old hangings. In the parlour there was only a table, a frame and a form. The principal bedroom was the parlour chamber, which had a joined bedstead with a featherbed, two blankets, a coverlet and a bolster, together with another frame table and form, a joined stool and more hangings. The hall chamber, which was larger, had three joined bedsteads with painted testers, one with a flock bed and two with mattresses, complete with bolsters and three 'old coverlets', a straw bed, a 'great joyned chest' and some more hangings.

In the chamber over the shop, there were three old chests, a further two straw beds, two truckle beds, and a small bedstead complete with featherbed, feather bolster, sheets, blanket, coverlet, pillow and pillowbere. The kitchen was well supplied with two iron pots, two kettles, a dripping pan, a basin and 'divers old tubbes', together with a range of platters, pewter dishes, saucers and spoons. This was the only room in the house apparently to be heated, and contained two spits for cooking purposes plus a pair of andirons, a fire rake and pair of tongs. Lighting was supplied by six candlesticks, stored in the buttery where there was also a frying pan and a chafing-dish used for keeping food hot at table. Seven spare pairs of sheets, some napkins, towels and four table-cloths completed the tally of his household goods. There is little indication here of any outward show of luxury. Bare functionality would appear to be the keynote even amongst skilled tradesmen.[38]

Living accommodation was often limited and on occasion had to serve as additional storage space. John Clarke, cloth merchant, who lived over his High Street shop, had to share his one bedchamber with 3,000 dried herrings, 20 seams of dorsers (fish baskets), 200 (ft) of new nets and a small barrell of vinegar. Peter Adrian, who had three chambers, used the chamber over the parlour to store two pieces of ordnance from his ship and a stallage, presumable for beer.[39]

Signs of comfort were a rarity and almost invariably came only with considerable wealth or status. An early example is provided by the vicarage, which on the incumbent, William Wykwyk's death in 1498 had a heated parlour, complete with andirons, fire fork, tongs, firepan and a brass chafer, together with red saye hangings and cushions of saye and leather in both hall and parlour.[40] Quality wooden furniture was another indication of wealth. Danske (Danzig) chests were a particular fashion of the Elizabethan era and are mentioned in six inventories. Ralph Rode, customer of the port of Rye, who died in 1563 left one, together with such other luxury items as a teak featherbed, some diaper tablecloths and a tapestry coverlet for a bed. Peter Adrian in 1577 also possessed a danske chest, together with a selection of high quality joinery including a wainscott press, a long settle, a settle

182

chest with a lock and a needlework chair. Francis Daniell, 1592, had a pair of playing tables, and Richard Wowan, 1590, had two danske chests, an old desk and a french (walnut) joined bedstedle.[41]

Eating and drinking vessels provide another measure of wealth, ranging from the handful of unspecified (probably wooden or earthenware) dishes of widow Prophette and the three pewter dishes of a rippier named Goodale, in 1567, to a range of over 60 pewter vessels in 1599 in the house of David Hewett. These included 21 assorted drinking vessels; an assortment of 28 plates, platters, dishes, saucers, bowls and basins and a pewter beaker, a bottle, two kettles, five salts (saltsellers) and eight chamber pots. Altogether 22 separate inventories out of 30 which listed dining utensils, specified pewterware, often in considerable quantity, ranging in date from the late fifteenth century (24 items) until the end of the sixteenth century. Other pewter items listed included a goblet, spoons, trenchers and a 'nut trimmed with pewter' all of which featured among the possessions of Richard Wowan; and two pewter candlesticks and two pewter flower pots among the goods of Robert Horsley distrained for house rent in 1566.[42]

Brass was rarer and usually confined to candlesticks and cooking utensils, mainly pots, pans and kettles. Of the 32 inventories which listed cooking equipment, fifteen specified items of brass, ranging from the single brass pot in the relatively well-stocked kitchen of widow Clarke, in 1581, to the 31 brass cooking utensils, comprising five pans, a great brass pot and eight others, five kettles, five stupnetts, two basins, two ladles, two skimmers and a collander, listed amongst the goods of James Pearsall in 1593. He also owned two brass andirons, three brass chafing dishes and six brass candlesticks.[43] Other items of brass occurring in Rye inventories included a 3 gallon pot in a late fifteenth century list of goods; a hanging candlestick among Robert Horsley's goods; and a brass mortar owned by John Clarke.[44]

Rarer still was laten, an alloy of copper, zinc, lead and tin, which was primarily used for candlesticks (five inventories mention these), although David Hewett possessed a laten pestle and mortar and a fifteenth century inventory also listed a laten chafing dish, two basins and two lavers. Widow Clarke's two laten candlesticks were described as old, so perhaps this alloy

183

was going out of use as the sixteenth century wore on.[45]

Probably the most common cooking utensils were made of iron, which could explain why there are so few specific references to iron cooking vessels. John Hamond had two iron cooking pots and Peter Adrian a pair of iron pothangers. Widow Clarke's pair of cob irons and pair of baking irons were presumably made of iron, as may well have been her frying pan, two dripping pans, five kettles, four spits and two gridirons. Certainly Francis Daniell's inventory specified an iron pot, two iron dripping pans, an iron kettle, two gridirons, and four brandirons (probably a sophisticated arrangement of pothangers over the fireplace). One household also had a 'pressinge iron', presumably for ironing clothes.[46]

The majority of fireplace accessories were almost certainly also made of iron including the pairs of andirons or firedogs specified in fourteen inventories, the chafing dishes specified in thirteen and the pairs of fire tongs specified in fifteen inventories. Five houses also had pairs of bellows. Presumably, since two andirons and three chafing dishes are specified as being brass, the remaining four andirons, tongs, fire rake and fire garth mentioned in James Pearsall's inventory were of iron. Firebacks, being regarded as fixtures, are not mentioned in these inventories, although according to a deposition relating to George Raynoldes's will (1579) his house had three and one fifteenth century Rye house still has a locally-made iron fireback dated 1564 apparently in situ in the hall fireplace. Two other households, those of Francis Daniell (1592) and David Hewett 1599, possessed warming pans, and Robert Horsley's house had a looking glass, which must all have been very much luxury items at this date.[47]

There is also evidence of home baking in at least some of the larger houses. Widow Clarke possessed a kneading trough as well as the cob irons and baking irons already mentioned. James Pearsall's kitchen also had a kneading trough and a boulting hutch, used for sifting corn, whilst Robert Wymond numbered among his possessions a kneading trough, two sieves, a boulting, two bunters, one lot of meal sacks and certain (unspecified) old bakehouse implements.[48] Three households possessed brine or salt tubs, one other had a tolvet of salt, and a further two had unspecified tubs. Four households had barrells or firkins, presumably of beer, and James Pearsall also had a firkin of butter.

184

David Hewett's house possessed a still, and James Pearsall's house a limback (another type of still). Four households possessed pairs of scales and sets of weights.[49] Bedding provides another measure of wealth, varying from the single flock bed and bolster with coverlet and a spare pair of sheets in the house of Henry Prescott in 1578 to the range of feather and flock beds with linen or canvas sheets, for family and servants respectively, found in houses of jurats and the wealthier sort, such as George Raynoldes. A good quality joined bedstedle complete with featherbed, bolster, pillow, blanket and covering might cost as much as 30s or more. Richard Godwin's feather bed, bolster and pillow fetched 16s 6d when it was copped in 1583. His bedstedle, which must have been very poor fetched 3s 2d. A flock bed fetched rather less. Widow Prophette's, together with two bolsters, was valued at 4s in 1566. Henry Prescott's flock bed and bolster was apprised at only 5s some 22 years later.[50] Nevertheless, the bed was the single most expensive item of household furnishing and provides a good indication of the level of wealth of its possessor. The more prosperous households included items such as tapestry or dornex coverlets, bed curtains or hangings, indicating four posters complete with accoutrements. Ralph Rode, customer, had a quilt; Thomas Forman had a valence. Robert Marchall, in 1560, left a silk sheet and three 'pillowcotes edged with silk lace', and Richard Wowan's walnut bedstead came complete with feather bedding 'a red rugge and a whit blanket'.[51]

Comfortable bedding was clearly a high priority among the inhabitants of sixteenth century Rye. Nicholas Morris, tailor, possessed two feather beds and a flock bed, complete with coverlets and spare pairs of sheets. John Hamond, carpenter, also had two feather beds together with a number of flock ones. A number of households also possessed large quantities of linen. John Clarke had fifteen pairs of linen sheets, together with a not inconsiderable collection of napkins, towels and tablecloths. Thomas Whitfield had 22 pairs of new sheets, together with 36 napkins, eight towels, five table cloths and five pillows of down. John Whiteman had 23 pairs of sheets, 18 pillowcotes, 36 napkins, five table cloths and two towels. The largest collection of linen was owned by James Pearsall. He had a staggering 37 pairs of sheets, 33 table cloths, 32 towels, and 112 napkins, plus assorted pillowcotes, cupboard cloths and table towels. His was clearly an exceptionally large house, with a total of eight joined bedsteads and two truckle beds in five chambers and a little parlour, together with a boarded truckle bed in store in the wheat loft. Yet Francis Daniell's house was larger still, with a total of twelve beds in six chambers and a downstairs parlour; and even John Hamond's house had seven beds, although only two of these had feather beds and three had straw mattresses.[52]

flock beds

In the case of John Hamond, the explanation for this number of beds is probably that he had several servants or apprentices, as well as his family, living on the premises which were over his carpenter's workshop. Certainly he had at least two apprentices in 1576 and took on two covenant servants and a further apprentice in 1585. He had only three bedrooms, so living accommodation must still have been cramped. In fact a considerable number of Rye households had servants or apprentices living in. The muster rolls for 1597–8 , which list able-bodied men above the age of sixteen, list 69 male servants in 47 households and there is reason to assume that there were as many female servants.[53] In 1597–8 in Middlestreet ward, Robert Swayne and Richard Stace each had three male servants and John Fowtrell, then mayor, had five. Allowing for female domestics and other servants under the age of sixteen such households must have been large indeed.

However, the explanation for the large number of beds in James Pearsall's and Francis Daniell's houses is rather different, for both were licensed victuallers. In 1585 the licences gave details of the numbers of beds in such premises and Francis Daniell was described as having six. James Pearsall was also one of the few innkeepers licensed to sell wines, which made his house in Market ward one of the principal inns of the town and helps explain such luxuries in the upstairs chambers as oil paintings, chairs with cushions and stools of needlework, bedcurtains of buckram, saye or of white and red cloth and a 'joyned garth to burne coles'.[54]

Downstairs, the hall, which was presumably used for dining, was dominated by a long table with a long settle and a form, a great cupboard, a joined chest, two chairs, and a stool. There were needlework and leather cushions, painted cloths on the walls and a curtain for the window and the whole was heated by a fireplace complete with andirons. The great parlour, with its brass andirons, assorted tables, chairs and stools, complete with pictures on the walls, buckram curtains and three nutcrackers must have been the main social area and was served by an exceptionally well-equipped kitchen and two butteries, together with ale and beer from the cellar. The entry contained two tables and a dresser and there was provisioning for the horses in the stable, complete with hay loft, wheat loft and ostry at the rear.

James Pearsall's house was clearly exceptionally well-appointed. What is perhaps slightly more surprising at first sight is the quantity of armour and weaponry stored in various rooms in the house. There was a caliver, complete with flask and touchbox, a sword and two headpieces in the Green Chamber, which most probably was Pearsall's own bedroom. There was another sword and a dagger in the hall, a halberd in the 'old chamber' and two horsemen's lances in the wheat loft.[55]

Elizabethan government, like its predecessors, placed obligations on its citizens, particularly the wealthier ones, to supply their own personal arms for defence, so it was quite normal at this time for houses to contain small quantities of arms. The 1597–8 and 1600 Rye muster rolls provide a comprehensive picture of individuals' arms within the town,[56] but a sound impression of the range of weaponry to be found in Rye houses at this time can be gained from the inventories. Altogether thirteen specify particular items of arms or protective clothing, ranging from the bows and arrows of John Clarke (1558) and Ralph Rode (1563) to the calivers with flask and touchbox of Francis Daniell, David Hewett, Richard Wowan and James Pearsall in the 1590s and widow Clarke's (presumably her late husband's) in 1581. Swords were also relatively common, being mentioned on four occasions: Francis Daniell had six; while David Hewett, Richard Wowan and Peter Adrian all had daggers and Ralph Rode also had a rapier. Among the more unusual weapons, George Raynoldes had five halberds (four of them gilded) and a gilded partizan; and Peter Adrian in 1577 had 'two old corselettes, viz two gorgettes, two pair of vanbrases and a paire of graunlettes' valued at 10s together with two 'handgonnes with fier lokes' valued at 14s in his hall.[57]

Calivers or other handguns because of their cost, are an indication of membership of the town's mercantile and trading elite. Yet the average total value of the household goods of the six whose handguns are mentioned in their inventories is little more than £20 ranging from the £13 0s 5d of Peter Adrian in 1577 to the £54 9s 4d of James Pearsall in 1593. Indeed, excluding the valuation placed on his horses, Francis Daniell's inventory total of £21 6s 4d is very similar to the £18 4s 4d and £17 8s 6d at which Richard Wowan's and widow Clarke's goods respectively were valued. Including his horses, Francis Daniell's gross inventory total rises to £34 19s 8d; and Peter Adrian's rises to £39 0s 5d when a lease on four messuages with 16 years still to run is taken into account. Ralph Rode, the customer's inventory valuation of £157 9s 3½d is similarly reduced to only £20 16s 4d when his household goods alone are taken into account and his outstanding debts and customs farms are excluded. Finally, John Clarke's inventory total of £63 5s 9d includes shop goods valued at over £32, leaving household goods valued at £30 8s 1d, which is further reduced by £5 5s 0d if his silver plate is excluded.[58]

Variations in wealth

It would seem, then, that even among the wealthier sort, household goods were in the range of little more than £20–£30 rising to a maximum of perhaps £50 in exceptional cases in the 1590s—a phenomenon at least partly due to inflation in the late Elizabethan period. Inventory totals above this level, indicate the inclusion of shop goods, outstanding trading or other financial transactions and plate, which was readily convertible into monetary value. Below these levels, household furnishings varied in value from the somewhat spartan comfort of houses such as John Hamond's, a master carpenter, to the bare necessities of those with goods valued like Thomas Robens', a fisherman, at 35s 4d or Alice Aubons', widow, at 34s 6d.[59] Below these levels, poverty was extreme.

An impression of these relative differences in wealth can be deduced from the surviving inventory totals which are written into the Lewes Archdeaconry probate registers for Rye. Unfortunately the inventories themselves do not survive.

Table 29 indicates the main divisions of wealth in the town. Only three people with goods valued at less than £1 either made wills or had probate granted on their estate. A further 38 had goods valued at less than £3. Below these levels is material poverty, whilst of those owning some property in the town, those valued at under £10 comprise the poorer sort. The largest group of inventories is for those with goods (including such items as

Table 29

Rye probate inventory totals 1541-1603

Years	under £5	£5-10	£10-20	£20-40	£40-100	£100+
1541-50	8	8	11	8	5	-
1551-60	10	12	16	15	20	1
1561-70	5	12	23	16	22	3
1571-80	16	18	18	18	11	7
1581-90	22	19	11	15	11	7
1591-1603	18	11	27	37	12	6
Total 479:	79	80	106	109	81	24

Source: Lewes archdeaconry probate registers W/A1-4 /A1-4; W/B1-3.

leases, business debts etc.) valued at between £10 and £40 which comprise almost half of the surviving inventory totals. These were the middle sort of Rye inhabitants, wealthier craftsmen and smaller traders. At the upper levels such individuals shade into the mercantile elite, or wealthier sort, who comprise roughly one quarter of those whose inventory totals survive. At the apex of this pyramid of wealth were men like John Mercer, a jurat, whose goods were valued at £547 18s ·8d at his death in 1588 and John Fisher, also a jurat, who died in 1603 leaving various leases, plate and other moveables, valued at £705 11s 0d.[60]

Unfortunately, the relatively small number of complete inventories in the corporation records has made it impossible to make direct statistical comparisons, although the general pattern, as described above, is clear. Only one of the complete household inventories lists plate, although nine partial inventories do. From these, it is clear that plate, as well as having its own intrinsic value was regarded as a source of ready exchange, odd or broken items being offered by weight in payment of debts. Among the goods 'late Mr. Passes' seized in payment of a debt in 1578, were 'a nut lipt and fotid with silver' valued at 20s, 'a salte with a cristall stone silver gilt' worth 26s 8d and three 'peces of broken silver' weighing 8 oz, which were apprised at 4s 4d per ounce. Similarly another debt, to Thomas Herste, baker, in 1566, was satisfied by an assortment of gold coins of several nations and a gold ring, while Johanne Banbrigge settled one of her outstanding debts in 1565 with a silver cup, valued at £10, a little silver pot, valued at £4 and two feet from silver cups and a silver lid, valued together at £6 10s.[61]

Items of plate disposed of in this way, ranged from silver cups and standing bowls, to gold rings and other items of jewelry. Augustine Swetinge had one of the former, a silver standing bowl, valued at £10 in 1565, six silver spoons and an assortment of gold rings, brooches and other jewels. In 1532 Thomas Byspyn, the son of a former mayor, gave Robert Barnes, a future jurat, one 'salt of silver parcel gilt' weighing 7¾ oz and 6 'spones parcell gylt' weighing 11¾ oz as security for a debt.[62] Such items alone were often in excess of the total value of the household goods of a poorer inhabitant. For example, Johanne Banbrigge's silver cup was worth more than the total moveable possessions of 159 out of the 479 Rye inhabitants for whom figures are available (i.e. approximately one third).

Among the wealthier inhabitants, possession of plate was the norm rather than the exception. Thirty-two out of the 62 surviving jurats' wills for the Tudor period make specific bequests of items of plate, in a number of cases indicating the existence within the household of considerably more such items than are specifically referred to in individual bequests. For example, John Fagge, in 1583, referred in his will amongst other items of plate, to his 'greatest goblet parcel gilt', implying that there was more than one; and John Baylye, in 1572, mentioned his 'best silver salt'.[63] Allowing for a degree of under-representation, the range of plate even apart from personal jewelry referred to in Rye jurats' wills is still considerable. Eighteen jurats left quantities of silver spoons in their wills, including three who left large silver 'Apostle Spoons'. A total of fifteen left drinking vessels of gold or silver of various types, including six who left goblets either of silver or silver gilt; seven left cups; three specified 'drinking peces' and three more drinking cruses and one referred to his three 'stone drinking pots footid in silver'. Eleven jurats referred to silver or silver gilt salts including in the will of Robert Swaine, his 'double salt, double gilt with a pepper box on top'.

Among those with notably large collections of plate, Adam Oxenbridge, in 1496, referred to his chalice, his gold chain, his diamond, sapphire, ruby and emerald gold rings, a gilt cup and six chased silver cups. Robert Bennett, a butcher, in 1564, left six apostle spoons, twelve 'silver spones with bellknopes', three gold rings and two silver gilt salts; while John Baylye in 1572, left six

Table 30

Distribution of household sizes of Rye ratepayers 1596

Number of persons in household	Number of households excluding servants			Number of households including servants		
	Poorer	Middle	Wealthier	Poorer	Middle	Wealthier
1	5	15	4	5	13	3
2	34	30	16	30	25	8
3	27	31	12	28	33	13
4	34	23	11	33	18	14
5	20	25	11	19	22	9
6	15	7	5	17	13	6
7	6	8	7	7	12	8
8	1	2	1	3	4	1
9	1	2	1	1	2	1
10	-	-	-	-	-	5
11	-	-	1	-	1	1
Total households	143	143	69	143	143	69
Total persons	539	517	278	560	567	329
Average household size	3.8	3.6	4.0	3.9	4.0	4.8

Notes: The poorer sort comprises those assessed at £1-2 in goods; the middle sort those assessed at £2+ to under £40; and the wealthier sort all those over £40.

Sources: PAR 467/1/1/1-2; RYE 1/3-7; RYE 85/2.

apostle spoons, ten other silver spoons, two gold rings, several silver bars, at least two cruses and two silver salts and several silver goblets.[64]

Households and families

The contrast between the different levels of material comfort of the main social groups in Rye was reflected also in the differing household sizes of the richer and poorer inhabitants of the town. Table 30 is an attempt at the reconstruction of the households of ratepayers listed on the town sesse of 19 March 1596. Despite its more obvious shortcomings, this household analysis provides clear evidence of the substantially greater size of richer, as opposed to poorer households. Much of this difference was accounted for by the considerably larger numbers of servants and apprentices living in the households of the wealthier inhabitants, where they represented just under one-sixth (15.5 per cent) of residents. But there was also a slight differential accounted for by the marginally greater numbers of children in the wealthier households. The actual size of Rye households in 1596 was probably rather higher than these figures suggest, since it has not proved possible to trace more than a fraction of the step-children of male householders brought into the household as a result of

191

second marriages, and it is clear that the numbers of female servants (6) as compared to male servants (120) are also substantially under-represented, by perhaps as much as 95 per cent.[65] Most of these servants came from outside Rye or from the poorer households in the town, although in a few cases, as for example with William Tolkin's two sons, boys were sometimes apprenticed to their fathers.[66]

The average household size for Rye in the late Elizabethan period derived from family reconstitution (4.1) although clearly an underestimate, does not compare too badly with the figures derived from the 1565 government survey (4.6) referred to in Chapter 1 above.[67] It is also possible to attempt a rough population estimate for the town as a whole based on these figures. Out of 419 resident householders, listed in the 1596 sesse, it proved possible to reconstitute the families of 355 (84.7 per cent) from the parish registers, with a reasonable degree of accuracy. By increasing the number of female servants to the rough equality shown to have existed between male and female servants from the burial registers and inflating the whole by 15.3 per cent to account for the remaining ratepayers and a further 28 per cent (the proportion of those described as householders buried during the 1596/7 plague epidemic not listed on the sesse) a total population for Rye of 2244, which, allowing for step-children would probably be nearer to 2500 in 536 households is arrived at. Such figures confirm the results of the aggregative analysis of the parish registers set out in Chapter 1. Since the five-year moving average for baptisms in 1596 was only 83.4 compared to 118.6 in 1576, a fall of some 30 per cent, the population of Rye prior to the decline of the 1590s was probably nearer 3300, possible rather higher in the 1550s and 1560s.

Nevertheless, the average (mean) household size in Rye in the late sixteenth century does seem rather low compared to the figures for Poole and Ealing for example (6.05 and 4.75 in 1574 and 1599 respectively), although substantially higher than Phythian-Adams's estimate for Coventry (3.7) at the height of its decline in 1523.[68] Much of the reason for this was probably the exceptionally high mortality rates prevailing in Rye as compared to the much smaller south-western port of Poole, Even Worcester, a town of some 4250 persons in 1563, only a little larger than Rye at that date, which experienced markedly higher mortality rates

Table 31

A comparison of the average numbers of children
listed in wills of Rye and Worcester testators 1540-1610

	RYE		WORCESTER	
Decade[1]	number of wills mentioning children	average number of children	number of wills	average number of children
1541-50	31	2.2	66	2.8
1551-60	22	2.3	108	2.6
1561-70	35	2.0	47	3.0
1571-80	36	1.9	50	3.4
1581-90	18	2.4	41	3.2
1591-1600	19	2.7	56	3.2
1601-10	22	2.4	76	3.2

Notes: [1] Figures for Worcester run 1540-9, 1550-9, etc.
Sources: W/A1-13; W/U5; W/C4 and C11. Figures for Worcester taken from A.D. Dyer: *The City of Worcester in the Sixteenth Century* (1973) table 2, p.35.

than its surrounding villages, does not appear to have suffered to the same degree as Rye. As Table 31 shows, at no time during the sixteenth century do the numbers of surviving children mentioned in the wills of Rye testators equal those listed in the wills of inhabitants of Worcester—a clear indication of the lower survival rates for infants and children prevailing in Rye. Indeed, if the figures for all Rye wills were to be taken, the average number of children falls much further, to a low 1.2 in the 1570s and 1580s and a high 1.8 in the 1590s, clearly demonstrating that at no time during the sixteenth century was the Rye population able to maintain itself except by the regular influx of substantial numbers of immigrants.

When the corresponding rates of baptisms per couple for Rye and Worcester are compared, the much higher rates of infant and child mortality in Rye become fully apparent. Between 1540 and 1619, Dyer found that Worcester families (excluding childless couples) baptised on average 2.6 children, compared to 4.0 children of first marriages (excluding childless couples) baptised in Rye over a similar period. Even with the inclusion of childless couples, the Rye figures still only fall to 3.4, substantially higher than those for Worcester families. These Rye figures, however, mask notable differences in fertility rates of rich and poor, the average number of children christened per couple by first marriage among the poorer sort being only 3.8 compared to 4.1 for the middle sort and 4.6 among the wealthier class of Rye

193

Table 32a
Infant and child mortality rates arranged by decade of baptism 1540-1609

Decade	baptisms	Under 1 year buried	%	1-9 yrs buried	%	10-21 yrs buried	%	Total 0-21 yrs buried	%
1540-9	424	66	15.6	89	21.0	47	11.1	202	47.6
1550-9	638	104	16.3	227	35.6	40	6.3	371	58.2
1560-9	613	125	20.4	126	20.6	41	6.7	292	47.6
1570-9	545	111	20.4	119	21.8	22	4.0	252	46.2
1580-9	631	72	11.4	112	17.7	61	9.7	245	38.8
1590-9	656	120	18.3	136	20.7	9	1.4	265	40.4
1600-9	572	65	11.4	72	12.6	2	0.3	139	24.3
Total	4079	663	16.3	881	21.6	222	5.4	1766	43.3

Notes: Figures for baptisms and burials based on a reconstitution of the families of 1595 ratepayers listed in one or more of the 10 town sesses 1554-1604.

Sources: PAR 467/1/1/1-2; RYE 1/1/-7; RYE 77/6.

Table 32b
Infant and child mortality rates by decade of baptism arranged by wealth 1540-1609

	Decade	baptised	Under 1 year buried	%	1-9 yrs buried	%	10-21 yrs buried	%
Poor	1540-9	70	12	17.1	11	15.7	10	14.3
	1550-9	194	31	16.0	79	40.7	14	7.2
	1560-9	277	63	22.7	56	20.2	25	9.0
	1570-9	209	48	23.0	56	26.8	8	3.8
	1580-9	274	25	9.1	47	17.2	26	9.5
	1590-9	294	49	16.7	63	21.4	4	1.4
	1600-9	272	36	13.2	34	12.5	1	0.4
	Total	1590	264	16.6	346	21.8	88	5.5
Middle	1540-9	214	34	15.9	40	18.7	18	8.4
	1550-9	312	52	16.7	109	34.9	18	5.8
	1560-9	239	49	20.5	48	20.1	12	5.0
	1570-9	225	46	20.4	48	21.3	12	5.3
	1580-9	269	36	13.4	56	20.8	24	8.9
	1590-9	269	56	20.8	61	22.7	5	1.9
	1600-9	240	21	8.8	31	12.9	1	0.4
	Total	1768	294	16.6	393	22.2	90	5.1
Wealthy	1540-9	140	20	14.3	38	27.1	19	13.6
	1550-9	132	21	15.9	39	29.5	8	6.1
	1560-9	97	13	13.4	22	22.7	4	4.1
	1570-9	111	17	15.3	16	14.4	2	1.8
	1580-9	88	11	12.5	9	10.2	11	12.5
	1590-9	93	15	16.1	12	12.9	0	0.0
	1600-9	60	8	13.3	7	11.7	0	0.0
	Total	721	105	14.6	143	19.8	44	6.1

Notes: Poor comprises those assessed at 2s or less (12d in 1604, worth 40s in 1596 and 1598).
Middle comprises those assessed at under 10s (under 5s in 1604, worth under £40 in 1596 and 1598).
Wealthy comprises those paying 10s or more (5s or more in 1604, worth £40 and over in 1596 and 1598).

Sources: PAR 467/1/1/1-2; RYE 1/1-7; RYE 77/6.

194

ratepayers.[69] This contrast between the experience of rich and poor in Rye is further borne out, although to a far lesser extent, by the infant and child mortality rates experienced by Rye ratepayers, set out in Table 32.

Table 32a shows the changing levels of infant and child mortality during the seventy years between 1540 and 1609. The worst decade was the 1550s, when a series of infuenza epidemics in the years 1557–60, compounded by an outbreak of plague in 1556, resulted in child and infant mortality rates of almost 60 per cent. The 1540s and 1560s (major plague outbreaks in 1544 and 1563) and the 1570s (a major plague outbreak in 1579–80) were only slightly less unhealthy, with mortality rates for the same age group of almost 50 per cent. Not until the relatively epidemic-free 1580s (a minor outbreak of, possibly, typhus in early 1590) did the figures fall to below 40 per cent of those under 21, rising to just over this level in the 1590s (a major plague outbreak in 1596–7 followed by a minor one in 1598).[70] Only in the first decade of the seventeenth century did mortality rates fall sharply to only 24.3 per cent, less than half the decennial averages for the period 1540–79, and coinciding with the collapse in Rye's economy and a sharp reduction in the town's total population. Probably, therefore, this sharp fall in mortality rates was due to the relief from overcrowding which a declining population brought. But even allowing for the much-improved figures for the early seventeenth century, the period 1540–1609 saw infant mortality rates (under one year) equivalent to almost one sixth of live births (16.3 per cent) and child mortality rates (1–9 years) which accounted for a further one in five of live births (21.6 per cent) or one in four of those who had survived their first year of life. Overall, some 43.3 per cent of those babies whose baptisms are recorded in the Rye parish registers appear in the burial registers of the town under the age of 21. Such figures, although considerably worse than those produced by Wrigley and Schofield for their selected parishes[71] appear not dissimilar to the experience of other larger English towns. At York, for example, Palliser has estimated that infant mortality rates in the decade 1591–1600 varied between 159 per thousand in the wealthier parish of St. Crux and 264–280 per thousand in the poorer parish of St Denys;[72] while at Worcester, Dyer estimated child mortality rates (1–24 years) varying between 30–35 per cent in the decade 1575–84 to just over 50 per cent in the 1590s before falling to below 20 per cent in the 1630s.[73] On the basis of such comparisons, Rye seems to have been rather less healthy than Worcester, but rather more so than York. Probably its experience was much the same as other larger south coast ports, such as Dover, Sandwich or Southampton.

However, as Table 32b indicates, these bare totals mask a number of interesting and significant variations in the life expectancies of children born into families with differing levels of wealth. Of those children born in the 1550s, the decade of highest infant and child mortality, almost two-thirds of the children of poorer parents (63.9 per cent) died without reaching maturity. The corresponding figures for children of parents of middling means and the wealthier sort were considerably lower (57.4 per cent and 51.5 per cent respectively). Indeed, in the first four decades under consideration, in only one, the 1540s, did mortality rates for poorer children fall below 50 per cent. In the 1570s, for example, they were running at 53.6 per cent compared to similar rates for the children of the wealthy of only 31.5 per cent. Overall, however, mortality rates for those aged up to 21 varied surprisingly little between the social groups, with the poor (43.9 per cent) suffering almost identical levels of mortality to the middling sort and only slightly more than the wealthy (40.5 per cent). This is particularly surprising in view of the significantly far greater differences in the levels of mortality in poorer, as opposed to wealthier households found during the major plague epidemics in Rye, when the percentages of poorer victims per household regularly ran at levels some 25–50 per cent higher than those from wealthier households. Indeed, during the 1579–80 plague outbreak, the number of victims per household from poorer households outnumbered those of the wealthier sort by 240 per cent.[74] The most likely explanation for this discrepancy lies in a combination of two main factors. Firstly, the figures in Table 32b taken over a number of years, may tend to underestimate the levels of mortality among poorer families, rather more of whom may have moved away from the town than those with more property, and so were no longer 'at risk'. Secondly, the figures themselves suggest that the children of wealthier parents died rather older than those from poorer households. It may be, therefore, that while epidemics and other infant diseases hit poorest families hardest, the generally insanitary nature of

196

conditions in Rye eventually weakened even the better-nurtured constitutions, so producing only the very slight differences in overall levels of mortality between the social classes indicated in Table 32b. Despite the obvious differences in housing and living conditions, in such relatively compact towns as Rye, rich and poor lived in close proximity to one another, very often in the same street.

The generally unhealthy conditions in Rye, which produced such high levels of mortality among the younger members of the population, had a similarly depressing effect on the life expectancy of adults. Of those aged 21 and upwards for whom it has been possible to establish age at death, only a handful reached old age, the average age at death being 40 years 1 month for males, 40 years 5 months for females. Slightly over 57 per cent of males and just under 55 per cent of females died before they reached the age of 40; while, conversely, only 2 per cent of males and 4 per cent of females reached the age of 70.[75] Since the average age at marriage was 22 years 6 months for females and 24 years 9 months for males the average duration of marriages was relatively short. Of 287 first marriages of both partners which it has been possible to trace among Rye ratepayers, the mean length of marriages was only 13.1 years, with notable differences between the wealthy (15 years 5 months) and the poor (10 years 2 months). A total of 82.6 per cent of these marriages lasted less than 20 years, with more than two in five (42.9 per cent) lasting less than 10 years. At the other end of the scale, only 20 marriages (7.0 per cent) lasted more than 30 years. Significantly only one of these was one of the poorer ratepayers.[76] Among the more common causes of death among women was childbirth itself, which in a sample of 271 burials of the wives of householders, accounted for 32 instances (11.8 per cent), rather more than one in nine.[77]

The relatively short duration of marriages led to frequent remarriages of the surviving partners. This is particularly noticeable after major epidemics, when the annual number of marriages might double. Following the plague of 1563, marriages in 1564 leapt to 91, compared to 50 the year before and 37 in 1562. Similarly after the 1579–80 plague, the number of marriages went up from 31 in 1579 to 82 in 1580. An analysis of the remarriages of male householders shows that the interval between the death of a spouse and the remarriage of the survivor might be as little as just over a month (12.8 per cent) while over a third of remarriages (34.4 per cent) took place in one to three months and just over two-thirds (68 per cent) in under a year. In all, 85.6 per cent of remarriages of male householders took place in under two years, while in only 4.8 per cent of cases where it can be shown that the survivor was alive for at least five years following the decease of his spouse, does it appear that a man did not remarry. The experience of men such as the jurat, Henry Gaymer, who waited 17 years and 8 months between the death of his second wife and his marriage to a third, or of Simon Vale, fletcher, who survived his only wife by almost 30 years until his death in June 1600, were very much the exception.[78] Out of the same 287 ratepayers whose first marriages were traced, in 79 instances (27.5 per cent) there is evidence of a second marriage, in 25 instances a third (8.7 per cent) and in four instances a fourth (1.4 per cent) Of the remaining 179 (62.4 per cent) for whom only one marriage is recorded, 113 predeceased their wives, one died on the same day and most of the others died shortly afterwards, certainly within two years. Remarriage was therefore the norm and a man (or woman) might expect in most cases to find a new partner within a relatively short time. This is reflected in the relatively low proportions of households headed by widows (26 of 419, or 6.2 per cent) and widowers (12 of 419, or 2.9 per cent) listed in the March 1596 sesse.

In such circumstances it was rare that both parents lived long enough to see their children reach adulthood. Of 190 wills of Rye testators between 1540 and 1609 mentioning children or step-children, in 134 instances, (70.5 per cent) some or all of these appear to have been still minors or unmarried accounting in all for 301 (68.9 per cent) of the 437 offspring listed. Rather more than two-thirds of children in a similar proportion of families experienced the loss of one or both parents. Excluding the wills of widows, these figures appear even more stark. Of 167 wills of fathers mentioning their children or step-children, in 126 instances (75.4 per cent) they were minors, accounting for 292 (72.3 per cent) of the 404 children listed. If the evidence of these wills is representative of the prevailing situation in Rye in the sixteenth and early seventeenth centuries, then something appro-aching three-quarters of children suffered the loss of their father before they had reached maturity.[79] Corroborative evidence is available from the 287 families whose first marriages were traced. Of these, 187 families had children who survived into adulthood. In only 26 cases (13.9 per cent) did the father survive long enough to see all his children reach the age of 21 and in only 50 cases (26.7 per cent) did he live long enough for the eldest to reach their majority. In 161 cases (86.2 per cent), fathers died leaving children under the age of 21 and in 111 instances (59.3 per cent) these children were all under the age of 14 years.

Life in sixteenth century towns like Rye was clearly extremely harsh, especially for the poor. Life expectancy at birth was poor and of those who reached adulthood few could hope to attain old age. Subsistence crises, poor sanitation and recurrent epidemics, ensured consistently high, although fluctuating, levels of mortality among children and adults alike. In over a fifth of all instances, parents died without any surviving children to succeed them.[80] In almost all of the rest, parents suffered the loss of as many as half of their children during the early years of life, while most children suffered the loss of one or both parents in childhood. In times of plague, sometimes complete households were wiped out in a matter of days or weeks. Often they suffered the loss of the main breadwinner. The annual rate of change in the names of householders recorded in the town sesses rarely fell below 6–8 per cent mainly through deaths and rose to as much as 20.8 per cent (96 of 326 ratepayers in the 17 months between April 1563 and September 1564) following the plague of the summer of 1563.[81] The difference was made up mainly by immigration into the town, largely from the surrounding countryside but also in some instances from further afield, attracted by the prospects for social and economic advancement. In all too many cases the reality awaiting immigrants was rather different.

CHAPTER 6

Crime and Social Order

An evell fact must by notable example be punished and not
with gentlenes of pardon forgeven. A man may through
mercie graunt an offendor of his goodnes that as he cannot
escape by justice.   c.1556
                                                                (RYE 57/4)

Moral considerations

The administration of justice in Tudor Rye was seen as a
necessary blending of justice with mercy, of exemplary punishment and mitigation or forgiveness. A number of recent writers
on crime and punishment in the early modern period have
remarked on this attitude of mind among sixteenth century
administrators of justice, seeing it as derived from the twin poles
of the Law of the Old Testament and its mitigation by Christ's
teaching of the need for mercy, in the New Testament.[1] St Paul in
particular, in his Epistle to the Romans made clear his belief that
under the Law of Moses, all stand condemned, for all are sinners.
Only through God's mercy, vouchsafed through Jesus Christ, can
man hope to be saved.

Such an outlook clearly influenced the attitudes to justice of
Rye's inhabitants and their neighbours in the sixteenth century.
Thus in January 1597, following a major plague epidemic in Rye,
the town corporation of Ashford wrote:

'whereas of late yt hath pleased God ... to vysytt your towne
with one of his greate roddes or scowrges wherewith he often
afflicted man for synn, wherof not long sythence wee of our
towne of Asheford have had manyfold experience and as yt
pleased hym of hys greate mercye then to rayse us up many
frendes to have a fellow feeling of our myseryes and to

200

contrybute towardes the necessyte of our poore ... so it hath now pleased hym to move our hartes to contrybute something ... towardes the releaving of the poore sayntes of God amongest you, the some wherof is fyve poundes ... And thus desiring God (for his Christe's sake) to loke downe mercifully upon you and in his good tyme to withdrawe his heavye hand of correction from you ...'[2]

The idea of divine punishment for sin falling on a community was commonplace, particularly in the Elizabethan period. The role of the magistrate in correcting evildoers was thus seen as part of the wider responsibility of a community to preserve a godly order in all its activities on pain of divine punishment. It was this outlook which moved an assembly in August 1572 to order public prayer and fasting for all inhabitants between the ages of 16 and 60 both morning and afternoon on Mondays and the attendance of one representative 'of sufficient discretion' of every household at the church in time of common prayer on Wednesdays and Fridays, 'till it please God to staie this unseasonable weather' 'token of God's great displeasure, threateninge no small miseries and calamities to fall upon us ... for our losse liff and neglectinge to do our duties'. In addition, all inns and tippling houses were to remain closed to inhabitants of the town on that day, although 'necessary work and labour' was enjoined 'after the prayer and sermon endid ... so all waies the same daie nor no parte therof be spent in plaies, pastimes of Idlenes, and much lesse in lewde, wicked or wanton behavior'. Finally, there was to be a weekly collection of alms for the poor and on the next Sunday 'a generall communion of all the honest inhabitauntes of the towne and their wyves and suche of their householde as they shall thinke moost mete, therby to declare to all the worlde a generall reconsiliation of all offences whatsoever passed betwene eny of the inhabitauntes of this towne, as also to protest a godly, christian and stedfast love and unitie betwene the inhabitauntes. And farther by such brotherly and Christian communicatinge togethers, to manifest their faith and godly agrement in the religion of Jesus Christe.'[3]

Such public manifestations of faith demonstrate the close interrelationship between religion and social polity, God's law and man's, in the minds of the inhabitants of late Tudor Rye. Sin, equated with 'loose life', drunkenness, idleness and lewdeness, was the responsibility of the whole community, which might itself suffer the divine consequences of tolerating such ungodly behaviour, as had happened even to God's chosen people, the Israelites, for their idolatry in making a golden calf to worship in the desert:

> 'soe sure as God is true, unless they repent and get pardon in Christ hath God plagued adulterers, thieves and prophane persons and sabbath breaking in former times. He is Jehova, let them look to it, it is his name and nature to hate and plague such everlastingly unless there be repentance on their part and pardon on his.'[4]

So wrote Richard Fletcher, Minister of the Word of God in Rye from 1574 until 1583, in a manuscript 'Treatise on the Commandments' still preserved among the records of Rye parish church, and which, from their argumentative style, no doubt formed the basis for many of his sermons.

For Fletcher, human laws were a mere reflection of the divine law set out in the Ten Commandments and imprinted in every man's conscience so as to 'serve to leave them without excuse and to condemn them' (i.e. evildoers). Yet if the main work of the divine law lies in 'denouncing the anger of God and eternal punishments to all that are not perfectly conformable to it' Fletcher recognised the role of God's mercy in the 'remission of sins and reconciliation by Christ our mediator', dependent, of course, upon man's repentance, which itself, often only came about as a result of God's punishment and correction:

> 'Therefore when any of his children have been brought into great misery and that for their sins as Manasses was ... for his great wickedness, yet when he repented and betoke himself to prayer we see God heard him and holpe him both out of his sins and misery ... he being Jehovah the same for ever ... must deliver us also when we call upon him.'[5]

Such attitudes were reflected in the daily administration of justice in Rye, both in the sentences imposed upon wrongdoers and in the responses of the defendants themselves. John Syms, sent to ward for abusing his wife in April 1593, on his appearance in the court hall, indicated his recognition of the principle that mercy should only follow true repentance in his promise henceforth to 'demeane himself honestly towardes his wyffe and children and in refrayninge dronkennes and common resorting to Alehouses. Otherwyse he desyreth no other favour of Justice but stryct punyshment according to his defect'.[6] However, where a merciful approach had clearly failed, the full severity of the law might follow swiftly. Usually, though, the threat of such exemplary punishment was sufficient, as in the case of John Mathew, arrested for abusing a jurat in September 1593. He was released with a caution, having made a full submission to the court. However, were he to offend again he was to be 'severlye whypped in example to others to be of good behaviour and to be imprisoned untyll he shall fynde good suretyes to be of good behaviour in tyme to come'.[7]

Occasionally even harsh measures such as these failed to bring about the desired amendment, as in the case of James Welles, a persistent minor offender with a drink problem. In February 1594 during one of his periodic appearances before the mayor and jurats 'for extreame dronkennes and horyble swearinge in so much as he was in danger' he promised 'to become a newe man and to forsake those dampnable synnes and offences'. This recognition of guilt and acknowledgement of sin was shortlived. In June of the same year, he was once again in prison for drunkenness, when he was bound over for his good behaviour. A year later in September 1595 he was fined 10s for breaking out of prison, where he found himself again, presumably for a like offence. The threat of a further bond if he did not behave in future seems almost a recognition of defeat on the part of the magistrates. The problem obviously ran in the family, since in June 1594 his son, William, was brought before the court for drunkenness. He also promised to reform, on pain of standing in the collar and a public whipping.[8] The exasperation of the magistrates in cases like that of James Welles can be seen in a certificate granted to Helen Frotier in May 1581, who sought to go to her family in Rouen to escape her husband, John Frotier, locksmith, 'a very drunken and beastly person and hath from tyme to tyme contynually beaten and marvailous evelly entreated the said Helen, his wiff, whereof she hath often complayned and we often tymes have ponished him for his lewdnes and yet no amendment followeth, but rather the poor woman in danger of her liff then otherwise.'[9]

Punishment was thus conceived as having a reforming function. Francis Brooke, accused of seditious libel against the mayor, the Queen's lieutenant and the minister of Rye church in 1598 was ordered to stand in the collar in the Market Place with a paper over his head signifying his offence, to be severely whipped and then returned to prison until he could find sureties for his future behaviour. Summarising the court's attitude to his behaviour 'whereby he spredeth rumors, dyscordes and mutenyes in the commen welth which is not tollerable or to be sufferedd', the sessions book entry set out the thinking behind his sentence: 'For reformacion whereof it is thought good yt discipline by myny-stredd unto him, yt he may be reformed and may be brought to lyve under lawe and government'.[10] In most cases the public shame of the offender was an integral part of the punishment. However, exceptions were made, in particular for the young. Two servants of Robert Blacke, shipwright, were in 1577 ordered to be thoroughly whipped in the Court House for a number of small pickeries (minor thefts) from their master 'and therby to take warninge of leike offences'.[11]

Second offenders inevitably received exemplary punishment. When, in 1589, Catherine Claise, a married woman, was found to have disobeyed an order not to frequent the company of Roger Justice, a sailor, with whom she had previously been found to have had illicit sexual relations, she was immediately ordered to be ducked.[12] Similarly Elizabeth Blakey, widow, for (sexual) incontinency, was in 1580 ordered to be severly whipped 'the rather for that this was the second tyme she was taken with this offence'.[13]

Such punishments were intended to serve as a deterrent both to the offender and to others who might contemplate a similar offence. When, in 1576, young Thomas Baddle, a servant, was ordered to 'be scorgid with roddes in the court House effectually' for petty pickery of lead, it was further ordained 'that their be present the schole boyes in the towne to take example by his ponishment'.[14] A similar instance is furnished by the fate of Richard Tate, servant, fined 3s 4d with imprisonment in 1591 for striking Mr. Grenewood, preacher, a considerable sum for someone of his status. This was clearly intended to warn others, since the sessions entry recorded of his crime, 'the example of this is very pernicious and not to be suffered in any well governed common welthe'.[15]

A range of exemplary punishments of a public, physical kind, was available to be employed against malefactors, chiefly for moral and behavioural crimes most commonly of a sexual nature, verbal abuse or petty thefts. The ducking stool, at the Strand, used for ducking obstreporous females, usually for verbal abuse, was in operation throughout the century. Also at the Strand, by the fishmarket, was the collar and the cage, the latter mainly used to exhibit women for various behavioural offences. In the Market Place, near the Court Hall was a pillory, stocks and whipping post, used for the punishment of male offenders. Vagrancy seen as stemming from idleness,[16] another moral offence, was generally punished by whipping about the town, usually at a cart's tail, a punishment also employed on occasion for sexual offenders who might alternatively be sentenced to ride in the cart. Rarer punishments included 'God's Yoke' employed in the punishment of riotous behaviour and disrupting divine service in 1594 and 1589 respectively, and being 'washed at a boat's tayle in the channel', inflicted upon Jone Benson in 1603 for her 'notorious scoldinge and abusing 2 jurats and others'.[17] In exceptional cases a special punishment might be devised, as in 1572, when it was ordered that 'Woddes wif shall go about the towne with a bason afore hir and a sword and buckler on hir shoulder, and hir husband to follow hir with a brome on his shoulder, which ponishment is for bytinge away a pece of hir husbandes eare and for fytinge with him and other beastly usinge hir self towardes him'.[18]

In order to ensure the maximum public impact, such punishments invariably took place on market days, the offender being held in prison from his sentencing until the next such day. For example, Philipe Wever, butcher, in 1581, for slandering the matrons and honest women of the town 'to the grete greiff aswell of them, their husbandes, and all other good people' was ordered to ward 'there to remayne untill some convenient tyme this weke followinge, and then to be sett in the fishmarket alofte upon some barrell or stoole, with a paper uppon his hed signifyinge his lewde offence, and from thence to retorne againe to the court house and there to remayne untill Saturday followinge, and then in the fulnes of the market to be sett on the pillory with a paper over his hedd.. and there to stand by the space of two houres and so from thence to be banished the towne, excepte he fynde two sufficient suerties for his good behavior.'[19] In a rather more unusual punishment, no doubt because of his office, William

Gere, sergeant at the mace, for speaking ill of the mayor, was committed to ward in August 1576 for two days and further ordered 'publicly upon the eleccion day next at the crosse in the churchyard at the time of the eleccion' when the freemen of the town would be expected to be present, to 'make suche recantation of his wordes and speeches as by the jurats shall be devised and delivered unto him in writing'.[20]

Further instances of the exemplary nature of justice in sixteenth century Rye are afforded by the burning of unlawful kilderkines in the Market Place 'in opyn market' in 1567 and of books employed in 'practizing inchantmentes and wichcraftes' in 1570. Such public manifestations of justice helped to establish social attitudes to particular crimes and to reinforce a healthy respect for authority in an age in which public ritual played an important role in the maintenance of the social order. An example of this is afforded by the arrest of a suspected priest in December 1578 who according to their report to the Bishop of London, 'the people very desirous to see him and his maskinge apparell' was dressed accordingly by the town authorities and led through the streets being 'beheld both of yonge and olde, to no small nomber, whos acclamations and disleikinge of suche vanityes we refer to the report of the messenger.'[21]

Perhaps the clearest indication of the importance placed by the town authorities on public shame as a deterrent to wrongdoers was the 'Decree against Whoredom' passed by the assembly in January 1581. It began by stressing God's displeasure at this fact and continued:

> 'It is orderid that all suche, as without the compas of matrimony shal be gotten with childe, or founde to offend that waye, shall have a partlet made of yellow and grene clothe, kersey or cotton which shalbe thought metest and the same to ware about their neckes uppermost uppon their garment, for by and duringe so longe tyme as they remayne in the towne, and by consideration of the Maior and jurates releasid. And if any suche person be founde without, to be sett in the Cage with godes yoke by the space of thre houres and afterwardes to ware againe the said partlet.'[22]

On March 3 the assembly books record the punishment of eight single women, probably all servants, who had the partlets put on them and were then committed to ward overnight before being brought to church the following day, being a Sunday, where they were to remain during the time of service before being dismissed to their homes. Further, their masters and mistresses were warned not to let them go at any time without those partlets but to inform the mayor so that further punishment might be ministered to them on pain of punishment themselves.[23]

Although the 'Decree against Whoredom' remained in force until at least 1589, following this initial drive against sexual immorality, the wearing of partlets seems only to have been ordered on three subsequent occasions, on the last two of which the guilty party was given the option of leaving town instead.[24] Men were generally treated with less severity, although on a number of occasions both guilty parties were carted together and in rare cases the woman rode in the cart while the man was whipped at its tail. More usually however, the man merely had to enter a bond to save the town from the charges of bringing up the child.

Social class and the ability to pay a substantial fine also affected punishments for sexual offences. In February 1581, William Scragge, a member of the common council was displaced from office for his 'notorious and apparent whordom ... committed with the wiff of Gabriell Gibbons ... and to be ponished as lawe will permit'. On his appearance before the mayor and jurats he humbly submitted himself and 'desired that it would please them to consider of him beinge an old man and his labor past, that he might not be in theies his old yeris too publiquely shamed emongest the people' and instead offered to pay a sum of money to the town's works, fixed by them at £10 which he duly paid 'and so to be remitted of his other ponishment before determined against him, which was to have rid in a carte with the wiff of the saide Gibbons, and tingid with a bason about the towne'.[25] Similarly, William Eaton a Dover merchant and a maidservant found asleep in bed together by the mistress of the house in July 1585, had their punishment of carting, with the maidservant whipped at the cart's tail, remitted to imprisonment 'for some consideration', presumably also financial.[26]

Capital offences

The ultimate exemplary punishment was execution, in theory the penalty for all felonies, but in practice inflicted only rarely. Nevertheless, Rye had its share of public executions in the Tudor period, ranging from the hanging of eight rebels, probably implicated in the attempted landing of Perkin Warbeck in July 1495, to the burning in the Market Place in June 1535 of Cornelius Johnson, a Dutch anabaptist, for heresy.[27] Such events were attended with considerable ritual, designed to increase the impact of such awesome punishments on the beholders. Twenty billmen had their ferry paid 'to se execucione done' on two pirates hanged at Rye in September 1566, having been previously taken for examination at Dover and paraded back by road through the Kent towns and villages in 'halters and trussyng lynes'.[28] Similarly, in April 1551, when three counterfeiters were tried and executed for treason at Rye the event was surrounded by elaborate preparations including a feast for the special commissioners, including Sir John Baker, Attorney General, Mr. Tufton and Mr. Thomas Darell, prominent county JPs. The chamberlains' accounts also include the stark entry 'Payd to thexecutyoner ye xth of Aprell for makyng ye pytt, burying and for poles to sett theire headdes on . And bearying one of theare headdes to Wynchellsey and settyng yt up iiij s'.[29]

Yet such punishments were rare and were reserved for exceptional offences, usually dealt with by special commissioners or by courts outside of the town. Rye's own courts record only nine death sentences in the 45 years between 1558 and 1603, five of which were for murder or infanticide. Out of a total of 114 persons accused or suspected of capital larceny, only three were actually sentenced to death and probably only two of these were executed, one of whom had already previously been granted benefit of clergy for an earlier offence and had also once been acquitted of felony. A summary of these proceedings is set out in Table 33.

The procedure in felony cases before a suspect might eventually be executed was lengthy and laborious. Following an accusation or suspicion, or, in the case of murder, the verdict of a coroner's jury, a suspect might be examined and sent to ward or bailed. In most cases he would then be proclaimed at successive hundreds (or sessions as they were alternatively known), which were specially convened for the purpose, usually at three week intervals. If no-one came to prosecute by the third occasion, the suspect was acquitted and delivered from gaol by proclamation.[31] As can be seen above, a considerable number, roughly one sixth,

208

Table 33

Felony cases before Rye Courts 1558–1603:
Judicial process and outcome

	Suspicion/Accusation	Proclaimed	Released	Indicted	Grand Jury Ignoramus	Grand Jury Reduction	Grand Jury True Bill	Plea Reduction	Trial Jury Acquittal	Trial Jury Reduction	Trial Jury Guilty	Bench Mitigation	Benefit of Clergy	Pardon	To hang	In burial Registers
Murder	11	7	1	6	-	-	6	1	2	1	4	-	2	-	2	2
Infanticide	5	4	-	4	-	-	4	-	1	-	3	-	-	-	3	1
Accessory	2	1	-	1	-	-	1	-	1	-	-	-	-	-	-	-
Larceny	114	95[2]	23	72[3]	4	4[4]	63[5]	-	38	1	18[6]	2[7]	11[8]	2	3	2[9]
Accessory	7	6	-	6	1	-	4[10]	-	3	-	1	-	1	-	-	-
Other	5	5	-	5	1	-	4	-	3	-	1	-	-	-	1	-
Total	144	118	24	94	6	4	82	1	48	2	27	2	14	2	9	5

Notes:
1. Burial register has gap for period covering one possible execution.
2. 3 suspected felons granted Royal Pardons while in prison on suspicion, probably during Queen's visit to Rye.
3. 5 indicted, fled or no further action.
4. From £160 to £34.
5. 2 released by proclamation; 3 no further proceedings.
6. 1 reduced to petty larceny.
7. 2 whipped.
8. 2 couldn't read, but not in burials.
9. 1 horse thief possibly pardoned. 2 other felons imprisoned at same time noted as having been granted Royal Pardons—1559.
10. 1 indicted, no further action.
11. 1 acquitted by trial jury of witchcraft; 1 grand jury ignoramus for buggery of a sowe; 1 acquitted by trial jury of rape; 1 sentenced to hang for highway robbery and 1 accomplice to same acquitted by trial jury.

Sources: RYE 1/2-6; PAR 467/1/1/1.

of those upon whom suspicion fell (26 out of 144) did not even reach this stage in the judicial proceedings, either having fled or it having been decided that there was little point in proceeding further. A further sixth (24 persons) were released on proclamation because no-one came to prosecute, including several who were clearly guilty such as the two apprentices of William Gilford apprehended and sent to prison by their dame for felony of their master's goods and conspiring to run away. They spent a month in prison until their release on 19 August 1564, their master and mistress presumably having decided this was sufficient punishment.

Those who were prosecuted were then indicted before a grand jury which had to decide whether or not there was sufficient evidence to proceed and could, if it were so minded, reduce the charge against the defendant, which was done in the case of four men jointly accused in June 1571 of the theft of unspecified goods of William Chapman of Rye, originally valued at £160 but reduced to £34, presumably in order to ensure that the men would qualify for a grant of benefit of clergy (only permissible in the case of thefts of under £40) should they be found guilty. In the event, two were released by proclamation on 14 August and the other two were acquitted on 27 August.[33]

Of the original 144 suspects, only 82 (57 per cent) had a true bill issued against them by the grand jury. Of these a further six (including the two above) were not proceeded against further; one was granted a plea reduction, from murder to manslaughter; two had the charges against them reduced by the trial jury and a further 48 were acquitted altogether, leaving only 27 out of an original 144 suspects (18 per cent of the original total, or 29 per cent of those indicted) who were found guilty. Of these, however, only one third (9) were actually sentenced to hang, two having received royal pardons, two having had their sentences reduced to whipping by the mayor and jurats and eleven having claimed benefit of clergy. Five were definitely hanged, their entries being recorded in the Rye burial register which in one case is defective, but in three cases no burial is recorded, suggesting that even at this late stage, there was a possibility of mitigation. Usually the execution took place within a few days of the actual sentence. An indication of the lengths to which the town authorities were prepared to go in order not to execute is therefore indicated by the case of two mariners who stole cloth valued at £3 from a ship in the Puddle in November 1558. Sentenced to hang on 27 January 1559, they were kept in prison until they were released by royal pardon on 3 June.[34]

In the case of murder or infanticide the proportion of those indicted actually receiving the death sentence (5 out of 10) was much higher than for property offences (3 out of 72). Even here, however, there is clear evidence of a deliberate policy of mitigation according to circumstances. Seven of the eleven murder cases related to fights, usually with daggers following arguments. In three cases the killer fled, and of the remaining four cases, in one a plea of manslaughter was accepted allowing benefit of clergy; in another, relating to a duel with rapiers on the Mountes, the trial jury reduced the charge to homicide by chance, also qualifying for benefit of clergy; in another case, involving a fight at the Conduit between two women the trial jury granted an acquittal and the guilty party was merely bound over; while in only one case, where there was evidence of premeditation, was the guilty party actually executed.[35] Social status may have helped William Tolkin junior, yeoman, whose plea of manslaughter and claim of clergy was accepted by the court in January 1591 following a dagger fight. This was the only plea reduction accepted during this period and his father was a jurat.[36] At the very least a knowledge of legal proceedings can hardly have been irrelevant to the conduct of his defence.

Those murderers who were executed either showed manifest proof of guilt or had committed a particularly brutal premeditated act, as for example Thomas Robinson, found guilty of having on 26 May 1594 conveyed into the body of Bridget his wife 'at her secret partes, certeyne broken glasse and poyson' which caused her a lingering death almost three weeks later. She died on 12 June, the inquest was held the following day and on 17 June her husband was indicted, tried and sentenced to hang. The burial register records that he was buried 'under the gallowes where he was hanged for poysening of his said wife' on 19 June.[37] In such a clear-cut case, justice was extremely swift.

The same was true of infanticide, which evoked a deep sense of horror in the community. In each of the four cases indicted, the defendant was a single woman (in one case a widow) suspected of having done away with an unwanted bastard child at birth. In the case of the acquittal, in 1570, Kateryn Herste, widow, and John Page were immediately carted and banished for 'their lewde act in whoredom', while on 3 February 1580, Margery Porter, single-woman, was sentenced to be taken from prison at nine in the morning on the following Saturday, being market day, and to be hanged, the father of her child, John Mody als Bylly, cockman, being taken from prison at the same time and whipped about the town at a cart's tail 'for his whoredom'.[38]

Over 80 per cent of felony cases at Rye related to property offences. In the 51 cases where the property is specified, cloth, or items of clothing (17 cases) and sheep (16) were the most common items mentioned, followed by household goods (5) and money (4). Eight of the accused were females and 113 males, including 19 from outside the town. The occupations of the accused, given in 85 cases show a clear relationship between poverty and crime. Simon Duron, a tailor, executed for felony on 1 October 1597[39] and Edward Harris, butcher, who forfeited 160 sheep, 7 kine, 9 weyners, a sowe and 6 pigs together with his household stuff, corn and hay, as a convicted felon in August 1599, were very much exceptions amongst those brought before the courts for capital property offences.[40] The largest single group of offenders were mariners and fishermen (27), followed by labourers (11), apprentices, boys or servants (8). The residue was chiefly composed of a range of poorer trades: cobblers (4), tailors (4), carpenters (2), rippiers (2), butchers (mainly employees of master butchers, 8) and other employees such as an ostler, a tapster, a servingman and a footman. Seven only can be identified as belonging to the wealthier sort, including two Dieppe merchants, a London stationer and four yeomen, all of whom were either not proceeded against or acquitted.[41]

Fishermen and mariners in particular were occupations liable to seasonal unemployment, and the evidence of the 1576 sesse demonstrates conclusively that they were among the poorest of Rye's inhabitants. These and other poorer inhabitants could easily find themselves driven to crime in order not to starve. This was especially true in years when poor harvests led to soaring corn prices and severe bread shortages. Figure 7 which relates the size of the 2d household loaf, regarded by the corporation as 'baked for the poore',[42] and the incidence of property felonies, suggests a close correlation between the high price of this item of the staple diet of the poorer classes and theft of property. The peaks of twelve felonies per year in mayoral years 1596–7 and 1597–8 and of eleven felonies in 1565–6 all coincide with acute reductions in the buying power of the poorer classes. The bad harvest of 1565 saw the reduction in size of a 3d loaf from 76 oz to 44 oz, while between September 1596 and May 1597 it fell from 30 oz to 16¾oz, recovering only slightly until January 1599 when it was set at 32 oz. Such sudden reductions in the purchasing power of those already barely at subsistence level inevitably led to an equally sudden spate of thefts. No doubt it was an awareness of this fact which led the authorities on all but one occasion during these years, to refrain from exacting the death penalty.

Minor offences – regulating conduct

The prosecution of felony was only a small part of the work of the courts in Tudor Rye and accounted for little over 5 per cent of business during the Elizabethan period, when records are

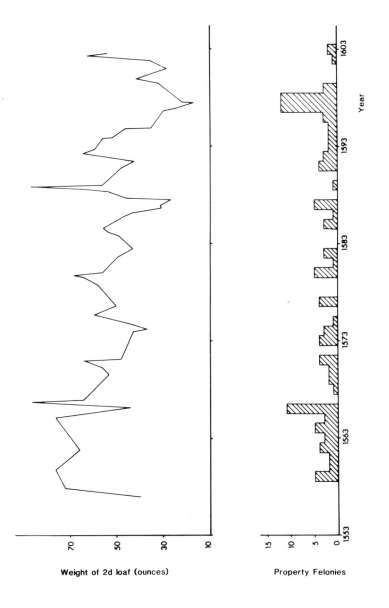

Weight of 2d loaf (ounces)   Property Felonies

Figure 7: Property felonies and the price of bread in Rye 1558-1603

213

Table 34
Crime and social control in Elizabethan Rye:
Annual totals 1558–1603

Year	Homicide	Capital Larceny	Other Capital	Petty Larceny	Economic	Behavioural	Affrays and Riots	Vagrants and Newcomers	Administrative	Other	Bonds
1558/9	1	5	-	-	5	-	22	1	43	-	-
1559/60	-	2	-	-	6	3	11	-	5	3	8
1560/1	-	2	1	-	3	3	17	-	-	-	1
1561/2	-	4	-	-	16	5	16	-	18	1	3
1562/3	-	3	-	-	2+	-	19	4	16	-	2
1563/4	-	5	1	-	2	-	15	-	71	-	-
1564/5	-	3	-	-	18+	4	35+	1	15	9	8
1565/6	2	11	-	-	3	7	28	5	9	-	4
1566/7	1	-	-	-	41	8	14	1	22	1	13
1567/8	-	1	-	1	16	5	14	-	20	-	5
1568/9	-	2	2	-	26	13	18	4	15	2	6
1569/70	1	2	-	-	11	18	39	3	8	1	1
1570/1	-	4	-	-	14	1	9^2	-	5	-	8
1571/2	1	-	-	-	18	9	17	-	7	4	15
1572/3[3]	-	4	-	3	2	6	1	1	11	-	4
1573/4	-	3	-	2	20+	2	21	5	13	2	11
1574/5	-	1	1	-	18	3	6 18^2	-	19	8	14
1575/6	-	-	-	-	23+	7	27	4	20	-	4
1576/7	-	4	-	4	12	7	19	1	-	-	7
1577/8	-	-	-	-	11	4	34	-	8	1	13
1578/9	-	-	-	-	+	8	33	-	6	1	9
1579/80	1	5	-	-	15+	6	10	-	4	-	9
1580/81	-	1	-	2	6+	29	19	1	17	2	12
1581/2	-	3	-	3	25+	8	26	-	12	-	5
1582/3	1^1	-	-	7	50+	6	14+	7	12	1	6
1583/4	2	-	-	-	43	7	9	1	18	1	6
1584/5	-	3	-	-	13	2	$-^2$	1	3	-	10
1585/6	2	1	-	1	45+	3	7^2	5	4	-	4
1586/7	-	5	-	2	9	1	$-^2$	-	2	-	4
1587/8	-	-	-	-	3	-	9^2	-	5	-	4
1588/9	-	1	-	1	1+	6	4^2	4	5	-	9
1589/90	-	-	-	-	12	4	1^2	-	18	2	-
1590/1	-	4	-	-	4+	1	12^2	3	29+	-	5
1591/2	1	3	-	-	7	5	5^2	3	6	-	7
1592/3	1	2	-	2	4	8	18	8	8	-	3
1593/4	1	2	-	1	4+	11	28	6	9	-	13
1594/5	-	2	-	-	6+	1	7	2	55+	-	10
1595/6	1	3	-	-	1	2	7	8	7	-	8
1596/7	-	12	1	2	22+	-	16	4	12	1	10
1597/8	1	12	-	2	25	-	11	5	38	-	4
1598/9	1	3	-	-	15+	5	8	-1	10	-	10
1599/1600	1	-	-	-	6	2	11	-	5	1	8
1600/1	-	-	-	4	10	1	14	2	9	-	9
1601/2	-	1	-	-	12	-	2^2	-	4	-	13
1602/3	-	2	1	-	-	1	3	-	13	-	4
Total	19	121	7	37	607+	222	658+	91	635+	41	309

Table 34

Notes
+ indicates reference to unspecified number of fines in addition to those totalled individually
delivered to High Sheriff's officers at boundary.
1 Outside the Cinque Port Liberty.
2 Figures clearly incomplete.
3 No chamberlains' accounts survive amongst the RYE MSS at E.S.R.O. for 1572/3.
Categories:
1 See Table 33
2 See Table 33
3 See Table 33
4 Includes petty pickery, attempted pickery of purses, petty bribery.
5 Includes bakers' fines (201 +), butchers' fines (72 +), regrating and ingrossing (21), Sunday
trading (2), fishing and unlawful nets (39), unlawful occupations (80), unlicensed victualling
(91), transporting prohibited goods overseas (34), false weights or measure (22), other (45).
6 Includes bastardy allegations (38), other sexual misdemeanours (80), evil/lewde demeanour
(24), unlawful gaming (24), victualling offences (17), drunkenness (23), apprentices' offences
towards masters (10), religious offences (5), maltreatment of child (1).
7 Includes frays and braches of the peace (589 +), scolding and verbal abuse (19), night
disturbances (23), other disturbances (28), shooting guns (4).
8 Includes vagrants (39), newcomers ordered to enter bonds or certificates of good behaviour or
depart (47), soldiers suspected returning without passports (5).
9 Includes non-attendance at assemblies or sessions (332), forfeit recognizances (35), attacks on
town officials (21), abuse/contempt of mayor/jurats or refusal to obey ordinances (42),
animals (mainly hogs) in the streets (32), fired chimneys (21), filth, washing at the conduit and
other nuisances (22), casting ballast (21), damage to roads by shoed carts (9), damage to
jetties and other shipping offences (18), thatch (2), papists' oaths (3), other (55), refusal to pay
sesse (3), refusal to pay other fines/dues levied (14).
10 Includes aiding freebooters (8), suspected piracy (2), arbitration of disputes (13), sedition
against the Queen (2), forgery of a will (1), witchcraft/sorcery (1), idiocy (1), other (13).
11 includes bonds to behave (101) and bonds to keep the peace (208).

Total 2750 cases not including bonds to appear and answer unspecified charges except where
covered by later court action, nor including unspecified fines entered in chamberlains' accounts.
As far as possible, individual cases have been checked in both assembly books (RYE 1) and
chamberlains' accounts (RYE 60) to prevent duplication.
Sources: E.S.R.O. RYE 60/4-7;1/1-7.

relatively complete. Much of the rest of that business was
regulatory in nature, enforcing the assize of bread and regulating
the price of beer, wine and beef; licensing inns and alehouses;
enforcing town ordinances against petty nuisances; as well as
punishing breaches of the peace and other behavioural offences.
The full range of these other functions can be seen in Table 34,
which lists 2747 individual prosecutions, including 309 persons
bound over to behave or keep the peace during the years
1558–1603.

From this it can be seen that economic offences, administrative
offences and affrays and riots accounted for the bulk of the courts'
activities, usually resulting in fines for the guilty parties. This was
particularly the case in respect of affrays and riots, which resulted
in fines in 603 of 658 instances. The chief exceptions to this were

night and other disturbances, usually the result of late night drinking, which in 31 instances resulted in the guilty parties being sent to ward overnight, in eleven cases additionally being fined and in a further eight cases also being bound over to behave; and the nineteen cases of scolding or verbal abuse, for which fourteen women and five men were arraigned. In this instance six cases resulted in an appropriate form of public exhibition of the offender, in three cases standing in the collar at Strand with a paper over their heads signifying the offence, in two others the cage,[43] plus on one occasion ducking as well. Ducking was also prescribed in two further instances and in another two cases offenders were banished.[44]

Such a sentencing policy indicates the greater seriousness with which verbal abuse and night disturbances were treated by the town authorites, who clearly saw them as a much greater threat to social order than the great mass of affrays and fights, which received only a summary fine ranging from 12d to 3s 4d or occasionally 6s 8d depending upon the date and whether or not a weapon was used, and only rarely above this rate. Probably the corporation realised that affrays and similar incidents were an inevitable feature of town life particularly in a large port and that no threat of exemplary punishment was likely to lead to any improvement in behaviour.

In the case of economic offences the preference for fines levied on 519 out of 607 occasions, suggests an attempt to make the breaking of market regulations unprofitable and hence to reduce the number of offences. There also appears to have been some attempt to graduate the level of fines according to the seriousness of the offence. This is most obvious in the case of infringements of the assize of bread, which resulted in over 200 prosecutions and 189 fines during the Elizabethan period. From at least 1569 onwards there is evidence that bakers were often fined at the rate of 12d per ounce for underweight bread and this was specifically stated on a number of occasions, as in December 1579, when it was ordered that 'the baker for every ounce so wantinge shall paye xijd for a fynne at the leaste; alwaies regarde to be had to the stallnes of the brede'.[45]

As a last resort against consistent major offenders there was the threat of the pillory, although it was never actually carried out. Thus Henry Ollyve was given the choice of the pillory or a 13s 4d fine in October 1567 for his 2d loaf which weighed only 42 oz, being 20 oz light; Thomas Heblethwaite in February 1586 was warned to keep the assize on pain of being put in the pillory because his bread was one-third below weight; and Roger Gylforde 'his ijd loffe being very unholsom and naughty bredd' as well as being 6 oz light, in September 1598 was fined 30s and given judgement of the pillory if he offended again.[46]

Sometimes, however, it was the mayor who had to adjust the assize in the face of the economic realities and the concerted opposition of the bakers. On 1 August 1586 six bakers were found with their 2d loaves 11–13 oz light. Heavy fines of between 10s and 17s and the threat of the pillory made little difference and on 6 September their 2d loaves were still lacking between 9½ and 12 oz. To make matters worse they had only 39 bushels of wheat and 81 bushels of meal between them 'and the rest of the bakers have no bread'. A month later on 8 October the situation had deteriorated still further and the bakers' 2d loaves ranged from 13 oz to 17 oz below the assize, which as a result was at last lowered, the new weight of the 2d loaf being set at just under 31 oz, the top weight at which bakers were still selling bread.[47]

Similar situations arose with regard to the price of meat, which was the main source of the 72 or more fines on butchers. Thus in December 1573 five butchers were accused of conspiring together not to kill beef except at 12d the naile. Although they had to enter into bonds to sell until Christmas at 11d the naile, they were promised that then a new price would be set. A rather more serious situation arose on 28 May 1586 when Edward and Thomas Harrys, Francis Daniell and Thomas Swifte, butchers, refused to sell at the prices set. They were committed to ward, but the following day they were released and the price of beef was raised to the unprecedented level of 16d the naile.[48]

Rather more than half of butchers' offences related to selling above price. Fines were also levied, however, for the killing of barrens after All Saints (10), the killing of hogs before All Saints (3), killing calves (13) and killing meat in Lent (2). Perhaps the most bizarre offence, however, was that committed by Thomas Harrys and Robert Bennett in December 1574 in 'sendinge a shoulder of a dogge, instead of a shoulder of venson ... to be baked', for which they were fined 6s 8d apiece, 3s 4d going in compensation to the aggrieved party and 10s to the poor.[49]

Other economic offences which mainly attracted fines were unlicensed victualling (91), for which fines were often set at penal rates and for which 16 persons had to enter bonds to desist; pursuing unlawful trades or occupations, for which 74 persons were fined and six others either given time to appeal or ordered to desist; false weights or measures (18 fined out of 22); fishing with unlawful nets or at unlawful times, for which 39 French fishing boats had their nets confiscated and in 33 cases were forced to enter into bonds; transporting prohibited goods overseas, mainly tallow or leather (30 fined); trading on the Sabbath (2); and forestalling the market or regrating and engrossing (21 cases including fifteen fines, four of whom were also sent to ward and two of whom together with six others had to enter bonds).

Administrative offences, although attracting mainly fines (487+ in 635+ cases), comprised a wide range of infringements of town regulations. Most common was non-attendance at an assembly or sessions, or failure to attend for service on a hundred or lenten jury, which resulted in 328 fines and four persons being sent to ward. In this instance fines were usually low, generally being fixed at 12d for a commoner or common council member and 2s for a jurat. Exceptionally, Richard Frenche and Henry Peck, commoners, were committed to ward for the offence, because, having been warned by the mayor's sergeant to attend a hundred on 16 December 1566, although nearby, 'did obstinately refuse to make ther appearance' Peck further compounded his offence by refusing to pay his fine, which was eventually fixed at the astronomical level of £5 and as a result of 'his obstinacye and stobernes' remained in prison thirteen days before he was prepared to submit. Richard Frenche submitted at once and paid 3s. [50]

Other administrative offences which normally resulted in fines included such minor nuisances as casting filth over the town wall and washing clothes at the Conduit, usually resulting in a fine of 4d, (22 fines in all); firing chimneys (21 fines ranging from 3s 4d to 10s); allowing hogs to wander in the streets (14 fines and 18 bonds to remove them, including 15 who were given three weeks to avoid them following a town ordinance of 25 July 1590); ships casting their ballast into the harbour (21 fines ranging from 12d to 53s 4d depending on the magnitude of the offence); damaging the streets with shoed carts or damaging the quayside with a ship (17 fines according to the scale of damage); encroachments on corporation property (7); and a range of other minor offences from laying thatch on house roofs contrary to the 1561 town ordinance (two fines of 16s each in May 1565) to failure to pay debts due to the town.

Three types of offences in this category of which a more serious view was taken, however, were refusal to pay a town sesse or other town duties, for which three freemen were disfranchised during the Elizabethan period; attacks on town officers, which resulted in two warnings, seven persons being sent to ward, eight fines, two bonds to behave and two persons being put in the stocks; and finally, contempt for or abuse of the mayor or jurats (47 cases in all, generally resulting in the offender being sent to ward, together with either a fine or some exemplary punishment).

The majority of cases involving abuse or attacks on town officers seem to have resulted from some other offence which the offender was in process of committing at the time of his or her detection by the town authorities or from a dispute over an official's authority in a particular circumstance. A typical instance is afforded by the prosecution of Edward Tyndall and his wife, brought before the mayor and jurats on 24 May 1594 following a dispute in the market, 'for revyleing John Engram, Clarke of the Markett, in provyding to see mackrell sold to thinhabitauntes ... And his wiffe also ... for fighting and scratchinge one Thomas Smyth for defending the said John Engram'. Both were released with a warning. Similarly, in April 1573, John Willes, lighterman of Playden, having brought unlawful billets into the town was brought before the mayor and jurats for 'misusing' the Clerk to the Market. Perhaps a more serious instance is afforded by the fate of two members of the town watch in May 1583, who, having come upon some leather being illicitly transported at night, seized it, only to have it taken again from them by force by Robert Farley and John Benbrick's son. The town watch, evidently, could be a hazardous occupation. John Peirs and Harry Strete, servants, were ordered to be set in the stocks with a paper over their heads signifying their offence 'for beatinge and misusinge the watche of the towne', presumably following some late-night revelry in October 1583.[51]

On other occasions, individuals or their relations protesting at the severity of a particular sentence of the court often launched into an attack on the administration of justice and verbal abuse of the mayor and jurats. Thus 'olde Bull', following his son's punishment for his part in the sexual abuse of a female servant in July 1593 was heard to say that his son 'was as honest a man as the best and that he cared not for the governors and that yf he were as his sonne, he wolde putt his cappe whereupon the paper stoode under his tayle'. Similarly, Robert Bennett, butcher, on hearing that his brother John, a tailor, had been called before the mayor and Richard Fletcher, minister, for being in a tavern house drinking during service time on Easter Monday 1576, as he was leaving the church 'sayd openly that he would call the church-warden knave of yt'. Both brothers were regular offenders, but Robert had the more abusive tongue. When called before the mayor and jurats in December 1575, to redeem his part in the recognizance for his brother John's good behaviour which the latter had forfeited by fraying with Richard Daniell, 'his wordes of defyance stretchinge to Mr. Maior syttinge in place of Justice in the presence of the jurates and Common Councell assembled, a matter odious and not sufferable', resulted in his being committed to ward, where he remained eleven days before he was willing to yield to his fault. He was fined 3s 4d, an additional 10s fine by way of damages to the mayor for his slander being redelivered to him 'by Mr. Maior of his courtesy', presumably because he recognised that it had been said in the heat of the moment.[52]

Not all instances of verbal abuse of the town authorities resulted from outbursts by those outside the political hierarchy. Relations between John Yonge, waterbailiff, and the mayor and jurats whose jurisdictions sometimes conflicted were never good. On at least five occasions they broke out into public conflict, resulting in Mr. Yonge being sent to ward. On 2 April 1575, he was committed to ward 'for abusing him self in the court hall in place of Justice before the Maior and jurates there assembled with blasphemeous wordes against god, with swaringe and other irreverent speches, and usinge untrue accusations against divers honest persons, wherby grete disquietnes did rise and blodshed leike to have ensued'. No sooner was he released than he was again committed to ward on 11 April 'for threateninge and misusinge the churchwardins and sidemen which were sworn to present defaulters unto the commisary'. In December 1578 he was once more committed to ward, this time for an unspecified misdemeanour against the mayor and jurats, and in March 1581 for 'his lewde wordes and ill speches' against a sidesman in the execution of his duty in presenting ecclesiastical offences. Finally, on 15 May 1581 he was sent to ward by the jurats 'for his slaunderous and evill wordes usid against Mr. Robert Jacson, Maior of Rye' and fined 5s to the town and 40s to the mayor for damages. This was almost the last time the magistrates had to deal with their recalcitrant neighbour, although he was bound over in the sum of £20 to keep the peace in July 1586 and in the sum of £60 , an unusually high figure, in December 1586. The mayor and jurats must, nevertheless, have been relieved, when in January 1587 he surrendered up his office to his namesake, John Yonge of Chichester, in return for a lump sum payment of £10 and an annual pension of £20 per year.[53]

Verbal abuse also served as a form of political protest when events went badly for the town. In 1514, for example, following the loss of the Mary Hankyng during the war with the French a woman is recorded as having been set upon the cucking stool 'for skolding with the Vice Admirall'.[54] As Rye's economic fortunes declined in the 1590s such protests occurred with increasing regularity. In 1594 a man found himself in the stocks for saying publicly that the next year he would rather have 'an innocent' (i.e. an idiot) as mayor. Then in the spring of 1597, acute grain shortage hit the town. Bread prices soared and many bakers had no bread at all. The resulting outcry took the form of abuse of the mayor. A shipload of grain, sent by Sir Henry Palmer in response to Rye's plight which arrived on 10 June, did little to allay the criticism and a week later when a Breton ship carrying grain had also come into the harbour, a woman was fined 20s, to be paid by her husband, for 'saying yt the wheate and Rye which of late was brought in ... came in against Mr. mayors will, contrarye to all truth'. Barely a month later, Richard Swanne, a freeman, appeared before the mayor and jurats for refusing to pay his town duties and trying to dissuade others from doing the same saying 'it were as good to compleine to noboddye' and 'yf any that shold be Maior were worse then he that now is Maior he wyshed that he were hanged at the Landgate'.[55]

The different types of behavioural offences elicited widely differing responses from the town authorities as can be seen from Table 35. In the case of the treatment of putative fathers in

Table 35:
The incidence of behavioural offences and their punishment 1558-1603

	Accused only	Examined only	To ward	Fined	Warned	Whipped	Carted	Publicly exhibited	Ducked	Other public	Banished with other public	Banished only	Bound	Other	Total
Bastardy	3	-	-	1[1]	-	2[1,2]	-	-	-	1[2]	-	-	28	3[3]	38
Other sexual	-	1	-	2	-	12[4]	30[5]	5[6]	1	9[7]	-	18[8]	6	1	80
Evil demeanour/lewdness	-	-	1	3	-	2	1[9]	-	-	2	2	12[10]	-	5	26
Gaming	-	-	-	19	-	-	-	-	-	-	-	-	4	1	24
Victualling	-	-	-	16[11]	-	-	-	-	-	-	-	-	-	1	17
Drunkenness	-	-	6[12]	1[13]	-	-	-	1	-	-	-	-	-	12[14]	23
Apprentices/Servants	-	-	-	-	-	3[15]	-	-	-	1[16]	1	-	2	6[17]	10
Religion	-	-	-	2[18]	-	-	-	-	-	-	-	3[19]	-	-	5
Maltreatment of child	-	-	-	-	-	-	-	-	-	-	-	-	-	1[20]	1
Totals	3	1	10	42	-	19	31	6	1	12	21	27	41	29	222

Notes:

1. led to infanticide.
2. includes ill treatment.
3. ordered/bound to marry.
4. includes 2 cases of perjury and adultery; 1 attempted rape by a male servant of his master's daughter (defendant also pilloried), 1 second offence and 1 case of having 2 wives.
5. 5 instances with collar.
6. in stocks includes 5 of 6 young men for sexually abusing a female servant (the sixth merely bound over).
7. wearing of parties of yellow and green outside houses.
8. 1 female suspected of incontinency, drunkenness and common railing
9. lewdness with 2 maidservants and wife beating.
10. includes 1 suspected bawde and 1 female dwelling in an alehouse.
11. includes 1 fined 40s and dismissed tippling for mayoral year for allowing dicing in service time.
12. includes also 2 bound.
13. plus banned from tippling houses.
14. banned from tippling houses.
15. 2 also dismissed service.
16. 'punished in Open Market'.
17. 5 dismissed from service, 2 of these and 1 other also punished (unspecified).
18. 2 Bretons fined for 'idolatrous idoles'.
19. 3 Dutch immigrants for 'misbelieves contrary to Christian religion'.
20. removed from custody and placed with another family.

bastardy allegations, for example, where the proof of the fact rested only on the evidence of the pregnant woman, the magistrates limited their action to safeguarding the town from the charges of childbed or of bringing up the child. In the case of the woman, however, whose pregnancy itself constituted manifest proof of guilt, punishment was of an exemplary nature; similarly in other cases where there was clear proof of guilt. William Hore, currier and Anthony Vyne's wife, for example, having been previously warned by the mayor and Mr. Fletcher, the minister, for their repeated sexual incontinency together, were carted in September 1576, having been 'by Mr. maior himself taken in Hore's chamber'.[56]

Gaming offences, on the other hand, rarely elicited more than a small fine, usually 12d, for those found at play, with a somewhat higher fine of 10s or, occasionally, more for the instigator, in whose house, usually a tippling house, the offence took place. An exception was the punishment meted out to John Rowland, a professional gambler previously banished for using false dice and now again entered into the town without permission 'and hath provoked many to playe at dyse and cardes with hym'. In July 1540 the mayor and jurats inflicted the full penalty of the law, ordering 'that the seyd John Rowland shall in the Market Place of Rye have a byllet naylyd to hys lyfte ere and so had round aboute the towne and a taber before hym and so had owt of the towne of Rye, never to retorne thyther ayene under payn of losyng both hys eres'.[57]

Suspected places and suspicious persons

Many of these offences, particularly gambling and drunkenness, but also night disturbances, many affrays and woundings, a number of sexual offences and even the occasional murder[58] were centred on unruly alehouses, which might also serve as havens for vagrants, bawds and others of a similarly lewd disposition. Evil rule, when detected, would result in fines of either 10s or 20s, or higher for repeated offences. Mercy Poskins, widow, had to pay a fine of £3 in April 1569 for having Frenchmen to tipple in her house after an assembly had banned them from there 'because of the evil rule and misdemeanour used in her house by them'. In other cases ill rule might be suspected but not proven.[59]

Single women given to frequenting alehouses, fell under

obvious suspicion. Thus Parnell Rubway, Frenchwoman, was, in June 1571, ordered 'no more to dwell in eny tipling howse but in some other honest mans house' or else to leave town.[60]

Frays, occasioned by some drunken quarrel, were a common occurrence, although few of those found guilty suffered the penalty inflicted on Richard Sadler, servant of Samuell Williams, rippier, in February 1583, who was fined 3s 4d and ordered thenceforth not to frequent 'eny victualling howse within the towne or liberties, but send for suche victuals as he hath nede of to his owne house, wherby his wiff may be the better relevid'.[61] On rare occasions, the consequences of such frays could be fatal, as, for example, on 25 March 1549 when:

> 'Hans Scryver mariner ... about v of the clok in the afternone came into one Fraunces Russells howse ... where in the compeny of others he founde one Adrian Dirik de Rover maryner sittinge by the fier with whom the said Hans assone as he came in picked a quarell and drew owt his rapier wherewithall the said Dirik crope under the table. And then the said Hans strok at one Laraunce Clayson, master of an hoy of Siricksey then present and wounded him and had killed him then if the aforesaid Fraunces Russell had not rescued the said Laraunce, and found meanes to convay both him and others that wer in the house out of the house. And when the said Hans saw the rest to begon he loked under the table and espied there the aforesaid Dirick, he strak at him beinge there and making no resistaunce he thrust him in the flanke with a fyne and gave him a wound of vi enchis diep upon the whiche wounde he died immediatly. At the doinge of the which murder ther was only ene the howse where the dede was don one Garrard Luksman ducheman who was in such feare of life that he dirst not uris to styr nor meddle ...'[62]

Although such fatalities were rare, late night drinking bouts could occasion a considerable amount of disturbance and damage to the property of law-abiding citizens. One such incident occurred on the night of Monday 26 September 1575, when Edward Harris, Robert and John Bennett and two men from Hythe met up with Thomas Mathew, painter, at the bench in the Market Place at about nine o'clock in the evening. Having gone back to Mathew's house and drunk 'three or four potts' of beer, they came out again at about eleven o'clock and went down to the Strand, one of them feeling 'skent well at ease'. From there they went on the rampage through the streets, throwing a piece of timber and some wheels over the cliff by Landgate, upsetting a cask in Watchbell Street and a tan vat in Okeman's Lane, breaking a window in Middle Street and pulling down the wall of Thomas Beveridge's kitchen and the lattice from Thomas Edolf's window, which they threw over the wall into the vicarage. Perhaps surprisingly, only Robert Bennett was fined (6s 8d) and in his case it was more for his perjury and attempts to obstruct evidence when he was first examined than for the actual incident itself. The other main participants seem merely to have been bound over to keep the peace, a relatively forlorn hope in the case of such regular offenders![63]

Drunkenness was evidently a major concern of the town authorities. In July 1581 decisive action was taken. Following a petition from the churchwardens and sidesmen to the mayor and jurats, twelve 'commen dronkerds' were banned from every tippling house in Rye. The seriousness of the penalties—anyone who served them was to be dismissed from tippling—indicates the gravity with which the situation was regarded. There was some justification for the concern. Over-indulgence might not just lead to violence. It could have severe economic consequences too. Cornelis Jacobson, master of a vessel of Rotterdam laden with white wines from Bordeaux came into harbour on 13 February 1576 to await a favourable wind to resume his voyage. However, when the wind changed, no amount of attempts at persuasion would move him, Jacobson answering that he 'wold take tyme when it pleasid him', meantime lying in the Three Kings 'being every daye very dronke'. During this time a man of war came into port, being stayed by order of the mayor and jurats. Jacobson now insisted he would not depart until he could have its protection. Meanwhile, every day for the next eight or ten days, 'Jacobson sufferid the said man of warr and his company to come aborde his vessell where they laye drinkinge of the said wynne untill he was released'. As a result, the Purveyors of Wines for the Queen's Majesty 'by reson of suspicion of his longe abydinge here at Rye' now came on board his vessel and confiscated '4 peces' of wine for the portions of the Lord Admiral and the Lord Warden. The subsequent correspondence with the owners of the cargo indicates that they were far from pleased.[64]

In addition to putting temptation in the way of those with weak wills and large capacities, alehouses also posed a more serious threat to order, by providing meeting places and accommodation for a whole range of suspicious or ill-disposed individuals, both newcomers and townsmen. Stolen goods, for example, might be disposed of in this way, as in July 1592, when one Charles Flahowe, Frenchman, caught trying to sell two pieces of canvas, claimed he had received them from a stranger 'at the Signe of the Three Mariners'.[65] Similarly, the gaming that went on in tippling houses provided excellent cover not only for the professional gambler and cheat, but also for disposing of counterfeit coin. According to three fellow participants in one such game in February 1555, a tailor from Cranbrook, a weaver from Sheppey and another man from Rye, their suspicions were aroused when one Peter Welden repeatedly 'wold use to lay downe his hole money of vjd and dyd use to take uppe the ijd pecys' laid down by the other players. When one of the other players told him that 'the Testers loke very evyll', Welden replied that 'they were in salt water'. The case came before the mayor and jurats, when Welden alleged he had received two of the testerns from 'olde Cater' and the rest had been uttered by the other players.[66]

Unlicensed alehouses were a particular problem, providing sanctuary for all kinds of ill-disposed persons. Against such places, the town authorities might occasionally take decisive action. One such establishment was run by an elderly man by the name of John Browne, sailmaker, and his wife, in a small tenement granted to them for the term of their lives 'of devocion and charity ... of the gift of the ... towne'. After repeated offences 'howstering and lodging of meny evill disposed persons and idell beggers' in December 1560, he was ordered to enter into a bond of £10 to cease from tippling on pain of forfeiture of his recognizance, loss of his tenement and banishment from the town.[67]

Few alehouses, however, can have had as bad a reputation as that owned by Richard Abbot at Playden, just outside the liberties of Rye, which was notorious for harbouring 'rogues, vagabondes, searovers and other ill livers' and which became the subject of a series of complaints from the parishioners of Playden and Iden and of correspondence from Rye to the county JPs at Lewes during the winter of 1575–6. In January 1576, in their third such letter of complaint, Rye informed the county justices that only recently:

> 'He harboured by the space of three dayes serteyn searovers
> as Blunt and Westone with others of theyre companye which
> for theyer misbehavior durst not come into ye towne of Rye.
> In sort that our townesmen watched theyre botes during
> theyre abode at Abbottes for feare least they should take any
> of theyre botes by stealt to sea as they were very lyke
> parsones to doe suche a facte because they at that tyme
> lacked a shippe'[68]

It is also clear that such alehouses provided ready shelter for
vagrants and other suspicious persons in their travels through the
countryside. Thus one Jone Hailie, widow, late of Winchelsea,
taken at Rye for a vagabond and rogue in September 1572 on
suspicion of theft of the new petticoat which she was wearing,
described her journey from London following her release from
prison where she had been held under suspicion of murder and
felony:

> 'that Monday at night she laie at Lion Key in London at one
> Abbotes. The Twesdaie she came downe to Gravesend and
> there laie at the Sarazens Hed and frome thence came to a
> farmors house within a mile of Tenterden on Wednisdaie
> followinge, and ther laie all night and on Thursdaie
> morninge, she tooke hir journy to Ry and cam thether before
> none, where she was apprehendid for a roge ...'

She was whipped at the cart's tail and her ear burnt according
to statute.[69]

Evidently Jone Hailie was only one of a number of suspicious
females coming to Rye in these years, for on 25 November 1562
the assembly decreed a 40s fine to anyone who 'dothe receive into
his or ther house or houses eny light personnes, harlottes, hores or
comon women resorting to the said towne or being before
remeninge in the same'. Those too poor to pay were to spend 40
days in prison without bail or mainprise.[70]

Alehouses, then, were a cause of considerable concern to the
town authorities. The extent of that concern and the dangers most
commonly perceived to stem from these institutions can be seen
in the clauses in the victuallers' recognizances which had to be
taken out annually, usually in September, at the start of the
mayoral year. In 1563 these recognizances included clauses
relating to the maintenance of good rule; 'not hoistering eny mens
servauntes or apprentyces eyther by daye or night'; 'not harbering

227

eny evill or suspectyd persons but imediatly geyve knolege therof' to the mayor and jurats; not suffering any unlawful games to be played in their house; not victualling in service time and selling only by lawful measures and at the prices set. In 1568 bowling alleys were added to the list of prohibitions. It was, however, not until the mid-1570s that the Rye victuallers' recognizances reached their fullest form, providing a detailed picture of alehouses in the town. Thus in 1575, additional clauses included not serving victuals after nine o'clock in the evening in summer or eight o'clock in winter, nor to receive any 'suspect persons' into the house to eat drink or lodge after that time without the express command of the mayor or a jurat; and not to 'suffer to remayne any idle person or persons longe to sitt singinge, drinkinge or idely, to the maytenaunce of idlenes and of idle persons'. The following year a further prohibition was added:

> 'Nether at any tyme (to) receyve into his house any mens servantes without the consent of their masters for some necessary busines ther to be don. Nor (to) suffer any laboringe person which livith by his daies labor, and hath wiff or children in the saide towne or liberties, to sit drinkinge, or to spende their mony within his said house.'[71]

There was evidently some concern that otherwise, servants might be taught to cheat their masters and day labourers be tempted to spend their wages before they reached home. But these clauses have a wider implication, singling out, as they do, specific categories of persons as potential offenders. Apprentices and servants on the one hand and vagrants, idle and other suspect individuals on the other were two groups whose offences and therefore proven criminality in the eyes of the magistrates were disproportionately high for their numbers.

Male servants and apprentices, generally in their teens or early twenties were particularly prone to fall into petty crime. Pay for apprentices was often only 2d or 4d a quarter until the end of their term and covenant servants generally received their wages at the end of the year's employment. An indication of the underlying frustration endured by many of Rye's young men is the occasional attempts to escape the system which came to the notice of the magistrates. Thus two apprentices of William Gilford in 1564 and another two apprentices and a servant at will of Robert Jackson's in 1576, appeared for conspiracy to rob their master and depart abroad, in the latter instance being whipped at the cart's tail, together with summary dismissal from his service in two cases.[72]

Evidence of a degree of friction between servants and their masters can be found in the dismissals from apprenticeships brought at their masters' requests, in a further three instances for unspecified causes and in one case in 1593 for 'froward demeanour towards his master and his mistress and his fellowes'.[73] Petty theft, often of their master's goods, by servants and apprentices was relatively commonplace. Eleven out of the 37 cases of petty larcenies were perpetrated by male servants or young men and a further three by female servants,. In addition, at least twelve of those accused of property felonies were servants or apprentices.

Servants and apprentices were often prominent among those committing other minor misdemeanours such as the four unnamed young men found abroad in the streets at night in July 1574 who were sent to ward and fined 12d each. Youthful high spirits, especially where they did no-one any harm, were of course tolerated to a degree, as in July 1593 when another four young men were reported 'for rydeinge and chaseinge Mr. Dydesburyes asse in the Montes', outside the Landgate, and for muzzling it. No action was taken.[74] Sometimes, however, crimes were of a more serious nature. Stephen Frencham's servant, for example, was fined 2s for shooting his gun in the Market Place in October 1569, and drunkenness could also be a problem. Drew Cornish, servant to Thomas Radford junior was ordered to leave town in May 1576 on pain of whipping and having a billet nailed to his ear for his 'dronkenness and evil demeanour'; and in the case of Richard Starne, servant to Margaret Danyell, widow, found to be drunk and disorderly in December 1593, it was evidently felt that a stricter control than his mistress could provide was needed. He was ordered 'within vij dayes to gett him into service to some honest man'.[75]

On rare occasions, such offences might be of a more serious nature, as in the case of Morrys Benyon, servant of Arthur Mekyns, shearman, imprisoned and afterwards pilloried, whipped and banished in October 1578, for 'mysusinge the doughter of the saide Mekyns beinge a childe of vij yeris olde, causinge hir to take his privie members in hir hande and afterwardes layinge hir uppon a bedd and attemptinge to ravishe hir'.[76]

Exposure to the temptation to commit sexual crimes was especially common in the larger households containing young servants of both sexes. Four such cases of fornication between two servants in the same household are recorded in the assembly books, usually resulting in banishment of the offending parties. Female servants were particularly at risk and pregnancies were high. At least ten of the 38 bastardy allegations related to female servants, in one case as a result of a liaison with a male servant in the same household and in another following the attentions of her master. The majority of those made to wear partlets following the 1581 Decree against Whoredom were female servants, and altogether, out of 80 behavioural crimes relating to sexual misdemeanours, fourteen were committed by female servants and seven by male servants, which, together with the twelve other individuals also charged as a result of these instances means that 33 prosecutions (41 per cent of the total) related to sexual offences in which male or female servants were involved.

Perhaps the worst such case was that of the female servant (un-named) of John Oliver, fisherman, who, in February 1580 'never beinge maried as she confessith' had three children. The moral dangers to which female servants could be exposed is well indicated by the case of John Milles, shoemaker, who in January 1560 was carted for his 'evill and lude demeanor' with Alis Adenton and Kateryn Noughty, his maidservants 'and with sundry others', and for beating his wife. Both maidservants were punished and banished. A similar situation arose in February 1577 when Mathew Button of Lewes, rippier, who had only recently hired a house in the town, together with his daughter and maidservant Alice, 'beinge his harlott', were carted and banished for incontinent living, it having been found that he 'lay with the said harlot and his doughter in one bedd'. Altogether four cases of illicit sexual relations between a master and his servants are recorded in these years, and there were no doubt others which were never detected.[78]

The other group which gave most cause for concern was vagrants and newcomers to the town. Altogether 91 such cases were dealt with during the Elizabethan period, in the case of vagrancy usually by whipping and banishment, in the case of other newcomers and their families mainly by bonds and recognizances for their good behaviour and to save the town charges (27 cases). Six newcomers were ordered to send for certificates of their good behaviour from their former abodes, in this instance including two Flemish merchants, who had to produce certificates from the Reformed Churches at London and Maidstone respectively in 1569. A further fourteen families were ordered to depart.

In October 1567 the assembly decreed that no landlord or tenant was to suffer a stranger to dwell above 24 hours in his property without licence of the mayor and jurats on pain of a 20s fine and prison, tippling houses already being under a similar restriction.[79] Even so, it was not always easy for the authorities to identify all those of suspicious character. Harry Oliffe and his supposed wife Elizabeth, for example, were only detected as living in adultery in May 1573, some years after they had moved into the town; and it was often the case that vagrants were only apprehended after they had committed some other offence, as in the case of Robert Fraye and John Morgayne, two vagrants apprehended for picking in June 1596. Altogether seven vagrants were apprehended for pickery and a further twelve for other offences, including five soldiers returning without passports and one with counterfeit money and two vagrants with false passports. It seems that both of them obtained these from one William Randall, clarke, of Udimore, 'a comen forger of passportes .. He is a very daungerous fellowe and wryteth many handes ...'[80]

The maintenance of order in Tudor Rye thus presented the authorities with a host of difficulties. In September 1568 a first step towards more effective policing was taken with the division of the town into six wards each allotted two jurats and four commoners to present strangers dwelling without licence and other defaults such as not coming to church. In February 1574 when the ward boundaries were finally fixed, two constables as well as two jurats were allotted to each ward with considerably increased responsibilities. Their charge reads like a catalogue of many of the most common offences in the town: arresting any 'that make any riotes fraies or assaultes'; presenting all 'common annoyances'; searching the taverns and victualling houses every Sunday and festival day 'to compell the people to come to chyrche'; presenting all 'rybawdes and evill lyvinge persons, or suche as be suspecte, common dronkerdes and troblesom persons'; presenting 'all incommers to dwell within the same warde, what they be and from whence they come with their names and facultie'; and finally signifying the jurats of their ward 'all such tiplers and huxters which are not lycenced. That they may present the same to Mr. Maior and have due correction for the same.'[81]

Such a long list indicates much of the range of concerns of the governors of sixteenth century Rye. The prosecution of common annoyances and other petty nuisances, economic and moral offences, as much as the more serious incidence of vagrancy, crimes of violence and property felonies were all integral parts of the overall task of maintaining a well-ordered commonwealth. As one sixteenth century town clerk wrote:

'it is not possible that that countrey shall well stand in good government and the people grow in welth where order in every state is not fitly observed and that body cannot be without mutch greafe of inflamation where any least parte is out of ioynt and not duly set in his owne naturall place.'[82]

CHAPTER 7

Trade and Decline

'The towne of Rye ... hath had such trade and traffick that it
hath paid 2000 li a yeare custome in Queene Elizabeth's time
... but of late yeares the harbour is much swarved with sand
... by which meanes the towne is impoverished for want of
trade and unpeopled, there being a hundred houses unin-
habited, there trade and shipping is decayed ... many ...
dayly fly from it by reason of the greate chardg the towne is
at for the maintenance of the jetties, keyes, groines and sea
walles ...'. Preamble to draft Parliamentary bill for amending
Rye haven, March 1624.

(RYE 47/98/15).

A major south coast port

A modern observer, visiting Rye, now situated some three miles
from the sea, its quaysides at the Strand, where once merchant
ships from many of the great ports of northern Europe docked,
little more than a muddy creek, might well be excused for
wondering whether this landlocked town could ever have been a
major port. He would probably readily agree with the diagnosis of
the reasons for decline put forward so insistently by the
corporation in the late sixteenth and early seventeenth centuries.
The evidence is there for all to see. Rye harbour has silted up and,
equally, it is clear from the surviving local and national customs
accounts that trade did leave during the closing decades of the
sixteenth century, with the resulting impoverishment of many
householders and the wholesale depopulation of the town, so that
by the 1620s Rye's inhabitants numbered little more that a
quarter of what they had done at its height.

233

By the mid-1590s the rapid decline in the town's fortunes was obvious to ordinary citizens. Henry Kennett, a shearman, on his death bed in December 1596, doubted whether a creditor would accept his three houses outside the Landgate in payment of a £40 debt and to allow his wife a £20 legacy, whom he advised 'to goe to London for this place will not bee for her to gayne any thing.'[1] From 1592 onwards as many as half of the corporation's tenants, including many of those with warehouses and shops at the Strand, defaulted on their rents, while others were able to pay only a proportion. In the financial year 1592/3, 43 of 65 properties at the Strand listed in the town rental defaulted on their rents. Stephen Harrison, land chamberlain for three years between 1596 and 1599, had to be allowed the rents of 27 defaulters in his first year, 32 in his second year and 49 in his third year, out of a total rent roll of 109 properties. His successor, Thomas Ensinge, was allowed £19 16s 0d, being the rents for 52 properties which had defaulted in 1600/1, compared to his receipts of £19 19s 11d from the remaining 57. Nor were those who failed to pay restricted to the poorer sort. Robert Carpenter, jurat, appears to have defaulted on his rents every year from 1592 onwards until his disappearance from the jurats' bench in 1601; Mr Belveridge, the customer and his deputy, Christopher Marshall, are reported to have owed £18 for six years' arrears of rent for the Customs House to Michaelmas 1600. At the time of their sale in April 1602 to help pay for the abortive harbour works, 26 out of the 32 shops in the two rows at Strand had defaulted on their rents, including most of the 11 which had been forcibly re-entered and re-let in 1596 and 1597[2].

However although the symptoms of decline are clear enough, the exact causes are less so. Other south coast ports, whose harbours were not subject to the progressive deterioration that Rye's suffered were also in difficulties. Southampton, for example, had undergone an equally spectacular decline, as indicated by the fall in its customs revenues in the first four decades of the sixteenth century of almost 95 per cent, from a yearly average of £10,342 (1504–9) to only £663 (1541–5). In this case the cause was the wholesale transfer of its trade to London, which experienced a quite phenomenal growth during the sixteenth century, a factor recognised by contemporary observers and modern economic historians alike as the major single cause of

Table 36

Changes in the amounts of customs revenues of the port of Chichester paid by Winchelsea and Rye 1489/90-1559/60

	Customs receipts								
Year	Port of Chichester			Winchelsea			Rye		
	£	s	d	£	s	d	£	s	d
1489/90	116	1	2¼	69	10	10¾	19	19	6
1490/1	136	4	8¾	88	16	7¾	12	8	1¾
1513/4	112	14	0	46	4	2¼	44	9	8¼
1528/9	404	12	6¾	51	12	3¼	206	10	10¾
1531/2	382	16	2	18	15	2¾	243	2	1
1537/8	240	14	1	31	8	9½	130	14	5¾[1]
1538/9	249	3	2½	17	1	4¼	103	5	7½
1543/4	124	14	0½	22	14	1	64	6	2½
1545/6	175	8	10¼	12	19	5½	113	19	3¼
1548/9	120	0	1½	10	16	3¾	80	19	0½
1549/50	164	11	2	1	4	9	96	14	6
1559/60	621	2	7¾	1	5	5	573	1	7

Notes: [1] Rye total incomplete. One entry (c.4s) partly illegible.

Sources: P.R.O. Customs Accounts E122 35/7-8; 36/1,7,10,13; 37/3-4; 38/11,13; 200/5,8-9.

the decline of its outports in the same period. Altogether it seems probable that it was a similar loss of its trade to London which led to the collapse of Rye's economy in the late sixteenth century, although a number of other factors played their part, chief among them, the departure of the French after 1589 and the increasingly onerous burden of taxation placed on the shoulders of a dwindling population by the town corporation in order to finance expensive and ultimately futile grandiose schemes for the improvement of the haven.

As we saw in chapter one, Rye experienced a relatively steady growth in wealth and population from the end of the fifteenth century until the peak middle decades of the sixteenth century. Much of this growth was probably due to the transfer of trade to the town from Winchelsea, which was suffering severe problems of silting in the early part of the sixteenth century. As Table 36 shows, the customs revenues from the latter town, which, during the early years of Henry VII's reign, was still the predominant trading centre among the Sussex ports, had declined to almost nothing by 1550. The same period saw Rye's rise to pre-eminence among the coastal towns included under the jurisdiction of the customs officials of the Port of Chichester (all ports between Folkestone and Chichester). The combined share of trade of the

Table 37

Total tonnage of merchant vessels of the larger English ports 1571-2

	Port	Tonnage		Port	Tonnage
1	London	12265	21	Hastings	514
2	Leigh (Essex)	2330	22	Cley (Norfolk)	497
3	Hull	2048	23	Dover	494
4	Yarmouth	1906	24	Woodbridge	444
5	Newcastle	1893	25	Lowestoft	436
6	Ipswich	1669	25	Faversham	436
7	Aldeburgh (Suff)	1268	27	Brightlingsea	435
8	Lynn	1140	27	Barnstaple	435
9	Dartmouth	1115	29	Hythe	418
10	Bristol	1040	30	Brighthelmstone	416
11	RYE	1015	31	Southwold	412
12	Colchester	1004	32	Newport	385
13	Harwich	891	33	Walberswick	344
14	Plymouth	890	34	Topsham	343
15	Southampton	790	35	Liverpool	338
16	Sandwich	729	36	Wells (Norfolk)	330
16	Poole	729	37	Northampton[1]	310
18	Maldon	599	38	Miltonshore[2]	300
19	Blakeney	595	39	Millbrook[3]	295
20	Chester	544	40	Lyme	292

Notes:
[1] Gloucestershire
[2] Suffolk
[3] Cornwall
Source: P.R.O. SP15/22

two towns situated on the Camber (77.2 per cent of the revenues of the Port of Chichester in 1489/90, 76.5 per cent in 1549/50) remained remarkably constant during this period of transition. The growing importance of Rye in the early Tudor period seems therefore to have been entirely due to the economic collapse of its neighbour. By the mid-1550s–1580s, Rye was at the height of its prosperity and, as Table 37 demonstrates, had the largest mercantile fleet on the south coast.

By the early 1570s, Rye's merchant shipping was roughly on a par with that of Bristol and was considerably greater than that of either Plymouth or Southampton (Portsmouth was listed 74th with only 95 tons). Among the other Cinque Ports, Rye's pre-eminence is clear, with a tonnage nearly half as large again as that of Sandwich and slightly larger than that of Dover and Hastings combined. Nor is there any reason to suppose that these figures for Rye were untypical during the mid-Elizabethan period. A similar exercise, carried out on the Rye port books for 1573/4 produced a combined tonnage of 992 tons for 36 ships, compared to the 1571/2 figures of 1015 tons and 32 ships. These figures reflect the volume of trade passing through the port at the time, customs revenues amounting to £1157 13s 2¼d in 1573/4. Among its Sussex neighbours, Rye enjoyed a substantial superiority in terms of trade, in these years accounting for up to three-quarters of the total receipts of customs for the Port of Chichester. The relative positions of the various other Sussex ports are set out in Table 38. As can be seen from these figures, Rye's revenues accounted for between 58.8 per cent (1549/50) and 79 per cent (1558/9) of the total customs dues collected from the various creeks of the Port of Chichester. Clearly, in the mid-sixteenth century, the trade of the Sussex ports was heavily concentrated in the Camber.

Table 38

**Customs revenues of Rye and other creeks
of the Port of Chichester 1549/50-1558/9**

	1549/50			1558/9		
RYE	£96	14	6	£499	11	6¾
Hythe	23	0	5	8	0	5¾
Pevensey	16	5	3½	5	7	0½
New Shoreham	9	2	7½	13	5	2½
Meeching and Lewes	6	10	1	35	2	6
Arundel and Littlehampton	6	7	8	4	20	2½
Chichester	4	11	0½	36	0	6
Winchelsea	1	4	9	7	0	5
Hastings		14	9	23	6	6
Total	£164	11	2	£632	4	5

Source: P.R.O. E122 37/4,38/11.

Patterns of trade

Rye's importance as a port rested on a number of factors, each of which contributed in various degrees to its economic prosperity. Locally it provided a distribution centre for goods for neighbouring parishes and small towns. Among the many goods passing through the port in 1582/3 for example was a shipment of wine and grocery wares in September 1582, destined for a number of small merchants at the neighbouring town of Lydd. A few months later a consignment of six hogsheads of wine arrived for one Buysshop of Battle.[6] Rye's position at the mouth of the Rother,which was navigable by lighter as far as Bodiam bridge, meant that it was also well placed for the import and export of raw materials and manufactured products for the cloth and iron industries which existed near the banks of the river and its tributaries. More important still, the Rother gave access to the vast, but dwindling, Wealden forests, which provided Rye's principal export, timber. The 1565 government survey of shipping lists five lighters operating from Winchelsea and a further four, in the range of 8–10 tons, based up-river from Rye.[7] Other goods which they carried included wine, beer and quantities of dyestuffs, principally woad, madder and brasell, destined for clothiers at Cranbrook, Tenterden and the surrounding area plus iron plates from Cardiff destined for the Robertsbridge ironworks to be made into steel and then re-shipped out of Rye to London.[8] Finally, by its daily provision of the London fishmarket, Rye was linked to London by an overland route served by trains of pack animals, who, having discharged their load, were able to bring back to Rye goods both for local consumption and for export. It was upon this link that Rye's role as a major outport for the shipment of cloth overseas in the 1570s and 1580s was based.

Between July and September 1572 for example, there was an almost daily traffic in horsepacks of cloth from a wide variety of London merchants to Rye, from where it was shipped, principally to Rouen, to which 28 ships sailed from Rye laden with cloth between 24 May and 24 November 1572, with a further one ship to Nantes. With the exception of October, in which ten ships sailed, there was an average of five sailings a month, the overwhelming majority in Rye ships (all but two of the 29 sailings in this five-month period), providing an important source of income and employment to Rye's shipowners and mariners.[9] Two years later, between Michaelmas 1573–1574, the Rye port books record the export of 676 horsepacks, 36 fardels, 15 trusses and 5 packets, all containing cloth, in 37 ships, paying £495 16s 10½d in duties, equivalent to 42.8 per cent of the total customs revenue of Rye during that year, and 99.3 per cent of duties on goods exported.[10] However, while the importance of the transit trade in cloth is undeniable, it took second place in terms of bulk to Rye's main export, billets (for fuel) and timber.

The survival of the returns of local customs dues (maltodes) for Rye, paid into the lesser box for 11 years between 1580/1 and the last year of the reign of Queen Elizabeth provides a detailed picture of the changing patterns of both coastal and overseas trade in these years, something impossible for the earlier Tudor period for which only the overseas customs accounts survive. The returns for the early 1580s, which are extant for each of the five years beginning at Michaelmas 1580 and ending at Michaelmas 1585 enable a reasonable picture to be built up of the traffic of goods at a time when the port was still of some importance (Table 39). During these years, exports appear to have been substantially greater than imports in terms both of the numbers of individual consignments and of the number of ships entering and leaving the port.

Table 39
Average yearly shipments of major commodities through Rye 1580/1–1584/5

Imports			Exports		
Commodity	Ships	%	Commodity	Ships	%
Grain	55	34.6	Billets	69	34.7
Coal	7.8	4.9	Cloth	29.8	15.0
Wine	7	4.4	Timber	13.4	6.7
Salt	5.6	3.5	Iron	10.2	5.1
Cloth	4	2.5	Horses	7	3.5
Hops	3.8	2.4	Grain	3	1.5
Dyestuffs	2.4	1.5	Dyestuffs	2.6	1.3
Iron	2.4	1.5	Herring	2.2	1.1
Timber	1.4	0.9	Beer	2	1.0
Bricks	1	0.6	Wine	1.8	0.9
Tar	1	0.6	Mixed—other	55.8	28.1
Livestock	1	0.6			
Mixed or other	66.6	41.9			
Average number of consignments	364.4		Average number of consignments	498.4	
Average number of ships[1]	159		Average number of ships	199	

Source: RYE 66/12-31
Notes: [1] Rounded up to nearest whole number.

On the whole, imports are more difficult to categorise than exports, a larger proportion of cargoes being of the mixed variety, or comprising relatively rare items ranging from baskets of quails or gulls (the former a regular import, usually of about 4 baskets in early May) to more intermittent items such as bags of pepper, barrels of soap, stools, chairs and grocery wares, quantities of wool cards and Purbeck stone, packs of paper and even elephant tusks. By far the major import was various types of grain, principally wheat and malt, chiefly from East Kent and West Sussex, but occasionally from further afield such as East Anglia or the West Country. Most of this grain was destined for Rye itself, whose large population was inadequately supplied from the neighbouring countryside which was predominantly sheep and cattle farming, but a small proportion was re-exported along the coast to neighbouring towns or upstream to Tenterden and Appledore. In the early 1580s, yearly imports of malt averaged 1850 quarters and of wheat, 755 quarters, making grain by far the largest bulk commodity imported. Such figures compare well to the 63 and 51 coastal shipments of grain recorded in the port controller's books for 1553/4 and 1555/6, which accounted for 1254 and 699 quarters of malt and 1779 and 762 quarters of wheat respectively, representing some 60 per cent of coastal imports during these two years.[11]

Another important bulk import was coal from Newcastle, of which an average 152 chalder was imported in the early 1580s, mainly in the summer months, the majority of it carried in barks of Hastings, some of which seem to have made a number of round trips for the purpose.[12] Most of it seems to have been destined for Rye itself, although small quantities (4½ chalder in 1581/2 and 1 chalder in 1582/3) were re-exported up river by lighter and 4 chalder in the autumn of 1580 and a further 20 chalder in the autumn of 1583 was sent by coastal vessels to London.[13] Much of the wine imported came from Rouen, brought back in ships engaged in the cloth trade, together with barrels of vinegar, sack, proynes, oil, ballots of woad, sacks of hops, pepper, brasell, nuts and raisins, some glass and regular quantities of Normandy canvas, much of it in mixed cargoes. Together with the cheaper French wines, imports of which averaged more than 80 tons a year in the early 1580s, there were occasional shipments of sack, basterd, malmesey and in 1601, muscadyne, some of which was transhipped up river to the clothing towns of the Kentish Weald. From Flanders came Flemish hops together with cargoes of tar, soap, salt fish and fresh vegetables such as onions and cabbages. The quantities of hops imported, particularly in 1583/4 and 1584/5 were substantial, averaging 115 pockets (about 8½ tons) in each of these two years, one pocket being the equivalent of 168lbs. Again, these figures are broadly comparable to those of the earlier period, the average during the years 1508/9–1543/4 being about 6 tons. A small quantity of this was shipped up river by lighter. More important still in terms of bulk were the large quantities of dyestuffs imported for the local cloth industry. The average quantity of woad, a blue plant dye, imported in the early 1580s was 178 ballots (equivalent to 70–120 lbs each) per year. Imports of brasell, a type of wood used for dyes ranging from peach colour

240

to bright red, averaged more than 20 tons a year, and there were smaller quantities of alum, madder (a plant used for a crimson red dye) and, in the 1590s, fustick (another type of wood giving a yellow dye) and cochineal (a scarlet dye made from dried insects from the New World) which first appears in the maltode books in 1601.[14] Also sent up river for Kentish clothiers was some of the quantities of oil imported and the occasional consignment of teasels, a dried plant used for burring cloth to give it a sheen.

From Flanders too came shipments of Flemish bricks, although the total quantity imported in the early 1580s (86,000 in five years) can scarcely have been sufficient for more than a few chimney stacks. The highest figure recorded was in 1508/9 (89,000), but generally imports of bricks averaged between 12–20,000 annually during the first half of the sixteenth century. Other imports included barrels of ale, beer and grocery wares shipped along the coast from London and quantities of wainscott, lathes, pales and deal board, some of it from the Netherlands. There were also occasional consignments of pitch and tar, including 3 barrels of pitch out of a French ship for 'the French shipwright' in August 1582 and of grindstones either for cornmills or the iron mills, barrels of broken glass, presumably destined for the glass works at Beckley which was in operation in the late 1570s or for the works of Andrew Harry, glasier, another Huguenot refugee, and, in the 1590s, occasional shipments of 'newland fish' from the West Country ports.[15]

Principal among exports were billets and timber. Shipments of the former averaged almost 1.1 million a year in the early 1580s, although as Table 40 shows, exports (chiefly to Calais) had occasionally reached over 4.5 million in the peak years of 1531/2 and 1549/50. By the 1580s most of the billets were going to the Low Countries, with regular shipments recorded to Flushing, Middleburg, Dunkirk, Bruges (4 shipments in the first three months of 1583 totalling 105,000) and occasionally, Amsterdam. Smaller quantities were also exported to Dieppe, together with coastal shipments to Sandwich, Thanet, Dover and London. Altogether, billets accounted for between one third and one half of all cargoes exported from Rye in the latter part of the period. Earlier, the figure had been even higher, accounting for over 90 per cent of overseas exports in 1513/4, 1531/2 and 1548/9. Other timber exports included considerable quantities of logs

Table 40

Timber exports from Rye 1489/90-1602/3

Year	Billetwood (1000)	Logs (Loads)	Timber (tons)	Total timber shipments	% all outward shipments
O1489/90	417	-	111	36	77
O1490/1	233	37	59	24	89
O1497/8	788	198	56	86	87
O1499/1500	904.5	223	106	102	84
O1508/9	1076	554	96	138	61
O1513/4	1186	499	157	166	95
O1528/9	2085	393	122	204	74
O1531/2	4722.5	847	225	362	95
O1537/8	549	230	134	56	65
O1538/9	761	169	97	57	68
O1543/4	908	631	27	69	79
O1545/6	874	60	115	81	70
O1548/9	2712	150	32	111	92
O1549/50	4686	318	18	176	78
OC1553/4	1023	162	30	50	50
OC1555/6	1210	60	40	46	39
OC1558/9	20	-	-	1	2
OC1560/1	966	41	-	NA	NA
O1561/2	15	-	-	3	6
O1566/7	1444	-	1892	NA	NA
OC1580/1	1158	162	161½	94	42
OC1581/2	1074	73	170	66	35
OC1582/3	1136	56	140	75	35
OC1583/4	926	55	48	78	44
OC1584/5	1093	4+	37+	99	54
OC1592	516	-	28	41	36
OC1593/4	285	32	1	29	34
OC1596/7	488	-	32	44	40
OC1599/1600	200	51	20	23	41
OC1600/1	234	6	38	29	55
OC1602/3	142	-	72	26	43

Notes: O Overseas
C Coastal

Sources: P.R.O. Customs accounts and port books E122 35/7-8,11,14,18; 36/1,7,10,13; 37/3,4; 38/1-2,6-7,11,13; 200/5,7-9; E190 737/24; Rye Chamberlain's accounts and quarterly Lesser Box returns RYE 60/7/241-3; RYE 66/12-69.

and building materials and, increasingly, during the 1580s, numbers of loads of spoke timber 'for her Majesty' and various timber frames, including one for a bridge, also for the Queen in 1599, and others for a house and a mill. Much of the residue of the timber exported was also destined for the Low Countries, as for example the 40 tons sent to Bruges in the spring of 1582.[16]

Cloth exports in the early 1580s continued to form the second largest number of bulk cargoes (15 per cent) with by far the greatest proportion of these being shipped out in Rye ships. Although annual totals of assorted horsepacks, packets, trusses and fardels exported through Rye fluctuated somewhat, they averaged 648 a year, only slightly down on the combined total of

732 exported in 1573/4, which was equalled in 1583/4 and surpassed (794) in 1580/1. Their importance as the principal cargo exported in Rye ships, however, was considerably greater than their overall share of exports suggests. In 1580/1 for example, while cloth shipments from Rye accounted for 35 out of the 217 outward movements recorded in the maltode books (excluding lighters), a proportion of slightly over 16 per cent, they accounted for almost half (48.6 per cent) of the 72 cargoes carried in Rye ships. In particular, they formed a regular source of income to masters such as William Morris, who carried five cargoes of cloth, mainly to Dieppe, in 1580/1, John Potten and William Harman, who each carried three and seven other ships' masters who each carried at least two such shipments in between coastal trading and other voyages, transporting iron, horses and other wares. Included among these were masters of merchant vessels such as Robert Holnes, who in addition to carrying two cargoes of cloth to France in 1580/1 also carried three shipments of mixed cargoes to London, two of them predominantly of cases of glass, one together with twelve tons of iron and both including loads of mats, the other a mixed consignment of mats, teasels, timber and brasell as well as one shipment of glass, barrels (possibly of herring) and old shoes to France. Others, such as William Harman, who in addition to transporting three cargoes of cloth, also shipped at least one cargo of horses overseas, as did William Morris on two occasions in addition to the five cargoes of cloth mentioned above.[17]

Next in importance after timber and cloth were the shipments of iron and cast ordnance, chiefly destined for London, which in the 1580s were running at about 185 tons a year. Other goods sent to the capital included annual summer consignments of mats, apparently made at Wittersham, a number of shipments of charcoals, a consignment of 12 loads of tann to a tanner at Barking (1602), occasional consignments of leather (in the 1590s) and various shipments of glass, amounting to 303 cases in the two years 1580/1 and 1581/2. Another important export, averaging 90 head a year in the early 1580s was horses, mainly to Dieppe, where they were probably destined for the knacker's yard. Again, these figures are broadly in line with those for the earlier period, when shipments generally ranged from between 70 to 150 horses annually. Local beer was also exported, averaging approximately

120 barrels a year in the early 1580s and reaching a peak of over 700 barrels in 1592, mainly to Flushing and Flanders, although there were other consignments to Plymouth and in French boats. Finally, herring, either salted (white) or smoked (red) was shipped out of Rye in barrels, chiefly to London, total shipments (usually in the autumn) in the first three years of the 1580s averaging over 400 barrels a year, with smaller quantities of barrels of sprats, some of which were exported to France. One major item missing from these late Elizabethan maltode books, which had formerly accounted for up to 10 per cent of Rye's annual exports was leather, which had averaged 85–140 diker a year (15–30 shipments) in the 1520s–1540s, together with large quantities of rabbit and 13 other skins, but which had become prohibited by proclamation later in the century.

Among the more irregular items exported in the 1580s was a variety of goods, indicating Rye's role as an entrepôt, with transhipments of oranges, apples, beans, raisins, sugar, wax, soap, Normandy canvas and even, on one occasion, 30 dozen pairs of bellows, almost certainly destined for the London market. The wide range of goods passing through the port in the early 1580s (156 separately identified items) contrasts sharply with the situation only twenty years later (93 items) when the contraction in trade passing through the port had severely restricted the range of goods entering and leaving the harbour. The overall impression of Rye from the middle years of Henry VIII's reign up to the 1580s, then, is of a relatively bustling port, acting not only as a distribution centre for its immediate hinterland but also as an important staging post for materials passing up and down river for the Wealden cloth and iron industries and as a transit port for goods passing to and from London overseas, with substantial fishing and mercantile fleets, the latter carrying a substantial proportion of the goods passing through the port. The impression is one of stability, but this was relatively short-lived, for, by the end of the century, much of the trade, and with it most of the merchant ships, had disappeared, leaving the town in a state of almost complete economic collapse.

The severing of connections

The causes of this rapid decline were essentially fourfold. In the first place, Rye's importance as an outport of London rested on the transit trade in cloth, which was almost wholly owned and directed from the capital. It was a traffic of relatively recent growth to its mid-Elizabethan levels, which, in so far as it had existed at all in the earlier part of the century, had been at a much lower level. In 1531–2, a peak year for cloth shipments in Henry VIII's reign, a total of 23 ships carried in association with other cargoes an assortment of 10 northern dozens, 5 short cloths, 3400 cotton goods, 534½ pieces of worsteds plus 43 yards of oddments to Dieppe from Rye, roughly equivalent to what was shipped out of Rye in one month in 1572 and little more than one average-sized cargo at that date.[19] The exact reasons for the transfer of this trade to Rye, which can be traced through the port books and the enrolled customs accounts for the Port of Chichester to the late 1560s and early 1570s[20], are not entirely clear, but were presumably linked to the religious conflicts in the Netherlands and in France, and the growing conflict with Spain. The revolt of the Netherlands seriously disrupted the traditional markets in cloth, particularly at Antwerp, which never recovered, and also led to a marked growth in privateering in the channel, the dangers of which were severely increased by the seizure of the Spanish bullion fleet in December 1568 and the threat of Spanish reprisals on English shipping which followed. During these years there was a definite shift in the pattern of trade away from the Flemish ports to other centres of the cloth trade principally Rouen, a pattern mirrored in the Rye port books, which would have made the much shorter sea-crossing from Rye more attractive to London merchants, both from a point of view of safety and also of cost. It seems not without significance that the effective departure of this transit trade from Rye, which can be charted in the maltode books to between 1593/4 when there were still 542 horsepacks and parcels of cloth passing through the town and 1596/7 when the figure had dropped to only 89, coincided with the effective end of any serious Spanish attempts to prolong the struggle against the Dutch and the end of privateering by the Catholic League in the channel following the entry of Henri IV into Paris which marked the end of the French religious wars in March 1594. A brief revival of the transit trade through Rye in the 1630s coincided with a renewal of the war between the United Provinces and Spain and with Charles I's pro-Spanish foreign policy, the effect of which again disrupted trade with the Netherlands.[21]

Table 41

Rye ships engaged in merchant trading from Customs Accounts
and Port Books 1489/90-1599/1600

Year	Number of ships	Tonnage	Voyages outwards	% total voyages outwards	Voyages inwards	% total voyages inwards
O1489/90	5		34	72	5	29
O1490/1	2		1	4	1	8
O1487/8	7		9	9	7	21
O1499/1500	2		3	21	2	8
O1598/9	5		6	3	18	13
O1513/4	3		1	1	2	4
O1528/9	27		43	16	27	19
O1531/2	12		3	1	16	7
O1537/8	23		32	37	41	60
O1538/9	15		14	17	22	27
O1543/4	7		4	5	5	12
O1545/6	20		32	28	5	10
O1548/9	6		7	6	1	5
O1549/50	11		18	8	4	10
C1553/4	30		37	37	17	19
C1555/6	40		52	44	24	26
O1558/9	28		56	59	37	76
O1559/60	26		32	84	41	60
O1561/2	14		41	77 .	54	57
O1573/4	36	992	41	76	47	77
O1588/9	24	562	33	92	29	35
O1599/1600	10	340	5	10	16	20

Notes:
O   Overseas
C   Coastal
Sources: P.R.O. Customs accounts and port books E122 35/7-8,11,14,18; 36/1,7,10,13; 37/3,4;
38/1-2, 6-7,11,13; 200/5,7-9; E190 739/16,740/26, 744/19, 745/15, 750/21,32.

Secondly, as a consequence of the ending of cloth exports from Rye, there was a dramatic fall in the number of local ships engaged in trade, which, as Table 41 demonstrates, had generally fluctuated between 20-30 vessels in any one year in peace time from the late 1520s onwards. Such trading activities had clearly provided a useful additional source of income and employment to many of the larger fishing vessels, principally those between 20-30 tons generally known as crayers. At least two of the merchant vessels listed for Rye in 1572, the Primrose and the Peter (both 25 tons) for example had appeared in the earlier, 1565 government survey under the heading of fishing boats. Most of the Rye ships listed in the earlier customs accounts are described as 'fishing boats' or 'crayers' (6 and 9 respectively, with one 'smack' and only 7 'naves' or merchant ships in 1537/8).[22]

By the end of the 1580s, the number and tonnage of the Rye ships still engaged in trade had fallen sharply. By 1600 the size of

246

Rye's merchant fleet was smaller than at any time since the early years of the sixteenth century (other than in time of war, when such vessels were engaged elsewhere, transporting troops and supplies). The extent of the collapse is further revealed by the sharp fall in the number and proportion of shipments carried in local vessels by 1600, which were down to less than a quarter of what they had been only 20 years earlier. The average number of voyages undertaken by each vessel was also sharply down on the early Elizabethan period when, on average, individual ships made three to four voyages a year. In 1599/1600, the ratio was down to barely two. By 1600, therefore, the whole of the growth of the previous century had been wiped out and it is extremely difficult to imagine that more than a handful of the remaining merchant ships could survive long in Rye in the prevailing economic climate.

In itself, such a reduction of the town's home-based merchant fleet might not have been totally catastrophic. During the reign of Edward VI, a time when Rye's trade was relatively buoyant, Thomas Barnabe, a London merchant writing in the early Elizabethan period, recalled having seen '37 hoys sail out of Rye at a single tide, laden with timber, and not one of the 37 was English'.[23] Although probably an exaggeration (the 1549/50 customs accounts show the largest timber fleet sailing to Calais as being 16 ships on 14 June 1550, the next largest being 11 on 11 September), Barnabe's account did serve to illustrate the loss of opportunity due to the lack of suitable English cargo vessels in the first half of the sixteenth century.[24] Nevertheless, the outlook for Rye in 1600 was quite different to that earlier. The dearth of merchant shipping revealed in the earlier period was little more than a reflection of the prevailing situation throughout England. By 1600 however, a substantial and continuing growth in the tonnage of English shipping had long been taking place. The collapse of Rye's merchant shipping in the concluding years of Queen Elizabeth's reign was therefore another symptom of the town's declining economic fortunes. The situation was most obviously apparent in Rye's overseas trade, as Table 42 indicates.

The most striking feature of this analysis is the sheer weight of numbers of ships entering Rye in the early part of the period and the heavy concentration of ships from Netherlandish ports, which alone accounted for just over half of incoming ships and a rather

Table 42:
Home ports of trading vessels carrying cargoes into or out of Rye from Customs Accounts and Port Books 1489-1600

a) Inwards

	1489/90	1490/1	1497/8	1499/50	1508/9	1513/4	1528/9	1531/2	1537/8	1538/9	1543/4	1545/6	1548/9	1549/50	1558/9	1559/60	1561/2	1573/4	1588/9	1599/1600
1: English ships																				
Rye	5	1	7	2	18	2	27	16	41	22	5	5	-	4	56	41	54	47	29	6
Winchelsea	-	2	-	-	-	-	-	-	-	-	-	-	-	-	-	-	-	-	-	-
Hastings	-	-	3	-	-	2	-	8	-	-	-	-	5	-	-	-	-	-	-	-
Other S'sx/Kent	-	-	-	-	2	-	-	-	1	3	2	-	2	2	-	2	2	2	3	-
London	-	-	-	-	1	-	1	-	1	1	-	-	5	-	-	-	-	-	-	-
Other English	1	6	-	-	1	2	2	5	3	2	-	1	1	4	-	2	-	-	-	-
Total English	6	9	10	2	22	6	30	29	46	28	7	6	13	10	56	45	56	49	32	6
2: Calais ships																				
Total Calais	8	3	14	-	14	5	6	3	9	4	9	-	9	-	-	-	-	-	-	-
3: Scottish ships																				
Total Scottish	-	-	-	-	-	-	-	-	-	-	-	-	-	-	-	-	-	-	-	1
4: French ships																				
Dieppe	-	-	1	13	15	2	28	57	8	17	2	18	-	16	-	2	12	9	35	13
Other Normandy	-	1	-	4	6	-	2	5	-	1	1	4	2	2	3	2	2	-	-	-
Other French	1	-	-	-	-	-	-	-	-	1	-	2	3	-	6	-	1	-	1	1
Total French	1	1	1	17	21	2	30	62	8	19	3	24	5	18	9	4	15	9	36	14
5: Breton ships																				
Total Brittany	-	-	-	-	14	4	32	50	4	10	13	8	32	2	4	1	3	-	-	-

248

Table 42:

a) Inwards (continued)

	1489/90	1490/1	1497/8	1499/50	1508/9	1513/4	1528/9	1531/2	1537/8	1538/9	1543/4	1545/6	1548/9	1549/50	1558/9	1559/60	1561/2	1573/4	1588/9	1599/1600
6: Netherlandish ships																				
Rosendale	-	-	-	-	14	4	32	50	4	10	13	8	32	2	4	1	3	-	-	-
Dunkirk	-	-	-	-	14	4	17	72	-	9	1	1	2	2	2	2	1	-	-	-
Tergow	-	1	3	1	18	6	2	5	-	1	2	-	10	1	8	5	3	-	-	-
Antwerp	-	-	-	-	3	-	3	-	-	1	1	3	13	-	2	2	3	-	-	-
Flushing	-	-	-	-	3	-	3	1	-	-	-	-	9	-	3	3	-	-	14	1
Ostend	-	-	-	-	3	9	10	-	-	2	3	-	4	-	2	1	6	-	-	-
Other N'lands	-	-	1	2	9	6	5	14	-	1	2	6	20	4	7	3	-	1	-	2
Total N'lands	-	-	4	3	64	29	72	142	4	24	22	18	90	10	28	17	17	1	14	3
7: Iberian ships																				
Total Spain/Portugal	1	-	-	-	2	4	-	1	-	-	2	-	-	-	-	-	2	1	-	2
8: Hanseatic ships																				
Total German Hanse	-	-	-	-	-	-	1	-	-	-	-	-	-	-	1	2	1	1	-	-
9: Other																				
unidentified	1	-	-	-	6	-	1	-	-	-	-	-	-	-	-	-	1	-	2	1
Total	17	13	33	26	134	47	141	240	67	80	43	50	114	40	94	68	95	61	84	28

Table 42:
Home ports of trading vessels carrying cargoes
into or out of Rye from Customs Accounts and Port Books 1489-1600

b) Outwards

	1489/90	1490/1	1497/8	1499/50	1508/9	1513/4	1528/9	1531/2	1537/8	1538/9	1543/4	1545/6	1548/9	1549/50	1558/9	1559/60	1561/2	1573/4	1588/9	1599/1600
1: English ships																				
Rye	5	1	9	3	20	1	43	3	32	14	4	32	7	18	37	32	41	41	33	3
Winchelsea	1	·	·	·	4	·	·	2	·	·	·	·	2	·	·	·	·	·	·	·
Hastings	·	8	4	·	3	3	6	1	·	4	2	1	5	26	·	2	·	·	·	·
Other S'sx/Kent	·	·	·	·	·	·	·	·	5	·	·	2	2	12	·	·	·	·	·	·
London	3	1	1	·	1	·	4	·	·	·	1	·	4	11	1	·	1	2	·	·
Other English	·	·	1	1	·	·	3	·	·	·	·	·	·	·	·	·	·	·	·	·
Total English	9	9	15	5	28	4	56	6	37	18	7	35	20	68	38	34	42	45	33	3
2: Calais ships																				
Total Calais	34	17	53	85	34	9	25	24	26	15	25	8	9	48	·	·	·	·	·	·
3: Scottish ships																				
Total Scottish	·	·	·	·	·	·	·	·	·	1	·	·	·	·	·	·	·	·	·	·
4: French ships																				
Dieppe	·	·	4	9	15	1	29	65	2	7	·	15	2	18	·	·	·	·	·	·
Other Normandy	·	1	·	4	17	2	4	5	·	·	2	5	·	·	·	2	·	·	·	14
Other French	·	·	1	·	1	·	·	·	·	·	·	·	·	·	·	·	·	·	·	·
Total French	·	1	5	13	32	3	33	70	2	7	2	20	2	18	1	·	2	3	2	14
5: Breton ships																				
Total Brittany	·	·	2	4	2	·	·	3	·	·	·	·	·	1	·	·	·	·	·	3

Table 42:

a) Inwards (continued)

	1489/90	1490/1	1497/8	1499/50	1508/9	1513/4	1528/9	1531/2	1537/8	1538/9	1543/4	1545/6	1548/9	1549/50	1558/9	1559/60	1561/2	1573/4	1588/9	1599/1600
6: Netherlandish ships																				
Rosendale			1		18	39	97	121	17	27	28	30	32	23			3			
Dunkirk			12		21	42	27	40	1	4		1	2	3	3					
Tergow			2	8	33	33	2	6		4	4	5	10	4	5	3				
Antwerp					10	1	2	4	3	1	3	4	13	16	1	1	1			
Bruges				1	5	1	3	14		1	6	1	1							
Flushing					4		3	14			2		9	2	1					
Ostend			1		6	9	8	4		1			4	1						
Other N'lands	1		7	6	16	34	17	72		4	10	11	19	39		4	3	4	1	2
Total N'lands	1		23	15	113	159	159	275	21	42	53	52	90	88	10	4	7	4	1	2
7: Iberian ships Total Spain/Portugal					1		1				2	1								
8: Hanseatic ships Total German Hanse																		1		
9: Other unidentified					16					1										
Total	44	27	98	122	225	175	274	375	86	84	87	116	121	223	49	38	51	53	36	19

Sources:
P.R.O. Customs accounts and port books E122 35/7-8,11,14,18; 36/1,7,10,13; 37/3/4; 38/1-2,6-7,11,13; 200/5,7-9; E190 739/16,740/26, 744/19,745/15,750/32,750/12.

higher proportion of outward bound vessels in the first half of the sixteenth century. Dieppe and Normandy, however, provided the second largest number of vessels, indicating that the close connections between the two towns were already well established. Among the imports which came from Dieppe were Normandy canvas, woad, wine, hops, barrels of proynes, apples, nuts, raisins, cases of glass, loaves of sugar, oil and vinegar. They also brought consignments of luxury goods, presumably destined for London, such as playing tables, ivory combs, a gross of spectacles, knives, porcelain ware, a variety of gold and silver jewellery inlaid with precious stones for women and inlaid daggers for men, together with a number of religious images and a large quantity of haberdashery such as several hundred dozens of assorted velvet and felt hats and caps (including ones for priests, night caps and children's caps), lace, gloves, satin sleeves, velvet sword girdles and quantities of sarcenet. To Dieppe went horses, English cloth and large quantities of leather and skins, together with some tallow, another traffic which became prohibited later in the century.

However, the bulk of the ships visiting Rye in the first half of the sixteenth century, particularly most of those ships from the Netherlands ports, came for billet wood and timber consign-ments, principally for Calais. All but 20,000 of the 908,000 billets exported in 1543/4 comprising 68 separate shipments were destined for Calais. Two years later the figures were 782,000 billets to Calais and 92,000 to Boulogne, recently captured by Henry VIII, in a total of 84 vessels which also carried 383 dozen loaves of bread, 66 sheep, 53 pigs, 46 quarters of beef, 14 bacon flitches, 504 poultry and a variety of barrels of cider, butter, flour, grain and salted fish towards the provisioning of the former town. During the renewed hostilities with France in 1548/9 the customs accounts reveal the export of 2,390,000 billets to Calais and 169,000 to Boulogne in 94 and 8 ships respectively. The following year the figures were 4,083,000 billets to Calais and a further 451,000 to Boulogne together with 48 bacon hogs, 30 bacon flitches and quantities of beef, butter, cheese and other necessities for the victualling of Calais, carried in 187 ships (155 to Calais, 32 to Boulogne) principally from the Netherlands but also from a number of East Anglian and south-eastern ports, presumably ordered to Rye for the purpose.[25]

With the loss of Boulogne in 1550 and Calais in 1558, there was a once and for all cut by about two-thirds in the number of ships recorded leaving the port of Rye, with a consequent loss in revenues to the townspeople (particularly the town's innkeepers and others engaged in the victualling trades) from the provisioning of ships and from sailors coming ashore. The impact of this reduction can be seen in the figures for outward shipments from 1558/9 onwards, which slumped to a lower level than at any time since the early 1490s. The effect on Rye itself was, however, only temporary and the billet trade seems largely to have recovered to its more usual peacetime level of about one million billets exported a year up to the 1580s, helped by an increase in coastal shipments and a revival of trade with the Netherlandish ports in the early Elizabethan period.

The renewed decline of the billet trade in the late 1590s to only about 200,000 billets a year, scarcely 20 per cent of its 1580s level was, however, an important third factor in Rye's ultimate decline as a port. The impact on the revenues of the town corporation and on the customs accounts was, however, slight, since billet wood was a relatively cheap bulk cargo, subject only to minimal customs dues, which, by the 1560s had been entirely abolished, and the town's own maltode of ld per thousand, introduced in 1560, scarcely brought in more than a few pounds a year.[26] However, it must have had a more severe effect on some of Rye's merchants, who were actively involved in the trade, as indicated by references in the chamberlains' accounts to Mr Birchett's and Mr Welles's 'woodhowses' (1545), at least two further woodhouses at the Strand (1564), and to a woodclose 'late James Milles' (1585). In 1581/2, for example, James Milles, who also imported hops and Flemish bricks and seems to have had a virtual monopoly on the timber trade at that date, paid maltode on 67 separate consignments of wood, consisting of 710,000 billets, 127 loads 21 of logs and 10 tons of timber, mainly to Flanders and Normandy. The virtual extinction of this trade in the 1590s, therefore, represented a further constriction in the scope of activity for Rye's merchants.

Fourthly, the influx of large numbers of Protestant exiles from France and the Netherlands in the late 1560s and 1570s, including numbers of merchants and skilled craftsmen, although providing a temporary boost to the town's economic fortunes, gave only a

253

brief respite from an underlying trend of economic decline. Their departure in the early 1590s,coinciding as it did with the end of the transit trade in cloth and a further decline in the export of billets merely served to reduce still further the population and level of economic activity in Rye at a time when the corporation was incurring increasingly heavy costs in the maintenance of a safe haven for the town's fishing vessels. A small part of the cloth trade, too, was attributable to their presence, at least in its initial stages. Between October and December 1572, for example, Cornelis Sohier, resident in Rye, had 15 horsepacks of cloth transported to him from Southwark for shipment overseas and what appears to have been two of his relations, Peter and Simon Soheire, dwelling in Fenchurch St, London, sent a further 9 consignments of cloth to Rye between July and November of the same year.[28] Among importers of goods into Rye, the Protestant exile community accounted for a small but significant proportion of shipments coming into the port, including such items as Normandy canvas, Lyons thread, silk, taffeta, felt, combs and brushes together with cheaper bulk items such as barrels of proynes and vinegar, and paying £42 13s 5d in customs dues, equivalent in value to 6.5 per cent of imports during the year. The loss of this trade was therefore a further blow to the economic fortunes of the town at a time when it could least be afforded.

The social and political upheavals in Rouen and elsewhere in Normandy following the murder of the Duke of Guise on Christmas Day 1588 now also began adversely to affect Rye's trade. Between 1588 and 1590 the revenues of the lesser box fell by more than half and in April 1591, Henry Gaymer, who only 18 months earlier had leased the town's storehouse at Strand for £32 10s a year for three years demanded to be released from his contract for, 'by reason of the trobles and warres in Fraunce ... little or no goodes of late have byn brought into the sayd howse.' During the next three years, no lessee could be found and the Storehouse remained in the town's hands and its dues were paid directly into the chamberlains' accounts. Receipts reached their lowest point in 1592/3, which coincided with a further fall in the revenues of the lesser box. In that year the total dues from goods left in the Storehouse amounted to a mere £4 3s 9d, little more than an eighth of its rent three years earlier. Although there was a recovery the following year to £15 15s 10d, preceding a new

Table 43:

The fall in quantities of goods imported and exported through Rye between the early 1580s and the late 1590s

Commodity	Average annual quantity		% change
	1580s	1590s	
Imports			
Wheat	755.4 qtrs	272 qtrs	−64
Malt	2857.6 qtrs	718 qtrs	−74.9
Salt	685 qtrs	528.8 qtrs	−22.8
Wine	85.8 tons	21.4 tons	−75.1
Woad	178.4 ballots	52.5 ballots	−70.6
Coal	152.4 chalder	111.8 chalder	−26.6
Iron	26.3 tons	14.5 tons	−44.9
Canvas	8.8 packs	2 packs	−77.3
Horsepacks/packs	27.2	17	−37.5
Total consignments	364.4	161.8	−55.6
Ships	159	74	−53.4
Exports			
Billets	1077.4 thousand	266 thousand	−75.3
Horses	89.4	94	+ 5.1
Iron	184.8 tons	133.5 tons	−27.8
Horsepacks/fardels	591.8	52.5	−91.2
Timber	111.3 tons	40.5 tons	−63.6
Total consignments	498.4	113.3	−77.3
Ships	198.8	70.3	−64.7

Sources: RYE 66/12-69.

lease for £20, which coincided with the brief revival in the transit trade seen in the 1593/4 lesser box returns, trade again slumped in 1595/6 and 1598/9, so that by the time of its sale in 1602, the rent of the Storehouse had fallen to only £7 a year.[30]

By the late 1590s therefore, Rye was suffering a severe trade depression, the effects of which can be seen in Table 43. Overall the greater effect was on exports which for the first time during the sixteenth century fell below the level of imports. In comparison to the 1580s the fall in trade was severe enough, but compared to the 1531/2 total of 613 ships listed in the Rye customs accounts, the fall to only 46 ships listed in the 1599/1600 port books (134 ships according to the maltode books which include coastal trade) represented the reduction of Rye's role in the maritime economy of England from that of a port of national importance to a minor port of merely local significance. Even as compared to the early 1580s, there was a combined reduction in the total number of ships entering and leaving Rye harbour of almost 60 per cent by the end of the sixteenth century.

Within this overall pattern of decline, by far the largest single reduction was in the export of cloth, represented by a fall in the average number of horsepacks and fardels exported from over 590 a year in the 1580s to only 52.5 in the 1590s, only 8.7 per cent of its previous level. Only slightly less severe was the fall in timber and billet exports, the latter down to only a quarter of its 1580s level. An indication of the severity of the general decline in Rye's trading position is the fact that even after such a fall in quantity, timber and billets still accounted for by far the largest proportion of Rye's exports (38.4 per cent of shipments leaving the port according to the maltode books). Among exports, only iron (down by a quarter) and horses, which alone showed a minor increase, showed any sign of maintaining their earlier levels; and in the case of iron the geographical situation of the industry left no alternative to Rye (except, possibly, Winchelsea) if a costly overland journey was to be avoided. Apart from a very local traffic, therefore, by the beginning of the seventeeth century, Rye's export trade had virtually ceased to exist.

Nor was the situation very different with regard to imports. Even the trade in dyestuffs, represented by a 70 per cent fall in woad imports, suffered major decline, indicating that by 1600, much of the Wealden cloth industry was being supplied overland from the Medway ports or direct from London. Other major falls, such as that in Normandy canvas, down to less than a quarter of its earlier level and accompanied by a similar drop in mixed cargoes and in wine imports, indicates the almost complete destruction of Rye's role as an entrepot, serving primarily as an outport of London for the importing of a variety of goods. The collapse in grain imports, down by more than two-thirds overall, reflects the fall in population in Rye at this time. Of bulk cargoes, only salt and coal showed any sign of maintaining their earlier levels and these were down by a quarter. In the case of salt the maintenance of this relatively high level of imports was largely due to three shipments, varying between 360–400 quarters each in 1600/1, by a group of Rye merchants headed by John Fisher, one of the jurats and his partners, probably for the purposes of salting herrings, since Fisher was also an ost.[31] It was however almost the only remaining example of local mercantile initiative in Rye at the end of the sixteenth century.

The loss of opportunities for mercantile profits by the end of the 1590s was very marked compared with earlier times. In the 1550s and 1560s, men such as John Fletcher's sons Thomas and

Richard had built on the family's fortunes by their trading activities. In the spring of 1553 for example, Richard Fletcher paid keyage on 40 tons of wine alone.[32] In the 1570s Rye's merchants had a wide network of trading connections, supplying neighbouring towns such as Winchelsea, Hastings, New Romney, Lydd, Hythe, Tenterden and Cranbrook. Farther afield they provided wine to Canterbury, and a range of goods by sea to Dover and Sandwich to the east and Chichester to the west. Some idea of the extent of these activities can be obtained from the annual files of letters of process among the corporation records, which record attempts to recover outstanding debts both to and occasionally from Rye's trading community. Thus, in the 1570s, Henry Gaymer claimed £100 of Alexander Minge of Dover (1572) and £20 of Thomas Collier of Sandwich (1576), both merchants, for goods supplied and was in turn charged with owing £60 to Humphrey Meade, merchant of Dover (1575). Robert Carpenter claimed £6 17s from a London grocer for grocery wares he had supplied; William Dabernell claimed £60 of Philip Morgan of Stepney (1575); Edmund Tindall and Nicholas Cheston claimed £80 from a Chichester merchant; James Pearsall claimed £23 6s from a Southampton merchant (1577) and William Bragden demanded £200 outstanding to him from Robert Gregory, merchant, of Weymouth (1577). Other outstanding debts included ones for fish supplied to London and Maidstone; for billets to various towns including Dover, Sandwich and Ostend; for tailors' wares supplied to Chichester; and a large number relating to goods supplied to Tenterden and Winchelsea.[33]

Among goods imported in 1573/4 for local traders were hops, lupins, canvas, Spanish wool, alum and straw stools and chairs.[34] Chief among the importers listed in the port books for that year was James Pearsall (variously described as of London or Rye), merchant, a member of the common council from 1578–1589, who imported goods to the value of over £450 including 3,400 lbs pepper, 3 tons brasell, canvas and salt, much of it destined for the London market. Other importers included Peter James, Robert Farley, Edmund Tindall, William Bragden and William Didsbury. Farley dealt in a number of commodities, principally glass, exporting 210 cases between September 1575 and April 1576 and importing 60 barrels of broken glass during the same period.

Didsbury, owner of the Mermaid Inn, imported mainly wine.[35]

Several of these men acted as factors for London merchants. Among those listed acting in this capacity in 1573/4, William Bragden, William Didsbury and Richard Daniell were the principal Rye agents for cloth exporters. They were also agents for London importers together with Robert Farley and Nicholas Harrold. Among the immigrant community, Cornelis Sohier and Vincent Dugard acted as factors for Dieppe merchants, importing a variety of Normandy cloth and other wares into England. Others, principally John Willes, who also traded on his own account, acted as factors for the sale of billets. The loss of the transit trade, coinciding with the general decline in the town's fortunes in the mid-1590s, thus had an additional effect on individual Rye merchants at a time when they could least afford it. It is therefore hardly surprising that no new generation of Rye merchants emerged in the closing years of Elizabeth's reign to rival the economic activities of their predecessors. Men such as Thomas Hamon, John and Thomas Fisher and James Appleton, son of the late town clerk, who continued to trade in the closing years of the sixteenth century, were fast becoming a dwindling band as the immigration of potential young recruits with some personal means to the town's merchant elite effectively dried up. The situation was made worse by the decline during the 1590s of the Rye fishing industry, which further depressed the incomes of those merchants who also acted as osts and feters.

The collapse of Rye's fishing industry

The decline in the Rye fishing fleet, referred to in chapter three, which was reflected in the fall of 27 per cent in the number of coastal fishing vessels operating out of Rye between the early 1580s and the last five years of Elizabeth's reign, had a dramatic effect on the sales of fish in the Rye fish market, as shown in Table 44. Sales of fish to osts, acting as agents for the London Fishmongers' Company, fell from an average 3624 seams a year in the five years ending in 1584/5 to only 1896 seams a year between 1596/7 and 1602/3, a drop of 47.7 per cent. The fall in the amount of fish sold to market men for local consumption fell even more sharply, from an average 4265 dossers a year to only 1863 dossers, a drop of 56.3 per cent. The rather larger fall in the totals of fish sold to market men probably reflects the preferential

Table 44

Annual totals of fish sold in Rye fishmarket 1580/1-1602/3

	Quantities of fish sold[1]	
Year	To Osts (seams)	To market men (dossers)
1580/1	2222	3980
1581/2	2837	4219
1582/3	3053	3708
1583/4	5693	5413
1584/5[2]	4317	4007
1592	2398	2167
1593/4	2156	1724
1596/7	1516	1020
1599/1600	1818	1788
1600/1	1992	2341
1602/3	2259	2304

Notes:
[1] Fish sold to osts for transportation to the London fishmarket was measured in seams, on which a maltode of ½d a seam was paid by freemen (double by unfree inhabitants); market men, who bought for the local market, had their purchases measured in dossers, on which they paid a ¼d maltode. According to the 1550 town ordinance, non-residents paid half as much again as non-free inhabitants. One seam was therefore probably equivalent to three dossers. Since, in 1580, the maltode on 7,000 herrings paid by a non-resident was 14d, a dosser seems to have been the equivalent of about 250 herrings and a seam approximately 750. RYE 57/1/67; RYE 66/12-15.
[2] Estimated from dues collected. RYE 66/31, covering June-August 1585 slightly defective.

Sources: RYE 66/12-69.

treatment accorded to the osts, who comprised a number of the wealthier of Rye's inhabitants, including several jurats. The effect of this fall can be seen both in the reduction in the number of osts trading in the Rye fishmarket and also in the average number of seams bought by the chief traders among them. The number of osts listed as paying maltode on seams of fish, which stood at 12 in the early 1580s, rising to 14 in the peak year 1584/5, had fallen to only 10 by 1596/7 and fell again to nine in 1602/3. Among the leading five osts in any one year, who accounted between them for a remarkably constant 65–66 per cent share of the market in ost fish, the average number of seams traded annually by each of them fell from 478 in the five years to 1584/5 to only 248 in the period 1596/7 to 1602/3, a drop of 48.1 per cent. The 1590s therefore must have represented a serious reduction in the levels of income and opportunities among the leading wholesalers of fish in Rye.

The dues on fish, together with (from 1568) the maltodes on goods and ships passing through the harbour, together, formed the revenues of the little box. Although the detailed quarterly

Table 45

The Rye lesser box returns: annual totals of maltodes on ships and goods passing through the port of Rye and on the sale of fish 1547-1603

Year	Grand Passage[1]	Petty Passage[1]	Keyage and Mesurage[1]	Osts	Market Men	Total
1547/8	-	-	2 2 2		37 19 6	
1548/9	-	-	3 7 4½		37 19 8	
1549/50	-	-	4 13 0		33 6 1	
1550/1	-	-	19 11 1		28 9 2	
1551/2	-	-	18 19 10½		40 8 1½	
1552/3	-	-	14 18 6		24 19 9½	
1553/4	-	-	13 8 5		24 12 5½	
1554/5	-	-	14 17 7		29 5 0¼	
1555/6	-	-	21 18 8		22 19 4¾	
1556/7	-	-	10 0 9		30 6 7	
1557/8	-	-	2 2 4½		20 8 9	
1558/9	-	-	10 11 5		23 2 5	
1559/60	-	-	18 1 10		23 11 8	
1560/1	-	-	33 14 6		21 1 10¼	
1561/2	-	-	20 16 4½		20 1 10½	
1562/3	-	-	22 0 4		22 11 5	
1563/4	1 19 8½	-	19 4 3		19 5 7½	
1564/5	10 5 8	10 5 8	19 14 4		18 15 1	
1565/6	10 17 6	3 1 5	28 18 7½		27 17 0	
1566/7	11 10 0	3 0 3	24 9 6½		22 10 4½	
1567/8	6 2 6	2 15 0	32 16 5½		18 1 9½	
1568/9						57 3 3
1569/70	11 5 4	2 12 11	22 10 6		21 6 2	
1570/1	15 17 6	4 11 8	30 16 0		20 8 1	
1571/2						86 8 4½
1572/3						n/a
1573/4						n/a
1574/5						57 6 11
1575/6						52 8 8
1576/7						58 2 4½
1577/8						62 5 6½
1578/9						68 2 6
1579/80						61 18 11½
1580/1	10 5 0	3 7 6	31 19 1½	7 15 8	8 5 10	61 12 1½
1581/2	10 12 6	3 6 8	41 13 4½	8 15 4½	8 15 9½	73 6 8½
1582/3	10 2 6	Farm	44 6 4	9 11 6	7 14 6	71 14 10
1583/4	12 5 0	Farm	39 10 5	27 8 2	11 5 6½	90 9 1½
1584/5	10 15 0	Farm	32 1 0½	16 12 3	8 6 11½	67 15 3
1585/6						69 18 1
1586/7						61 14 9
1587/8						106 7 0½
1588/9						91 16 9½
1589/90						80 10 6
1590/1						54 5 6
1591/2						63 0 10½
1592/3						49 7 11
1593/4	8 15 0	Farm	21 10 8½	8 17 8	3 11 10	42 15 2½
1594/5						34 13 4
1595/6						9 18 11
1596/7	6 7 6	Farm	17 18 7	6 8 8	2 3 2	32 17 11
1597/8						33 4 2½
1598/9						12 16 6½
1599/1600	1 2 6	Farm	11 16 3½	8 5 5	3 14 6	24 18 8½
1600/1	1 5 0	Farm	11 3 1	8 19 0	4 18 10½	26 5 11½
1602/3	1 17 6	Farm	22 7 5	15 7 9	11 9 10	51 2 6

Notes: [1]Until 1571/2 only the dues on osts and market men were included in the lesser box. From 1571/2 the lesser box also included payage and mesurage, grand and petty passage. From 1582/3 the petty passage was let out to farm and not included in the lesser box returns. The detailed figures for totals for these years, taken from the same source, differ slightly from the amounts recorded in the chamberlains' accounts volumes (RYE 60/9-10).

Sources: RYE 60/6-10; RYE 61/1-4; RYE 66/12-69.

returns only survive from the early 1580s, the total revenues of the lesser box were included separately in the chamberlains' accounts. Until 1568 keyage and measurage (which first appears to have been taxed significantly in 1550/1, following the introduction of a set of maltodes in September 1550) was listed separately, enabling a comparison of the relative fortunes of trade and fishing. The results are set out in Table 45.

The situation is, however, made more complex by a number of increases in the rates of maltodes on particular goods and by the addition of new items to the list of those subject to maltode. Thus in January 1567 the assembly decreed that the rates for keyage and measurage previously agreed should apply not only to goods passing overseas, but also to goods shipped along the coast or to London; and they further decreed a maltode of ½d a thousand billets or ton of wood to be paid by freemen, inhabitants to pay 1d and strangers 2d, confirming a local tax which had been collected since 1560, but which does not appear in the 1550 list of maltodes.[38] There was evidently some resistance to the imposition of charges on goods passing to and from London, since a further decree was issued by the assembly in January 1575 confirming their previous decision.[39] In the same year, a new maltode of 3s 4d a ton towards the maintenance of the quays and jetties was introduced on the sale of London beer and the following January the masters of any vessels bringing beer from London or elsewhere were to certify the fact to the mayor and jurats before it was landed.[40] In December 1578 the rates for keyage and measurage of grain were increased and it was specified that any that was re-exported should be charged maltode both in and out.[41] The effect of these various decrees was probably only slight, especially as they largely restated existing practice. However, the temporary increase between March and August 1584 from ½d to 1½d a seam in payments by osts for fish sent to London and elsewhere, almost trebled the dues from ostage in 1583/4.[42] Similarly, in 1587, when the town was in some financial difficulties over its provision of a ship for service against the Spaniards, the imposition of a tax of 6d on every bonne of beer laden or transported overseas by way of trade, seems to have been the main reason for an increase of over £40 in the revenues of the lesser box in 1587/8. Even in 1592, when the number of ships coming into the port was well down as a result of the French wars, the proceeds from the new imposition on beer exports still amounted to £17 18s, equivalent to 53.9 per cent of the total dues on keyage and measurage collected in that year. In January 1593 the dues payable on both the export of beer and of iron were reduced by the assembly, in the first case to 2d a bonne and in the second from 4d to 2d a ton, possibly as a result of competition from Winchelsea, whose exports particularly in iron, seem to have increased at this time. By 1599 either beer exports had dried up or a decision had been taken to end the export duty, since there is no mention of any duty paid on beer exported from 1599/1600 onwards.[43]

By the end of the sixteenth century, the parallel decline in Rye's trade and in fishing was having a severe effect on the receipts of the corporation from the lesser box at a time when expenditure on the harbour was increasing. In October 1602, therefore, the maltodes on osts and market men were increased, from $\frac{1}{2}$d to 3d a seam and to 1d a dosser. A month later a new set of maltodes was issued, which concentrated increases in rates on such staple items of Rye's trade as the export of timber and billets, mats and iron, and the import of dyestuffs, barrels of prunes, wine and hops. The effect, once again, was almost to double the receipts from the lesser box as compared to the previous year.[44] However, as Table 38 shows, the decline in Rye's economy still left the total receipts of the lesser box at a lower level than they had been at any time since the 1560s, while in real terms the fall in revenue was much greater.

A bankrupt corporation: the harbour works of the 1590s

The decline in the Rye fishing industry, though not the decline in trade, was closely connected with the gradual silting up of Rye haven, which, from the 1570s onwards, was causing increasing problems to Rye's fishermen in the provision of a safe anchorage for their vessels. The problem of silting was well enough known on both sides of the Channel and in itself is unlikely to have been sufficient to account for the almost total collapse of the town's economy in the 1590s. In the case of trading vessels entering the harbour, a light at Camber Castle and another at Dungeness, and the appointment of a pilot to guide ships into the harbour in 1589 appear to have provided a workable solution, although it is the case that an 80 ton merchant vessel leaving Rye ran aground in

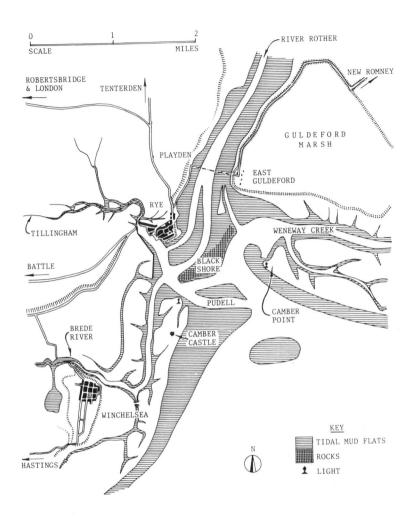

Figure 8: Rye harbour in the late sixteenth century
(based on P. Symondson's map of Rye harbour, Rother levels, Walland and Romney Marshes 1594 (ye 132/6) and John Prowze's map of Rye harbour 1572 (PRO MPF 212))

263

the Camber in October 1574 and its cargo had to be discharged before it could be re-floated, and a number of other vessels seem to have come to grief in the Camber during winter storms.[45] The situation here, however, seems little different from that further along the coast at Newhaven, where at least six ships came to grief between 1576 and 1578.[46] There were, however, some limitations placed on the length of time during which ships were allowed to remain at the quayside in lading and unlading, which in 1564 was set at no more than four days and nights at the quays between the ferry and the old quay and in 1575 was restricted to no more than one tide after a ship had completed lading or discharging at the new quay, but this may just as easily be an indication of the pressure on the port by the growth of the transit trade during these years as an indication of any serious reduction in actual harbourage. Certainly there appears to have been sufficient safe anchorage for larger vessels in the Puddle throughout the sixteenth and seventeenth centuries, although the loss of the Camber itself does appear to have reduced this anchorage from sufficient for over 400 vessels to little more than 40 by the mid-seventeenth century.[47] Nevertheless, the continuing use of the port by the 120 ton Hercules throughout the 1590s and the reappearance of the passage trade in the 1630s make it clear that the silting of the haven had little practical consequences for trade.

The situation for Rye's fishermen was however rather different. As early as 1576 they had complained of the lack of a safe anchorage for their vessels, chiefly as a result of the increased force of the sea following the wearing away by the Camber itself, of a sandbank or spit of land which had previously guarded the entrance of the tidal lagoon at the mouth of the Rother, at the north end of which Rye was situated. According to the fishermen's petition, 'we lose and are in damaged among all our said craft, for want of good harboringe in one fowle night more than we are able in one hole yere to gett uppe agene.'[48] For a remedy they proposed the construction of a wooden jetty on the west side of the entrance to Rye creek, which appears on subsequent maps opposite the southernmost end of the new quay at Strand in order to narrow the entrance and give greater force to the ebb tide to wear away the sand at the creek's mouth. This and subsequent descriptions of the works undertaken for the amending of Rye haven make it clear that what primarily concerned the townspeople was not the main channel of the River Rother from Rye to the sea, but the harbour formed by the mouth of the Tillingham where it joined the Rother by the Strand quay. The ultimately fruitless attempt to maintain this haven increasingly preoccupied the town corporation over the next three decades and led to virtual corporate bankruptcy.

At least part of the problem of silting in this particular channel was caused by the gradual inning of the marshes both above and below Rye, which had the effect of severely reducing the flow of the sea through the main channels. In 1548, therefore, Rye and Winchelsea had jointly promoted a bill in Parliament to enable the construction of a number of sluices to improve the scouring action of the ebb tide.[49] Further proposals in 1561 included a sluice west of Dimsdale bridge to pen up the water in the River Brede, which joined the Rother near the mouth of the Tillingham.[50]

During the ensuing three decades a series of abortive attempts were made to improve the haven at Rye. In 1571 a sesse of £95 7s 8d was made for a ninety foot long and twelve foot high stone quay at Strand, following discussions between the Lord Warden and the corporation about the amending of the haven. In 1574 it was agreed to build a new timber quay at Strand, and the following year the town agreed the erection of a groine from Gateborough marsh wall to the north jetties at a cost of £16 plus materials. Early in 1576 the first of another series of Parliamentary bills was ordered to be drawn up for the amending of the haven, which culminated in the bill drawn up for the 1601 Parliament which provided for an additional national customs levy (much as had been agreed for Dover harbour) to pay for the projected works.[51] All that could be achieved in 1576, however, despite a series of appeals to the Council, was the grant of a commission of sewers to examine the problem, which Robert Carpenter, one of Rye's MPs, writing from London, advised the corporation to accept for the time being, 'for that we perceive her majestie will d⟨ ⟩arte from no money for the doeng therof.'[52] In March of that year, for the first time, there was a suggestion for turning Appledore water into Rye creek, and in August three engineers from Dunkirk and Nieuwport in Flanders were invited to Rye by the corporation to advise on new harbour works. Their main recommendation was the construction of a groine between the Black Shore and the town to stop up a minor channel which flowed out of the creek above the main entrance and 'to guyde the water gently to your Creke wher it shall ronne' and the lengthening of the jetty at the entrance of Rye creek by a further 12 feet, with another jetty opposite, sloping inwards so as to create a narrow entrance to the harbour where the water would run faster and therefore deeper.[53] The following June the engineers returned and the work of construction went ahead and was completed during the autumn.[54] These works seem to have been temporarily relatively successful, since there is little further about the problems of the haven until 1589, when, once again, serious problems, largely related to further inning of the marshes, seem to have been encountered.

At first the main proposals under consideration seem to have been for a new sluice to be placed in the marshes on the west side of Rye creek, towards Winchelsea, where a 'great scluse' was set up in February 1589, and for the purchase of St Mary's Marsh 'for penninge of water or otherwise for the amendinge of the sayd harbour of Rye', on the advice of John Stonham, one of three engineers consulted at this time by the corporation. At the end of 1590 it was agreed to construct a new wall on the west side of the creek against the millbank and the following summer another groine was erected at the head of this wall on the west side of the ferry way. In July of 1591, however, the corporation came to hear of the works elsewhere of an Italian engineer by the name of Frederico Genebelli. Over the next two years the assembly books and correspondence files are full of discussions concerning his plans for the amendment of the haven, culminating in his arrival in the town in March 1593, when he seems to have convinced the corporation of his ability to carry out the works, although without actually revealing his precise plans. The assembly was evidently sufficiently impressed by his references to special 'engines' for the more speedy completion of the work to have written to the Lord Warden offering to meet half of Genebelli's proposed total expenditure of £2000 by way of annual sesses of £200 a year for five years if Lord Cobham could prevail upon the Privy Council to find the rest. Cobham's request that they ask him to prepare a 'plott' to show his precise intentions and appear with it before the Council was evidently more than the mayor and jurats had done, since, when it was produced, it at once became apparent that his plan was to make a new cut of almost two miles in length from

Dimsdale Creek through the marshes to the sea between Winchelsea and Camber Castle, which would have made Winchelsea the main beneficiary. This provoked the immediate response from Rye corporation that it was 'a thing lykelie to proffytt others of other places and very preiudycyall to us; for which cause it is not lyked that this towneshipp shalbe at greate charges to worke their owne decaye' and that he had 'most trecherously abused this towneshipp', the town clerk recording in the margin of the assembly book 'Ser Jenabell, his lewde dealing discovered'.[55]

With the collapse of these grandiose schemes for the amendment of Rye haven, the corporation reverted to the more traditional remedy of trying to improve the scouring action of the tide in Rye creek. In the spring of 1594 £65 was spent on stopping another breach in the Black shore. Later in 1594 and again in 1595, the corporation consulted Philip Symondson of Rochester, who was commissioned to draw a plan of the town and surrounding countryside to indicate how best the harbour could be amended. In January 1595 John Stonham was also once again consulted. As a result the 'Great Scluse' in Mr Tufton's marshes was once again repaired and set going again and a new wall was constructed to help pen in the water there.[56]

Finally, in May 1596, the corporation embarked on a major new scheme for a sluice, 60 ft across, with two gates each 10ft wide and 17ft deep, the whole being 21ft deep across the channel immediately to the west of the windmills at the Strand and for the turning of Appledore water into the newly deepened channel through a new cut to the west of the town. A contract was entered into with Thomas Bridges of Nedesham Market, Suffolk, carpenter, for £600 for the completion of the scheme by Christmas. By January 1597, the project had so far cost £445 and was still far from completion. In March a system of forced labour was introduced, with householders in each of the wards in turn being ordered to work on the haven at Strand or else to find a substitute on pain of a 2s fine for every day defaulting. Between April and December a further £133 was accounted for, including payments to Noye Radford for playing the drum 'for the caling of the pepell to the workies and from the workies'. The works were still not complete by the beginning of November, when it was agreed to pay Mr Bridges an additional £28 and to provide him with eight labourers at the town's charges in order to finish the west wall between the sluice and Cadborough Hill to pen in the water. Throughout this period the forced works continued. In September 1597 it was decreed that for the more speedy completion of the west wall of the work at the Strand, the wards were to work alternately. At the end of December it was decreed that they should work for a week out of hand for the strengthening of the south wall at Strand. The following July, when a breach appeared in the new works, all householders of ability were ordered to work there, one or two wards a day, or pay 6d per person in default. In August the penalty was raised to 12d as the commissioners of sewers were expected shortly to view the progress of the works. By June 1599 a total of £1407 16s 7d had been spent compared to only £1165 0s 10d received, leaving a substantial deficit at a time when the town was under financial pressure from other quarters[57]

As a result of these expenses, which came on top of heavy demands for ship service in 1596 and 1597, the corporation found itself virtually bankrupt, and in February 1597 agreed to sell off or mortgage any of the town lands that could be sold in order to raise the necessary money for the completion of the project. At the same time, Thomas Hamon, the mayor, agreed to lend the town a further £200 in addition to the £80 already owed to him, William Ratliff agreed to loan a further £20 and in August 1597 a further £100 was borrowed, partly for the finishing of the sluice and partly to repay the mortgages when due on the Storehouse and the Vine. In December a series of leases on minor items of town property were sold off to the value of £30 13s 4d because the cost of the works to amend the harbour 'doth growe to a farre greater charge than was expected and ... this corporation is very greatly indebted.' Yet despite a benevolence from London, Kent and Sussex, a £50 gift from Sir Henry Guldeforde and the imposition of two sesses and a range of special taxes, from the raising of the maltodes to an imposition of 4d a turn on lighters and cockboats using the harbour and of 6d a bonne on beer sold in the town's tippling houses, the corporation was forced to liquidate a whole range of corporate assets between 1600 and 1602, including the ferry, the two rows of shops at Strand and the town's storehouse, which went to Thomas Hamon for £400, the Vine, which was sold to Stephen Harrison for £56 and the custom house, which was sold to Robert Ireland's heirs. Altogether over £600 worth of the corporation's lands and buildings had to be sold. Yet despite all this expenditure, early in the new reign the corporation lamented 'the mynet daunger' that the town stood in 'of beinge utterly lost by reason of the violence of the sea and great ruyne and decaye of the jetties, keyes, caulsers, seabanckes and other defences about the same, whereby it is alredy well neere not onelie severed from the mayneland, but very likelie to be altogethers undermynded', its revenues small, 'and the howses and tenementes now inhabited very meanlie rentid'. Nevertheless, in 1610 the corporation had to find a further £100 by way of sesse to repair the jetties, causeways and other defences against the sea.[58]

Altogether, between 1596 and 1600 Rye spent at least £1400 and perhaps considerably more on works to its harbour at a time when trade was declining, the French immigrants were leaving, some of the fishing boats and much of Rye's merchant shipping were moving elsewhere and the town's population was in general decline. Under these circumstances the increasing exactions placed on the shoulders of the dwindling number of wealthier inhabitants, both by way of sesse and through increased dues on trading, coupled with the imposition over a two-year period of a policy of forced labour, had the effect of still further reducing the town's fortunes by driving away those who could take their remaining wealth with them elsewhere and by discouraging potential immigrants from coming to dwell in a town so obviously in deep economic crisis. In this sense, then, however necessary they may have appeared, the harbour works embarked upon in 1596 were the final, contributory factor to the irreversible decline of a once proud town. The crisis of the 1590s thus marked the beginning of the transformation of Rye from a major English port to a minor market town.

Appendix 1:
Annual levels of christenings, marriages and burials in Rye 1539-1607

Year	C	M	B	Year	C	M	B
1539	92	24	86	1573[3]	26	30	91
1540	84	43	208	1574	107	36	110
1541	97	46	147	1575	142	32	98
1542	114	37	93	1576	110	48	101
1543	96	47	121	1577	125	34	94
1544	126	47	440	1578	109	21	95
1545	112	46	143	1579	109	31	271
1546	87	34	131	1580	93	82	556
1547	64	28	56	1581	112	46	53
1548	114	44	120	1582[4]	106	42	101
1549	140	46	95	1583[4]	60	25	43
1550	110	44	91	1584	68	26	53
1551	86	31	78	1585	124	30	99
1552	108	30	89	1586	100	20	70
1553	121	43	120	1587	95	28	126
1554	126	42	122	1588	111	42	122
1555	138	20	106	1589	98	27	79
1556	134	38	188	1590	86	50	233
1557	92	35	266	1591	107	29	96
1558	106	46	331	1592	101	49	178
1559	75	61	257	1593	108	39	124
1560	134	73	219	1594	96	47	76
1561	133	56	140	1595	103	32	71
1562	100	37	127	1596[5]	81	25	422
1563	116	50	771	1597	68	23	138
1564	99	91	81	1598	69	19	73
1565[1]	116	37	110	1599	76	21	42
1566[1]	49	19	-	1600	77	18	57
1567	79	35	-	1601	72	30	39
1568[2]	89	24	62	1602	80	24	51
1569[3]	45	26	57	1603	93	33	86
1570[3]	-	43	163	1604	80	28	100
1571	-	52	113	1605	86	29	44
1572	-	52	163	1606	71	19	90
				1607	75	24	120

Source: E.S.R.O, PAR 467 1/1/1-2.

Notes: entries missing:
[1] CM Oct 1565-Apr 1566, B Nov 1565-Jul 1568.
[2] C May-Aug, M Mar-Sep.
[3] C Jun 1569-Nov 1573, B Sep 1569-Mar 1570.
[4] C Nov 25 1582-10 Mar 1583.
[5] C Oct 24 to end Dec.

Appendix 2:
Annual income and expenditure from Rye Chamberlains Accounts 1485-86

Mayoral year[1]	Income			Expenditure			Surplus/Deficit		
	£	s	d	£	s	d	£	s	d
1485/6	51	19	6½	50	19	8	+0	19	10½
1486/7	50	17	10	53	8	10½	-2	11	0½
1487/8	54	17	3½	44	7	9	+9	19	7½
1488/9	34	5	8	35	18	6	-1	12	10
1489/90	63	13	1½	55	14	7½	+7	18	6
1490/1	71	4	1½	69	2	6	+2	1	7½
1491/2	67	17	7½	52	17	4½	+15	0	3
1492/3*	108	18	8½	93	17	2	+15	1	6½
1493/4	78	4	11	74	17	2½	+3	7	8½
1494/5	63	12	11½	62	3	10½	+1	9	1
1495/6	63	17	8	63	12	7	+0	5	1
1496/7	63	10	6½	61	9	7	+2	0	11½
1497/8	72	9	3½	66	7	6	+6	1	9½
1498/9	69	9	2	51	7	2	+18	2	0
1499/1500	88	7	10	81	3	6	+7	4	4
1500/1	81	12	6½	65	16	3½	+14	16	3
1501/2	78	1	0	61	8	1	+16	12	11
1502/3	71	15	0½	67	12	2½	+4	2	10
1503/4	70	13	9½	-	-	-	-	-	-
1504/5	87	7	1½	72	6	8½	+	0	5
1505/6	82	0	5	67	11	6	+14	8	11
1506/7	106	15	5	96	18	8½	+9	16	8½
1507/8	88	14	4½	89	8	7	-0	14	2½
1508/9	83	2	6½	78	12	11	+4	9	7½
1509/10	95	16	2½	90	3	7½	+5	10	7
1510/1	81	16	4	72	15	7½	+9	0	8½
1511/2	119	16	10	101	3	9	+18	13	1
1512/3	113	16	6	99	5	5	+14	11	1
1513/4	210	1	9½	205	13	8	+4	8	1½
1514/5	119	9	10	104	5	0	+15	4	10
1515/6	119	16	7½	91	18	0½	+27	18	6½
1516/7	119	4	8	119	17	10½	+9	6	9½
1517/8	137	1	9½	-	-	-	-	-	-
1518/9	93	0	10	93	10	11	-0	10	1
1519/20	82	19	6½	66	11	11	+16	7	7½
1520/1	99	10	5	82	2	1	+17	8	4
1521/2	96	6	7½	88	14	8	+7	11	11½
1522/3	122	16	3	124	6	1½	-1	9	10½
1523/4	99	4	3½	99	16	2	-0	11	10½
1524/5	171	11	11	161	3	9½	+10	8	1½
1525/6	123	12	3	114	10	4	+9	1	11
1526/7	107	5	9½	92	0	2	+15	5	7½
1527/8	152	8	7½	169	0	8½	-16	19	6
1528/9	105	3	3						
1529/30	128	1	10½	108	16	1	+19	5	9½
1530/1*	158	7	8	142	18	6½	+15	5	9½
1531/2	111	18	4	111	17	4	+0	1	0
1532/3	138	0	10½	133	13	10½	+4	7	0
1533/4	139	6	7						
1534/5	144	4	10	142	6	1	+1	18	9
1535/6	133	9	9½	133	0	10½	+0	8	11
1536/7	135	8	3½	120	3	0½	+15	5	3
1537/8	153	14	5	141	19	2½	+11	15	2½
1538/9	169	9	0	154	3	0⁰	+15	5	11½
1539/40	185	17	9½	175	5	1½	+10	12	8
1540/1	132	18	3½	122	10	9	+10	7	6½
1541/2	147	15	10½	141	6	1	+6	9	9½
1542/3	176	0	4½	169	0	1½	+7	0	3
1543/4*	337	12	1	337	17	8	-0	5	7
1544/5*	289	19	11½	316	18	5	-26	18	5½
1545/6	203	14	10¹	203	18	7		n/a	
1546/7	179	3	0½	182	0	11½	-2	17	11

271

Appendix 2 (continued):

Mayoral year[1]	Income			Expenditure			Surplus/Deficit		
1547/8	170	2	2½	149	4	0	+20	18	2½
1548/9	223	18	4	248	18	5½	-25	0	1½
1549/50	278	17	10[1]	240	12	2[2]	+38	5	8
1550/1	208	5	8½[1]	211	1	4½[1]	-2	15	8
1551/2	271	15	10	245	11	8	+26	4	2
1552/3	220	17	6	236	2	8½	-15	5	2½
1553/4*	319	3	11½	330	13	3	-11	9	3½
1554/5	313	14	6	302	14	7½	+10	19	10½
1555/6	283	14	1	272	17	1	+10	17	0
1556/7	323	10	8	307	14	9½	+15	15	10½
1557/8*	634	11	11	605	5	0	+29	6	11
1558/9	306	16	11	297	11	0	+9	5	11
1559/60	272	8	11½	259	6	2	+13	2	9½
1560/1	372	12	6½	380	0	3	-7	7	8½
1561/2	295	0	9	263	14	9	+21	6	0
1562/3*	248	14	4½	264	5	2½	-15	10	10
1563/4	277	10	0	276	5	2	+1	4	10
1564/5*	305	6	3	281	10	5	+23	15	10
1565/6	259	18	8	241	1	3	+18	17	3
1566/7	283	16	1	263	14	7	+47	1	6
1567/8	317	8	5	298	9	7½	+18	18	9½
1568/9	280	1	8½						
1569/70	311	13	0[1]	316	13	3	-5	0	3
1570/1*	337	17	8[1]	388	0	4½[1]	-50	3	8½
1571/2	327	12	0[1]	272	17	5[1]	+49	14	7
1572/3		n/a			n/a			n/a	
1573/4	522	11	3	477	4	4½	+45	6	10½
1574/5	376	15	2½	350	3	0	+26	11	11½
1575/6*	330	15	9	358	6	3	-27	10	6
1576/7	299	4	6	221	9	7	+77	14	11
1577/8	537	5	2½	547	8	8	-10	3	5½
1578/9	287	4	5	303	12	4½	-26	7	11½
1579/80	285	17	11½	279	14	4½	+6	3	7
1580/1*	320	13	6	338	14	7	-18	1	1
1581/2	265	11	1½	239	12	8	+25	18	5½
1582/3	308	4	1	183	15	7	+124	8	6
1583/4	429	18	10	353	11	1	+76	7	9
1584/5	345	19	8½	220	1	0½	+145	18	8
1585/6	384	3	4	355	12	5	+28	10	11
1586/7	291	16	11	286	5	1	+5	11	10
1587/8	297	15	0½[1]	345	8	8[1]	-47	13	7½
1588/9	466	12	9½[1]	357	12	3½[1]	+109	0	6
1589/90	249	9	4½[1]	280	16	10[1]	-31	7	5½
1590/1	289	15	6[1]	207	11	10[1]	+82	3	8
1591/2	276	10	4[1]	243	0	5[1]	+33	9	11
1592/3	323	10	5½	275	3	3[1]	+48	7	2½
1593/4	291	4	1½[1]	288	2	1[1]	+3	2	0½
1594/5	408	13	11[1]	337	6	4[1]	+71	7	7
1595/6	104	1	0[1]	77	8	9[1]	+26	12	3
1596/7	235	19	3	207	14	6½	+28	4	8½
1597/8*	208	13	11	182	16	7	+25	17	4
1598/9	166	10	0	138	4	4	+28	5	8
1599/1600	336	10	4[1]	321	1	1[1]	+15	11	3
1600/1	158	13	9[1]	194	16	3[1]	-36	2	6
1601/2	227	12	7½	207	9	1½	+20	2	6
1602/3	180	18	5½	139	0	0	+41	18	5½

Notes: * income for year inflated by sesse money.

[1] Land chamberlain's accounts only. Note that Sea chamberlain's income ranged between £15-25 and expenditure ranged between £6-22 in period 1569-1603.

Source: RYE 60/3-10; 61/1-9; 62/1-6.

1535 1525 1515 1505 1495 1485

Thos Litherlond
Adam Oxenbridge (w.1496)
John Sutton (w.1506)
Robert Croche (w.1497)
Henry Baly
Stephen Wayte
John Usant
John Tregosser
William Pernell
William Eston Snr
William Barnham
John Baker (als Chesman) (w.1504)
Henry Swan (w.1503)
Nicholas Sutton
Robert Wymond (w.1510)
Thomas Oxenbridge (w.1502)
Clement Adam
John Oxenbridge
William Stonacre (w.1517 Winchelsea)
John Shurley (w.1529 Isfield)
Robert Bawdwyn (w.1510)
Richard Barkeley
Giles Love
Thomas Basden[1]
Nicholas Whyte
John Carpenter
Robert Mede
John Dyrrykson
Gabriel Wayte
George Mercer
Richard Pedyll
William Clerke

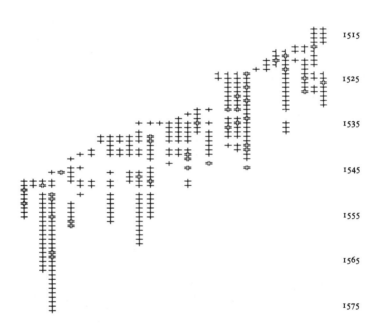

William Byspyn² (w.1535)
Thomas Baker (als Chesman)¹
John Wymond¹ (w.1529)
Thomas Whyte¹
John Edolf
William Browning
John Peers (w.1524)
William Brown
John Fletcher (b. 27.4.46)
Richard Inglett (b.21.4.44)
John Swan (b.16.4.42)
Robert Jerves
Richard Nycoll (b.19.7.48)
James Jetter
Alexander Wulphyn (b. 28.9.49)
John Marche (b.2.2.43)
William Oxenbridge (b.22.8.45)
John Lympeny
Thomas Birchett (b.30.10.56)
Robert Barnes (b.13.5.63)
Robert Wymond (d.1548)
William Mede (d.1548)
Robert Wood (w.1558)
Robert Marden (b.8.7.41)
John Cornysshe (b.27.7.52)
Clement Cobbe (w.1557)
Alexander Welles (b.21.11.58)
William Roberthes
George Raynoldes (w.1577)
Thomas Fletcher (w.1508)
William Wymond (w.1551)
Richard Rucke (b.30.8.57)

1515
1525
1535
1545
1555
1565
1575

274

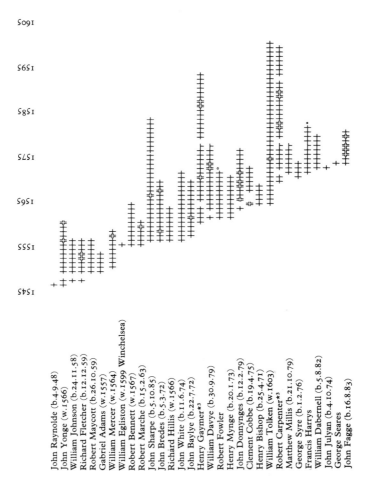

1605

1595

1585

1575

John Mercer (w.1587)
Robert Jacson (b.8.12.86)
Thomas Edolphe[3] (b.11.11.95)
William Ratcliff (b.2.8.1603)
John Bruster (w.1592)
William Didsbury (b.25.12.93)
Thomas Colbrand (w.1622)
Francis Smith
Davy Hatchard*
Robert Bett
Thomas Belveridge[4]
Clement Hopper
William Coxson (b.15.8.95)
Edward Beale (b.9.7.96)
Thomas Mathewe (b.15.3.90)
Richard Rucke (b.13.6.92)
Thomas Hamon (b.29.7.1607)
Thomas Chiswell (b.2.10.1603)
Robert Woode (w.1605)
John Fowtrell (b.20.4.1609)
Richard Portryffe (w.1614)
Thomas Fysher*[5] (b.3.3.1604)
John Fysher[5] (b.3.3.1604)
William Mellow[5]
Robert Swayne (b.14.4.1609)
John Styner[5] (b.24.7.1609)

276

Notes:

w. Date of will
d. Date of death
b. Date of burial
ꝼ Mayor
ʳ Served incomplete year as mayor
✓ Served complete year as jurat
+ Served incomplete year as jurat
○ Expelled
* Date of probate administration
¹ Resigned
1 Expelled at election day 1519. Barden, Wymond, White reappointed at All Saints; Cheseman after Christmas
2 Previously dismissed.
3 Refused oath on John Fagge's election as Mayor for third consecutive term
4 Never took oath
5 Chosen 1596, not sworn until 1598 (except John Styner, 'recusat')

Source:
RYE 1/1-7; RYE 60/3-10; RYE 33/7; PAR 467/1/1/1-2; W/A1-12; W/B1-6; PRO PROB 11/-.

Appendix 4
Occupations of ratepayers from the January 1576 Rye town sesse (RYE 1/4/228)
Landgatewarde

From Sawnders on the hill beinge the fyrst house of the warde, and so frome there unto the gate thorough the netherstret on both sides thereof and the same warde to take his ende at Mr Heblethwaites house on the other side with the friars & conteynith in houses—lxx.

	Name		
	John Saunders yeoman	iiis	
	Widowe Yonge	xiiis	iiiid
s	John Welles smith	iiis	iiiid
t	John Symes lighterman	vs	
	Thomas Vymie feter	vs	
ts	Symon Vale (CC) fletcher	xiiis	iiiid
t	Nicholas Fowle	xiiis	iiiid
s	John Tyler	vis	viiid
s	Henry Nashe upholsterer	iiis	
	John Bruster (CC) brewer	xxxs	
s	William Butcher mercer (French)	xxs	
s	Anthony Cocke merchant (French)	xiiis	iiiid
s	Thomas Radford junior (F) cordwainer	iiis	iiiid
t	Robert Farley (G) merchant	xxxs	
	Edward Engram mariner	iiis	iiiid
t	Thomas Simpson (F) cordwainer	xiiis	iiiid
	Allen Harry merchant (French)	xs	
s	Edward Suringe (F) tailor	vs	
s	Thomas Fisher (F) mercer	vis	viiid
	Thomas Hubberd cowper	iiiis	
s	Simon Ewen fisherman (O/M)	xvs	
	Robert Castleton shoemaker	iis	
s	John Fisher feter	iis	iiiid
	Thomas Cuthorne fisherman	vs	
	Arnold Maxsted carpenter	iiis	iiiid
	John Ball fisherman (M)	iis	
s	John Pedell mariner	iiis	iiiid
	John Taplin (CC) fisherman (O)	xxvis	viiid
	Thomas Potten (CC) fisherman (M)	xxs	
	Edward Beale (CC) fisherman (O/M)	xxvis	viiid
	Ellis Goodwin	xs	
	Arthur Beson mariner	iis	
	William Aprice basketmaker	iis	
s	William Yonge	iis	iiiid
	Peter Johnson carrier	iiis	iiiid
	Thomas Chamberlaine blacksmith	xiid	
	Richard Beale carpenter	iis	
	Lewis Sohier merchant (French)	xxs	

Robert Farley, Thomas Simpson

	Name		
T	Richard Sampson innkeeper	iis	vid
	John Worgar fisherman (M)	iis	xiid
	Prest		
	Daniell Mynge (F) merchant	iis	
	John Mosse (CC) beerbrewer	xiiis	iiiid
	Mr Tolkin jurat feter	xviis	viiid
V	Ellis Eliard merchant	iiiii	
	Robert Jacson (CC) beerbrewer	xs	
	William Morris mariner (M)	iis	
S	John Frotier locksmith (French)	iis	
	William Gold baker	iis	
S	Esay Kingwod (F) mercer	vis	viiid
S	John Freman mercer	vis	viiid
	Robert Mordock mariner (O)	iiiis	
TS	Raynold Jacob tailor	vs	
	Mathew Flory surgeon (French)	iis	
S	Andro Harry glasier (French)	xs	
	Thomas Pitt	iis	
	Mr Heblethwaite beerbrewer	xxs	
	Jerrom Bayes mariner	iis	
	Widow Fyrrall	xxs	
	Allen Gribbel mariner (M)	iis	
T	Edward Bching	iis	
	Thomas Foster innholder (1570)	iis	xiid
	William Partridge mariner (M)	iiis	iiiid
	John Thornton	iis	
T	Hugh Harrison baker	iis	
	Thomas Robins baker		
	Thomas Cable (F) husbandman/Town porter	iiis	xiid
	Robert Newton yeoman	iiis	xiid
	Olyver ye carpenter	xiid	
	Robert Pacnet sailor	xiid	
	Arnold Joyner joiner	iiii	iiid
	Peter Hubberd (Spaniard)	iiis	iiiid
	John Welles (F) mariner	iis	
	Robert Skalles mariner (M)		
	Mr Oxenbridge¹ for the Friors	xxs	xiid

Collectors for this warde

Market warde

To begyn at John Dowces and Peter Somlers Corners with Okmans Lane through the Market Place downe to John Bulles and Robert Goodwins Corner upward againe to the Vicaridge & there to ende conteyninge in houses lxiii.

	Andro Ramsey fisherman (M)	iis	vid
	John Bull fisherman	vs	
	Thomas Edwardes shipwright	iiis	iiiid
	Robert Goodwin mariner	iis	
T	Mr Sharpe jurat butcher	ls	
	Owen Milles shipwright	xxs	
	Thomas Baker labourer	iis	
	Robert Bennet (G) butcher	xs	
S	John Bennet (F) tailor	vis	viiid
	Mrs Bennet widow	xiiis	iiiid
V	Mrs Fordman widow of Thomas, merchant	xvs	
	James Persall innkeeper/merchant	xs	
	Robert Bradford carpenter	iis	
	John Rolf yeoman/mercer	xvs	
	Mr Fagge jurat (O) butcher	iiiii	
T	Thomas Beacon tapster with John Prowze	iiis	iiiid
	William Swifte butcher	vs	
	John Prowze(r) innholder/scorer with the butchers	vis	viiid
	Manasses Enge	iiis	iiiid
	William Scrage (F) cutler/mayor's sergt	xiiis	iiiid
S	John Spilsted yeoman	xls	
S	Anthony Boniface (F) mercer	xiiis	iiiid
S	Henry Mere (F) jeter	iiis	iiiid
	John Stonham carpenter	vis	viiid
	Mr Shepperd¹ (of Playden, Gent)		
	The heires of Thomas Byrchet for their tenementes	iiii	
	Mr Taillor¹ (?of Willesborough, Kent, Gent) for his tenementes	xxvis	viiid

	Mr Chatfild¹ for his tenementes	xvs	
	Nicholas Wolpet mason	xs	
S	Gabriell Gibbons (F) blacksmith	viiis	
	John Dallet merchant (French)	ls	
T	Stevin Frencham mercer	iis	vid
S	Mr Syre jurat merchant	xxvis	viiid
	John Palmer cordwainer	iis	iiiid
TS	Mr Davy maior fisherman (O)	iiiivis	viiid
	John Englet (F) shipwright	iiis	iiiid
	Roger Bartlet blacksmith	iiis	iiiid
	John Dowce (F) capper	vs	
	Richard Cooke (CC) beerbrewer	xxvis	viiid
	John Duron beerbrewer	xxxiiis	iiiid
	Robert Aderfold hookmaker	iis	iiiid
	John Holnes mariner	iis	iiiid
	William Englet	vs	
	John Duffet fisherman (O/M)	iiis	iiiid
	Raynold Dunmold fisherman (O/M)	iiis	iiiid
	Frebody for Okemans heires	xiis	iiiid
	Mrs Sheperd¹ for the tenementes betwene her & Mr Maior & theme at the cliff	xiiis	iiiid
	Mrs Sheperd¹ for the tenementes without Landgat		
	Mr Easton¹ for his tenementes	xxs	
S	Robert Harward¹ for their	xxvis	viiid
	Goddard Harward¹ tenementes		
	Mr¹ Mynges heires for their tenementes	xs	
	Henry Gibbons¹ of Rolvenden for his tenementes	iiis	iiiid

John Spilsted   Robert Bennet   Collectors for this warde

278

Strandgat warde

To begin on the one side of the streate at the house of Thomas Tokaey and on the other side of the streate at the Red Lyon, and so alongest both sides of the streate, Poundgardin & thorough the Strandgate with the newe buildings without the saide gate under the west cliff & so to Fraunces Christmas house and conteynith in houses 1xx.

	Mr Wymond, ?Paul, Gent	xls
	Mr Carpenter jurat brewer	xxxiiis iiiid
	Anthony Vines chief brewer	xiid
	Peter Joye	vs
	William Hore currier	iiis iiiid
	John Pye carpenter	iis
	Clement Hopper (CC) merchant	xxs
	James Potten fisherman (M)	iis
	Thomas Stride fisherman (O/M)	vs
S	James Hubberd fisherman	iis
S	Thomas Tokey (F) tailor	xs
	John Donke (F) tailor	xxs
	John Gilmer	iis
	John Forsett fisherman (M)	iis
	Robert Bennet (F) fisherman (M)	vis viiid
	John Potten (F) fisherman (M)	vs
S	Robert Wodd merchant	vis viiid
	Richard Badcocke shipwright (O)	vis viiid
	Robert Wilson baker	xiiis iiiid
	John Tailler fisherman (M)	vis viiid
S	John Tippe fisherman (O/M)	xiiis iiiid
	Edmond Tindall (F) tailor	vis viiid
	Edward Hurrocke fisherman	iis
	William Fyrroll (F) fisherman (O/M)	xs
	Roger Nonten fisherman (M)	xs
S	George Philips cooper	iiis iiiid
	Mr Mercer jurat brewer	xvs
	Mathew Wodd fisherman (O/M)	vis viiid
S	William Tharpe draper	iiis iiiid
T	John Hamond innholder	iiis iiiid
	Richard Breker	vis viiid
S	John Scrugham brasier	vis viiid
	Thomas Kynge mercer	vis viiid
	Edward Turner baker	iiis iiiid

S	John Pynner	vs
	James Welles (F) baker	xvs
	James Gonby	iiis
	Edward Gilbart	iiiid
	William Hurleston mariner	iis iiiid
	Peter Philipe mariner (O/M)	iiis iiiid
	Henry Gray mariner	iis iii?
S	Lawrence Whitman (F) cordwainer	xvs
S	Thomas Benbrick goldsmith	iiis iiiid
	The owner of Benbrikes house	iiis iiiid
	Jeffery Asby	xiid
	Thomas Firrall	vs
T	John Lawrence (F)	vis viiid
T	William Ratliff (CC) tailor/vintner	ls
	Richard Bushops heires	iiis
S	William Berworth (F)	iiili iiiid
	Raph Simondes¹ for his tenementes	xs
S	John Awodd fisherman (O/M)	xvs
	John Benbrick goldsmith	iiiis
	Stevin Welshe (F) feter/ost	vis viiid
S	James Christmas	iis
	John Mills (F) mercer	vs
T	Nicholas Harrold (F) yeoman/merchant	xvs
	Alexander Lyndsey (F) shoemaker	vis viiid
	John Rawson lighterman	iis iiiid
S	Stevin Dyne (F) fisherman (M)	vs
T	Peter Kelinge (F) yeoman/merchant	xiiis iiiid
T	Eliz Carr wife of Cuthbert, fisherman	iiis iiiid
	John Sparrowe	iis vid
	Andro Barnet marriner	iis vid
T	Fraunces Christmas (F) innholder (O)	xs
	William Davy¹ of Brede for his tenementes	
	widowe Bell	xs iiiid

Robert Wilson Laurence Whitman   Collectors for this warde

279

Middlestret warde

To begin at William Burdites house in the Churchyard & frome thence to John Skalles house and so directly downe the streat to Mr Whites Corner and frome thence into the Middlestret on both sides and so ende at John mercer thelders house besides Strandgate conteyning in houses lxv.

	Name			
	Mr Henry Gaymer jurat ost/feter	iiii	vis	viiid
	William Whitwodd		xvs	
	John Nicolls		vis	
S	William Burdet tallow chandler		vis	viiid
	Robert Mason			xiid
	Robert Welles (F) gent/baker	xxvis		xiid
	John Marshall draper	xxxs		viiid
	Fraunces Maquery merchant (French)	xxvis		
S	Andro Forgison tailor	iiis		viiid
	Richard Bennet	iis		iiiid
V	Mr Raynoldes jurat	xls		vid
	Robert Wymond for his			
	tenementes (F) baker	xs		
	Thomas Honnam	iis		
	William Lucas			
	Richard Wright mariner (O/M)	iis		xiid
	William Roades (F) fisherman (M)	iis		iiiid
	Thomas Hinson fisherman			xiid
	Thomas Nicols mariner (M)	iiis		iiiid
	Nicholas White feter	vs		
	Thomas Harman (F) fisherman (O/M)	xvs		
	John Gilbert fisherman	vs		
	Mr Edolf jurat gent (O)	ls		
	Robert Marche (F) butcher	xiiis		iiiid
	Mr Yonge (F) waterbailiff	xs		
TV	William Didsbury (F) merchant (O)	xxxs		
	Mr Donnynge jurat customer	xls		
	Richard Portriffe beerbrewer	xiiis		iiiid
	Rede¹ of Bennenden for the house that Portrif occupieth	vs		
S	William Bellington	iis		vid
	Michael Bennet (F) fisherman	iis		
S	Samuell Reade	vis		viiid
S	Nicholas Purvage (P) yeoman/merchant	xiiis		iiiid
S	Henry Holstock (F) tailor	iiis		iiiid
S	Robert Daniell (CC) tailor	xxxiiis		iiiid

	Name		
S	Thomas Radford (CC) merchant	vis	viiid
	John Albons fisherman	vs	
	Thomas Goodwins mercer	vis	viiid
	William Harmon (F) fisherman (O/M)	xxxs	
T	Widowe Medcalfe widow of		
	Michael, Town Sergt	vs	
	William Bocher sailor (French)		xiid
	Fraunces Canche merchant (French)	xvs	
	Richard Cromwell fisherman	vs	
T	Peter Robertes yeoman/chandler	iiiis	
	John Abury (CC) feter	vis	viiid
	George Bagwell fisherman (M)	iis	vid
	Richard Holbroke (F) mariner (O/M)	iis	vid
	Edward Ostler fisherman	xiiis	iiiid
	Allen Bennet fisherman	xiiis	iiiid
	Mr Harris jurat mercer	xlvis	viiid
TV	William Allen (F) merchant	vs	
	James Milles (F) merchant	xiiis	iiiid
T	Alexander Goldsted	iiis	iiiid
	James Oxley (F) mercer	xs	
	Thother scholmaster	iis	
	Robert Bett (CC) fisherman (O/M)	xs	
	John Sole cordwainer	xs	
	George Raynoldes tailor	iiis	iiiid
S	John Fraunce fisherman	iis	iiiid
	Thomas Colbrand (CC) yeoman	xvis	viiid
S	Richard Thorpe (F) fisherman	xs	
	Edward Whithed tailor		xiid
	James Cowley mariner	vs	
S	Thomas Blacke	iis	
	Crottinden¹ of Burwashe for		
	his tenementes	iiis	iiiid
S	John Mercer senior (F) mercer	iiis	iiiid
	Simon Marche yeoman	xvis	viiid
	Frenches heires	vs	

James Oxley Samuel Reade Collectors for this warde

280

Baddinges warde

To begyn at Thomas Foglers Corner alonge the Baddinges & thorough the whole streat called the Watchbell strete with Durickes Lanne and to end at Edmond Johnsons & James Bastians house and conteynith in houses lxxv houses.

	Name		
	Edmond Johnson fisherman (M)	vs	
	James Bastian (F) fisherman (M)	vs	
	John Porter fisherman (M)	iiis	iiiid
	William Berde (F) mariner	vs	
	Edmond Harber mariner (M)	iiis	iiiid
	John Pen	iiis	iiiid
	Old Tomlen, butcher	iis	
	Younge Tomlen butcher	iis	
	Edward Edmondes mariner	iis	vid
	Thomas Piers mariner	iis	
	Robert Swayne fisherman (M)	iis	iiiid
	Stevin Amiat	iis	
	Philipe Winterborn (F) fisherman (O/M)	iis	
	Thomas Browninge fisherman		xiid
	John Philips (F) cooper	iis	vid
T	Thomas Belveridge (F) yeoman/gent	xls	
	Richard Daniell (F) feter	xs	
	John Belveridge (F) fisherman (O/M)	xiiis	iiiid
	Gilles Harrison yeoman	xiiis	iiiid
	Robert Gillam feter	iis	vid
	Adam Smith (F) fisherman (M)	xiiis	iiiid
	Widow Julians widow of John, jurat	xiiis	iiiid
	William Bragden merchant (O)	xiiis	iiiid
	Robert Walker (F) feter	iis	iiiid
	Richard Eles mariner (M)	vs	
	James Almon fisherman (O/M)	vis	viiid
	William Love fisherman		xiid
	William Hilles fisherman (M)	iis	
	Thomas Johnson fisherman (M)	iis	iiiid
	Robert Clement (F) fisherman (M)	vs	
	John Erle fisherman (M)		xiid
	John Leny butcher	iis	
	Thomas Benkin	iis	
S	Thomas Chiswell (F) fisherman (O/M)	xs	
	Robert Browne (F) feter		xiid
	John Thorpe (F) mercer	iiis	iiiid

	STV		
	widowe Chapman widow of Wm. merchant	iiis	iiiid
	Mr Milles jurat gent/feter	vs / xxvis	viiid
	John Rowes (F) fisherman (M)	xs	
	William White (CC) fisherman (O/M)	xxs	
	John Smith (CC) feter	xvs	
	Robert Holmes (CC) fisherman (O/M)	xiiis iiiid	xiid
	Simon Gogle fisherman (M)		
	Mr Daburnell jurat mariner (O)	xxxs	
	John Cheston (CC) mariner (O)	xvs	
	Gregory Davy mariner	iis	vid
	Thomas Wayt mariner		
	Robert Henson fisherman (M)	iis	xxd
T	George Brigges feter	vs	
	William Coxson fisherman (O/M)	iis	vid
	John Fateley mariner (M)	iis	iiiid
	Nicholas Fryor butcher	vis	
	Thomas Bennet[2] fisherman (O/M)	iis	iiiid
	Nicholas Kempe fisherman (M)	vis	viiid
	Jesper White	iis	vid
	John Vincet[1] for his tenementes	vs	
	Mr Haynes[1] for his tenementes	xs	
	Robert Milles carpenter	iiis	
	John Herle	iis	
	John Convers (F) deputy waterbailiff	iis	vid
	Robert Brickenocke	iis	
	John Colton mariner		
	Robert Bryce fisherman (M)	iis	
	Thomas Marshall mariner	iis	
	Edward Harrys (F) butcher	iis	vid
	Mr Tufton[1], of		
	Peasmarsh, gent, his tenementes	xs	
	Hugh Whit mariner	iis	
S	Robert Cotman		
T	William Lyndson mariner		xiid
	Richard Rotherman		xiid
T	Thomas Mathew (F) painter	vis	viiid

281

Baddinges warde (continued)

	Name		
	William Charles labourer		xiid
	Philipe Cardy baker (French)		xiid
	Thomas Noven fisherman (M)	vs	
	Henry Kyte (F) fisherman (M)	vis	viiid
	Richard Almon (F) fisherman (M)	vs	
T	Thomas Holstock (F) innholder	iis	
	Cutbert Carr (F) fisherman (O/M)	iiis	iiiid
	Mrs Bushope widow of Henry	xs	
	Michael Bushope (F) tailor	iiis	iiiid
	Henry Byler joiner	iis	
	George White baker	iis	xiid
	Thomas Swaine (F) fisherman		xiid
	John Bewlie	iis	xiid
	John Hamond carpenter	iis	vid
	Gilles Johnson		xiid
	William Robson		xiid

Name		
Thomas Fogler (CC) merchant	vs	
John Stacy	iis	
Richard Esterfild butcher	iis	
William Geire (F) tailor/mayor's sergt	vs	iis
John Versey		xxd
Richard Franke cobbler	iis	
Richard Frankes sonne shipwright	iis	iiiid
Nicholas Flemynge	iis	
William Mellowe chandler	iis	
John Dugard mariner (M)	vis	viiid
at Owen Milles (shipwright)		
Richard Swayne feter	vis	xiid
The heires¹ of Cowchman for		
Mrs Chapmans house	vs	
Partridge¹ of Ewhurst for		
Anthony Qoc house	iiis	iiiid

Thomas Mathewe Richard Daniell Collectors for y^t warde

To begyn at Bawdwins wishe at Rawlins house & so alongest the West Cliff and from Strandgate unto Richard Mynions house thorough the Fishe market the old wishe on both sides the same strete with all the newe buildinges alonge the towne dike conteynith

	Name		
	John Hobbes	iis	
	Robert Hubberd (F) fisherman (M)	viiis	
	Nicholas Fowler fisherman (O/M)	iiis	iiiid
	widowe Terry wid of Ri, merchant	vs	
	Joan Marche¹ for her tenementes		
	that the widowe Terry dwellith in		
	Roger Michill	iis	
	Mr Fowler (F) fisherman		
	(Warden of Company)	xxs	
	William Waters fisherman (M)	iiis	iiiid
	Simon Smith (F) fisherman (O/M)	iiiis	
	William Halliard fisherman (O/M)	iiis	iiiid
	Richard Patten baker	iis	
	George Thorpe fisherman (O/M)	iis	
	John Sawnder fisherman (O/M)	iiis	iiiid
T	Robert Clerke	xs	
	John Harry mariner		xiid
	Thomas Smith mariner		xiid
s	John Ivy blacksmith		xiid
T	John Dollinge	iis	vid
	John Allen goldsmith	iis	vid
	Richard Mailler fisherman (O/M)	xs	
	widowe Hayes	iis	vid
	Alexander Quarry (F) fisherman (M)	xiiis	iiiid
T	John Boycott (F) feter (town serg't)	iis	vid
	Robert Bushope shipwright		xiid
	Robert Blacke shipwright (O)	xiis	iiiid
	Thomas Bushope (F) shipwright (O)	iiis	iiiid
	Thomas Hewson shipwright	iis	
	Thomas Sly fisherman	iiis	iiiid
	Osmond Bennister fisherman (M)	iis	vid
	John Fraunces fisherman	iis	
	John Parkes fisherman	iis	xiid

	Name		
	George Lockewod mariner	iis	
	Simon Farne shipwright	iiis	iiiid
	Andro Roche fisherman (M)		xiid
	Thomas Aves		
	Bartholomew Cater cockboatman	iis	xiid
	Thomas Rose	iis	vid
	John Ball fisherman	iis	iiiid
	John Chaundler fisherman	iis	xiid
	John Walne		
	John Blackeford feter	iis	
	William Browne fisherman	iis	
	William Blacke	iis	
	John Emery for his tenementes		
	(als Wattes) mariner		
	Henry Godsmarke feter	xvs	xvid
	William Anderson		xiid
	Richard Knight fisherman	iiis	iiiid
	Noye Lanson (F) for his		
	tenementes baker	xiiis	
	Richard Goddins		iiiid
	widowe Whit		xiid
	Thomas Delman (CC) mercer	xxxs	xiid
	Richard Tomson	iis	
	Humfrey Knolles mariner	iiis	iiiid
	Thomas Notty	iis	
	Richard Jacobs mariner	iis	
T	Robert Chaundler feter	iis	
	John House shipwright	iis	
	William Cole labourer		
T	Thomas Fryor blacksmith		xiid
	Lawrence Wibley rippier	vs	
	John Belgrave	iiis	iiiid
	Thomas Gibson mariner	vs	xiid

283

Watchbell warde (continued)

Name	s	d	Name	s	d
John Engram mariner	vis	viiid	William Nicholson		xiid
John Oliver mariner (O/M)	vis	viiid	James Barneby mariner		xiid
Davy Hatchet (F) fisherman (O/M)	xiiis	iiiid	John Foster mariner	xiid	
George Harrison	iis		John Barnabe	iis	
John Blacke	iis		Robert Ball		
John Boys mariner	iis		Thomas Ball		xiid
Richard Barnes	iis		John Maidman fisherman		xiid
Nicholas Bonde fisherman	iis		Robert Tokey[1] for his tenementes	iis	vid
Thomas Savy fisherman	iis		yeoman of Winchelsea	iiis	iiiid
Robert Wilson fisherman		xiid	Blacke Barnes tenement mariner	iis	vid

John Engram   Robert Black   Collectors for this warde

This cease to be gathered in forme following viz: the fyrst payment of the cease to begin th fyrst weke in Lent next and the seconde payment to begin the next weke after Whitsonday nexte.

Notes:

1	Non-resident
S	shop
T	beer tipler
(F)	Freeman
(CC)	Common Councillor
(O)	Owner or part-owner of fishing or merchant vessel
(M)	Master of merchant or fishing vessel
	Names of Jurats are in italics

Sources: As for Table 11.

284

Appendix 5:
Rye Fishing Fleet 1485–1602

a) Quarterly payments by masters of fishing boats 1485–1554

Mayoral Year	Number of masters paying quarterly maltode				Mayoral Year	Number of masters paying quarterly maltode			
	1	2	3	4		1	2	3	4
1485	20	14	20	18	1520	20	19	24	25
1486	14	17	21	22	1521	25	31	25	26
1487	20	20	23	22	1522	19	25	24	24
1488	14	17	20	20	1523	24	22	24	21
1489	15	19	22	20	1524	17	25	23	22
1490	20	21	25	24	1525	26	20	29	26
1491	21	22	25	25	1526	24	28	25	21
1492	17	16	22	25	1527	17	17	20	16
1493	16	17	22	13	1528	20	21	23	18
1494	16	20	24	17	1529	22	21	22	18
1495	23	20	25	24	1530	25	27	27	11
1496	21	20	24	25	1531	24	24	26	21
1497	19	20	24	25	1532	27	29	27	23
1498	18	19	24	25	1533	30	26	28	27
1499	20	21	24	24	1534	26	27	33	23
1500	19	19	25	24	1535	27	28	25	21
1501	19	19	28	27	1536	28	17	30	20
1502	25	22	27	22	1537	25	32	26	19
1503	23	20	23	21	1538	26	25	29	13
1504	21	17	26	24	1539	28	31	33	21
1505	21	21	28	26	1540	29	40	35	20
1506	24	21	27	28	1541	28	32	41	18
1507	24	20	31	30	1542	26	34	31	20
1508	27	25	28	28	1543	-	-	-	-
1509	22	19	29	-	1544	19	27	27	21
1510	22	29	33	30	1545	23	17	-	-
1511	22	26	29	31	1546	11	28	36	21
1512	27	28	32	31	1547	22	26	35	32
1513	29	31	35	22	1548	34	42	36	23
1514	28	29	32	38	1549	31	39	48	29
1515	27	28	37	32	1550	32	26	37	13
1516	28	34	33	23	1551	21	30	42	23
1517	29	34	32	29	1552	35	16	-	7
1518	22	34	34	11	1553	44		-	21
1519	-	-	19	-	1554	27	51		33

Notes:
Mayoral year runs from Sunday following St Bartholomew's Day (25 Aug).
First quarter 25 August–27 December (St John the Evangelist).
Second quarter January–Easter.
Third quarter Easter–24 June (Nativity of St John the Baptist).
Fourth quarter end June–St Bartholomew's day.

Appendix 5:
Rye Fishing Fleet 1485–1602

b) Numbers of vessels engaged in North Sea and Channel fisheries 1530–1602

Year[1]	Coastal trammelers		Scarborough	Boats	Yarmouth			
					Masters	Men	Boys	Total
1530	23		-	9				
1531	23		-	6				
1532	27		-	10				
1533	24		-	12				
1534	25		-	12				
1535	24		-	14				
1536	22		-	10				
1537	21		-	16				
1538	19		-	10				
1539	22		-	15				
1540	20		-	10				
1541	23		20	22				
1542	29		23	-				
1543	17		11	13				
1544	28		-	20				
1545	-		5	14				
1546	15		-	24				
1547	28		21	15				
1548	19		4	10				
1549	22		17	14				
1550	-		-	15				
1551	-		31	-				
1552	-		23	-				
1553	30		32	38				
1554	-		31	41				
1555	-	(32)	41	-				
1556	27	(29)	34	-				
1557	29	(34)	-	16				
1558	27		-	21				
1559	24	(36)	-	27				
1560	23	(28)	14	25				
1561	17	(32)	17	29				
1562	21	(25)	16	30				
1563	21	(24)	-	6				
1564	-	(31)	10	26				
1565	23	(29)	15	28				
1566	26	(28)	14	27				
1567	27	(26)	12	21				
1568	25	(28)	11	17				
1569	23		4	16				
1570			-	-				
1571			-	19				
1572			-	22				
1573			-	22				
1574		(23)	-	21				
1575		(23)	2	22	22	237	44	303
1576			11	22	22	226	43	291
1577		(27)	-	21	21	228	2	251
1578		(25)	7	22	22	206	45	273
1579		(22)	10	27	27	342	38	407
1580		(23)	10	25	25	296	42	363

1581	(21)	5	25	25	280	35	340
1582	(22)	7	27[2]	27[2]	284[2]	49[2]	360[2]
1583	(19)	6	28	28	287	47	362
1584	(23)	7	25	25	264	37	326
1585	(21)	8	29	29	300	46	375
1586	(18)	1	24	24	235	47	306
1587		3	22	22	221	40	283
1588		-	23	23	232	42	297
1589		-	-	-	-	-	-
1590	(19)	-	-	-	-	-	-
1591		5	25	25	251	46	322
1592		-	26	26	246	57	329
1593		-	23	23	266	34	323
1594		-	25	25	244	48	317
1595		-	26	26	247	61	334
1596	(16)	-	26	26	258	42	326
1597	(13)	3	23	23	235	40	298
1598		8	21	21	213	35	269
1599		-	20	20	193	34	247
1600		-	17	17	195	42	254
1601	(15)	-	18	18	196	30	244
1602	(18)	5	18	18	194	29	241

Notes:
[1] i.e. calendar year beginning 1st January. Scarborough voyage took place in the early summer, Yarmouth voyage in early September. The figures for coastal trammelers are for the year of the accounts beginning September.
[2] RYE 47/30/95 gives 27 fishing boats with 27 masters, 266 men and 50 boys.
The main series of figures for coastal trammelers are taken from payments to the churchwardens. Those in brackets ( ) are from the maltodes paid by masters of coastal trammelers in the chamberlains' accounts volumes.

Sources: RYE 1/1/4-7; RYE 60/3-10; RYE 62/2-3; RYE 147/1.

Appendix 6
Inventories of goods of Rye inhabitants 1485-1603

a) Complete inventories

RYE 138/6	late 15C	unknown	*	
P.R.O. PROB 2/141	1498	William Wykwyk, vicar	£4	0s 4d
RYE 33/9/148v	1537	Nicholas Morris, tailor	*	
RYE 35/9	1551	William White		47s 2d
P.R.O. PROB 2/328	1558	John Clarke	£63	5s 9d
RYE 1/3/41-2	1563	Ralph Rode, customer	£257	9 3½d
RYE 1/3/186-7	1567	Prophyttes wife		55s 4d
RYE 113/160	1566	Robert Horsley	£7	14s 9d
RYE 47/13/7	1575	John Hamon, carpenter	*	
RYE 35/31	1576	John Palmer		55s 0d
RYE 35/31	1577	Peter Adrian	£13	0s 5d
RYE 35/33 (2 docs)	1578	Henry Prescote	£2	8s 7d
RYE 35/33	1578	Mr Passes	£9	15s 3d
RYE 35/33	1979	Edmond Mathew	£4	1s 8d
RYE 47/23/18	1580	Alice Aubons		42s 0d
RYE 35/35	1581	Mildred Clarke, widow	£17	8s 6d
RYE 35/36	1583	Richard Goodwins	£4	9s 6d
RYE 47/40/14	1589	Richard Wowan	*	
RYE 47/42/7	1590	Richard Wowan	£18	4s 4d
RYE 47/46/10	1592	Francis Daniel	£34	19s 8d
RYE 35/42	1593	James Persall, gent	£54	9s 4d
RYE 47/51/39	1594	Thomas Roben, fisherman		35s 4d
RYE 137/37-40	1595	Mrs Castleton	£73	2s11d
RYE 47/58/16	1599	David Hewett	*	

b) partial inventories

RYE 35/2	1537	Thomas Byspyn	£32	13 8d
RYE 35/16	1560	Robert Marshall	*	
RYE 35/16	1560	John Whiteman	£15	3s 4d
RYE 35/19	1565	Augustine Swetinge	£14	10s 0d
RYE 35/19	1565	Johane Banbrigge	£20	10s 0d
RYE 35/20	1566	William Fynall		51s 4d
RYE 35/21	1567	William Coppinger	£13	18s10d
RYE 35/23	1568	John Wodd, mariner	£4	19s 8d
RYE 35/27	1572	Robert Wymond	£6	3s 4d
RYE 35/34	1578	Thomas Whitfilde	£52	8s 8d
RYE 35/37	1579	Francis Maquery	£12	
RYE 25/34	1580	John Jenevere, carpenter	*	
RYE 35/34	1580	Alexander Goldsted	£6	3s10d
RYE 35/34	1580	Raynolle Jacobe	£10	12s 4½d
RYE 35/39	1588	John Oliver	£60	
RYE 35/46	1595	Thomas Forman	£12	

* No valuation

Notes and references

Introduction

1 C. Phythian-Adams: *Desolation of a City: Coventry and the Urban Crisis of the Later Middle Ages* (1979); A.D. Dyer: *The City of Worcester in the Sixteenth Century* (1973); W.T. MacCaffrey: *Exeter 1540–1640* (1975); D.M. Palliser: *Tudor York* (1979).

CHAPTER 1 Footnotes 1

1 I. Nairn and N. Pevsner: *The Buildings of England, Sussex* (1965) p594.

2 *Letters and Papers, Foreign and Domestic, of the Reign of Henry VIII* ed. J. Gairdner et al, (hereafter referred to as L.P.) Vol 4, pt 2, nos 4627,5031; Public Record Office (hereafter referred to as P.R.O.) State Papers (hereafter referred to as SP) 12/254/75(1).

3 For the ferry to East Guldeford see e.g. the costs for ferrying the mayor and other representatives to the Brotherhood at New Romney 28 May 1556 RYE 60/7/126; for the Town Ferry, or West Ferry see RYE 1/2/53v; RYE 1/4/175: Inhabitants of Rye parish living on the far side were to have their ferry free for coming to church on Sundays and holy days and for weddings, churchings, christenings and burials, according to an assembly Decree 4 September 1574.

4 SP12/38/28.

5 For the Chichester assessments see J. Cornwall: *The Lay Subsidy Rolls for the County of Sussex 1524–5*, Sussex Record Society 56 (1956) pp 2–6.

6 Sandwich and Dover had very similar levels of tonnage and numbers of ships in 1587. See above Table 5.

7 RYE 77/3; RYE 81/1–2; RYE 1/6/30–43.

8 P.R.O. E179/231/218; E179/190/197, 199–202, 225.

9 J. Cornwall, op.cit. pp xxiv, 2–6.

10 A.J.F. Dulley, 'The early history of the Rye fishing industry', *Sussex Archaeological Collections* 107 (1969) p 49 argues the figure of 450 servants is too high and probably a scribal error; however his own estimates of Rye's population, op.cit. p 63 are extremely impressionistic.

11 See my article in *S.A.C.* 124 (1986): 'Epidemic mortality in sixteenth century Rye'.

12 RYE 47/24/7; R.F. Dell: *Rye Shipping Records 1566–90*, Sussex Record Society 64 (1966) p xxxv.

13 RYE 85/2. At Southampton a local census gave a population of 4200 in September 1596, with 784 able men, a ratio of 1:5.4 *The Population of Southampton: A Historical Survey*, Southampton City Record Office (1978) p 2.

14 An indication of the extent of this immigration is that less than half of the surnames listed in the 1596 sesse appeared in 1576.

15 The impact of epidemics caused a substantial decennial surplus of burials over baptisms throughout the sixteenth century, as in other towns. The urban experience is clearly quite different to that of the country as a whole. See e.g. E.A. Wrigley and R.S. Schofield : *The Population History of England, 1541–1871* (1981) Table A3.1, p 528.

16 RYE 77/3; RYE 60/5/143v; RYE 60/6/53v, 87: RYE 60/7/162v; RYE 1/1/22–26; RYE 1/2/10–16; RYE 1/3/38v, 43–48, 94, 97v–102; RYE 1/4/228–32, 353–6: RYE 1/6/30v–43; RYE 77/6.

17 The chamberlains' accounts run from September to September each year.

18 Figures based on the volumes of chamberlains' accounts RYE 60/3–10. For the increase in rates see RYE 1/7/446–8. The assembly books also record earlier lesser increases in rates in January 1567 (RYE 1/3/183v–4), December 1578 (measurage of corn and keyage of goods entering the port, RYE 1/4/297), March 1584 (rates of osts, RYE 1/5/35v) and January 1599 (RYE 1/6/272v). These and earlier impositions are listed in the schedules of the 'Maltode Droits and Dues payable to the Corporation of Rye for Passengers Goods and Merchandises Exported and Imported there' of which the earliest is 1689 RYE 79/4–6.

19 For the annual income and expenditure totals for Exeter see W.T. MacCaffrey: *Exeter 1540–1640* (1975) pp 55–7.

20 See G.J. Mayhew, 'Rye and the defence of the Narrow Seas: a 16th century town at war', *S.A.C.* 122 (1984) esp pp 107–11.

21 RYE 60/3/51–56; RYE 60/9/239v–250.

22 RYE 60/3/6v–18v, 55–57; RYE 1/4/227–232, 237; RYE 1/6/112.

23 RYE 60/7/101–128; RYE 1/1/33v, 42; RYE 1/2/58v.

24 RYE 60/5/97; RYE 60/7/8–10; RYE 60/6/42v, 55, 56, 165–6; RYE 1/3/63v, 94; RYE 1/4/66, 69v.

25 RYE 1/3/106v. In January 1569 the assembly agreed that Mr Customer would have the keys to open the cocks of the Strand Conduit, RYE 1/4/35; and in April 1570 a man was employed to keep the conduits clean and to open and shut them with other duties at 8s.4d quarterly. RYE 1/4/64v.

26 RYE 60/3/54v, 69; RYE 60/9/246.

27 RYE 60/4/292v–3; RYE 60/5/7; RYE 60/6/222v; RYE 1/3/74v; RYE 1/5/32v.

28 RYE 60/3/53v–6; L.A. Vidler 'St Bartholomew's Hospital at Rye', *S.A.C.* 83 (1943) pp 73–99; RYE 57/1/48v–49; RYE 111/1. The land conveyed to the corporation by Welles in 1551 appears to be the same as that left by John Raynoldes, jurat, in his will in 1548 for the purposes of building an almshouse. Welles was one of his executors. P.R.O. PROB11/33/11; RYE 60/7/41–55; RYE 1/4/339; RYE 1/6/229, 232v; RYE 1/2/25.

29 RYE 60/3/53v; RYE 60/7/140; RYE 60/6/141v.

30 RYE 60/4/30,31; RYE 60/7/203v; RYE 1/6/185.

31 RYE 60/4/82v–3, 85v–6, 87v–8; RYE 60/7/12v; RYE 60/7/227; RYE 60/10/31v.

32 RYE 60/3/70; RYE 60/6/180–1, 187.

33 RYE 1/4/140, 156v, 162v; RYE 60/9/12. The cost of making each coat was 2s.8d. plus materials.

34 RYE 1/5/304v.

35 RYE 1/4/248; RYE 1/4/164v–5; RYE 1/5/140v–142; RYE 47/21/77; RYE 60/5/83; RYE 147/1/2v.

36 RYE 47/25/2; RYE 47/13/64.

37 RYE 47/46/35; RYE 47/25/9; RYE 47/46/65.

38 RYE 1/1/31v; RYE 1/3/33; RYE 1/4/158, 190v; RYE 1/5/50v.

39 RYE 47/10/19–20; RYE 47/7/97; *Royal Commissions on Historical Manuscripts Report* (hereafter referred to as H.M.C.Report) 13, Appendix IV (1892) p 65.

40 RYE 1/3/57v; *H.M.C. Report* 13, Appendix IV (1892) pp 88–9.

41 J. Stow: *A Survey of London* (1603 edition, Everyman 1912) p 168.

42 RYE 60/6/2–6. There is a later copy of these ordinances in the Entry Book of Decrees RYE 57/7/4–5. For a different interpretation of these articles see A.J.F. Dulley op cit.

43 RYE 33/10/1v–2; RYE 1/4/7; RYE 1/4/347v; RYE 1/5/88.

44 RYE 132/15; RYE 47/71/20; RYE 47/75; RYE 1/6/107v–8.
45 RYE 60/4/321v–323; RYE 60/5/10; RYE 1/2/46; RYE 1/3/11v; RYE 1/3/124v; RYE 1/5/134; RYE 60/9/192–3; RYE 60/4/238v, 256v.
46 RYE 1/3/11v, 162v; RYE 1/5/134; RYE 1/4/115v, 331; RYE 1/4/6; RYE 1/4/331v; RYE 1/5/102v, 159; RYE 1/4/357.
47 RYE 60/5/358v–9; RYE 1/1/21v; RYE 1/3/92v; RYE 60/4/29–34; RYE 60/9/23.
48 RYE 35/34; RYE 1/3/200v; RYE 1/4/286v; RYE 7/1; RYE 1/5/173.
49 RYE 7/1–3.
50 RYE 7/3; RYE 1/4/317v; RYE 1/5/23.
51 RYE 1/5/24; RYE 7/3; RYE 1/5/43.
52 RYE 1/4/165v, 167v.
53 J.F.D. Shrewsbury, *A History of Bubonic Plague in the British Isles* (1971), pp 232, 234; *L.P.* 5 no 1231; *L.P.19* pt 2 no 253; RYE 1/3/153; RYE 1/4/309; RYE 1/6/66, 83, 87, 88, 249; RYE 47/101/22; RYE 47/39/21–2; RYE 60/5/40v; PAR 467 1/1/1–2.
54 PAR 467 1/1/1–2.
55 RYE 1/3/51.
56 RYE 1/4/309–12.
57 RYE 1/6/66; RYE 60/10/51v.
58 RYE 1/6/83.
59 RYE 1/3/65 records the imposition of a 40s fine by the town assembly in December 1563 on any jurat absenting himself from the town for more than a month without licence during future epidemics. Entries in the assembly books for the period July–December 1563 show the continual postponement of business due to the lack of attendance by jurats and freemen at assemblies and sessions.
60 RYE 1/4/81, 274, 292.
61 RYE 1/4/157; RYE 1/5/77; RYE 1/3/68; RYE 1/5/154; RYE 1/5/122v.
62 RYE 1/4/369v; RYE 1/3/206v; RYE 1/5/27v.
63 RYE 60/6/138v, 139v, 171v; RYE 47/23/34; RYE 60/4/157v; J.S. Cockburn, (ed) *Calendar of Assize Records : Sussex Indictments Elizabeth I* (1975) pp 92–3.
64 G.J. Mayhew, 'Rye and the defence of the Narrow Seas', *S.A.C.* 122 (1984) pp 107–8, 117–9; RYE 1/4/376–v.
65 RYE 60/4/299.
66 G.J. Mayhew 'Rye and the defence of the Narrow Seas', *S.A.C.* 122 (1984) pp 108–9.
67 M. Mollat: *Le Commerce Maritime Normand a la fin du Moyen Age* (Paris, 1952) p 257; RYE 1/4/340v.
68 RYE 47/25/182.
69 RYE 60/5/133, 155v.
70 RYE 60/5/107, 109v, 146v; RYE 60/7/57–58.
71 RYE 48/30–33.
72 RYE 1/3/73v–74; RYE 1/4/198, 230v.
73 Details of the expenditure by Rye's two MPs in 1548 on the promotion of their parliamentary suit are contained in the churchwarden's accounts for that year, the costs being met from the sale of church plate. RYE 147/1/114–v. A draft of the original bill put forward survives, RYE 99/1. For later parliamentary activity by Rye's MPs see RYE 1/4/232v, 352, 361–3; RYE 1/5/ 51v, 151, 276–7v; RYE 1/7/385v–6; RYE 47/2/35; RYE 47/24/4; RYE 47/25/60; RYE 47/47/6–7; RYE 47/63/73–4.
74 D.M. Palliser : *Tudor York* (1979) pp 51, 58, 188, 215, 218–9, 228, 242.

York's MPs, like Rye's, 'were never instructed to take a stand on the national issues which dominate Sir John Neale's *Elizabeth and her Parliaments,* but rather to fight for local statutes, for reductions in the city's tax, or for sympathetic government action over local problems' ibid p 58. Parliamentary bills on such issues as the removing of obstacles to navigation in the Ouse, the amalgamation of parishes and the diversion of chantry lands to the corporation, and the takeover by the corporation of vacant building, were promoted in 1532, 1536, 1540, 1543, 1547, 1548, 1553, 1555 and 1556.
75   RYE 1/5/142v.

CHAPTER 2

1   RYE 60/3–10; RYE 147/1 passim, but especially RYE 60/7/135v; RYE 147/1/19–20, 140.
2   The annual appointment of the Lenten Inquest, to search the butchers and victuallers to ensure compliance with these regulations is included in the Rye assembly Books RYE 1/2–7.
3   RYE 147/1/20,92.
4   RYE 147/1/10v.
5   RYE 147/1/39–v, 50v.
6   RYE 60/7/125v, 224; E.R. Chambers: *The Medieval Stage* (1903), I, p 399; RYE 60/4/264v. For a description of Robin Hood's part in the May Games in London in 1515, in which Henry VIII took part see J. Stow op. cit. pp 90–1.
7   RYE 60/3/55; RYE 60/4/32v, 50v, 197, 212, 229v, 295; RYE 60/5/37v, 206v.
8   RYE 60/4/198v, 216, 247, 317, 323; RYE 60/5/24, 104v, 261v.
9   RYE 60/3/56, 68v; RYE 60/5/81, 207; RYE 60/7/224. Altogether, in the period 1485–1560 players from the following towns and villages are listed as having visited Rye; Appledore 1488, 1517, 1521; Ashford 1503; Benenden 1500, 1523; Bethersden 1508; Brookland 1506, 1508, 1511, 1519, 1520, 1521, 1527, 1534; Canterbury 1488, 1503/4, 1518, 1526, (waits 1533, minstrels 1550, 1551); Charte 1507; Chichester 1505; Cranbrook 1504, 1527; Dover 1506, 1508; Faversham 1525, 1526; Frittenden 1488, 1490; Goudhurst 1504; Halden 1527; Harysham 1509; Hastings 1533; Hythe 1519, 1520; Ivechurch 1522, 1531; Lews (Lewes?) 1526; Lydd 1486, 1503 1509 1531 1532; Lydenden 1507; Maidstone 1492; Malling (Kent) 1498, 1505, 1507, Mersham 1523; Peasmarsh 1524, 1525; Reding 1492; Robertsbridge 1525; Rochester 1521; Romney 1496, 1503 (twice), 1510, 1517, 1526, 1540, 1560; Sittingbourne 1518, 1520, 1521; Tarring 1512; Tenterden 1494, 1504, 1510, 1519, 1521; Winchelsea 1490, 1502, 1503. In addition, players from Billericay, Essex, were listed in 1525 and (one player only) in 1527; and minstrels from Colchester in 1520. For a similar list of players visiting New Romney, see E.K. Chambers op.cit. II pp 385–6. The Rye players were recorded at Lydd in 1480 and at New Romney in 1489. Ibid p 393.
10   G.J. Mayhew, 'Religion, Faction and Politics in Reformation Rye : 1530–59', *S.A.C.* 120 (1982) pp 142–6, 154; RYE 47/77/2.
11   See e.g. the charges for lighterage of 50 tons of iron plates from Rye to Bodiam for Robertsbridge steelworks (July 1566) in D.W. Crossley (ed): *Sidney Ironworks Accounts 1541–1573* (Camden Fourth Series Vol 15, 1975) p 214.
12   John Foxe, *Acts and Monuments,* ed Rev. J. Cumming (1875) Vol 2, pp 724–7; P. Collinson, 'Cranbrook and the Fletchers: Popular and unpopular religion in the Kentish Weald', in P.N. Brooks (ed), *Reformation principle and practice* (1980) esp pp 176–7.
13   *L.P.* 4 pt 2 , no 4017; *L.P.* 9 no 1424.

14 C.E. Welch 'Three Sussex Heresy Trials', *S.A.C* 95 (1957) pp 59–70; J. Foxe op.cit. Vol 2, pp 348–9.

15 W/A3/100.

16 For a fuller analysis of the changing nature of religious preambles and testators' bequests in wills from Rye and other East Sussex towns, see my article, 'The Progress of the Reformation in East Sussex 1530–1559: the evidence from wills' in *Southern History* 5 (1983) pp 38–67.

17 *L.P.* 12 pt 2 no 505; P.R.O. SP1/113/106–9; SP1/124/21. The events leading to Inold's removal, contained in correspondence preserved among the State Papers have been detailed by G.R. Elton, *Policy and Police* (1972) pp 85–90.

18 For a discussion of the role of preachers licensed by Cranmer in spreading Protestantism in Canterbury diocese including Cinque Port towns such as Sandwich, see P. Clark: *English Provincial Society from the Reformation to the Revolution* (1977) (hereafter referred to as Clark: *English Provincial Society* pp 38,60ff; also P.Clark: 'Reformation and radicalism in Kentish Towns c1500–1553' in *The Urban Classes, the Nobility and the Reformation*, Publications of the German Historical Institute, 5 (1979) (hereafter referred to as Clark article) pp 114–5.

19 P.R.O. SP 1/113/106–9.

20 Clark: *English Provincial Society*, pp 41–4, 57–9, 67–8.

21 RYE 60/5/335v; RYE 60/6/167v. The election of Gabriel Adams and John Younge to replace Robert Wymond and John Raynoldes who died during the year was opposed by Thomas Fletcher who accordingly did not reappoint Adams, choosing instead his own younger brother Richard. RYE 60/6/202; RYE 33/7/42v.

22 P. Clark: *English Provincial Society* pp 39–40 shows the personal antagonisms of the rival political factions in Canterbury manifested in civil law suits.

23 *L.P.* 14 pt 2 nos 341, 546. For an earlier example of the hostility between the two factions see the conflict between John Fletcher and John Eston, cousin of William Wymond and another of Birchett's associates, Robert Cooke the younger in 1531, 'I tell thee, Cooke, and I would thou shouldest know it, that I have a sword of vengeance in my hand and I may strike and will strike the proudest of you all. when I list'. *L.P. Addenda* 1 pt 1 no 739; F. Hull (ed): *A Calendar of the White and Black Books of the Cinque Ports 1432–1955* (1960) pp 214–5, 217–8, 223.

24 W/A2/9; W/A7/67. For a fuller discussion of the personal interrelationships of Rye jurats during this period see my article 'Religion, faction and politics in Reformation Rye: 1530–59' *S.A.C.* 120 (1982) pp 144–7.

25 ibid. p 148.

26 *L.P.* 12 pt 1 no 1150; Clark, article, pp 119ff.

27 RYE 60/5/335v.

28 RYE 60/6/9–12.

29 RYE 12/1–8; RYE 60/5/344v, 356v.

30 Payments for their Parliament wages are entered in the chamberlain's accounts for 1538–9 and 1539–40.RYE 60/5/344v, 356.

31 RYE 60/5/361.

32 *L.P.* 16 no 1308 (45).

33 PAR467 1/1/1. He was presented to the vicarage of Boughton Aluph by the College of Wye in November 1537 and had a dispensation to hold a second benefice granted in December 1539. Lambeth Palace Library, Reg. Cranmer fol 362v; D.S. Chambers (ed), *Faculty Office Register* (1966) p 202. I owe these references to M.L. Zell.

34 Payments for their Parliament wages were made on 20 November 1545 and

20 January 1546. RYE 60/6/122.

35 RYE 60/6/119.

36 West Sussex record Office Register Bp. Day 30b. For an account of Scambler's later career, see the *Dictionary of National Biography*, 17 (1909) p 885.

37 RYE 147/1/111v.

38 RYE 147/1/116.

39 RYE 147/1/116v.

40 RYE 60/6/167v.

41 RYE 60/6/167v, 180.

42 RYE 60/6/165v. Normally churchwardens were appointed for two years each, one retiring per year. RYE 147/1/114.

43 RYE 147/1/122, 123.

44 RYE 147/1/124, 127, 128, 129.

45 RYE 147/1/129v–130.

46 RYE 147/1/130.

47 RYE 60/7/58, 59.

48 RYE 147/1/135.

49 RYE 147/1/135; RYE 60/7/77.

50 RYE 147/1/134, 135, 136.

51 RYE 147/1/133, 135.

52 *Acts of the Privy Council of England* ed J.R. Dasent (hereafter referred to as *A.P.C.*) 1552–4, Nos 387, 391, 395.

53 RYE 147/1/133v, 134 135v, 136.

54 G.S.Butler 'The vicars of Rye and their patrons', *S.A.C.* 13 (1861) p 273; RYE 147/1/136.

55 RYE 1/1/31v, 38v; *House of Commons Members. Parliaments of England* 1213–1702 (1878), p 391. The returns of members elected from all of the Cinque Ports to this Parliament were tampered with. From 1554 notices of elections and names of elected members appear in the assembly books. Prior to that date MPs can be identified from entries for Parliament wages in the chamberlain's accounts. The intervention of the Lord Warden, Sir Thomas Cheyney, in the election to Mary's first Parliament in October 1553 had led to a protest from all the Cinque Ports towns which resulted in an uneasy compromise whereby the Lord Warden was usually granted one nomination and individual towns the other: RYE 60/7/59. For a copy of Cheyney's letter on that occasion, see Winchelsea Corporation court book, E.S.R.O. WIN 51/123. For an earlier attempted intervention (January 1553), see 'Notes from an old record book', 11–13, unlisted MSS among the Hastings Corporation records, held in Hastings Museum, and placed with the earliest court books (C/A(d))—quoted in J.M.Baines, *Historic Hastings* 2nd edn (Hastings, 1963) pp 45–6.

56 RYE 1/1/47; *A.P.C.* 1552–4 p 391; J. Foxe, op.cit. Vol 3 p 947. An entry in the Rye parish register PAR 467 1/1/1 for the marriage of Margery Ravynsdale to Symon Johnsone on 16 November 1559 confirms the presence of a family of that name in Rye at this time; RYE 147/1/140v, 142.

57 RYE 147/1/140v; RYE 60/7/127v, 128.

58 *A.P.C.* 1554–6, p 327; RYE 60/7/129.

59 RYE 147/1/140, 144.

60 *A.P.C.* 1556–8, pp 112, 166, 182, 185, 214; RYE 1/2/6v, 15v.

61 RYE 1/2/5.

62 RYE 1/2/7v, 25.

63 RYE 1/2/ 23v; PAR 467 1/1/1.

64 RYE 147/1/154v, 159v, 160v, 162v, 165v, 167; RYE 1/2/54v, 79v.
65 H.M.C. Report 13, Appendix IV (1892) pp 6,14; RYE 1/4/171v, 252v; RYE 1/5/149, 193v; RYE 47/25/27.
66 H.M.C. Report 13, Appendix IV (1892) pp 46–7, 80; RYE 1/5/83v, 138, 149, 168v, 194.
67 RYE 1/5/264, 274v, 332–4; PAR 467 1/1/2. He was buried 30 October 1596.
68 H.M.C. Report 13, Appendix 4 (1892) pp 120–2.
69 ibid p 99.
70 RYE 47/2/6 8, 13, 16 18 19, 21, 22, 23.
71 RYE 47/2/31, 33.
72 J. Cornwall, op.cit. pp 164–5; L.P. Vol 14 pt 2 no 349.
73 W.D. Cooper 'Protestant Refugees in Sussex', S.A.C. 13 (1861) pp 181, 187; PAR 467/1/1/2.
74 W.J. Hardy 'Foreign Refugees at Rye', Proceedings of the Huguenot Society of London, 2 (1887–8) pp 414 567–8; RYE 47/2/12; H.M.C. Report 13, Appendix IV (1892) p 63.
75 W.D. Cooper op.cit. pp 195–9; RYE 1/4/158; H.M.C.Report 13, Appendix IV (1892) p 37.
76 W.D. Cooper op.cit. p 199; RYE 66/32; P.R.O. SP12/187/1.
77 RYE 66/1–39; Anthony Coq's patent of denization was enrolled in the assembly records, 30 January 1569 (RYE 1/4/32); Francis Maquery's denization is recorded 15 November 1566 (RYE 1/3/175v). He died, apparently by misadventure, in suspicious circumstances, standing up in a cockboat in the Puddle alongside one of her Majesty's pinnaces immediately in front of one of its guns at the moment of firing, 18 September 1586. (RYE 1/5/93v–94). H.M.C. Report 13, Appendix IV (1892) p 62; RYE 47/10/32.
78 RYE 65/1–40 esp 65/5, 12, 39.
79 RYE 1/4/284, 323; RYE 1/5/119v, 283, 310; RYE 65/38–40.
80 RYE 1/5/89v, 113, 160.
81 RYE 1/5/155v.
82 ed R.B. Wernham: List and Analysis of State Papers, Foreign Series, Elizabeth I, preserved in the Public Record Office (3 vols 1964–80) Vol 2 p 231.
83 RYE 47/6/7, 21, 22a,23, 27, 28, 29, 35, 41; RYE 47/7/1, 94; RYE 47/9/12, 14, 18a–b.
84 H.M.C. Report 13 Appendix IV (1892) pp 40,60,62; and see also R.F. Dell, op.cit., p xliii n2.
85 H.M.C. Report 13, Appendix IV (1892) pp 60–2; RYE 1/4/168.
86 W.J.C. Moens, 'Remarks upon Mr Hardy's Paper, "Foreign Refugees at Rye"', Procs Hug Soc London, 2 (1887–8), p 426; H.M.C. Report 13, Appendix IV (1892) pp 22 42, 62; RYE 47/13/64.
87 H.M.C. Report 13, Appendix IV (1892) pp 62–3.
88 W/A7/194; W/A8/210.
89 PAR 467/1/1/1–2; W.J.C.Moens op.cit. pp 424–7. For an account of the Rye church in the context of other foreign churches at this time see J.S. Burn: The History of the French, Walloon, Dutch and other Foreign Protestant Refugees settled in England from the Reign of Henry VIII to the Revocation of the Edict of Nantes (1848). A recent survey of the Huguenots in Britain, which adds little to the accounts of the Rye church in Burn, Hardy and Cooper is R.D. Gwyn: The History and Contribution of the Huguenots in Britain (1985). Drawing largely from these earlier sources, Gwyn places too much emphasis on the fluctuating size of Rye's alien Protestant community and tends to underestimate its size and contribution to the urban economy.
90 RYE 47/10/32: RYE 47/27/25,36; Cornelius Sohier disappears from the

lesser box returns after the quarter ending January 1579 and Wm Bucher's widow appears in the great and lesser box returns from August 1580. RYE 65/12–16; RYE 66/9–11. For Francis Maquery see above n 75.

91 H.M.C. Report 13, Appendix IV (1892) pp 106, 124–5; RYE 1/6/42.

CHAPTER 3

1   RYE 57/1/1–38v.
2   RYE 57/1/39v–49v.
3   RYE 1/3/192; RYE 1/7/474v–5.
4   RYE 60/4/145v.
5   RYE 60/4/204; RYE 60/4/252; RYE 60/5/73 and see also G.J. Mayhew: Religion, faction and politics in Reformation Rye: 1530–59. S.A.C. 120 (1982), hereafter referred to as 'Reformation Rye', esp pp 156–8; RYE 1/4/175. On a number of other occasions, as in 1536, when the leading local Protestant Thomas Birchett, made a jurat in 1535, seems not to have been reappointed, relatively junior jurats seem to have been temporarily displaced, but in the above cases specific mention of expulsion or dismissal for particular causes was made.
6   RYE 57/1/39v.
7   RYE 33/8/59v; RYE 1/4/305v.
8   RYE 1/5/305v; RYE 1/5/115.
9   RYE 1/4/233, 246, 279, 333, 373.
10 P.R.O. PROB 11/39/24; RYE 1/5/92v, PAR 467/1/1/2; RYE 1/7/345, W/B3/180.
11 F. Hull: A Calendar of the White and Black Books of the Cinque Ports 1432–1955 (1966) pp 200–2.
12 RYE 60/5/167,179; RYE 60/6/167v; and see G.J. Mayhew: 'Reformation Rye' p 155.
13 RYE 47/22/22.
14 RYE 1/4/321v–22.
15 RYE 1/4/332.
16 See e.g. RYE 1/4/307, 333; RYE 1/5/1, 70.
17 RYE 57/11.
18 RYE 33/12; RYE 1/3 passim.
19 W/A1/77; W/A5/206; P.R.O. PROB 11/42A/1; RYE 139/28.
20 RYE 47/25/98.
21 RYE 47/61.
22 RYE 57/9.
23 G.J. Mayhew: 'Reformation Rye' pp 148–58 passim.
24 RYE 1/4/175; RYE 1/5/180, 184v.
25 RYE 1/2/51v.
26 RYE 1/5/3; RYE 1/4/125; RYE 1/5/3; RYE 60/9/62–7. The chamberlain's accounts for 1575/6 show the scorer in receipt of a quarter of the poundage on the great box, the mayor's sergeant in receipt of half and the town porter in receipt of a quarter.
27 RYE 1/3/57v; RYE 1/4/100; RYE 1/5/76 provides another detailed set of the town porter's rates for carriage for 1585.
28 RYE 1/3/31v.
29 RYE 1/4/80; RYE 1/4/109, 156, 274; RYE 1/4/156v.
30 RYE 1/4/133.
31 RYE 1/3/141.
32 RYE 60/3–10 passim.
33 RYE 57/11.

34 A list of these in 1582 consisted of the following:
'One pyle called haber de poys weightes conteyninge xvi li weight beinge xii peces
One troy waight conteyninge viii li troy havinge ix severall waightes small and greate
One Leaden waight conteyninge di C
One other waight of leade conteyninge vii li
A beame and skalles
A brasse quart and a brasse pynte One standard of Iron with ell and yerdd uppon it'. RYE 1/5/3.

35 RYE 60/3–10; RYE 1/2–6.

36 RYE 1/2/25; RYE 1/4/37Ov and see above Chapter 6 : Crime and social order.

37 RYE 1/2/30; RYE 1/4/380; RYE 151/1 is a surviving late sixteenth century rate for Landgate Ward amounting to 16s 8d.

38 RYE 7/4.

39 See e.g. the jury list for 1580, RYE 1/4/322v.

40 e.g. in 1571 and 1573 the mayor, jurats and commons are referred to and in 1572 and 1578 the election is said to have been made by the parishioners. RYE 1/4/105, 128, 147, 294.

41 After 1590 the assembly books do not record the michaelmas elections of churchwardens, only the auditing of their accounts. It is therefore not always possible to identify all of those who held the office in the 1590s. A volume of churchwardens' accounts survives 1513–70 with odd gatherings 1577–97. RYE 147/1–13. The information on individual churchwardens is based on these accounts plus the details of those elected in the assembly books RYE 1/1–7.

42 RYE 1/4/358v.

43 RYE 1/4/13v, 336.

44 RYE 1/5/104v–105.

45 RYE 1/5/113.

46 An earlier attempt to establish a common council was made in September 1563, half to be appointed by the mayor and jurats, half to be chosen by the commons, to meet every Monday and with an additional responsibility for the auditing of the accounts and to oversee the payments made by the chamberlains. However this appears to have been only a temporary expedient, since the order was to continue only from 15 days to 15 days, indicating that it was only to last a short time. By December nothing further was heard of the institution.

47 RYE 1/4/187v–189.

48 RYE 1/4/187v, 193v, 194.

49 RYE 47/6/54 and RYE 1/4/148v.

50 RYE 47/12/3.

51 RYE 1/5/184–185.

52 That the terms 'freemen' and 'commons' are interchangeable is clear from a letter to the Privy Council following the mayoral election of 1579 which refers to 'the men of the commonaltie ... which freemen are called the commons and none other'. RYE 47/25/22.

53 RYE 1/3/26v.

54 RYE 57/1/67.

55 RYE 1/3/183v–184; RYE 1/4/203; RYE 60/5/232.

56 RYE 57/1/1–38v.

57 RYE 47/30/107.

58 RYE 57/1/43.
59 Decrees relating to the admission of freemen are : RYE 1/3/12 (1562); RYE 1/4/64v–65 (1570); RYE 1/4/124 (1572) and RYE 1/4/384 (1582).
60 RYE 33/7/69v; RYE 60/7/160v.
61 RYE 60/5/329, RYE 358v; 61/1/2v.
62 S.P.Hipkin: 'Class Structure and Social Control in Rye. 1600–1660: A paper delivered to the early modern history seminar, Oxford University, October 1980, p 8.
63 The domination of the early modern urban economy by a single trade or function is well-known from many other towns. Hoskins noted over 33% of traders in Coventry in 1522 were involved in textiles, whilst in Northampton and Leicester, leather accounted for 23% and 19% respectively. Pound found a similar proportion of 30% involved in textiles in Norwich in 1525, but few towns experienced the almost complete domination of their economies by a single function to the degree that Rye experienced. See e.g. W.G. Hoskins, 'English provincial towns in the early sixteenth century' and J.F. Pound 'The social and trade structure of Norwich 1525–1575' in ed P.Clark: *The Early Modern Town* (1976), D.M. Palliser: *Tudor York* (1979) p 157 and Table 1 'Leading trades in eight towns' in *The Fabric of the Traditional Community* Course Unit 5 of A 322 *English-Urban History 1500–1780* edited for the Open University by C. Phythian-Adams et al (1977).
64 RYE 46/5; RYE 99/5: RYE 65/1; RYE 66/1.
65 RYE 1/1/22–26 ; RYE 1/4/227v, 228v–232; P.R.O. PROB 11/66/14v; PROB 11/38/21.
66 P.R.O./PROB 11/11/7; PROB 11/23/13.
67 P.R.O.PROB 11/66/14v; W/A7/67; P.R.O. PROB 11/43/2; P.R.O. PROB 11/110/ 399; W/All/2O8.
68 G.J. Mayhew 'Reformation Rye' esp pp 146–8; RYE 81/1–2; RYE 60/4–6.
69 W/A1/102; P.R.O. PROB 11/44/10; RYE 47/2.
70 P.R.O. PROB 11/21/11; P.R.O. E 179 190/200 and G.J. Mayhew: 'Reformation Rye'. pp 151, 154.
71 P.R.O. PROB 11/38/21.
72 RYE 13 and see K. Thomas: *Religion and the Decline of Magic* (1971) p 758. The trial of Ann Bennett and Susan Swapper is discussed at length in A. Gregory: 'Slander accusations and social control in late 16th and early 17th century England with particular reference to Rye (Sussex), 1590–1615', University of Sussex, unpublished D.Phil. Thesis (1985),
73 RYE 33/7/69v; PAR 467 1/1/1; RYE 1/1/23 ; RYE 1/2/14, RYE 1/3/149v; RYE 1/4/288v, 312 ; RYE 1/6/32 ; P.R.O. PROB 11/110/399.
74 For a similar discussion of the Tudor York office-holders, see D.M. Palliser: *Tudor York* (1979) pp 92–110; and for Exeter see W.G. Hoskins: 'The Elizabethan Merchants of Exeter' in P. Clark (ed): *The Early Modern Town* (1976) pp 148–67.
75 P.R.O. PROB 11/23/77v–78; PROB 11/14/101; PROB 11/13/129v–30; PROB 11/25/183; RYE 33/7/21; RYE 60/4/187.
76 P.R.O. PROB 11/48/11.
77 P.R.O. PROB 11/35/8.
78 P.R.O. PROB 11/49/14; PROB 11/33/11.
79 J. Foster (ed): *The Register of Admissions to Gray's Inn 1521–1889* (1889) pp 5–37; H.A.C. Sturgess (ed): *Register of Admissions to the Honourable Society of the Middle Temple* (1949) p 31; J. Venn: *Alumni Cantabrigienses* Part I Vol I (1922) p 155.

80   W/A6/333.
81   P.R.O. PROB 11/39/34; PROB 11/56/1; PROB 11/33/11.
82   PAR 467/1/1/1; P.R.O. PROB 11/39/34; PROB 11/40/39; W/A1/23; PROB 11/ 42B/11; W/A1/204.
83   Donnynges, like Shurley, was an outsider, coming to Rye as Customer in 1565. He apparently did not leave a will and he does not appear as a witness, overseer or recipient of a bequest of any of his contemporaries among the Rye magistrates.
84   The names of godparents of children, baptised, are given in the Rye parish register June 1556–February 1561. PAR 467/1/1/1.
85   Ibid.
86   For a discussion of prevailing mortality rates see G.J. Mayhew: 'Epidemic mortality in sixteenth century Rye' in *S.A.C.* 124 (1986).
87   P.R.O. PROB 11/42A/1.
88   P.R.O. PROB 11/44/10; RYE 47/2; PAR 467/1/1/1.
89   RYE 47/24/7.
90   For Birchett see G.J. Mayhew: 'Reformation Rye', *S.A.C.*120 (1982) esp pp 144–6; RYE 139/25; W/Al/102–3; W/A1/44; P.R.O. PROB 11/49/14; PROB 11/66/14v; PROB 11/14/101; W/A8/173.
91   RYE 139/12,55.
92   RYE 1/4/140v, 282; RYE 1/6/118v–9.
93   RYE 65/8, 33, 36, 55; RYE 1/4/216, 219; RYE 1/5/107.
94   RYE 65/1.
95   RYE 79/1.
96   RYE 147/1/2v; W/Al2/l; RYE 60/2–4.
97   RYE 1/4/210.
98   RYE 66/1,7,22. The three fishing masters who are recorded as paying for their 'hepe of ostage' are William Clerke (1516), Nicholas Whyte (1496), and Robert Mede (1509). RYE 60/4–5.
99   See e.g. the bonds of ships' masters and owners for April and July 1495, RYE 60/3/116–117v; the survey of ships and mariners belonging to the south coast ports, December 1565, which lists masters and owners, SP 12/38/28; and the similar return of November 1580, RYE 47/24/7.
100 RYE 47/9/28; RYE 47/24/7 and RYE 47/25 pt II/ll, RYE 47/27/39, 42, 43.
101 RYE 1/2/7v, 58v; RYE 1/4/175; RYE 1/7/344; RYE 1/2/2v.
102 RYE 85/2.
103 See G.J. Mayhew 'Reformation Rye' passim.
104 RYE 1/4/99, 175, 214v–215v.
105 RYE 137/36.
106 P.R.O. STAC 5 H32/29.
107 P.R.O STAC 5 H76/38.
108 RYE 137/36; P.R.O. STAC 5 H76/38.
109 RYE 47/24/6.
110 RYE 47/2; P.R.O. PROB 11/44/10; W/A6/333; PAR 467 1/1/1; RYE 1/2/5v; RYE 1/4/246; P.R.O. PROB 11/49/14; P.R.O. PROB 11/42A/1.
111 RYE 47/21/49; RYE 47/25/4. The dispute between John Mercer and Rye corporation is both complex and highly documented. For Mercer's views see P.R.O. SP 15/28/112. The proceedings of Rye corporation against Mercer, together with his letters to the town clerk, are contained in the General Files of the corporation. See especially RYE 47/23/114; RYE 47/25 pt I/1, 2, 13, 18, 20, 22, 23, 25; RYE 47/pt II/3, 4, 27, 33, 38, 42, 47, 65, 66, 78, 90, 98, 105. The case became the subject of a decree of the Brotherhood of the Cinque Ports, confirming Mercer's disfranchisement. See F.Hull op.cit. pp

311,314–5,318–9,323,329.

112 P.R.O. PROB 11/66/14v; W/A7/274; P.R.O. PROB 11/83/6; W/A11/208; P.R.O. PROB 11/86/217; W/A12/1; W/A8/173. For other examples of wills drawn up by Robert Convers see e.g. those of Thomas Hamond, P.R.O. PROB 11/110/ 399 and of William Tolken, W/A12/64.

113 RYE 1/5/306; RYE 47/57/4–5; RYE 47/70/2–3; RYE 1/9/475v. A. Gregory; thesis pp 139–140 has wrongly identified Thomas Fisher junior with his namesake, Thomas Fisher the jurat.

114 RYE 47/24/6; RYE 47/25/22.

115 RYE 1/5/180. According to a letter from William Appleton written in 1581, Robert Carpenter and his brother John had set their sights on the mayoralty and town clerkship as early as the latter year. RYE 47/25/23. A statement of accounts 1592–3 headed 'My nephew Bolton' is endorsed 'My unckell Dydsburye his reconinge'. RYE 145/1.

116 RYE 47/25/22; P.R.O. PROB 11/66/14v; PAR 467/1/1/2; W/A11/208.

CHAPTER 4

1 See e.g. P. Clark and P. Slack : *English Towns in Transition 1500–1700* (1976) pp 111–3; D.M. Palliser: *Tudor York* (1979) pp 134–9; C. Phythian-Adams: *Desolation of a City: Coventry and the Urban Crisis of the Late Middle Ages* (1979) pp 128–36; W.T. MacCaffrey: *Exeter 1540–1640* (1975) pp 247–51; W.G. Hoskins : 'English provincial towns in the early sixteenth century', in P. Clark (ed) *The Early Modern Town* (1976) pp 101–2; J.F. Pound: 'The social and trade structure of Norwich 1525–1575' in ibid pp 129–33.

2 The account of the ward boundaries in Rye differs materially from that given in H.P. Clark: *Guide and History of Rye* (Rye 1861) pp 83–4 and the account given in W. Holloway: *History and Antiquities of the ancient Town and Port of Rye, in the County of Sussex* (1847) pp 326–7, which relate to the late seventeenth century.

3 RYE 127/10.

4 According to W.G.L. Gilbert, 'The Street Names of Rye', *Rye Museum Association Newsletter* (October 1959) pp 13–16, Dyrrickes Lane retained this name as an alternative to Sharp's Lane, which it is shown as on Samuel Jeake's map of Rye, 1667, (copy by William Wybourn, 1728, RYE 132/15). This map is invaluable in identifying many of the places referred to in the 1574 decree establishing Rye's ward boundaries.

5 In 1513 John Bawdwyn paid 2s rent to the parish church for his principal tenement at the west cliff. RYE 147/1/2v.

6 In January 1585 John Leny, butcher, was ordered to enter into a £10 bond not to keep his butcher's shop at the house where he then dwelt, or elsewhere 'excepte suche shoppes as are commonly usid and occupied in the Market Place of the same towne, commonly called the Bochery'. RYE 1/5/56.

7 Includes lightermen and cockboatmen. It is not always possible to distinguish mariners and fishermen separately as in a number of cases individuals are described as both at different times. Only those whose names appear among the lists of fishing masters, or served an apprenticeship to a fisherman or are elsewhere specifically described as such have been classified as fishermen. The remainder, including those who are specifically described as mariners or masters/crew of merchant vessels have been placed in the latter category.

8 William Radclyffe, jurat (also a vintner, 1603, W/B3 22); William Frenche (1603, W/B3/16); Robert Daniell (1580, W/B1/84v); Henry Upjohn (1595, W/B2/215); John Bennett (1579, W/B1/75).

9 RYE 1/3/164v, 179; RYE 1/4/211v, 212, 213–4. Among brewers objecting to

this decree were John Mercer and Robert Jacson, the latter obtaining a letter from the Lord Warden to enable him to continue baking until the following March. He evidently continued well beyond this date as in October 1576 and January 1577 he took on two apprentices in baking. RYE 1/4/257v. In 1579 Jacson and Mercer were still listed among the bakers whose bread was weighed, RYE 1/4/309. For the annual lists of bakers presented for occupying the trade without having been apprenticed to it, see RYE 7/1-4.

10   RYE 1/4/195, 198v, 204v.
11   RYE 46/5; RYE 47/25/71; RYE 1/4/210; RYE 47/9/28; RYE 47/24/7; RYE 47/ 25ptII/11; RYE 47/27/39,42-3.
12   Tables 21-22, which give primary occupations of ratepayers, list under victuallers only those for whom victualling was the primary or only known occupation, in order to prevent duplication.
13   RYE 1/2/76; RYE 1/5/13v.
14   RYE 1/4/251. In the seven years prior to September 1576 only 13 fishermen's apprenticeship indentures are recorded.
15   RYE 47/24/7.
16   RYE 60/9/61-4.
17   RYE 47/5/69.
18   5 Eliz c.4. *Statutes of the Realm* 4 (1816) pp 414-22. For comparable wage rates in other counties and towns see P.L. Hughes and J.F. Larkin (eds) *Tudor Royal Proclamations Volume II : 1553-1587* (1969) especially nos 502, 503, 512, 536, 544, 545.
19   P.L. Hughes and J.F. Larkin op.cit. no 502.
20   Ibid no 536.
21   RYE 1/5/71v-72; RYE 1/5/57.
22   RYE 1/3/204; RYE 1/4/297v; RYE 1/4/43; RYE 1/4/260v; RYE 1/5/289.
23   RYE 1/5/73v, 75, 77; RYE 1/4/286.
24   RYE 1/5/56v; RYE 1/5/329; RYE 1/5/364; RYE 1/5/130v-1.
25   There is a distinct widening of the differentials between ordinary mariners and ships' officers in Table 25, which may be related to the increase in the size of the vessels. Thus in 1544 the master received twice the amount paid to ordinary crew members. In 1588 and 1596 he received four times that amount. Throughout the period boys seem to have been paid half the wages of a mariner.
26   RYE 1/3/20v; RYE 1/3/75v; RYE 1/4/307v; RYE 1/4/358v; RYE 1/3/93v; RYE 1/5/331; RYE 1/5/274v; RYE 1/4/252v.
27   RYE 35/23.
28   RYE 1/5/308v; RYE 1/4/134; RYE 1/4/46, 51v, 143; RYE 1/4/316v; W/A1/168; RYE 1/5/61.
29   RYE 1/3/133; RYE 1/5/79,130; RYE 1/5/24v, 168; RYE 1/3/88, RYE 1/5/24v.
30   RYE 35/34.
31   5.Eliz.c.4(20); RYE 1/5/62; RYE 1/4/376v.
32   RYE 1/2/68-9v.
33   RYE 139/28.
34   RYE 1/5/118v, 363v; RYE 47/37/2; RYE 1/4/43; RYE 1/5/355v; RYE 1/4/383. For a summary of the surviving accounts of the voyages of the town ship see R.F.Dell : op.cit. p 42.
35   RYE 47/10/68; RYE 47/10/74; RYE 47/25/6; RYE 1/4/383.
36   P.R.O. SP 12/38/28; SP 15/22; RYE 47/24/7; RYE 60/7-9; RYE 147/1; RYE 1/2-4 passim.
37   RYE 1/2-4; RYE 60/7-9; Rye 147/1 passim.

38 RYE 47/98/15; P.R.O. SP 12/38/28. In 1580 the figure for those engaged in merchant trade was 20 masters, 108 mariners and 10 boys, although for two ships the number of crew members was not specified. RYE 47/24/7.
39 RYE 1/3/189; RYE 99/5–6.
40 W/A5/302; P.R.O. PROB 11/55/131–2v; W/A6/351; W/A7/67; RYE 1/4/138; RYE 99/6; RYE 47/26/12; RYE 1/5/13v.
41 RYE 1/4/100v; RYE 1/4/204v; RYE 47/9/32. The chamberlains' accounts record the payment of 40s a year by the Company of Tailors and Woollen Drapers between 1573 and 1581 and of £4 annually by the Company of Mercers from 1575 when this grant was sealed until 1580. RYE 60/9 passim.
42 RYE 47/15/25.
43 RYE 47/9/32; RYE 1/4/204v.
44 RYE 1/4/195–6; RYE 1/4/213–4; RYE 1/4/218v.
45 RYE 1/4/213–v.
46 5.Eliz.c.4(24); RYE 1/3/165, 178v, 206; RYE 7/1–4; RYE 1/5/16v.
47 RYE 60/4/270,289,290,306; RYE 60/5/144.
48 RYE 1/4/165.
49 See for example J. Youings: *Sixteenth Century England* (1984)Chapter 6: 'Inflation of Population and Prices'; Y.S. Brenner; 'The Inflation of Prices in Early Sixteenth Century England', *Economic History Review*, 2nd series, 14 (1961–2) pp 225–39; Y.S. Brenner, 'Inflation of Prices in England, 1551–1650' ibid, 2nd series, 15 (1962–3) pp 266–84; F.J. Fisher, 'Influenza and Inflation in Tudor England', ibid, 2nd series, 18 (1965) pp 120–9.
50 E.H. Phelps Brown and S.V. Hopkins, 'Seven Centuries of the Prices of Consumables, compared with Builders' Wage Rates', *Economica* 23 (1956) pp 296–314; E.H. Phelps Brown and S.V. Hopkins, 'Wage-rates and Prices: Evidence for Population Pressure in the Sixteenth Century', ibid, 24 (1957) pp 289–306.

CHAPTER 5

1 The timber-framed buildings of Rye are at present the subject of detailed individual surveys by the Rape of Hastings Architectural Survey (hereafter referred to as R.O.H.A.S.) chiefly D. and B. Martin, to whose reports this author is indebted.
2 There are also two probate inventories surviving in the Public record Office, that of William Wykwyk, vicar of Rye 1498 (PROB 2/141) and of John Clarke, 1558 (PROB 2/328).
3 For a full list of these inventories see Appendix 6.
4 RYE 35/42.
5 RYE 139/37,43.
6 RYE 139/13.
7 RYE 1/5/339v.
8 RYE 1/3/121.
9 RYE 139/9,20.
10 RYE 139/17,38.
11 RYE 139/16,35.
12 RYE 139/59.
13 RYE 139/18.
14 RYE 139/15.
15 As at St Antony of Padua, Church Square. See R.O.H.A.S. Report No 356.
16 RYE 33/7/159.
17 RYE 60/7/54v; W/A7/67; RYE 139/20.
18 RYE 35/34; RYE 1/4/168; RYE 1/5/30; RYE 7/1–4.
19 RYE 1/2/76v; RYE 1/3/92v; RYE 1/5/112v.

20 St Antony of Padua, Church Square, has one such surviving unglazed window in situ at first floor level in what was originally the rear wall and now separates the stair passage from a bathroom.

21 RYE 1/4/268; RYE 139/2.

22 W/A11/208; W/A7/67.

23 RYE 139/9,17,18,38; RYE 35/27.

24 RYE 35/34; RYE 1/5/211v; RYE 91/1–2.

25 RYE 139/10; W/A7/67; RYE 139/11.

26 P.R.O. PROB 2/328; RYE 47/46/10; RYE 35/42; RYE 35/33 (inventory of goods of Mr Passes 1578) specifies a sorrell gelding valued at £4; RYE 47/58/16 (inventory of the goods of David Hewett 1599) lists 2 geldings, one dark grey and one bay; W/A1/102.

27 The will of George Raynoldes, W/A7/67 refers to such a passage between his principal tenement and a smaller one which he bequeathed to an adopted daughter, reserving 'the way to my stable and garden as is now used which belongs to my principal tenement'.

28 RYE 139/6 and 43 relate to the sale in 1586 of a property on the south side of Middle Street which consisted of a messuage or tenement with gardens and backsides together with a cellar under the (adjoining) tenement of Cuthbert Carr and a chamber over his kitchen.

29 RYE 124/13–18.

30 R.O.H.A.S. Report No 359, Rye – the Custom House, Church Square.

31 RYE 1/6/328v; RYE 135/26; R.O.H.A.S. Report No 506 Rye—the Mermaid Hotel.

32 RYE 35/42.

33 As at St Antony of Padua where such decoration (raised wavy lines caused by running a comb across the still wet plaster) survives in a stairwell and in an upstairs chamber. See R.O.H.A.S. Report No 356.

34 See *S.A.C.*50 (1907) pp 116–37, P.M. Johnston, 'Wall Painting in a house at Rye formerly known as the Old Flushing Inn'; R.O.H.A.S. Report No 744 Rye–16/16A West St.

35 RYE 1/5/35; RYE 1/5/44 (goods of Robert Battel, fisherman).

36 RYE 1/3 preceding fol 187.

37 RYE 35/36.

38 RYE 47/13/7. The inventory, dated 24 October 1575, was taken by virtue of a writ directed to the mayor and jurats from the Admiralty court at Dover.

39 P.R.O. PROB 2/328; RYE 35/31.

40 P.R.O. PROB 2/141.

41 RYE 1/3/41–2; RYE 35/31; RYE 47/46/10; RYE 47/40/14 and 47/42/7.

42 RYE 1/3, preceding fol 187; RYE 33/12/133; RYE 47/58/16; RYE 138/6; RYE 47/40/14 and 47/42/7; RYE 33/12/160. Other inventories specifying large quantities of pewter include those of Nicholas Morris, taylor 1537 (40 items) RYE 33/9/148v; Richard Goodwins, 1583 (21 items) RYE 35/36 and John Oliver, 1588 (30 items) RYE 35/39. Finally 5 inventories listed pewter candlesticks.

43 RYE 35/35; RYE 35/42.

44 RYE 138/6; RYE 33/12/160; P.R.O. PROB 2/328.

45 RYE 47/58/16; RYE 138/6; RYE 35/35. Other references to laten candlesticks occur amongst Richard Godwin's goods RYE 35/36; the goods of Alexander Goldsted, 1580, who also had 2 tin candlesticks as well as 2 laten ones RYE 35/34; and in the will of George Raynoldes, 1577, which lists 3 laten candlesticks, W/A7/67.

46 RYE 47/13/7; RYE 35/31; RYE 35/35; RYE 47/46/10; RYE 33/12/17v.
47 RYE 35/42; St Antony of Padua, Church Square. See R.O.H.A.S Report No 356; RYE 47/46/10; RYE 47/58/16; RYE 33/12/160.
48 RYE 35/35; RYE 35/42; RYE 35/27.
49 P.R.O. PROB 2/328; RYE 35/33; RYE 47/40/14 and 47/42/7; RYE 47/46/10; RYE 35/42; RYE 47/58/16; RYE 33/12/133 and RYE 35/27.
50 RYE 35/33; W/A7/67; a 'joyned bedstedell' complete with 'fether bed, a blanket and a coveryng a boulster (and) a pillow' belonging to Francis Daniell was apprized at 30s in 1592, RYE 47/46/10; RYE 35/36; RYE 1/3 preceding fol 187.
51 Thomas Byspyn, 1537, had a tapestry coverlet RYE 35/2; Robert Horsley had a dornex coverlet and bed curtains, RYE 33/12/160; an unknown debtor possessed a coverlet of 'lyftes' and 8 cushions of this material in 1563 RYE 33/12/17v; RYE 1/3/41–2; RYE 35/4/6; RYE 35/16; RYE 35/36.
52 RYE 33/9/148v; RYE 47/13/7; P.R.O. PROB 2/328; RYE 35/34; RYE 35/16; RYE 35/42; RYE 47/46/10.
53 RYE 1/4/237v, 253v; RYE 1/5/329,364; RYE 85/2.
54 RYE 1/5/74; Pearsall was left his licence to sell wines by George Raynoldes in his will in 1577 W/A7/67.
55 RYE 35/42.
56 RYE 85/2–3.
57 P.R.O. PROB 2/328; RYE 1/3/41–2; RYE 47/46/10; RYE 47/58/16; RYE 47/42/7 and RYE 47/40/14; RYE 35/42; RYE 35/35; RYE 35/31; W/A7/67.
58 RYE 35/31; RYE 35/42; RYE 47/46/10; RYE 47/40/14; RYE 47/42/7; RYE 35/35; RYE 1/3/41–2; P.R.O. PROB 2/328.
59 RYE 47/13/7; RYE 47/51/39; RYE 47/23/18.
60 W/A8/173; W/Al2/l; W/B3/28.
61 RYE 35/33; RYE 33/12/159v; RYE 35/19.
62 RYE 35/19; RYE 33/9/53v.
63 P.R.O. PROB 11/66/14; PROB 11/56/4.
64 P.R.O. PROB 11/11/7; PROB 11/49/14; PROB 11/56/4.
65 During the 1596–7 plague cutbreak,19 male and 20 female servants were buried, indicating a rough equality in numbers between the sexes. G.J. Mayhew 'Epidemic Mortality in sixteenth century Rye', *S.A.C.* 124 (l986), Table 3.
66 An analysis of the 447 apprenticeship indentures recorded in the Rye assembly books for the period 1562–1602 indicates that at least a quarter came from outside the town, mainly from Kent and Sussex parishes within a 10–15 mile radius. RYE 1/1/3–7.
67 See above Table 4.
68 P. Laslett 'Size and Structure of the Household in England Over Three Centuries', *Population Studies* 13 (1969) p 204; C. Phythian-Adams *Desolation of a City. Coventry and the Urban Crisis of the Late Middle Ages* (1979) p346.
69 For an explanation of these categories see Table 32b, notes.
70 For details of these epidemics see G.J. Mayhew 'Epidemic Mortality in sixteenth century Rye', *S.A.C.* 124 (1986), passim.
71 Their figures show infant mortality rates of 14.3% and 12.7% and child mortality rates (age 1–9) of 14.2% and 12.3% for males and females respectively in the period 1550–99. E.A. Wrigley and R.S. Schofield *The Population History of England 1541–1871: a reconstruction* (1981) Table 7.19 based on the results from 12 parishes of widely differing sizes and locations. However, these are not a random sample and 'the average measures are

unlikely to be representative of the country as a whole'. Ibid p 248.

72   D.M. Palliser *Tudor York* (1979) p 119. These findings contrast sharply with the very much higher levels of infant and child mortality suggested by U.M. Cowgill 'Life and Death in the Sixteenth Century in the City of York', *Population Studies* 21 (1967) pp 53–62. However,the methods employed by the latter are open to serious question. See L. Henry 'Some comments on Ursula M. Cowgill's article,' *Population Studies* 22 (1968) pp165–9.

73   A.D. Dyer *The City of Worcester in the Sixteenth Century* (1973) pp 39–43.

74   G.J. Mayhew 'Epidemic mortality in sixteenth century Rye', *S.A.C.* 124(1986) Table 5.

75   These figures are based on a relatively small sample of 143 males and 75 females which were identified from the 1595 households of Rye ratepayers between 1554–1604. They can be contrasted with Dyer's findings at Worcester,where the average age at death of those reaching the age of 20 was 46 years for men and 49 years for women. A.D. Dyer, op.cit.p43.

76   Age at marriage based on a sample of 127 males and 176 females identified from the 1595 households of Rye ratepayers. The figures indicate that marriages in Rye took place at a slightly younger age than at Worcester or than has been posited nationally. See A.D.Dyer op.cit. p37 where he suggests female age at marriage fluctuated bet ween 22 and 26 years in the period 1560–1609 and male age at marriage rose from 23 years in the 1560s to an average 29 years in the period after 1580. The mean length of marriage in Rye is significantly shorter than studies of other places have revealed. See R.A. Houlbrooke *The English Family* (1984) p 208. At Colyton the mean length of marriages was 20 years.

77   The criteria used for assessing death as a result of childbirth was to include all instances in which burial of the wife occurred on the same day as the baptism or burial of a newly-born infant (10),cases where burial followed the latter within a week (15) and up to one month after a birth (7 cases,5 within 13 days). These figures are more than three times the level suggested by Houlbrooke op.cit. p129.

78   Based on analysis of the 287 male householders whose first marriage was traced. Of these 125 either remarried or can be shown to be still alive at least five years after the death of their spouse. The results broadly confirm the figures for Clayworth, Nottinghamshire in 1688. P. Laskett *The World We Have Lost—further explored* (1983) p113.

79   Such a proportion is not dissimilar to the experience of medieval London where 60 per cent of surviving sons of aldermen were under 21 when their fathers died in the years 1318–1497. At Ealing in 1599 the figure is lower. There, 21 per cent of children under ten had lost at least one parent. R.A. Houlbrooke op.cit. p 217.

80   In 61 instances out of the 287 households.

81   RYE 1/3/43–8,97–102.

CHAPTER 6

1   C. Herrup: *The Common Peace: Legal structure and legal substance in East Sussex 1594–1640*. Unpublished PhD dissertation, Northwestern University, Evanston, Illinois (1982) esp Ch 7: Law and Morality in Early Modern England. See also the discussion on the contemporary equation of crime with sin in the 16th and 17th centuries in J. Sharpe: *Crime in Early Modern England 1550–1750* (1984) esp pp 4–6, 151–4.

2   *H.M.C. Report* 13, Appendix IV (1892), 113.

3   RYE 1/4/121–2.

4   PAR 467/7/9.
5   ibid.
6   RYE 1/5/283v.
7   RYE 1/5/307.
8   RYE 1/5/324v, 337v, 339 ; RYE 1/6/1v.
9   *H.M.C. Report* 13, Appendix IV, p77.
10 RYE 1/6/257.
11 RYE 1/4/257.
12 RYE 1/5/153-4.
13 RYE 1/4/322.
14 RYE 1/4/247.
15 RYE 1/5/214v.
16 Amongst the collection of contemporary comments on the state of society
    c1556 in the Rye Precedent Book, (RYE 57/4) is the following comment on
    idle and vagrant persons: 'Loyterers leaving labor which they like not will
    follow idlenes which they shold not. Some men will geve almes to them
    bicause they more suspecte theyre strength then pittie theire neede. And
    sutch content themselves better with idle beggery then with honest and
    profitable Labor being a waster of money a spoyler of vitaile a sucker of blode
    a breaker of orders a seaker of breakes a queller of life and a basiliske of the
    common welthe'. RYE 57/4/24.
17 RYE 1/5/155v-156, 341; RYE 1/7/468.
18 RYE 1/4/122.
19 RYE 1/4/367.
20 RYE 1/4/244.
21 RYE 1/3/182v; RYE 1/4/68v; RYE 47/20/3.
22 RYE 1/4/345.
23 RYE 1/4/348v.
24 RYE 1/4/357; RYE 1/5/90v, 157.
25 RYE 1/4/347v, 348.
26 RYE.1/5/65v.
27 RYE 60/4/21; RYE 60/5/266-7.
28 RYE 60/8/45,58v.
29 RYE 60/7/11v-12v.
30 Simon Duron, tailor, was found guilty of felony 13 December 1596 and
    claimed benefit of clergy which was granted to him. He was tried on two
    separate charges of felony 26 September 1597, acquitted of the first and
    found guilty of the second and was sentenced to hang. He was executed and
    buried 1 October. RYE 1/6/96, 106v, 178v-9v; PAR 467 1/1/2.
31 See for example RYE 1/6/213, 217v, 224 for the case of Hugh Buckland of
    Rye, sailor, and James Heyward of Battle, labourer, suspected of felony.
    Proclamation was made in hundred courts on 6,20 March 1598 and 3 April,
    when they were acquitted, no-one having come to prosecute.
32 RYE 1/3/84v,85,86,88.
33 RYE 1/4/97,98,99.
34 RYE 1/2/23v, 24v, 28,31v.
35 RYE 1/5/233, 235v, 236 ; RYE 1/6/274, 276v-277, 279 (following a dispute
    in a victualling house); RYE 1/6/14, 19-20; RYE 1/4/117-9.
36 RYE 1/5/233, 235v, 236.
37 RYE 1/5/338; PAR 467 1/1/2.
38 RYE 1/4/66v-7, 68v; RYE 1/4/319v-321.
39 See above n. 30.
40 RYE 1/6/291v-292, 293.

41 See for example the preceedings against the 2 Dieppe merchants 1/2/48v–49, 51v, 52v, 54.

42 RYE 1/4/117.

43 Jonne Wibley 'for hir common scoldinge, fightinge and brallinge aswell with hir husband as other hir neighbors' and in this instance with Dollinges widow 'whom she hath hurt in the hedd with a stonne' was ordered on 9 June 1582 to be 'sett in the Cage, and afterwards at full sea duckid.' Her husband was also ordered to pay the medical expenses 'for hellinge the said Dollinge widowes hedd.' The latter was merely set in the cage 'for hir disorder'. RYE 1/4/380.

44 RYE 1/5/343v; RYE 1/2/34v.

45 RYE 1/4/317.

46 RYE 1/3/202v; RYE 1/5/81; RYE 1/5/161v.

47 RYE 1/5/90,93,96v–97.

48 RYE 1/4/149; RYE 1/5/85.

49 RYE 1/4/183v.

50 RYE 1/3/179v.

51 RYE 1/5/336; RYE 1/4/135v; RYE 1/5/17; RYE 1/5/26.

52 RYE 1/5/302v; H.M.C.Report 13, Appendix IV, p52; RYE 1/4/223v.

53 RYE 1/4/194v,196,297v, 350v, 358; RYE 1/5/88, 102, 103–5.

54 RYE 60/4/314v.

55 RYE 1/5/332v; RYE 1/6/144v, 149.

56 RYE 1/4/252.

57 RYE 33/7/57v.

58 See above n. 35.

59 RYE 1/4/41; in July 1591 John Goffe was ordered to cease frequenting the houses of John Weekes, James Hurlestone or others suspected of ill rule. RYE 1/5/214v.

60 RYE 1/4/96v.

61 RYE 1/5/13.

62 RYE 1/1/4–5. An alien, having been found guilty and sentenced to hang he claimed the King's pardon and abjured the realm 1/1/6v.

63 RYE 1/4/214v–215, 217v–218.

64 H.M.C. Report 13, Appendix IV, p74; RYE 1/4/360v; RYE 47/13/68.

65 RYE 47/46/65.

66 RYE 1/1/34; and see above.The activities of coiners are a recurrent theme in the Rye records. See e.g. the examination of Captain Grammont, suspected of 'washinge and dimmyshinge the Quene's Majesties quoyne' in September 1571. He had with him three melting pots which he purchased in London and had been melting money for the previous half year. H.M.C. Report 13, Appendix IV,p 2. One of the more unusual trials held in Rye for which a special commission of Oyer and Terminer had to be obtained, was that of David Hewett, pewterer, for making counterfeit shillings and 6d pieces. The grand jury returned a bill of ignoramus on 30 March 1597. RYE 16/2; RYE 1/6/128.

67 RYE 1/2/55v.

68 47/13/17,42.

69 RYE 1/4/125v, 126.

70 RYE 1/3/32.

71 RYE 1/3/55; RYE 1/4/22v; RYE 1/4/216; RYE 1/4/248v.

72 RYE 1/4/242v; and see above n. 32.

73 RYE 1/5/288.

74 RYE 1/4/171; RYE 1/5/302.

75 RYE 1/4/57v; RYE 1/4/239v; RYE 1/5/315.
76 RYE 1/4/294.
77 Thomas Petty, for example, servant to Richard Mailler, was whipped at the cart's tail and Jone Humfry, a servant in the same household, rode in the cart for fornication, in September 1578. RYE 1/4/290. Other instances are RYE 1/4/380 and 1/4/374v (bastardy allegation), while George Allen and Margery Saunders were imprisoned and fined 10s to the poor, and ordered to provide for the child if there was one, for 'inordinate dalliance' in the house of Boniface Honnynges, their master, in August 1583. RYE 1/5/23.
78 RYE 1/4/321; RYE 1/2/43v; RYE 1/4/257v.
79 RYE 1/3/205.
80 RYE 1/4/136v; RYE 1/6/61; H.M.C. Report 13, Appendix IV, 104.
81 RYE 1/4/23; RYE 1/4/158v.
82 RYE 57/4/24v.

CHAPTER 7

1   W/A10/21.
2   RYE 60/9/322v–4; RYE 60/10/50, 59–60, 73v–4, 83v–4v, 91v–2, 99–100. 103–5v, 115v–6v, 129.
3   RYE 60/10/99–100, 115v–6v.
4   A.Ruddock : 'London capitalists and the decline of Southampton in the early Tudor period', Economic History Review, 2nd series, 2, (1949–50) p 147. Ruddock's analysis of the ownership of the cloth transported through Southampton from the mid-15th century onwards shows that, as in the case of Rye's transit trade a century later, it was almost wholly owned by London merchants. For a late sixteenth century defence of the role of London in England's trade from the viewpoint of a Londoner, see J.Stow : A Survey of London (1603, Everyman edition 1912, pp 495–7.
5   In the 1590s, Winchelsea experienced a minor recovery in its economic fortunes by exploiting its jurisdiction of the Puddle at the mouth of the Rother, where vessels were occasionally laded and unladed from lighters. See e.g. the entry in the quarterly lesser box returns for September to December 1600 (RYE 66/59) for 20 October 1600 which records he payment of 20d for the export of 10 tons of iron in John Sanders' ship and 'the rest of his lading in the puddle' for which no maltode was payable. It is interesting to note that a fall in the numbers of coastal shipment at Rye in the 1590s is matched by an increase in shipments from Winchelsea. This is most marked in the case of iron shipments, see C.E.Brent thesis tables 23,45c (pp 141 and 299).
6   RYE 66/20,22.
7   P.R.O. SP12/38/28.
8   In 1566, for example, 103 tons of plates were brought by lighter from Rye to Bodiam bridge for the Robertsbridge ironworks and 23½ tons steel was shipped out of Rye to London. In 1568 80 tons of iron was recorded as having been shipped from Cardiff to Rye and by lighter to Robertsbridge. There are similar references in the accounts for 1542–3 for lighterage from Robertsbridge to Rye in 1542–3. D.W. Crossley: Sidney Ironworks accounts 1541–1573 (Camden Fourth Series 15, 1975) pp 52n13, 208–19,246.
9   P.R.O. E122 147/18–19.
10 P.R.O. E190 739/16; E190 740/26.
11 P.R.O. E122 38/1–2,6–7.
12 Brent implies that the seasonal distribution of imports of coal from the north-east was a result of Rye and Hastings boats returning from the Scarborough voyage. C.E. Brent thesis p 315. An analysis of the ships carrying coal to Rye,

listed in the Rye maltode books 1580/1–1584/5 provides no clear evidence to support this view.

13   RYE 66/12,16,18,20,24.
14   RYE 66/60. However the Rye port books record occasional shipments of cochineal as early as 1571. R.F. Dell: *Rye Shipping Records 1566–1590* (Sussex Record Society 64, 1966) pp 65,109,112,139–41.
15   For the glass works at Beckley, see *H.M.C. Report* 13 Appendix IV (1892) pp 62–3,75–6. For a fuller discussion of this glass works and of the trade in glass through Rye, see G.H. Kenyon: *The Glass Industry of the Weald* (1967) pp 18n,113,211–2.
16   RYE 66/17,47,48,55.
17   RYE 66/12–15.
18   RYE 66/12–19,23,27,42,48,55,62,66,69.
19   P.R.O. E122 200/8.
20   The enrolled customs accounts show the customs revenue for the port of Chichester (including Rye) more than doubling, from an average £548 a year in the 6 years 1564–70 to £1375 a year in the 4 years 1578–82. Unfortunately those for 1570–78, when the cloth trade at Rye was probably at its height, have not survived. E 356/28.
21   For this later temporary revival in the transit trade in cloth, see C.E. Brent *thesis* pp 298, 302. For a recent study of Rouen's trade in the late sixteenth century, see P.H. Benedict, 'Rouen's Trade during the Era of the Religious Wars (1560–1600)' in *Journal of European Economic History* 13 (Rome, 1984) pp 29–74.
22   P.R.O. SP12/38/28; SP15/22; E122 200/9.
23   Quoted in L. Stone: 'Elizabethan Overseas Trade', *Economic History Review*, 2nd series, 2 (1949–50) p 41 from R.H. Tawney and E. Power: *Tudor Economic Documents* Vol 2 (1924) p 97.
24   P.R.O. E122 37/4.
25   P.R.O. E122 36/10,13; 37/3,4.
26   The earliest reference to the collection of local maltodes on the export of billets was in the chamberlains' accounts for 1560/1 RYE 60/7/241v.
27   RYE 60/6/95,96v,106v; RYE 60/7/317; RYE 60/9/242. The trade in billets seems to have been particularly lucrative, with profits of almost 100%. According to a letter of process on behalf of Robert Jacson and James Milles against William Jarvis of Tenterden for non-delivery of 110,000 of 160,000 billets sold to the former in April 1573 at 2s 6d a thousand to be delivered at Reding flotte the following Michaelmas, they were selling for 5s a thousand in Rye that winter. RYE 47/11/66.
28   P.R.O. E122 147/18.
29   P.R.O. E190 739/16; E190 740/26.
30   RYE 1/5/162v,203v; RYE 60/9/306v,315–6,322: RYE 60/10/1–2,20–1; RYE 1/5/352v: RYE 1/6/178; RYE 1/7/344,412. The detailed accounts for the Storehouse for the period 4 May 1591–1 January 1592 indicate that the length of time most of the goods were deposited there varied from three days to eight weeks, with the majority being removed within a week. Among items deposited in the Storehouse during this 8-month period were 40 assorted horsepacks and other packs; 3 sacks or pockets of hops; 2 barrels of pitch and 2 barrels of soap with other wares for a Tenterden merchant; an unspecified quantity of woad for certain Cranbrook clothiers; 2 loads of madder, a wagon and a variety of trunks, hampers, baskets and barrels of different sizes, worth £2 11s 9d in dues. Almost as much was earned from the fees for weighing various goods (1d a hundredweight), amounting to £1 17s 1d during the

same 8-month period, principally 25s from a Southampton merchant for an unspecified quantity of woad (probably 15 tons), 106 hundredweight of hops, 14 hundredweight of prunes, 13 hundredweight of madder, 5 hundredweight of cheese and 4 hundredweight of brasell. RYE 60/9/307v–8,315.

31 RYE 66/58,59,62.
32 RYE 60/7/48.
33 RYE 47/4/10; RYE 47/11/76; RYE 47/11/18; RYE 47/4 (unnumbered); RYE 47/11/4; RYE 47/17/51; RYE 47/18/5; RYE 47/18/84; RYE 47/4/89; RYE 47/4/18; RYE 47/18/31; RYE 47/18/83; RYE 47/18/36; RYE 47/4/65; RYE 47/11/56; RYE 47/14/13; RYE 47/11/81; RYE 47/17/45.
34 P.R.O. E190 739/16; E190 740/26.
35 RYE 66/1,5–6.
36 P.R.O. E190 739/16; E190 740/26.
37 RYE 66/12–69. Thus the average number of seams sold by William Tolkin, jurat, and Henry Godsmarke, who traded throughout the period fell from 376 and 499 respectively in the early 1580s to only 217½ and 251 respectively in the latter period.
38 RYE 1/3/183v–4; RYE 57/1/66v–7v.
39 RYE 1/4/186.
40 RYE 1/4/203,227.
41 RYE 1/4/297'
42 RYE 1/5/35v,43v; RYE 66/24–7.
43 RYE 1/5/120; RYE 66/33–36; RYE 1/5/274; RYE 66/55–69. For exports of iron from Winchelsea and Rye during this period see C.E. Brent *thesis*, table 23, p 141. For the Rye assembly's attempts to stop the trading of billets by Rye inhabitants outside of the town's liberties in order to avoid paying maltode 24 July 1591 see RYE 1/5/213–v.
44 RYE 1/7/446–7v. At the same time quarterly charges for craftsmen (master carpenters, shipwrights, masons etc) were introduced, payable into the great box. RYE 1/7/448.
45 RYE 1/5/28; RYE 99/6; RYE 47/10/70; RYE 47/39/1; RYE 1/5/181v. In November 1590 the assembly ordered a new light to be erected near the old light by Camber Castle for the better direction of the fishermen (who were to contribute £4) and others. Foreign vessels entering the harbour were to pay 12d each towards the light and English vessels under 40 tons 6d, or over 40 tons 12d. For other examples of shipwrecks in the Camber see RYE 47/25, pt 2 no 12, RYE 47/30/40, RYE 47/30/97b and 106. An inventory of the goods remaining in the Storehouse from the Nightingale of London, which ran aground in the Camber in October 1574, reveals that she was carrying 68 chests of sugar, 27 hogsheads, 2 butts and 3 pipes of (wainscot) panels, 17½ hogsgeads of gum and 9 hogsheads of molasses. RYE 47/10/93. The Lesser Box returns also record the keyage of 16 qtrs of 'wrack grain' (21 November 1580) and 15 tons of 'wrack wines' (27 November 1582) RYE 66/12,20.
46 S.A.S. A593–7.
47 RYE 1/3/92v; RYE 1/4/207; RYE 47/145; RYE 99/1.
48 RYE 1/4/227; RYE 99/5.
49 RYE 99/1. However only a provision for the prevention of the dumping of ballast in the Camber was actually passed into law (2/3 Edward VI, c.30).
50 RYE 99/4.
51 RYE 1/4/72v,80v,84,88–95,155v,156,192,232v; RYE 1/7/385v–6; RYE 47/63/73–4.
52 RYE 1/4/235,241v,252v; RYE 47/13/69.
53 RYE 1/4/246v–8.

54 RYE 1/4/263,264,274v. The works were evidently still far from completion in December 1577, when it was decreed by the assembly that 'for the better furtherance' of the works at Strand for the amendment of the haven, 'one person of every house beinge able, shall fynde an able person to worke eche daye that their turne shall come at the said worke at their owne charge', young men working for themselves, included. RYE 1/4/276v.

55 RYE 1/5/149v,150v,165v,177–8,185,211v,215v,276v–7,281v–2v,321–v, 325; RYE 47/51/72–3. Genebelli, who had previously been employed in the royal service, in return for his services to Rye, requested the grant of a pension for 25 years equivalent to a proportion of the increased dues resulting from the improved harbour and also a monopoly during his lifetime of the amendment of any other havens in England by the methods he intended using. RYE 47/45/1a, 6. There is a considerable amount of other correspondence relating to Sr Genebelli's scheme, principally in the files of correspondence for 1592/3 and 1593/4. RYE 47/48 and RYE 47/51, together with a map showing the state of the harbour which was attached to his original demands in August 1591 RYE 47/45/1a.

56 RYE 1/5/331, 337, 339v, 362, 366; RYE 72/2–4.

57 RYE 99/11; RYE 1/6/112, 123v, 137v, 146–v, 171v, 192, 202, 235–6, 239, 250, 262; RYE 1/7/329.

58 RYE 1/6/114v–5,118v–9,137v, 168, 198v–201; 25/v 255v; RYE 1/7/311, 324v–8v, 412, 437v, 464; RYE 99/13; RYE 77/7. According to a royal licence for the collection of a benevolence throughout the southern and eastern counties in 1628, the cost of repaving Rye's walls, quayside and jetties was estimated then at not less than £3,000. RYE 99/14.

59 Ultimately the sluice proved a failure and was dismantled in 1610. C.E. Brent, *thesis*, pp 324–5. Another even more grandiose scheme, also aimed at diverting the Appledore channel of the Rother southwards along the western side of the town so that it would flow out through Rye harbour, costing some £60,000 similarly failed in the early 1770s. L.A. Vidler: *A New History of Rye* (Rye, 1934) pp 104–7.

Select Glossary

Most of the definitions have been taken from the *Oxford English Dictionary* (Oxford, 1971), supplemented by C. Cross: *York Clergy Wills 1520-1600) : I : Minster Clergy* (York, 1984), with additional information from W.D. Parish and H. Hall: *A Dictionary of the Sussex Dialect* (Chichester, 1957) and R. Bird: *The Journal of Giles Moore* (Sussex record Society Vol 68, Lewes, 1971).

Aleconner Officer appointed at the annual hundred court each December to inspect the quality and maintain the assize of ale.

Alum White mineral salt used in dyeing cloth.

Andiron Firedog.

Angel Gold coin,originally worth 6s 8d, rising to 10s in the early 1550s.

Apostle spoons Often large silver spoons with figures of the apostles on the handle.

Assembly Meeting of the mayor, jurats and freemen at which the administrative business of the corporation was transacted. Between 1575 and 1590, consisted of the mayor, jurats and common councillors.

Assize of bread, ale, beer. Regulation of the price and quality of these commodities in relation to the price of grain.

Ballot A small bale of 70-120 lbs.

Barke A small ship.

Barrel A cylindrical wooden cask, of specific capacity: beer: 36 gallons; ale: 32 gallons; soap: 30 gallons or 256lbs.

Bearward Keeper of a performing bear.

Billet Wood cut for fuel, firewood of a standard measure.

Bonne Beer cask, measure of capacity equivalent to a tun or 252 gallons.

Boulting hutch Wooden box for sifting grain or flour for baking bread.

Brandiron Iron framework for supporting cooking vessels over a fire.

Brotherhood Meeting of representatives of the 7 head ports of the Cinque Ports Confederation twice-yearly at New Romney on the second Tuesday after Easter and the third Tuesday in July to transact customary business and to appoint bailiffs to go with the fishing fleet to Great Yarmouth.

Buckram Coarse linen or cloth stiffened with gum.

Budge barrels, carts, used for carrying water.

Cage Literally a cage, used for the public exhibition of malefactors, mainly females.

Caliver Light musket or harquebus with a $\frac{2}{3}$ inch bore, about 3ft in length.

Cesse, sesse Town rate, literally a*sess(e)*ment.

Chafer, chafing dish Vessel to hold burning coals to heat anything placed upon it.

Chalder Measure of capacity, especially of coal, usually 36 bushels.

Clothes press Moveable clothes chest.

Cobiron Iron uprights on an open hearth on which spits were placed.

Cochineal Scarlet dyestuff composed of dried insects similar to wood-lice, imported from the New World.

Cockboat Small boat, mainly used in and around the harbour, manned by one person. The smallest type of fishing vessel, also used for lading goods into larger ships.

Collar Iron collar fixed to a post for public exhibition of petty criminals, usually males.

Conduit Water pipes conveying the town's water from springs to the taps or cocks from which it flowed out. Also used to denote the places where water could be collected from the cocks.

Corselet Piece of armour protecting the body as distinct from the limbs.

Cotton goods Coarse woollen fabric or type of frieze.

Crayer Small trading vessel also used as a larger fishing vessel, generally about 25-30 tons.

Cruse Large drinking vessel, otherwise a pot or tankard.

Cucking stool Wooden chair for public exhibition and ducking of disorderly women.

Diaper Linen with a diamond patterned weave.

Diker A lot of ten, used with reference to leather hides or skins.

Dosser Pannier or basket, generally slung in pairs over the backs of packhorses used to transport fresh fish overland to London. A unit of capacity, 3 dossers = 1 seam.

Fardel Small pack or parcel.

Fell Sheepskin with fleece left on.

Feter Wholesale fishmonger.

Firkin Small barrel of 8 gallons (ale) or 9 gallons (beer). A thirty-second of a tun.

Flock Coarse tufts and left-overs of wool used for stuffing mattresses, pillows etc.

Fustick Type of wood used to produce a yellow dye.

Fyndall Literally 'that which is found'. Items of flotsam and jetsam picked up by mariners and fishermen, their servants or apprentices.

Garth Hearth or enclosure for a fire.

Gorgett Piece of armour for the throat.

Grand jury Jury sworn to enquire into an indictment before it is submitted to a trial jury.

Graunlet Gauntlet.

Great box Quarterly receipts of dues for the exercise of the following land-based occupations : shops, beer tiplers, bakers, brewers, feters, butchers, vintners and occasionally artificers.

Guestling Special brotherhood, called to transact urgent business. The first reference to the term occurs in August 1526. It was at these meetings that the limbs, or minor ports, came to be represented.

Heap, hepe Payment to town made on admission as an ost.

Hogshead Large barrel equivalent to a quarter of a tun or 72 gallons (beer), 64 gallons (ale).

Holberd, halberd Long-handled spear with a lateral axe-blade.

313

Horsepack Large pack, generally of cloth or wool, approximately 240-280 lbs weight.

Hostler, ostler Man employed at an inn to attend to horses.

Hoye Small merchant or passenger vessel.

Hundred Ultimate judicial and legislative organ of corporation, comprising mayor, jurats and freemen. Summoned to elect mayor and town officers, to choose parliamentary representatives, grant cesses and approve major administrative decisions. Sometimes used to describe court summoned for trial of felonies, for which *see* sessions.

Ignoramus Bill of Verdict of Grand jury dismissing an indictment.

Indenture Deed or agreement between two or more parties, so called because each copy is executed on the same piece of parchment, then cut in a wavy line for proof of identity.

Inned, inning Reclamation of marshland, reclaimed marshland

Jurat One of up to 12 magistrates chosen by the mayor to 'assist in justice' and matters of administration. Equivalent to an alderman in some other corporations.

Keyage Dues on goods and livestock passing through the port.

Kilderkine Barrel holding 16 gallons (ale), 18 gallons (beer). A sixteenth of a ton.

Laver Wash basin.

Lesser box Quarterly receipts of maltodes or dues on goods passing through the port, including grand and petty passage (tolls on ships and passengers),keyage, measurage, dues on fish of osts and marketmen and on wood.

Limback Alembick or still for making spirits.

Madder Vegetable dyestuff from the roots of the madder plant producing a red dye.

Maltodes Local customs dues imposed by the corporation on a variety of goods passing through the port.

Manfare Amount of nets appertaining to one fisherman.

Mark 13s 4d.

Measurage Charge levied by the corporation for weighing certain bulk items, such as salt and grain entering the port.

Messuage Land or property comprising a dwelling house, its appurtenances and curtilege.

Musters Annual review of able-bodied men between 16 and 60, together with their weapons. Also the occasions for the exercise of their military skills.

Nut Goblet made from a coconut shell.

Ost Wholesale fishmonger or feter appointed as an agent of the London Company of Fishmongers to supply fish to the London fishmarkets.

Ostry Stables or harness store.

Painted cloth Cheap wallhanging common in the sixteenth century used as a substitute for tapestry.

Partizan Long-handled spear with a lateral blade similar to a holberd.

Partlet Outer garment worn by women about the neck and upper part of the chest, a neckerchief.

Pickery Pilfering.

Pin Small barrel of $4\frac{1}{2}$ gallons (beer), 4 gallons (ale). A sixty-fourth of a ton.

Platt Plan or map.

Pocket Bag or sack, usually of specific measure. In the case of hops, 168lbs or 12 stone.

Pottle Pot or vessel containing the measure of a pottle, or 2 quarts.

Presentment Verdict or finding of a Grand jury. In Rye the hundred jury was sworn annually in December to present a range of petty offences ranging from highway encroachments and leaky gutters to unapprenticed tradesmen and unlicensed alehouses.

Proynes Prunes.

Rippier Carrier of fresh fish overland from Rye and other ports to London by pack-horses.

Sarcenet Very fine and soft silk material.

Saye Cloth of fine texture resembling serge.

Seam In local usage equivalent to a quarter or 28lbs of grain or 3 dossers of fresh fish.

Sessions Quarter sessions.

Settle Long wooden bench seat with arms and high back and a box under the seat.

Soler Loft, attic or garret.

Stupnet Saucepan.

Taffeta Glossy silk or similar fabric.

Tapster One who draws beer or ale at an inn.

Teasel Dried prickle or burr used for teasing or dressing cloth.

Tester The ceiling or canopy of a four-poster bed. Also a sixpence piece.

Ton, tun Liquid measure equivalent to 252 gallons wine, 288 gallons beer. One ton equals 2 pipes or butts, 3 puncheons, 4 hogsheads, 6 tierces, 8 barrels, 16 kilderkines, 32 firkins or 64 pins. Also used to measure the capacity of the holds of ships.

Trammell Long narrow fishing net.

Trencher Large plate or platter of wood, metal or earthenware often used for serving meat.

Truckle bed Low bed on truckles or castors, stored underneath an ordinary bed.

Truss Bundle, generally 56-60lbs.

Vanbrase Piece of armour covering the fore-arm.

Wainscot Oak panelling.

Weyner Calf or lamb weaned during that year.

Withernam Legal process in cases of outstanding debts for goods or services supplied to non-residents whereby continued refusal to pay results in the distraint of goods to the same value as the outstanding debt from any fellow townsman of the debtor. Notification of such debts was made to the town authorities of the debtor's home town, who would then examine the offending party, and in default of a satisfactory explanation, compel payment in order to avoid retaliation against their fellow townsmen.

BIBLIOGRAPHY

a) **Manuscript sources**
i) **East Sussex Record Office, Lewes.**

Rye Corporation MSS

RYE 1/1-7 Hundred, sessions and assembly books 1546-1603.

RYE 33/6-17 Court of record: roll and books 1487-1603.

RYE 35/1-51 Court of record: plea rolls 1536-1603.

RYE 42/1-8 Court of record: case papers 1486-92.

RYE 47/1-100 General files: correspondence, depositions of witnesses, royal proclamations and other papers 1495-1624.

RYE 48 Royal proclamations 1559-1660.

RYE 57/1-14 Charter, custumals, oaths and precedent books 15c-1 7c.

RYE 60/3-10 Chamberlains' account books 1479-1606.

RYE 61/1-12 Land chamberlain's rough accounts 1570-1603.

RYE 62/1-3 Sea chamberlain's rough accounts 1589-98.

RYE 65/1-79 Great box: quarterly receipts 1573-1603.

RYE 66/1-69 Lesser box: quarterly receipts 1573-1603.

RYE 147/1-13 Churchwardens' accounts 1513-97.

RYE 7/1-4 Grand jury presentments 1579-86.

RYE 8/1-2 Indictments, late 16c.

RYE 12/1-8 Treason trial papers of Randall Bell, capper, 1539.

RYE 13/1-27 Witchcraft trial papers of Susanna Swapper and Anne Taylor, 1607-9.

RYE 14/1-21 Victuallers' recognizances 1586.

RYE 15/1 Rough list of residents (preparatory to drawing up a sesse) 1488, amended 1491/2.

RYE 16/1-2 Miscellaneous quarter sessions papers 1555, 1597.

RYE 28/1-12 Bonds for maintenance of orphans, bastards and apprentices 1567-1603.

RYE 45/1-20 Crown grants, writs, 1382-1569.

RYE 46/1-9 Borough grants and bonds 1519-97.

RYE 50/1-2 Miscellaneous correspondence and papers c1590.

RYE 58/9 Agreement between Lord Warden and Cinque Ports 1574.

RYE 71/1-17 Minor accounts 1590-1603.

RYE 72/1-8 Harbour and military accounts 1588-99.

RYE 77/3-7 Borough sesses 1491/2-1610.

RYE 79/1-6 Schedules of dues payable to bailiff and corporation, 17c.

RYE 80/1-15 Billets for allowance of tenths and fifteenths 1488-1603.

RYE 81/1-2 Receipts for benevolence, 1523.

RYE 85/1-3 Muster lists late 15c, 1598-9.

RYE 91,123-7,130-1, Deeds, draft deeds and agreements relating to Rye, 135,137,139-140 1486-1611.

RYE 95-8 Commissioners of Sewers: minutes, draft minutes, decrees, petitions and evidence 1595-1604.

RYE 99/1-15 Draft bills, petitions and agreements concerning Rye harbour 1548-1628.

RYE 111/1 Deed of feoffment, Welles's almshouse, 1551.

RYE 119/1-5 Town rentals and arrears, 1586-1600.

RYE 132/2-15 Maps and plans of Rye and Rother levels, late 16c-1666.

RYE 145/1-8 Accounts of Francis Bolton, town clerk, 1592-7.

Rye Parish records

PAR 46711/1/1-2 Registers of baptisms, marriages and burials 1538-1635.
PAR 467/7/9 Treatise on the commandments by Richard Fletcher, minister, c1580.

Lewes Archdeaconry Probate Records

W/A1-18 Registers of wills 1540-1624.
W/C4,11 Registers of wills 1535-45, 1567-9.
W/B1-5 Registers of administrations 1570-1627.

Winchelsea Corporation Records

WIN 51-5 Court Books: assemblies, hundred, record and Strangers 1527-1627.
WIN 62 Extracts from Winchelsea court books 1430-1767 (nd, c1770).

ii) West Sussex Record Office, Chichester

Lewes Archdeaconry court records
Ep II/5/1-6 Deposition books 1580-1604.

iii) Kent Archives Office, Maidstone
Cinque Ports Archives

CP/N2 Accounts and bills for naval expedition to Cadiz 1595-6.

iv) Public Record Office, Chancery Lane, London

E122 Customs accounts.
E179 Lay subsidy rolls, benevolences and forced loans.
E190 Port books.
STAC 5 Court of Star Chamber, proceedings (Elizabeth 1).
SP 1 State Papers, Henry VIII. General.
SP 12 State Papers Domestic, Elizabeth I.
SP 15 State Papers Domestic, Addenda, Edward VI to James I.
PROB 2 Prerogative Court of Canterbury: early probate inventories.
PROB 11 Prerogative Court of Canterbury: wills registers.
MPF/212 Map of Rye harbour and Rother, 1572.

b) Printed sources, calendars, etc.

W. B. Bannerman (ed): *The Visitations of Sussex, 1530 and 1633-4* (Harleian Society 53, 1905).
J. S. Brewer, J. Gairdner and R.H. Brodie (ed): *Letters and papers, foreign and domestic, of the reign of Henry VIII, preserved in the Public record Office, the British Museum, and elsewhere in England.* (23 vols 1862-1932).
D. S. Chambers (ed): *Faculty Office Register* (1966).
A. C. Chibnall and A. V. Woodman (ed): *Subsidy Roll for the County of Buckingham Anno 1524.* (Buckinghamshire record Society, 8, 1950).
J. S. Cockburn (ed): *Calendar of Assize records: Sussex Indictments, Elizabeth 1* (1975).
J. Cornwell (ed): *The Lay Subsidy Rolls for the County of Sussex 1524-25* (Sussex record Society, 56, 1956).
D. W. Crossley (ed): *Sidney Ironworks accounts 1541-1573* (Camden Fourth Series 15, (1975).
J. R. Dasent (ed): *Acts of the Privy Council of England 1542-1604* (32 Vols, 1890-1907).
R. F. Dell: *Rye Shipping records 1566-90* (Sussex Record Society, 64, 1966).

R. F. Dell: *The records of Rye Corporation: A Catalogue* (Lewes, 1962).
R. F. Dell: *Winchelsea Corporation records: A Catalogue* (Lewes, 1963)
B. Dietz (ed): *The Port and Trade of Early Elizabethan London: Documents.* (1972)
J. Foster (ed): *The Register of Admissions to Gray's Inn 1521-1889.* (1889).
John Foxe: *Acts and Monuments* (3 Vols (ed) Rev J Cumming 1875).
House of Commons Members. Parliaments of England 1213-1701 (1878)
P.L. Hughes and J. F. Larkin: *Tudor Royal Proclamations.* (2 Vols 1964 and 1969).
F. Hull: *A Calendar of the White and Black Books of the Cinque Ports 1432-1955* (1966).
S. Jeake: *Charters of the Cinque Ports, Two Ancient Towns, and Their Members* (1728).
R. Lemon M. A. Everett-Green (ed): *Calendar of State Papers, domestic series, of the reigns of Edward VI, Mary, Elizabeth, preserved in the State Paper Department of Her Majesty's Public record Office* (12 Vols 1856-72).
Royal Commission on Historical Manuscripts: *Calendar of the Manuscripts of the Marquis of Salisbury* Pt 5 (1894).
Royal Commission on Historical Manuscripts: *Fifth Report* (1876)
Royal Commission on Historical Manuscripts: *Thirteenth Report* Appendix IV (1892).
The Population of Southampton: A Historical Survey. (Southampton City Record Office, 1978).
Statutes of the Realm 4 Pt 1 (1819, reprinted 1963).
J. Stow: *A Survey of London* (1603 edition, Everyman 1912).
H. A. C. Sturgen (ed): *Register of Admissions to the Honourable Society of the Middle Temple* (1949).
R. Tittler (ed): *Accounts of the Roberts Family of Boarzell, Sussex. c1568-1582* (Sussex Record Society 71, 1979).
C. Webb and A. E. Wilson (eds): *The Ancient Customs of Brighthelmstone 1580* (Brighton, 1952).
R. B. Wenham (ed): *List and Analysis of State Papers, Foreign Series, Elizabeth 1, preserved in the Public Record Office* (3 Vols 1964-80).

c) Unpublished articles, reports and theses

C. E. Brent: *Employment, Land Tenure and Population in Eastern Sussex 1540-1640.* Unpublished D. Phil. thesis, University of Sussex (1973)
A. Gregory: *Slander accusations and social control in late 16th and early 17th Century England with particular reference to Rye (Sussex), 1590-1615.* Unpublished D. Phil. thesis, University of Sussex (1985).
C. Herrup: *The Common Peace: Legal structure and legal substance in East 1594-1640.* Unpublished PhD dissertation, Northwestern University, Evanston, Illinois (1982).
S. P. Hipkin: 'Class Structure and Social Control in Rye: 1600-1660'. A paper delivered to the early modern history seminar, Oxford University, October 1980.

d) Secondary sources, books

S.T. Bindoff (ed): *The House of Commons 1509-1558* (3 vols, 1982).
P.J. Bowden: *The Wool Trade in Tudor and Stuart England* (1962).
J.S. Burn: *The History of the French, Walloon, Dutch, and other Foreign Protestant Refugees settled in England from the Reign of Henry VIII to the Revocation of the Edict of Nantes* (1846).
E.M. Carus-Wilson and O. Coleman: *England's Export Trade 1275-1547* (1963).
E.K. Chambers: *The Medieval Stage* (2 vols 1903).

H.P. Clark: *Guide and History of Rye* (Rye, 1861).
P. Clark: *English Provincial Society from the Reformation to the Revolution* (1977).
P. Clark and P. Slack (ed): *Crisis and Order in English Towns* (1972).
P. Clark and P. Slack: *English Towns in Transition 1500-1700* (1972).
H. Cleere and D. Crossley: *The Iron Industry of the Weald* (1985).
J.A. Collard: *A Maritime History of Rye* (Rye, 1978).
H.M. Colvin: *The History of the King's Works, IV, 1485-1660: Pt 2* (1982).
C. Creighton: *History of Epidemics in Britain* (2 vols, 1891 and 1894).
D. Cressy: *Literacy and Social Order* (1980).
H.C. Darby (ed): *A New Historical Geography of England Before 1600* (1976).
Sir L. Stephen and Sir S. Lee (ed): *The Dictionary of National Biography* 22 vols (1917 on).
A.D. Dyer: *The City of Worcester in the Sixteenth Century* (Leicester, 1973).
G. Elton: *Policy and Police. The Enforcement of the Reformation in the Age of Thomas Cromwell* (1972).
J. Foster: *Alumni Oxonienses 1500-1714* (1892).
R.D. Gwyn: *The History and Contributions of the Huguenots in Britain* (1985).
P.W. Hasler (ed): *The House of Commons 1559-1603* (3 vols, 1981).
W. Holloway: *The History and Antiquities of the Ancient Town and Port of Rye, in the County of Sussex* (1847).
W.G. Hoskins: *Local History in England* (1959).
R.A. Houlbrooke: *The English Family 1450-1700* (1984).
G.H. Kenyon: *The Glass Industry of the Weald* (1967).
P. Laslett: *The World We Have Lost—further explored* (1983).
Local Population Studies Supplement: *The Plague Reconsidered: A new look at its origins and effects in 16th and 17th Century England* (1977).
W.T. McCaffrey: *Exeter 1540-1640* (1975 edition).
J.D. Mackie: *The Earlier Tudors 1485-1558* (1957).
R.B. Manning: *Religion and Society in Elizabethan Sussex* (Leicester, 1969).
J. Meryon: *An account of the Origin and Formation of the Harbour of the Ancient Town of Rye; of the causes of its present decay and of the means whereby it may be restored to its pristine depth and capacity, so as to become a considerable tide-harbour, and a useful harbour of refuge* (1845).
M. Mollat: *Comptabilité du Port de Dieppe au XVe siècle* (Paris, 1951).
M. Mollat: *Le Commerce Maritime Normand à la fin du Moyen Age* (Paris, 1952).
I. Nairn and N. Pevsner: *The Buildings of England: Sussex* (1965).
D. M. Palliser: *Tudor York* (1979).
C. Phythian-Adams: *Desolation of a City: Coventry and the Urban Crisis of the Later Middle Ages* (1979).
C. Phythian-Adams et al (ed): *The Fabric of the Traditional Community* (Open University Course Unit 5, A322, 1977).
G.D. Ramsay: *English Overseas Trade during the Centuries of Emergence* (1957).
H.R. Schubert: *History of the British Iron and Steel Industry from c450 B.C. to A.D. 1775* (1957).
J. Sharpe: *Crime in Early Modern England 1550-1750* (1984).
J.F.D. Shrewsbury: *A History of Bubonic Plague in the British Isles* (1971).
C. De Smedt: *De Engelske Natie Te Antwerpen In de 16e Eeuw (1496-1582)* (2 vols, Antwerp, 1954).
L. Straker: *Wealden Iron* (1931).
K. Thomas: *Religion and the Decline of Magic* (1971).
J. Venn and J.A. Venn: *Alumni Cantabrigienses: Pt. 1, From the earliest times to 1751* (4 vols, 1922).
W. Page and L. Salzman (eds): *Victoria County History, Sussex* (1905-37).

L.A. Vidler: *A New History of Rye* (Rye, 1934).

J. de Vries: *European Urbanization 1500-1800* (1984).

R.B. Wernham *After the Armada* (1984).

T.S. Willan: *Studies in Elizabethan Foreign Trade* (Manchester, 1959).

E.A. Wrigley and R.S. Schofield: *The Population History of England 1541-1871: A reconstruction* (1981).

e) **Secondary sources, articles**

J.H. Andrews: 'Rye Harbour in the reign of Charles II' *Sussex Archaeological Collections*, 94 (1956) pp.35-42.

J. Manwaring-Baines: 'The Ships of the Cinque Ports in 1586/7' *Sussex Notes and Queries*, 13 (1952) pp.241-4.

P.H. Benedict: 'Rouen's Trade during the Era of the Religious Wars, (1560-1600)', *Journal of European Economic History*, 13 (Rome, 1984) pp.29-74.

Y.S. Brenner: 'The Inflation of Prices in Early Sixteenth Century England' *Economic History Review*, 2nd Series, 14 (1961-2), pp.225-39.

Y.S. Brenner: 'Inflation of Prices in England, 1551-1650' *Economic History Review*, 2nd Series, 15 (1962-3), pp.266-84.

C.E. Brent: 'Devastating Epidemic in the Countryside of Eastern Sussex between Harvest Years 1558 and 1640', *Local Population Studies*, 14 (1975) pp.42-48.

C.E. Brent: 'Urban Employment and Population in Sussex between 1550 and 1660', *Sussex Archaeological Collections*, 113 (1976) pp.35-50.

G.S. Butler: 'Notes on Rye and its Inhabitants', *Sussex Archaeological Collections*, 17 (1865) pp.123-36.

G.S. Butler: 'The Vicars of Rye and their Patrons', *Sussex Archaeological Collections*, 13 (1861) pp.270-6.

P. Clark: 'Reformation and Radicalism in Kentish Towns c.1500-1553', *The Urban Classes, the Nobility and the Reformation, Publications of the German Historical Institute*, 5 (1979) pp.107-27.

P. Collinson: 'Cranbrook and the Fletchers: Popular and Unpopular Religion in the Kentish Weald', P.N. Brooks (ed): *Reformation Principle and Practice. Essays in honour of Arthur Geoffrey Dickens* (1980) pp.173-202.

W.D. Cooper: 'Notes of Winchelsea in and after the Fifteenth Century', *Sussex Archaeological Collections*, 8 (1856) pp.201-34.

W.D. Cooper: 'Protestant Refugees in Sussex', *Sussex Archaeological Collections*, 13 (1861) pp.180-208.

J. Cornwell: 'English Country Towns in the Fifteen-twenties', *Economic History Review*, 2nd series, 15 (1962) pp.54-69.

J. Cornwell: 'English Population', *Economic History Review*, 2nd series, 23 (1970) pp.32-44.

J. Cornwell: 'Forestry and the Timber Trade in Sussex, 1560-1642', *Sussex Notes and Queries*, 14 (1955) pp.85-91.

U.M. Cowgill: 'Life and Death in the Sixteenth Century in the City of York', *Population Studies*, 21 (1967) pp.53-62.

D. Cressy: 'Levels of Illiteracy in England 1530-1730', *Historical Journal*, 20 (1977) pp.1-24.

A.J.F. Dulley: 'The Early History of the Rye Fishing Industry', *Sussex Archaeological Collections*, 107 (1969) pp.36-64.

F.J. Fisher: 'Commercial Trends and Policy in Sixteenth-Century England', *Economic History Review*, 10 (1939-40) pp.95-117.

F.J. Fisher: 'Influenza and Inflation in Tudor England', *Economic History Review*, 2nd series, 18 (1965) pp.120-9.

W.G.L. Gilbert: 'The Street Names of Rye', *Rye Museum Association Newsletter*,

4 (Rye, October 1959) pp.13-16.

J.J. Goring: 'The General Proscription of 1522', *English Historical Review*, 86 (1971) pp.681-705.

W.J. Hardy: 'Foreign Refugees at Rye', *Proceedings of the Huguenot Society of London*, 2 (1887-8) pp.406-24, 567-77.

M.F. and T.H. Hollingsworth: 'Plague Mortality Rates by Age and Sex in the Parish of St Botolph's without Bishopsgate, London, 1603', *Population Studies* 25 (1971) pp.131-46.

W.M. Homan: 'The Marshes between Hythe and Pett. An attempt at the reconstruction of their topography as it was in the Middle Ages', *Sussex Archaeological Collections*, 79 (1938) pp.199-223.

P.M. Johnston: 'Wall Painting in a House of Rye formerly known as the Old Flushing Inn', *Sussex Archaeological Collections*, 50 (1907) pp.116-37.

P. Laslett: 'Size and Structure of the Household in England Over Three Centuries', *Population Studies*, 13 (1969) pp.199-223.

H. Lovegrove: 'Remains of Two Old Vessels Found at Rye, Sussex', *Mariner's Mirror*, 50 (1964), pp.115-22.

G.J. Mayhew: 'Epidemic Mortality in Sixteenth Century Rye', *Sussex Archaeological Collections*, 124 (1986).

G.J. Mayhew: 'Religion, Faction and Politics in Reformation Rye: 1530-59', *Sussex Archaeological Collections*, 120 (1982) pp.149-60.

G.J. Mayhew: 'Rye and the Defence of the Narrow Seas: a 16th century town at war', *Sussex Archaeological Collections*, 122 (1984) pp.107-26.

W.J.C. Moens: 'Remarks upon Mr Hardy's Paper, "Foreign Refugees at Rye"', *Proceedings of the Huguenot Society of London*, 2, (1887-8) pp.424-7.

M. Mollat: 'Anglo-Norman Trade in the Fifteenth Century', *Economic History Review*, 17 (1947) pp.143-50.

D. Palliser: 'Epidemics in Tudor York', *Northern History*, 8 (1973) pp.45-63.

E.H. Phelps-Brown and S.V. Hopkins: 'Seven Centuries of the Prices of Consumables, compared with Builders' Wage-rates', *Economica*, 23 (1956) pp.296-314.

E.H. Phelps-Brown and S.V. Hopkins: 'Wage-rates and Prices: Evidence for Population Pressure in the Sixteenth Century', *Economica*, 24 (1957) pp.289-306.

G.D. Ramsey: 'The Distribution of the Cloth Industry in 1561-2', *English Historical Review*, 57 (1942) pp.361-9.

F.W. Reader: 'Report on the Wall Painting at the Old Flushing Inn, Rye', *Sussex Notes and Queries*, 5 (1934) pp.116-8.

A. Ruddock: 'London Capitalists and the Decline of Southampton in the Early Tudor Period', *Economic History Review*, 2nd Series, 2 (1949-50) pp.137-51.

L. Stone: 'Elizabethan Overseas Trade', *Economic History Review*, 2nd Series, 2 (1949-50) pp.30-58.

L. Stone: 'State Control in Sixteenth Century England', *Economic History Review*, 17 (1947) pp. 103-20.

L.A. Vidler: 'The Fifteenth Century House in Rye now known as the Old Flushing Inn', *Sussex Notes and Queries*, 5 (1935) pp.147-51.

L.A. Vidler: 'An Inquest at Rye in 1581', *Sussex Notes and Queries*, 7 (1939) pp.139-45, 177-81.

L.A. Vidler: 'Rye Foreign', *Sussex Archaeological Collections*, 92 (1954), pp.125-56.

L.A. Vidler: 'St Bartholomew's Hospital at Rye', *Sussex Archaeological Collections*, 83 (1943) pp.73-99.

L.A. Vidler: 'Some Leaves of an Early Service Book Once in Use in Rye Church',

Sussex Notes and Queries, 7 (1938) pp.33-5.

C.E. Welch: 'Three Sussex heresy trials', *Sussex Archaeological Collections,* 95 (1957) pp.59-70.

A.F. de P. Worsfield: 'The Court House, Rye', *Sussex Archaeological Collections,* 66 (1925) pp.208-16.

INDEX

Thomas III, 117-18, 174;
William (curate), 61
Blacke, John, 284;
Robert (shipwright), 204, 283-4;
Thomas, 280;
William, 283
Blackeford, John (feter), 283
Blackshore, 263, 265, 267
blacksmiths, 73, 109, 123, 146, 148,
150, 154-5, 168, 277-8, 283-4
Blakey, Elizabeth (widow), 204
Blakeney, 236
Blundell, Nicholas, 38
Blunt (pirate), 227
Bocher, William (French sailor), 280
Bodiam, 13, 60, 237, 292, 308
Bolton, Francis (town clerk), 87, 96,
98, 119, 136, 300;
widow Margery, 119
Bonde, Nicholas (fisherman), 284
Boniface, Anthony (mercer), 278
bookbinders (aliens), 82, 84
booksellers/stationers, 41, 71;
London, 212
Bordeaux, 225
Boston, 15
Boughton Aluph, 68, 293
Boulogne, 37;
provisioning of, 8, 252-3
Boycott, John (feter, town sergeant),
283
Boys, John (mariner), 284
Braband, Captain, 87
Bracegirdle, Mr (vicar), 134
Bradford, Robert (carpenter), 278
Bragden, William (merchant,
shipowner), 50, 152, 257-8,
281
brasiers, 146, 148, 162, 279
Brazil, 51, 86
Bramber, 17-18
bread, 41-2, 71, 75, 95, 100, 169-70,
172, 212-13, 215-17, 221, 30,
312;
prices, 169-70, 172, 212-13, 221,
312
Brede, 13-14, 263, 265, 279;
forge, 13;
Brede Place, 112
Bredes, John (J), 65, 275
Breker, Richard, 279
Brensett, 13, 94
brewers, 25, 47, 80, 95-6, 108-9,

111, 114-5, 122-5, 146, 148-51,
153-7, 162-3, 167-9, 277-80,
300-1, 313;
beercarts, 50, 163;
brewhouses, 114, 163;
equipment, 114, 151, 162-3;
wages (foremen/journeymen),
154-6
Brickenocke, Robert, 281
bricklayers, 154-6, 159;
brickmakers, 154
Bridges, Thomas (carpenter of
Nedesham Market, Suffolk),
267
Brigges, George (feter), 281
Brightlingsea, 20, 236
Brighton (Brighthelmstone), 55, 236
Brill (Netherlands), capture of, 79
Bristol, 15, 22, 87, 113, 178, 236
Brittany, 89, 221, 248, 250;
Bretons in Rye, 222;
Breton ships, 221, 248, 250
Broadhurst, 113, 128
Brooke, Francis, 203-4
Brookland, 13, 59, 292
Broomhill, 13
Brown, William (J), 274;
John (vicar), 73;
Robert (feter), 281;
William (fisherman), 283
Browne, John (sailmaker, unlicensed
victualler), 226
Browning, William (J), 274
Browninge, Thomas (fisherman),
281
Bruges, 241-2
Bruster, John (J, brewer) 125, 131,
276-7
Bryant, Anthony (French mariner),
90
Bryce, Robert (fishing master), 281
Buckland, Hugh (sailor), 306
building trades, 19, 28-9, 31-2, 35,
37, 84-5, 109-10, 124, 145-50,
153-7, 159, 161, 169-70, 174-5,
181-2, 185, 188, 212, 241, 277-8,
310
Bull, John (fisherman, shipmaster),
164, 278
Bull, 'old' and son, 220
Burdet, William (tallow chandler),
280
Burwash, 280

Bury St. Edmunds, 15
Bushope, Henry (J), 275, 282;
  widow, 282;
  Michael (tailor), 282;
  Richard's heirs, 279;
  Robert (shipwright), 283
Butcher, John (carpenter's apprentice),
    157;
  William (French merchant), 82,
    88-9, 277;
  widow, 296
butchers, 25, 35, 41-2, 56-7, 95,
    98-9, 101, 108-9, 111, 123-5,
    146-52, 154-5, 157, 190, 205,
    211-12, 214-5, 217, 220, 278,
    280-2, 292, 300, 313;
  scorer with, 98-9, 101, 296;
  slaughterhouses, 123;
  wages (foremen/journeymen),
    154-5
Button, Matthew (Lewes rippier),
    230;
  maidservant Alice, 230
Buysshop (of Battle), 237
Byler, Henry (joiner), 161, 282
Byspyn, Thomas, 190, 288, 304;
  William (J), 93, 190, 274

Cable, Thomas (husbandman, town
    porter), 277
Cadiz expedition (1596), 51
Calais, 8, 33, 36, 50, 52, 241-2, 247,
    252-3;
  provisioning of, 52, 241-2, 247-8,
    250, 252-3
Call, Edward (shoemaker, victualler,
    owner of the Swan), 37
Camber, 11, 14, 70, 80, 87, 236-7,
    263, 264, 310;
  Castle, 13, 166, 262, 263, 267,
    310
Cambridge, 15, 298;
  Jesus and Christ's Colleges,
    117-18
camel, 58
Canchie, Francis (Huguenot
    merchant), 88, 280;
  daughter Martine (wife of Francis
    Ma?), 88
candles, 170-1
Canterbury, 6-7, 15, 89, 257, 292-3
  Archbishop of, 39, 78-9, 293;

Cranmer, Thomas, 62, 293;
  Homilies, 71, 77;
  Warham, William, 60;
  Prerogative Court, 6, 130
canvas/sailcloth, 30, 160, 226;
  Normandy, 240, 244, 252, 254-7;
  sailmaker, 226
capital offences (see also, executions),
    91, 207-12, 306-7
cappers, 67-8, 109, 146-8, 152, 154,
    167, 278
Cardiff, 238, 308
Cardy, Philipe (French baker), 282
Carpenter, John (J), 116, 273;
  John (brother of Robert jnr), 98,
    128-31, 136, 300;
  Robert, snr, 120;
  wife Elizabeth (Woode), 120;
  Robert jnr (J), 43, 54, 94, 96-8,
    102, 116, 120, 122, 129-33,
    136-8, 234, 257, 265, 275,
    279, 300
carpenters, 19, 29, 32, 37, 109, 124,
    146, 148, 150, 153-8, 161,
    169-70, 174, 181-2, 185, 188,
    212, 267, 277-9, 281, 288, 310;
  tools detained for debt, 161
Carr, Cuthbert (fishing master), 279,
    282, 303;
  wife Elizabeth, 279
carriers, 19, 146, 148, 277
Cartoall, Matthew (Huguenot
    minister), 89
carvers, 154-5
Castleton, Mrs (widow, shopkeeper),
    174;
  Robert (shoemaker), 277
Cater, Bartholomew (cockboatman),
    283;
  olde Cater (alleged issuer of
    counterfeit coin), 226
Cecil, William (Lord Burghley), 81
Chamberlain, Thomas (blacksmith),
    277
chandlers, 108-9, 124, 146, 148, 153,
    168, 280, 282;
  candle prices, 170-1
Chapman, Thomas (vicar), 69;
  William (merchant), 209, 281;
  widow, 281-2
Charles I, 245
Charles V (Holy Roman Emperor), 51

327

328

Coq, Anthony (French merchant), 83-4, 89, 175, 277, 282, 295; denization, 83, 89, 295; Moyses (son of Anthony), 89
cordwainers/shoemakers, 38, 84, 109, 146-8, 150, 152, 157, 166-7, 212, 230, 277-80, 282; Cordwainers/Shoemakers Gild, 166-7; French shoemakers, 84, 167; shoeseller, 41
Cornish, Drew (servant), 229; John (J), 65, 274
corn millers, 154-5; corn mills, 241
Cotman, Robert, 281
covenant servants, see apprentices
Coventry, 6, 15, 192, 289, 298, 300, 304
Cowchman's heirs, 282
Cowley, James (mariner), 280
Coxson, Jane, 130; William (J, fishing master), 122, 276, 281
craftsmen, see artificers
Cranbrook, 37-8, 60, 131, 133, 135, 226, 238, 257, 292, 309
Croche, Robert (J), 273
Cromwell, Richard (fisherman), 280; Thomas (Earl of Essex), 62, 64, 66-8, 114
Crottinden (of Burwash), 280
curriers, 109, 150, 223, 279
cutlers, 41, 73, 84, 109, 146-7, 149, 155, 168, 278; French, 84, 168
Cutthorne, Thomas (fisherman), 277

Dabernell, William (J, shipowner), 93, 131, 133, 257, 275, 281
Dacre of the South, Lord, 36
Dallet, John (French merchant), 278
Daniell, Francis (butcher, innholder), 60, 179, 183-4, 186-8, 217, 288, 304; Richard (feter agent of London clothiers), 220, 258, 281-2; Robert (tailor and woollen draper), 104, 156, 280, 300
Danner, Edward (town preacher), 77-8
Dannett, Audley esq (MP), 54

Danyell, Margaret (widow), 229
Danzig, 86; Danzig chests, 182
Darell, Mr Thomas (JP), 208
Dartmouth, 236
Davison, Mr, 77
Davy, Gregory (mariner), 281; William (J, fisherman), 98, 127, 130-1, 135, 275, 278; William (of Brede), 279
Dawson, John (fisherman's apprentice), 160; Thomas (scavenger), 43
Day, George (Bishop of Chichester), 73-4, 294
Deal, 20
Deane, Richard (sawyer, carpenter's apprentice), 157
De Falloyse, John (Valenciennes), 81; Mighell, 81
defence, 8, 11-12, 14, 18, 20, 24, 26-7, 30, 34-6, 43, 47, 49-53, 110, 143, 158-9, 163, 166, 176, 208, 221, 261, 269, 283, 290-1, 311, 314; town ordnance (see also weapons), 34, 99, 109, 159, 210-11
De la Place, Robert (Hugenot refugee), 88
Delman, Thomas (mercer), 283
De Moye, Ambrose, 88
Denis, M. (Huguenot minister), 89
denizens, see aliens, resident
Didsbury, Cicely (Jurat's widow), 136; William (J, merchant, owner of Mermaid, shipowner), 36, 125-6, 131, 133-4, 136, 152, 162, 174, 229, 157-8, 276, 280, 300; Widow Cicely, 136
Dieppe, 37-8, 50-1, 84-6, 88-9, 111, 212, 248, 250, 252, 258, 307; exports to, 241, 243, 245, 247, 252; imports from, 252; merchants from, 212, 258, 307; Protestants from, 81-2, 111; ships from, 51, 248, 250, 252; shipwrights, 85; yarnspinner from, 84
Dimsdale, bridge, 64; creek, 267

Dirik, Adrian, de Rover (mariner), 224, 307
Dollinge, John, 283, 307;
  widow, 307
Donke, John (tailor), 279
Donnynge, John (J), 50, 91, 103, 119, 131, 135, 275, 280
dossermakers, *see* basketmakers
Dove, Richard (carpenter), 157
Dover, 8, 14-16, 20, 22, 34-5, 52, 54, 58, 64, 80, 91, 196, 207-8, 236, 241, 257, 265, 289, 292, 303;
  Admiralty Court, 303;
  Castle, 52, 64;
  Lieutenant of Castle, 34, 80
Dowce, John (capper), 85, 152, 167, 278
Drake, Sir Francis (circumnavigation), 51
drapers (*see also* tailors), 109-10, 146, 148, 156, 162, 166-7, 279-80;
  French linen retailer, 85
drunkenness, *see* inns/alehouses
Du Cheyne, Nicholas (Huguenot refugee), 87
Duffet, John (fisherman), 278
Dugard, John (shipmaster), 282;
  Vincent (factor for Dieppe merchants), 258
Dugrange, Nicholas (French merchant, seacaptain), 83-4, 87
Dungeness, 13, 38, 262
Dunkirk, 50, 135, 241, 249, 251, 265
Dunmold, Raynold (fisherman), 278
Durham, 15
Duron, John (brewer), 163, 278;
  Simon (tailor), 211, 306
Duval, Nicolas (of Dieppe, owner of the *Loup*), 51
Dyne, Stephen (fisherman), 279
Dyryckson, John (J), 93, 273

Ealing, 192, 305
earthenpotters, 154-5
East Anglia, 239, 252
East Grinstead, 17
East Guldeford, 13-14, 30, 61, 115, 263, 289
Easton, Mr, 278
Eaton, William (Dover merchant), 207
Edmondes, Edward (mariner), 281

Edolphe, John (J), 39, 65, 274;
  Thomas, gent. (J, shipowner), 93-4, 120, 122, 126-7, 130-2, 134, 136, 152, 225, 276, 280
Edward VI, 52, 61, 69-71
Edwardes, Thomas (shipwright), 278
Egliston, William (J), 65, 75, 275
Eles, Richard (mariner), 281
Eliard, Ellis (merchant), 277
Elizabeth I, 24, 27, 35-6, 123
Emery alias Wattes, *see* Wattes
Emery, John (sailed to Guinea), 51
Enge, Jone, 130
  Manasses, 278
Englet, John (shipwright), 278;
  William, 278
Engram, Edward (mariner), 277;
  John (mariner, fishing boat owner), 163, 284
Ensinge, Thomas (land chamberlain), 234
epidemics, 7, 22-3, 35, 42, 44, 46-8, 53, 79, 115, 132, 163, 192, 194, 196-7, 199, 201, 289, 291, 299, 304-5
Erasmus, Desiderius, *Paraphrases* 69, 71, 75
Erle, John (fishing master), 281
Essex, 58
Esterfild, Richard (butcher), 282
Eston family, 120;
  John, 117, 293;
  William snr (J), 273;
  Eston's Kyllne, 32
Etuere, John (brasier's apprentice son of London merchant), 162
Ewen, Simon (fisherman), 277
Ewhurst, 282
executions, 95, 103, 207-8, 210-11, 221, 306-7;
  gallows, 91, 211;
  heresy, 60, 74, 208;
  murder, 208, 210-11;
  piracy, 208
Exeter, 6, 10, 15, 27, 289-90, 292, 300
exports;
  beer, 239, 243-4, 261-2;
  cider, 89;
  cloth, *see* cloth/clothing industry;
  fish, *see* fishing industry;
  glass, 84, 257;
  horses, 42, 239, 243, 252, 255-6;

iron, 238-9, 243, 255-6, 261-4, 308, 310;
leather, 243, 252;
prohibited exports (mainly tallow or leather), 214-15, 218;
wood;
   billets, 8, 28, 219, 239, 241-2, 252-8, 261, 309-10, 312;
   timber, 238-9, 241-2, 247, 252-3, 255-6

Fagge, John (J, butcher, shipowner), 44, 94-5, 112-3, 123, 125-36, 152, 190, 275-6, 278
Fairlight, 13, 166
Fanefield, Philip, 35
Farley, Robert (merchant, glass importer/exporter, agent for London clothiers), 44, 219, 257-8, 277
Farne, Simon (shipwright), 283
Fateley, John (shipmaster), 281
Faversham, 20, 236, 292
Fawcett, John (shipmaster), 164
fire hazards;
   chimneys, 176-7, 214-15, 218;
   thatch, 107, 177, 214-15
Firrall, Thomas, 279
Fisher, John (J, ost), 36, 116, 125-6, 131, 134-5, 189, 256, 258, 276-7;
   Thomas snr (J), 116, 136, 258, 276-7, 300;
   Thomas jnr, 134-5, 300
Fisher, widow (innholder), 152
fishing industry, 6, 11, 18-20, 25, 28, 32-4, 36, 38-43, 52, 81-2, 84, 100-1, 105, 108-11, 114, 123-4, 126, 145-51, 153, 156-7, 159-61, 163-6, 174-5, 177, 180-1, 185-6, 188, 205, 212, 214-15, 218-19, 230, 241, 244, 246, 252, 254, 256, 258-63, 269, 277-88, 299-301, 303, 308, 310, 312-15;
   fishermen (and apprentices), 19-20, 25, 36, 39-41, 100, 108-11, 114, 123-4, 145-51, 153, 156-7, 159-61, 164-6, 174, 177, 180-1, 185-6, 188, 212, 230, 264, 277-89, 299-301, 303, 310, 313-14;
   Rye Company or Fellowship of, 165-6, 264, 283;

benefactors, 166;
   seamen's hall, 166;
   wardens, 166, 283;
fishmongers;
   London (company of), 25, 38-9, 41, 258, 314;
   Rye;
   feters (local wholesalers), 25, 39, 108-10, 116, 124, 145-52, 161, 175, 258, 277-83, 313-14;
   osts (of London fishmongers' company), 25, 38-41, 108-11, 124, 126, 145-52, 159, 256, 258-62, 279-80, 290, 299, 310, 313-14;
market;
   Rye, 39-43, 101, 105, 205, 219, 258-60, 283;
   London, Rye exports to 6, 11, 18, 25, 38, 238, 244, 257-9, 261, 313-15;
nets (flewes, tramells), 81, 160, 164, 181-2, 214-15, 218, 314-15;
   trammel fayre, 157;
purveyor, royal (*see also* Angell, William; Fletcher, John; Gaymer, Henry; Haynes, Mr; Millis, Matthew), 25, 39-41, 109, 114, 124, 126;
   King's shop, 40;
vessels, 6, 18-20, 28, 39-40, 105, 108-11, 126, 150, 163-5, 246, 254, 258, 264, 269, 284-7, 312-13;
   barkes, 19, 312;
   crayers, 19, 246, 313;
   masters, 36, 105, 108-11, 114, 116, 124, 126, 150, 156, 164-6, 175, 281-5, 299-300;
   unlicensed French vessels, 218
Flahow, Charles (French seaman, stolen canvas), 37, 226
Flemynge, Nicholas, 282
Fletcher, John (J, merchant, seacaptain), 51, 64-6, 66, 68, 113-5, 117, 120-1, 123, 126, 132, 179, 256, 274, 293;

336

limeburners, 154-5
Lincoln, 15
literacy (*see also* clergy, benefit of), 53
Litherlond, Thomas (J), 273
Littlehampton, 237
Liverpool, 236
liveries, 34-5, 99, 290
livestock, 42, 48, 211-12, 214-15, 217-18, 229, 239
Lockewod, George (mariner), 283
locksmiths, 82, 146-8, 203, 277;
    French, 82, 203, 277
Lollardy, 55, 60
London, 6, 11, 15-16, 18, 22, 25, 29, 31, 37-40, 53, 74-5, 79, 86-7, 113, 117-8, 231, 234-6, 238, 240-1, 243-5, 248, 250, 254, 256-8, 263, 265, 292, 305, 307-8, 310, 313-15;
    Bishop of, 78, 133, 206;
    Fenchurch Street, 254;
    Fleet prison, 75;
    Gray's Inn, 117;
    Inner Temple, 118;
    Leadenhall market on Cornhill, 38;
    Reformed church in, 231;
    Tower, 118
    Rye as outport for (*see also* cloth/clothing industry; fishing industry; iron industry), 6, 11, 18, 25, 38, 238, 240-6, 254-8, 261, 308, 313, 315;
    pack-trade (*see also* rippiers), 38, 238, 242, 245, 254-6, 313, 315;
    seaborne traffic, 240-4, 248, 250, 261, 310;
    migration/family connections with Rye, 113, 117, 133-4, 162, 257;
    London merchant's son apprenticed in Rye, 162;
    London pavers/plumbers in Rye, 29, 31
    London stationer, 212
Lord Admiral, 59, 133, 225
Lord Warden, *see* Cinque Ports
Love, Giles (J), 273;
    William (fisherman), 281

Lowestoft, 236
Lucas, William, 280
Luksman, Garrard (Dutchman), 224
Lutterworth (Leics.), 113
Lydd, 13, 20, 30, 59, 87, 113, 131, 156, 237, 257, 292;
    town clerk of, 131
Lydenden, 292
Lyme, 236
Lympeny, John (J), 274
Lyndsey, Alexander (shoemaker), 279
Lyndson, William (mariner), 281
Lynn, 15, 22, 236
Lyons, 254

    Reformed church in, 231;
    Tower, 118
    Rye as outport for (*see also* cloth/clothing industry; fishing industry; iron industry), 6, 11, 18, 25, 38, 238, 240-6, 254-8, 261, 308, 313, 315;
    pack-trade (*see also* rippiers), 38, 238, 242, 245, 254-6, 313, 315;
    seaborne traffic, 240-4, 248, 250, 261, 310;
migration/family connections with Rye, 113, 117, 133-4, 162, 257;
    London merchant's son apprenticed in Rye, 162;
    London pavers/plumbers in Rye, 29, 31
    London stationer, 212
Lord Admiral, 59, 133, 225
Lord Warden, *see* Cinque Ports
Love, Giles (J), 273;
    William (fisherman), 281
Lowestoft, 236
Lucas, William, 280
Luksman, Garrard (Dutchman), 224
Lutterworth (Leics.), 113
Lydd, 13, 20, 30, 59, 87, 113, 131, 156, 237, 257, 292;
    town clerk of, 131
Lydenden, 292
Lyme, 236
Lympeny, John (J), 274
Lyndsey, Alexander (shoemaker), 279

Lyndson, William (mariner), 281
Lynn, 15, 22, 236
Lyons, 254

Maidman, John (fisherman),
    284
Maidstone, 231, 257, 292;
    Reformed church in, 231
Mailler/Mayler, Richard (fishing
    master), 174, 283, 308
Maldon, 15, 236
Malling (Kent), 58, 292
maps, 40, 159-60, 267, 300,
    315
Ma?, Francis (French merchant), 83,
    85, 87-9, 280, 288, 295-6;
    denization of, 83, 89, 295;
    wife Martine (Canchie), 88;
    son William (of Dieppe), 89
Marchall, Robert, 185, 288
Marche, Ellen, 118;
    Joan, 283;
    John (J), 65, 116, 274;
    Robert snr (J), 33, 65, 75, 116,
        118, 125;
    wife Anys (Woode), 118;
    Robert jnr (butcher), 280;
    Simon (yeoman), 280
Marden, Richard, 117;
    Robert (J), 65, 117, 274;
    widow Jone, 119
Margate, 20
mariners, 8, 19-20, 22, 36,
    51-2, 89-90, 109-10, 124, 145-50,
    153, 157-60, 174, 204, 210, 212,
    238, 243, 253, 277-84, 288,
    299-302, 306, 313;
    alien, in Rye, 36-7, 83, 86-8, 90,
        224-5, 280, 307;
        French, 83, 86-7, 90, 280;
        Netherlanders, 36-7, 88,
            224-5, 307;
    clothing, 158, 160-1;
    compasses, 160;
        cards for the sea, 160;
        mappe for the sea, 160;
    pressed to HM ships, 52, 90;
    sea chest, 160;
    wages, 157-9, 301
marketmen (non-resident
    fishmongers), 25, 41, 258-60,
    262, 314

Marshall, Christopher (deputy
    customer), 234;
    John (draper), 280;
    Thomas (mariner), 281
Martin, Bawdwyn (Rotterdam
    merchant), 84, 88-9;
    wife and servants, 89
Mary I, 52, 66, 71-3, 75, 294;
    Marian religious reaction, 51, 61,
        66, 69, 71-7, 114, 294
Mason, Robert, 280
masons, 109, 146-8, 153-4,
    169-70, 175, 278, 310
Mathew, Edmond, 288
Matthew, John, 203;
    Thomas (painter), 224-5, 282
Matthewe, Thomas (J), 125,
    276
Maxsted, Arnold (carpenter),
    277
May Game, 7, 57-8, 292
Maycott, Robert (J), 65-6, 113,
    118, 275
Mayfield, 58
Maynerd, Philip (bricklayer),
    156
mayor, *see* Rye Corporation
Meade, Humphrey (Dover
    merchant), 257
Medcalfe, Michael (town
    sergeant), 280;
    widow, 280
Mede, Robert (J, fishing
    master), 93, 116, 273, 299;
    William (J, fisherman), 65, 68,
        116, 123, 274
Medway Ports, 256
Mekyns, Arthur, (shearman),
    229
Mellowe, William (J,
    chandler), 119, 123, 276, 282
Mercer, George (J, town
    clerk), 96, 116, 273;
    John snr (mercer), 280;
    John jnr (J, beerbrewer, mercer),
        116, 122-3, 125, 129-34, 151,
        153, 189, 276, 299-301;
    Nicholas (J), 32, 65, 96, 116
mercers, 5, 35-6, 85, 103,
    109-11, 122-4, 128, 141, 143,
    146-8, 150-2, 157, 162, 166-9,
    173, 253-4, 256-8, 277-83, 288,
    302;

339

341

widow of, 177;
son Thomas (fisherman), 160,
277
Poynings, Lord, 33;
Mr, 33-4
Prescott, Henry, 185, 288
John (vicar), 78-9
Prest, 277
prices, 169-72, 212-13, 221,
302, 312
Priclove, John, 176
priest, suspected, 206
privateering (see also
Sea-Beggars), 51, 86-7, 245
privies, 43-4, 178
Privy Council, 62, 64, 68,
72-4, 80-1, 87-8, 114, 294, 297
proclamation, prisoners freed by,
208-10, 306;
proclamations, royal, 52-3, 301
Prophette's widow, 181, 183,
185, 288
Protestantism (see also Lollardy;
Reformation);
origins of, in Rye, 8, 51, 55,
59-63;
Prowze, John (innholder, scorer,
keeper of town ordnance), 159,
278
punishments;
abjuring realm (alien offender
pardoned on), 307;
banishment, 205, 214-15, 222-4,
226, 229-30;
billet nailed in ear, 223, 229;
cage, 12, 205-6, 216, 307, 312;
carting, 205, 207, 211, 222, 308;
collar, 203-5, 216, 222, 313;
death, see under executions;
ducking stool, 204-5, 216, 222,
307, 313;
fines, 91, 97, 101, 103, 105, 108,
168-9, 204, 107, 211-12,
214-22, 224-5, 227, 229, 231,
291, 308;
God's Yoke, 205-6;
imprisonment, 79, 84, 103, 107,
166, 202-3, 205-11, 216,
218-21, 227, 229, 231, 308;
pillory, 91, 205, 216-17, 222,
229;
stocks, 91, 205, 219, 221-2;
whipping, 203-5, 207, 210, 222,

227, 229, 308;
whipping-post, 205
Purbeck, 239
Purvage, Nicholas (Huguenot
merchant, yeoman), 87, 280
Pye, John (carpenter), 153,
157, 279
Pynner, John, 279
Quarry, Alexander (fishing
master), 283
Queen's Lieutenant, 203
Quilleboeuf, 163
Quock, Anthony, see Coq,
Anthony

Radford, Thomas snr
(merchant), 280;
Thomas jnr (cordwainer), 229,
277;
Noye (town drummer), 267
Ramsey, Andrew (fisherman),
278
Ramsgate, 20
Randall, William (Udimore
clerk, forger of passports), 231
Randolph, Thomas (controller of
HM Posts), 38
Ratliff, William (J, tailor,
vintner), 36, 43-4, 107, 113,
126, 131, 133-6, 152, 175, 178,
268, 276, 279, 300
Rawson, John (lighterman),
279
Ravensdale, Margery (widow),
294;
Thomas (shoemaker, burned for
heresy), 74
Ravin, John (tailor, from Great
Yarmouth), 153
Rawlins, 283
Raynold, Thomas (fisherman's
covenant servant), 157
Raynoldes, George (J), 65-6,
70, 74, 77, 94,113, 116, 118, 122,
127-8, 130-1, 135, 166, 176,
178-9, 184-5, 274, 280, 303-4;
George (tailor), 280;
Johane (wife of Alexander Welles),
118;
John (J), 65, 116-8, 121, 275,
290-1, 293;
John (of Broadburst, Kent), 113,

343

waits, 34-5, 99;
ward constables, 44, 47, 101, 231-2;
watch, 49, 101, 219;
waterbailiff, *see* bailiff;
Rye, cross-channel passage *(see also* Dieppe), 33, 37-8, 50-2, 147, 245, 252;
   military 47, 50-1;
   provisioning of Calais and Boulogne, 8, 52, 241-2, 247, 252-3;
   news/intelligence, 51-3, 71, 114;
   posts, 37-8, 51
Rye harbour, 6-7, 11-12, 14, 24, 27-8, 37, 54, 70, 110, 123, 139, 147, 159-60, 165, 205, 214-15, 218-19, 233-5, 253, 255, 261-8, 310-11, 313;
   customer *(see also* under Belveridge Thomas; Donnnynge, John; Marshall, Christopher; Oxenbridge, Adam; Rode, Ralph), 53, 103, 109, 124, 146, 234, 280, 288;
   customs accounts, 6, 235, 238-9, 242, 245-6, 248-51, 253, 255, 309;
   customs house, 103, 234, 268;
   port books, 6, 236, 238, 240, 242, 245-6, 255, 257, 309;
   port controller *(see also* under Holmes, John), 73
   port searcher *(see also* Welles, Robert), 93, 103, 109;
   Puddle, 210, 263, 295, 308;
   sea wall, 14, 233, 265-9;
   wrecks, 91, 262, 310
Rye hinterland *(see also* under Kent, Sussex and neighbouring towns/villages by name);
   local trade *(see also* cockboats; cockboatmen; lighters; lightermen), 6-7, 11, 237-40, 256-8;
   foodstuffs, 33-4, 41-2, 237, 239-40;
   fish, 11, 18, 25, 244, 257-8;
   industrial equipment/ materials/produce *(see also* cloth/clothing industry; glass; iron industry), 84, 238-41, 243-4, 252, 255-7,

292, 308-10;
   marshes, 11, 13-14, 54, 103, 263, 265-6, 314;
   migration/family connections, 7, 66-7, 112-13, 115-16, 119, 133, 175, 278, 280-2, 284, 304;
   players (local companies), 58-9, 292
Rye parish;
   church (St Mary the Virgin), 6, 22, 49, 56, 59-60, 67-75, 77, 85, 88, 102, 104, 114, 143, 173, 206-7, 289, 300;
   choir, 56-7;
   plate, 68-75, 77-8, 291;
   services 49, 55-8, 67-72, 92, 102, 201, 207, 231, 289;
   churchwardens, 27, 56, 67, 69-70, 72, 74-5, 77, 101, 220, 225, 294, 297;
   churchwardens' accounts, 5-6, 27, 56, 69-72, 108, 286-7, 291, 297, 302;
   churchyard, 29, 35, 41, 55, 92, 102, 142-3, 173, 175, 177, 180, 206, 280;
   curate, 59, 61-2, 67, 74;
   minister, *see* town preacher;
   parish clerk, 79;
   parish registers, 6, 21-2, 24, 46, 88, 94, 118, 140, 192, 194, 210-11, 294, 299;
   patrons, 68, 78;
   property, farm/lease of, 78, 109, 177, 300;
   sexton, 70, 78-9, 101, 159;
   sidesmen, 72, 74, 101, 220-1, 225;
   town preacher, 50, 77-9, 129-34, 160, 202-3, 220;
   vicar, 60, 68-9, 72-3, 78, 96, 114, 134, 174, 288, 294, 302;
   vicarage, 12, 78, 143, 182, 185, 225, 278

Sackville family, 78
Sadler, Richard (rippier's servant), 224
saddlers 109, 155
sailmakers, 226
St Albans, 15, 106

hoys, 247;
royal and other ships on military
    service, 11, 50-2, 89, 158-9,
    163, 225, 247, 261;
Regent (king's warship under
    construction at Reding),
    34;
Rye ships, 37, 51, 158, 160, 163,
    221, 246, 248, 251, 264, 301;
Blessing of God (merchantman,
    town ship), 163, 301;
    pinnace to, 163;
Ellin, 160;
Helen, 37;
Hercules, 51, 158, 264;
James Potten's boat, 158;
Mary Hankyng, 221;
Peter, 246;
Primrose, 246;
Savyor, 51, 158;
William (town ship), 158
shipmasters, 22, 109-10,
    157-8, 160, 164, 243, 277-84,
    286-7, 299, 301-2;
    French, 37-8, 83-4, 86;
    Rotterdam, 36-7, 88, 225
shipowners, 5, 51, 152-3, 163,
    238, 277-84, 299, 308
ship provisioning, 110, 147,
    259, 253
shipwrights, 85, 109, 145-8,
    152, 154-6, 161, 204, 278-9,
    282-3, 310;
    French, 85, 241;
    London, 114
Shoreham, 17
Shrewsbury, 15
Shurley, John (J, of Isfield
    Place), 113, 119, 176, 273, 299
Simondes, Ralph, 279
Simpson, Thomas
    (cordwainer), 277
Siricksey (Zeeland), 224
Sittingbourne, 292
Skalles, John, 280;
    Robert (mariner), 277
Skynner (householder), 177
slander, *see* verbal abuse
sluices;
    proposed, 265-6;
    1596, 12, 267-9
Sly, Thomas (fisherman), 283
Smallhythe, 13

Smith, Adam (fishing master),
    281;
    Francis (J), 119, 131, 276;
    George (sawyer, carpenter's
        apprentice), 157
    John snr (feter), 99, 281;
    Ottywell, 86;
    Roger (vicar), 79, 134;
    Simon (fishing master), 283;
    Thomas (mariner), 283
Smyth, Thomas, 219
Sohier, Cornelis (Netherlander,
        factor for Dieppe merchants),
        88-9, 254, 258, 295-6;
    Lewis (French merchant), 277;
    Peter (Fenchurch St, London)
        254;
    Simon (Fenchurch St, London),
        254
Snodden, Thomas (joiner), 85
soldiers, 34-5, 47, 50-2, 208,
    214-15, 231, 247
Sole, John (cordwainer), 280
Somler, Peter, 278
Somerset, Duke of, 27, 29, 34,
    64, 66, 69, 94, 114
Southampton, 8, 15, 22, 61,
    196, 234, 236, 257, 289, 308, 310
Southwark, 15, 112
Southwold, 236
Spain, 53, 245, 249, 251, 257
Sparrowe, John, 279
Spilsted, John (yeoman), 177,
    278
sports/pastimes (*see also*
        inns/alehouses);
    bowls, 50, 228;
    tennis, 50;
    quoits, 50;
    restraints and prohibitions, 50,
        60, 201
spurriers, 154-5
Stace, Richard, 115, 186
Stacy, John, 282
Stamford, 15
Stanley Abbey, 68
Starne, Richard (widow's
        servant), 229
Stepney, 257
Steyning; 17
Stonacre, William (J), 273
Stonham, John (carpenter),
        153, 266-7, 278

349

Woodbridge, 236
woodcloses, woodhouses, 179,
    253
Woode, Robert snr (J), 31, 63,
    65, 116, 120, 123, 126, 274;
    daughter Anys, 118;
    daughter Elizabeth, 120;
    Robert jnr (J, merchant), 116,
        118, 127, 276, 279
Worcester, 6, 15, 193-4, 196,
    289, 305
Worgar, John (fisherman), 277
Wowan, Richard, 183, 188,
    288
Wright, Richard (mariner),
    280
Wulphyn, Alexander (J), 65-6,
    274
Wybourn, William (1728), 300
Wye College of, 293
Wykwyk, William (vicar), 182,
    288, 302
Wyllison, Robert (fisherman),
    160
Wymond family, 115-6, 120;
    John (J), 115-16, 121, 274, 276;
    Paul, 176, 179, 279;
    Robert I (J), 92, 115, 273;
    Robert II (J), 63, 65, 67-8, 115,
        122, 274, 293;
    Robert III, 99, 178, 184, 280,
        288;
    Robert of Midhurst, yeoman,
        175-6;
    William (J, shipowner), 51, 65,
        115-17, 274, 293

Yarmouth, Great, 15, 20, 32-3,
    54, 208, 153, 160, 164-5, 236,
    286-7, 312;
    bailiffs to, 32-3, 312
yarnspinner (French), 84
yeomen, 109, 123, 175,
    211-12, 218, 277-81, 284
Yonge, John snr (J), 53, 65,
    72-3, 75, 77, 81, 102, 117, 275,
    293;
    John jnr (bailiff), 102-3, 117,
        220-1, 280;
    John (of Chichester), 103, 221;
    son Charles, 103;
    Richard, 117;

William, 277;
Yonge widow, 277
York, 6, 15-16, 54, 192, 194,
    289, 291-2, 298, 300, 305, 312

Zeeland, 80